A DEFENCE OF PRETENCE

A Defence of Pretence

CIVILITY AND THE THEATRE
IN EARLY MODERN ENGLAND

INDIRA GHOSE

PRINCETON UNIVERSITY PRESS
PRINCETON & OXFORD

Copyright © 2025 by Princeton University Press

Princeton University Press is committed to the protection of copyright and the intellectual property our authors entrust to us. Copyright promotes the progress and integrity of knowledge created by humans. By engaging with an authorized copy of this work, you are supporting creators and the global exchange of ideas. As this work is protected by copyright, any reproduction or distribution of it in any form for any purpose requires permission; permission requests should be sent to permissions@press.princeton.edu. Ingestion of any IP for any AI purposes is strictly prohibited.

Published by Princeton University Press
41 William Street, Princeton, New Jersey 08540
99 Banbury Road, Oxford OX2 6JX

press.princeton.edu

GPSR Authorized Representative: Easy Access System Europe - Mustamäe tee 50, 10621 Tallinn, Estonia, gpsr.requests@easproject.com

All Rights Reserved

ISBN 978-0-691-26999-3
ISBN (pbk.) 978-0-691-26998-6
ISBN (e-book) 978-0-691-27000-5

British Library Cataloging-in-Publication Data is available

Editorial: Ben Tate and Josh Drake
Production Editorial: Jenny Wolkowicki
Cover design: Katie Osborne
Production: Lauren Reese
Publicity: William Pagdatoon and Charlotte Coyne
Copyeditor: Joseph Dahm

Cover credit: The Picture Art Collection / Alamy Stock Photo

This book has been composed in Arno

10 9 8 7 6 5 4 3 2 1

To Walter

CONTENTS

Illustrations   ix

	Introduction	1
1	Castiglione, *The Merchant of Venice,* and the Imperative of Style	29
2	Manners and the Market	69
3	Theatricality and Lies in *Coriolanus*	109
4	*Sejanus* and the Degradation of Civility	148
5	Wit and the Art of Jesting	185
	Conclusion	223

Acknowledgements   231
Bibliography   233
Index   257

ILLUSTRATIONS

1. Giovanni Battista Moroni, *The Knight in Black* (ca. 1567) — 2
2. Raphael, *Portrait of Baldassare Castiglione* (ca. 1514–15) — 30
3. John Massey Wright (1777–1866), scene from *The Merchant of Venice* — 55
4. Hans Holbein the Younger, *Portrait of Desiderius Erasmus of Rotterdam with Renaissance Pilaster* (1523) — 70
5. Title page of *A Fair Quarrel* (1622) by Thomas Middleton and William Rowley — 104
6. Jacopo Pontormo, *Monsignor della Casa* (1541–44) — 110
7. Soma Orlai Petrich, *Coriolanus* (1869) — 129
8. Paul van Somer I, *Portrait of Francis Bacon* (1617) — 149
9. Jan Luyken, *Sejanus, Favourite of Emperor Tiberius, Strangled, and at the Gemonian Stairs, Miserably Abused* (1698) — 167
10. Andrea del Sarto, *Portrait of a Lady with a Book* (ca. 1528) — 186
11. Michele Beneditti, *Falstaff at Herne's Oak* (1793) — 213

Introduction

CIVILITY, WE ARE TOLD, is in crisis. In an increasingly polarised world, the ability to live together in civil society with a modicum of cordiality appears to be receding. Common courtesy is in decline, as is the willingness to interact with those outside our own cohort and engage with views that contradict our own. Outrage and anger dominate discourse on social media. In public debate, speakers regularly hurl accusations of incivility in the teeth of those with whom they disagree.[1] Others argue that civility itself is the problem, deeply implicated as it is in the history of Western colonialism and social injustice.[2] Some critics claim that civility is inevitably linked to white supremacy and is an expression of structural racism. Civility, they allege, serves only to perpetuate everyday discrimination. It is a mode of violence, used to mask 'the ugly acts of white supremacy, ableism, misogyny, or compulsory heterosexuality'. Civility, they declare, should be jettisoned. Instead, marginalized groups should be granted the dignity and equality that are their inalienable human rights, inherent in their humanity.[3]

Current debates about civility play out a tension that has been at the heart of the discourse and practice of civility throughout history. Civility, this book argues, is radically ambiguous: it can relate either to social distinction or mutual respect, partisan interests or the wider community. What is often overlooked is that the debate about civility encapsulates what Charles Taylor has defined as the greatest conflict in modernity—the diverging demands of particularity and

---

[1]. For a sample of recent work on the crisis of civility, see Boatright et al., *Crisis of Civility?*, and Hudson, *Soul of Civility*. For an incisive discussion that turns to early modern debates to shed light on our current predicament, see Bejan, *Mere Civility*.

[2]. See, for instance, Simpson, *Engaging Violence*, and King, *Civil Vengeance*.

[3]. Itagaki, 'Long Con of Civility', 1185. Also see Zamalin, *Against Civility*.

FIGURE 1. The art of *sprezzatura*. Giovanni Battista Moroni, *The Knight in Black* (ca. 1567). Museo Poldi Pezzoli, Milan.

universality, self-interest and community, or tribalism and the common good. It is a conflict that defines our world today as do few others.[4]

In this connection, why does literature matter? The premise of this book is that the early modern theatre in England played a pivotal role in shaping these debates. The drama of Shakespeare's time offers a prism through which to scrutinize aspects of civility from a variety of perspectives. At the most mundane level, the early modern theatre, a hub of literary and social activity, served as a conduit of civility and purveyed the latest styles and fashions even as it mocked them. But the plays also shed a light on the deep ambivalences within civility by testing the precepts of civility against scenarios that, however fictitious, comment on real life. Crucially, literature reveals the confusion and complexity of human life—and undermines our conviction of moral rectitude. Moreover, in the face of virulent antitheatrical attacks, the drama of Shakespeare, Jonson, and Middleton developed into an extraordinarily self-conscious medium, reflecting on its own status as fiction and on the notion of theatricality itself, in the sense of both performance and pretence. It is an ideal tool to gauge the role social performance and fictions play in human lives.

This book argues that in its exploration of social theatricality, the early modern theatre, in a range of plays from city comedies to tragedies, puts forward a number of remarkable propositions. It indicates that for all the tensions with which civility is fraught, pretence is an inescapable element in social life. As members of civil society, we are always role players. This does not mean that the plays offer a blithe endorsement of rank hypocrisy or a defence of untrammelled opportunism. Instead, they query our hankering after moral purity. Grappling with the vexed issue of dissimulation, lies, and social performance, they question the idea of a clear-cut boundary between sincerity and dissembling, truth and lies. Perhaps, they suggest, what is decisive is the use to which our play-acting is put: rampant self-interest or the common good—the notion that there is a common purpose we share. As a corollary, in a world riven by antagonism, an ironic pretence of mutual respect might be indispensable to facilitate an engagement with other members of society. At the same time, anticipating insights later articulated by Hobbes, the plays intimate that civil

---

4. See Taylor, *Sources of the Self*, 101. In the recent past, a number of thinkers have voiced their concern about the rise of solipsistic concepts of identity, amongst others, Sen, *Identity and Violence*; Lilla, *Once and Future Liberal*; and Appiah, *Lies That Bind*. I use the term 'self-interest' broadly to refer to any form of behaviour that serves our own interests, not specifically in the sense of economic advantage.

society is built around narratives, stories we create and that shape our ends. While some of these have a deleterious effect on the social fabric, some beliefs are indispensable to foster our shared stake in social life. The concept of the common good might be a fiction, but it is one that is crucial for human society.

It is undoubtedly the case that throughout history, the rhetoric of civility has been pressed into service by powerful groups to entrench hierarchies and repress dissenting opinions. However, what critics of civility fail to acknowledge is the wider meaning of civility as bound up with a community and a shared notion of the common good, or 'common weal', as early moderns put it. It is assumed that civility is merely a matter of manners or etiquette. What has largely faded from awareness are the conjoined implications of the term 'civility': as relating to good manners as well as to the civil community. As philosopher Cheshire Calhoun has pointed out, at the nub of civility is the idea of mutual respect, according to others precisely the same dignity and inalienable rights as human beings which we claim for ourselves—and on which the critics of civility rightly insist. Manners are only the conventional form we use to express our respect for each other. Civility is a matter of performance, a display of reciprocal esteem. It is a mode of communication which conveys mutual respect precisely in order to enable a dialogue with other members of society, people who are not part of our circle of family and friends and with whom we might have very little in common.[5] Like every form of language, civility is open to abuse: it has been consistently appropriated as a marker of social prestige and wielded as a weapon of exclusion. But norms are not graven in stone; they have been contested throughout history.

The idea that civility is a form of communication would come as no surprise to early moderns, for whom rhetoric manuals frequently double as courtesy books. Civility was the rhetoric of behaviour with which members of society signalled reciprocal esteem through civil courtesies, presented themselves as men and women governed by the virtue of restraint, themselves worthy of esteem, and aimed to create goodwill by accommodating themselves to others. As early modern historians have shown, a concern with civility, often subsumed under terms such as 'honesty' or 'good neighbourhood', was by no

---

5. Calhoun, 'Virtue of Civility'.

means restricted to the aristocracy and gentry.⁶ Admittedly, this is the impression evoked by the genre of courtesy literature, in the business of purveying social distinction as a commodity. It is in the most thoughtful literary texts of the time that we find an engagement with both the ideational as well as the dark side of civility: a way of living together in mutuality grounded in the sense of a shared purpose, or the instrumentalisation of social norms as a means of debarring outsiders.

Needless to say, civility did not originate in early modern Europe, nor even in Europe. Rules of conduct and social norms are to be found in every age and culture, as are codifications of ideal behaviour.⁷ The guidelines for social interaction delineated by Confucius in the fifth century BCE have left an indelible mark on East Asian culture, while *Cyropaedia*, one of the earliest examples of the advice genre of 'mirror for princes', compiled by the Greek writer Xenophon around 370 BCE, presents Cyrus the Great, sovereign of Persia in the sixth century BCE, as the model of virtues such as self-restraint and decorum. Asoka, the Buddhist ruler of the Mauryan Empire in the third century BCE, a state that stretched from present-day Afghanistan to South India, formulated a series of precepts of good behaviour that he had inscribed in the vernacular on stone tablets, rocks, and pillars which were erected throughout the length and breadth of the realm, thirty-three of which survive to the present day.⁸ The tenets set out in the inscriptions, outlining his notion of *dharma* or duty, in which consideration for others plays a central role, bear a remarkable affinity to the principles formulated by Stoic philosopher Panaetius a century later and transmitted to us by Cicero in his *De officiis* ('On Duties')—a text from which all European conceptions of civility derive.⁹

Equally striking, as Peter Burke notes, is the fact that throughout the ages and in widely divergent cultures, refined manners have been adopted as a

---

6. See, for instance, Thomas, *In Pursuit of Civility*, and Withington, *Society in Early Modern England*. On civility in civic societies, such as trade associations and guilds, and in more informal settings, such as alehouses, see Withington, 171–201.

7. Thomas, *In Pursuit of Civility*, 20.

8. See Sen, *Argumentative Indian*, 15–16.

9. The influence of Buddhist ideas on Greek culture is evidenced by the thriving Buddhist community established by Indian merchants in Alexandria in the second century BCE, impelling the governor to lament that 'the Greeks stole their philosophy from the barbarians'. See Zubrzycki, *Shortest History of India*, 52–53. And as William Dalrymple has recently shown, in the first century BCE the greatest trading partner of the Roman Empire was India. See his *Golden Road*, 53–74.

social strategy by elites or by those who aspired to elite status, be it the 'magnanimous man' of Aristotle or the ideal gentleman in Confucius's teachings.[10] Civility has been consistently entangled with elitist privilege. The impulse at stake is pithily summed up in the slogan 'manners makyth man'. This was the adage chosen by William of Wykeham, Bishop of Winchester and Chancellor of England in the late fourteenth century, to be appended to his coat of arms as well as to serve as the motto for Winchester College and New College, Oxford, both of which he founded.[11] To be sure, at the time 'manners' would have referred to moral comportment rather than to refined forms of behaviour, although the two concepts were closely entwined. The adage reflects the exciting ferment of thought emerging with the birth of humanism in Italy and specifically, the discussion centred on what constituted true nobility. In his *Convivio* (ca. 1304–7), Dante, inspired both by classical ideas and by Boethius, made the claim that it was not birth or wealth that defined an aristocrat. True nobility consisted in virtue. The idea that virtue alone was the title to rule became axiomatic for generations of humanists. Wykeham himself was a self-made man who rose up the echelons of political and ecclesiastical power. Significantly, at a time when most mottos were in Latin or French, Wykeham devised one in English. The maxim neatly sums up the meritocratic impulse that underlies humanist political thought, but also hints at less high-minded ideas—the assumption that cultivated behaviour is the key to social elevation and that being adept at creating a good impression is the most important skill that one acquired through schooling.

While actual social mobility in this period might have been limited in scope, broad swathes of early modern English society seem to have shared the fantasy of climbing the social ladder.[12] This meant that acquiring polished manners as a form of cultural capital was widely regarded as desirable.[13] Social performance, however, implies awareness of an audience: since everyone was performing, everyone was watching everyone else. It is also inevitably shadowed by anxiety, the suspicion that one's presentation was not quite up to the

---

10. Burke, *Fortunes of the Courtier*, 154–55.

11. In the following I am indebted to Griffith, 'Language and Meaning of the College Motto'.

12. Based on the sale of land, Lawrence Stone identifies an unprecedented surge in economic mobility between the mid-sixteenth and mid-seventeenth centuries. See his 'Social Mobility in England'.

13. The idea of 'cultural capital', a term coined by Pierre Bourdieu for apparently insignificant details of dress, bearing, and manners that nonetheless confer social prestige, is discussed in his *Distinction*.

scrutiny of one's peers. These undercurrents in social life are investigated by playwrights in a series of scenarios. The metatheatricality with which early modern drama is permeated makes it ideally suited to anatomize social spectatorship, ironically pointing to the startling resonances between a fictional arena in which all characters are busy observing one another and the surveillance—and self-surveillance—that characterise social life. Furthermore, it suggests that a measure of detachment from our roles might be the way to live together amicably.

The remarkable self-consciousness of early modern drama, its propensity to reflect on its own status as fiction, was not only a result of a preoccupation with social performance and spectatorship. The theatre of the time was mired in contentious discussions about the role of illusion and dissimulation. Antitheatrical writers fulminated against the stage as catering to a slew of sins. The illusions it staged served to seduce spectators to indulge in lust and idleness and most perniciously, gratified their vanity and pride, undermining their humility before God. The Aristotelian notion of mimesis encompassed both imitative practice and representations.[14] In the light of a widespread Calvinist suspicion of all products of the human imagination, some plays probe the very nature of fictions. Attacks on the theatre as based on a tissue of lies are a staple of moral discourse, harking back to Plato's disdain for art as merely an imitation of an imitation, a poor reflection of the truth, and, frequently, a distortion of the truth. They appealed to the senses and catered to the lower passions, he argued.[15] Following St Augustine, who for his part was strongly influenced by Plato's critique of images as at a third remove from the truth, many Calvinist reformers insist that fictions serve, at best, merely frivolous ends, pandering to our pride and self-regard instead of providing a conduit towards the divine.[16] Others point to the Bible as a storehouse of literary forms and tropes to be emulated in the quest for the divine.[17] Both schools of thought propagate

---

14. See Aristotle, *Poetics*, 1448b.

15. For Plato's view on art, see especially the *Republic*, books 3 and 10. No doubt the close link between fictions and lies stems from Plato's disapproval of fictions in the *Republic*, which found a new lease of life in the revival of Augustinianism in the Reformation. As scholar F. M. Cornford pointed out in his edition, *The Republic of Plato* (1941), the term Plato favours, *pseudos*, is far wider than the term 'lie' and applies to all works of the imagination. See Dombrowski, 'Plato's "Noble Lie"', 568.

16. On Augustine's debt to Plato, see Smith, 'Staging the Incarnation'.

17. For many of these thoughts I am indebted to Kahn, *Trouble with Literature*.

a cult of sincerity, stressing the Augustinian injunction to turn one's gaze inward to gain access to the truth.

It is undeniable that the discourse of civility is haunted by dissimulation as its dark double. Some plays, however, suggest that sincerity might be a myth.[18] Proposing that the individual good and the common good are tied up with each other, they indicate that in human relations, there might be no escape from performance. They reveal how in different spheres of life, we play a range of often radically contradictory roles.[19] What I show is that in a number of plays, the writers implicitly offer a defence of role-playing in social life as a variety of dissimulation that draws on the Ciceronian definition of irony as a mode of urbane pretence—'being mock-serious in your whole manner of speaking, while thinking something different from what you are saying'.[20] By holding up its own medium to question, the theatre creates a sense of ironic distance to the roles we play and our immutable conviction of certainty. In a world roiled by religious conflict, in which increasingly rigid group loyalties spurred deep hostility to other members of society, the plays suggest that a pretence of respect in mutual awareness of its status as a performative practice might fulfil a valuable function in maintaining a fragile framework of comity.

These ideas are indebted to the early modern revitalization of rhetoric, which vividly highlighted the ambivalence inherent not only in language but in concepts and values. Similarly, despite the miasma of scandal that surrounded Machiavelli's name, his thought circulated widely. Machiavelli had hollowed out the foundation of normative values, insisting that in political life, qualities such as generosity or fidelity to one's word were not inherently virtuous, but contingent on the effect they created.[21] The most reflective

---

18. Sincerity, Erving Goffman suggested, might simply be the term we use for 'individuals who believe in the impression fostered by their own performance'. See Goffman, *Presentation of Self in Everyday Life*, 28.

19. Ludwig Wittgenstein would formulate the idea of separate language games that govern our lives in his *Philosophical Investigations*; Erving Goffman elaborated similar ideas using the concept of 'frames' in his *Frame Analysis*.

20. Cicero, *On the Ideal Orator*, 2.269. All further references to cited sources are given in parentheses. Cicero distinguishes between a narrower concept of irony as saying something different from what one means (a concept subsequently expanded upon by Quintilian) and Socratian *dissimulatio* ('dissimulation'), a term he uses to render the Greek *eirôneia*. On irony, see especially Muecke, *Irony and the Ironic*, and Rorty, *Contingency, Irony, and Solidarity*. Also see chapter 5.

21. On Machiavelli and rhetoric, see Kahn, *Machiavellian Rhetoric*, and most recently Skinner, 'Machiavelli on Misunderstanding Princely Virtue'.

playwrights of the period go further: they explore the notion that dissimulation might in fact bear an ethical charge. Recently philosopher Kwame Anthony Appiah has made the case for the value of make-believe in our moral and political life. He argues that acting as if others are rational agents while being aware that this is not the case can serve a tactical purpose in civil society and might even motivate our behaviour towards the good.[22] The plays discussed in this book are less sanguine about the effect of pretence in shaping the self. Instead, they posit the use of dissimulation as a means to live together in society.[23] At the same time, they point to the role of fictions in social life.

In civil society, fictions play a crucial part. We impose meaning on the world in the form of belief and values. As Hobbes would point out, civil society itself is an artefact, a fiction in which we jointly acquiesce. The ideal of a common endeavour and the idea that our interests are indissolubly linked to those of our fellow beings are nothing but fictions that we collectively agree to believe in. In its insistence on its own nature as fabrication, the drama of the time hints that many of the beliefs a society claims as immutable truths might be constructions too. Nonetheless, some ideals might serve a vital function in underpinning our communal lives. It is in fictions such as the notion of a shared human bond that civil society is grounded.

The Origins of Renaissance Civility

At the root of European ideas of civility lies the notion of decorum articulated by Cicero in his *De officiis*, a book whose influence remained salient until far into the Age of Enlightenment.[24] In medieval Europe, rules of good behaviour did not, as is generally believed, originate at court, but were first formulated as a guide to regulate communal life in monasteries.[25] The best-known of these works are the fourth-century adaptation of Cicero's *De officiis* by St Ambrose, Archbishop of Milan, and the sixth-century *Rule of Saint Benedict*. At the royal courts, courtesy literature as a genre emerged in the twelfth century.[26] The

---

22. See Appiah, *As If*. Appiah makes it clear that stressing the role of enabling fictions in political and social life does not mean endorsing a Platonic 'noble lie' imposed by the rulers of a given society (*Rep.* 414b–415c). In a just society, beliefs would be grounded in the shared reason of all members of society and would be open to deliberation.

23. See Bybee, *How Civility Works*, to which I am greatly indebted.

24. The text will be discussed in detail in chapter 1.

25. See Knox, '*Disciplina*', and 'Erasmus' *De civilitate*'.

26. See Gillingham, 'From *Civilitas* to Civility', and Nicholls, *Matter of Courtesy*.

influential treatise *Urbanus Magnus* by Daniel of Beccles is believed to be one of the first courtesy books to appear in England. In the thirteenth century, courtesy texts, often in the form of poems, circulated in Anglo-Norman, the language of the elite; versions in English appeared only in the fourteenth and fifteenth centuries. These writings disseminate the ideals of courtesy that were inculcated into members of the aristocracy. They often centre on rituals in the noble household, above all during communal meals.[27]

The Renaissance concept of civility was decisively shaped by the humanist polymath Erasmus. His little treatise, *De civilitate morum puerilium* ('On good manners for children'), became one of the first bestsellers; it is hard to overstate its print popularity, with twelve editions in 1530 alone, and more than thirty editions in the first six years of its publication. Published by Johann Froben in Basel, its influence was rapidly felt throughout Europe. In 1531 it was translated into High German, in 1537 into French and Czech. Dutch, Swedish, and Finnish translations followed. In 1532, two years after its appearance, a English-Latin version by Robert Whittington was published, entitled *A lytell booke of good maners for children*.[28] Eighty editions, translations, and adaptations appeared in the sixteenth century. Shorn of references to Catholicism, it became a standard pedagogical text in Protestant schools; purged of the name of Erasmus, whose works had been placed on the Index, it was used in Catholic schools throughout Europe. The book spawned a spate of epigones, directed at children or at adults. The dissemination of civility was galvanized by the spread of literacy and the burgeoning print market. A second French translation of Erasmus's text in 1558, published by Robert Grandjon, even introduced a new typeface later known as the *lettre de civilité*.[29]

Many of the precepts set out in *De civilitate*—as in other early modern treatises of civility—are taken verbatim from medieval manuals of courtesy. As John Gillingham points out, 'In essence the ideas in *De Civilitate* were medieval commonplaces'.[30] Nonetheless, Erasmus introduced a radically new dimension in the history of civility. While his ideas on education bear the

---

27. See Bryson, *From Courtesy to Civility*, 68–74.

28. Brian McGregor, 'Introductory Note', in Erasmus, *On Good Manners for Boys*, 272. In the early modern period the term 'manners' referred predominantly either to mores and habitual conduct or to morals, although increasingly the current meaning of polite social behaviour gained prevalence. See *OED*, s.v. 'manner, n.'.

29. Chartier, 'From Texts to Manners', 76–77.

30. Gillingham, 'From *Civilitas* to Civility', 278.

stamp of his broadly rational Christianity, they were also imbued with the legacy of civic humanism, a term, attributed to historian Hans Baron, to describe the revival of classical notions of civic engagement in fifteenth-century Italy.[31] For Erasmus, the minutiae of everyday life are inextricably bound up with the community of citizens at large. Keen to evade the aristocratic connotations of medieval *courtoisie*, he draws on the Ciceronian ideal of a civil society (*societas civilis*), a community which reconciled individual interest with the common good or the well-being of the community as a whole.[32]

It is true that for Cicero, the community of citizens was tantamount to the Roman polity (the *res publica*)—the common good was congruent with the good of Rome. But it was by no means always the case that civil society was aligned with the state and its interests.[33] Long before eighteenth-century philosophers formulated a theory of civil society, Anna Bryson argues, the early modern period, informed by the ideas of civic humanism, saw the emergence of a sense of commonality that undergirded all social relations, a notion that was promulgated in manuals of civility.[34] The broad purview of civil manners they outline is epitomized in the term 'civil conversation', defined by Stefano Guazzo in his *Civile Conversation* (1574) as courteous commerce with 'all sortes of persons of what place, or of what calling soever they are'.[35] Only later would Hegel formulate a definition of civil society as a network of social relations that constituted a realm of social life between the state and the family.[36]

De civilitate is part of Erasmus's larger agenda to inculcate virtue into the elite by means of a rigorous regime of education. In northern Europe, it was Erasmus who spearheaded the movement whose watchword was the notion

---

31. See Baron, *Crisis of the Early Italian Renaissance*.

32. Cicero, *De oratore* 2.68, *De re publica* 1.49. Although in the Renaissance the latter was available only in fragments, Cicero's ideas were well-known from other sources, such as Augustine's *City of God*.

33. For a history of the concept of 'civil society', see Ehrenberg, *Civil Society*. The humanist debate about the 'common weal' or 'commonwealth', a conflicted term that could define the common good as identical with the good either of the polity or of the commonalty, runs through Tudor political discourse about the commonwealth, as exemplified in the divergence between Thomas Starkey's Ciceronian views, articulated in his *Dialogue between Pole and Lupset* (1529–32), and the work of Sir Thomas Smith, notably his *De Republica Anglorum* (1565, pub. 1583). On the concept of the commonwealth, see Early Modern Research Group, 'Commonwealth'.

34. See Bryson, *From Courtesy to Civility*, 43–74.

35. Guazzo, *Civile Conversation*, vol. 1, 1.56.

36. Hegel, *Grundlinien der Philosphie des Rechts*, §§182–256, pp. 142–80.

of true nobility (*vera nobilitas*), the insistence that virtue, not birth, was decisive in defining nobility. Like so many other radical humanist ideas, these views were appropriated with alacrity by the ruling classes, who set out to acquire civil manners as a mode of signalling their virtue. If the humanists failed dramatically in their goal of indoctrinating their noble charges with virtue, their campaign to make education a sine qua non in elite circles was a spectacular success, with the nobility and gentry flocking to universities to hone the skills expected of a gentleman.[37] The belief that virtue was achieved, not innate, became a truism; noble status, like virtue, was not a birthright, but needed to be displayed in one's actions, demeanour, carriage, and gestures.

In Middle English, 'civility' referred to citizenship and civil order, to a body politic, or, alternatively, to secular office. In the course of the sixteenth century, the signification of 'civility' as relating to polite behaviour emerged in a variety of European vernaculars.[38] The earlier term 'courtesy', with its connotations of chivalric courtliness, continued to be in circulation, and throughout the early modern period 'civil' and 'courteous' were used interchangeably, although in the seventeenth century 'civility' became the more frequently used term. Sir Thomas Elyot's Latin-English *Dictionary* of 1538 lists both 'courteysy' and 'civilitie' as synonyms for *civilitas*, as does John Florio for *civilità* in his Italian-English dictionary, *A Worlde of Wordes* (1598). A sixteenth-century courtesy book plays it safe by opting for the title *The Courte of Civill Courtesie* (1577).[39] The word 'politeness' as a synonym for good manners became widely current only in the eighteenth century.[40]

Inevitably, 'civility' was linked to the conduct of a gentleman: one of the earliest English dictionaries, Robert Cawdrey's 1604 *Table Alphabeticall*, defines 'civilitie' as 'honest in conversation, or gentle in behaviour', neatly encapsulating the nexus between civility, honour, and gentility.[41] In the early

---

37. The seminal work in this field is Skinner, *Foundations of Modern Political Thought*. Also see Brett and Tully, *Rethinking the Foundations of Modern Political Thought*.

38. *OED*, s.v. 'civility, n.'.

39. Elyot, *The Dictionary of Syr Thomas Eliot knyght*, D2v; Florio, *A Worlde of Wordes*, G1v; R[obson], *The Courte of Civill Courtesie*.

40. See Thomas, *In Pursuit of Civility*, 2–7, 15–17, and Withington, *Society in Early Modern England*, 186–88. For a discussion of a similar trajectory of the term *civilité* in France, see Chartier, 'From Texts to Manners'.

41. Cawdrey, *A Table Alphabeticall*, C3r. In citing early modern texts, u, v, i, and j have been normalized and contractions have been expanded. The term 'honest' is derived from 'honour'. *OED*, s.v. 'honest, adj. and adv.', 2.a.

modern era, the term also took on the wider connotations of a highly developed culture, as opposed to the backward manner of life of ostensibly more barbarous nations. The word *civilisation* emerged in French only in the 1750s and in English at the end of the seventeenth century, and subsequently replaced 'civility' for a culturally advanced way of living. But an enduring feature of the European discourse of civility was the opposition between what were regarded as cultured societies and barbaric peoples. A legacy of the ancient Greek concept of civility, which was defined in contrast to barbarism, and transposed to the medieval conflict between allegedly civilized Christian nations and a barbarous Islam, this distinction played a crucial role in encounters with non-European nations. In his *Race and Rhetoric in the Renaissance: Barbarian Errors* (2009), Ian Smith has meticulously traced the root of the notion of barbarism to the Greek exaltation of rhetoric and a culture of debate as the main marker of Hellenic identity. The fifth-century conflict with Persia, he argues, led to the emergence of a vision of Greek civilization as defined against inferior barbarian cultures which lacked the political system and linguistic skills that the Greeks boasted. As Keith Thomas has shown in his magisterial work, *In Pursuit of Civility: Manners and Civilization in Early Modern England* (2018), the putative superiority of Western manners and civilization of European societies was used to justify the colonisation of large parts of the world.

Rhetoric, Theatricality, Print

In this book, the focus is on a different set of oppositions that shapes civility—the divergence between commonality and a shared purpose on the one hand, and unbridled individualism or rigorous partisan interests on the other. Erasmus might have set the course for the early modern concept of civility, but equally influential for the Renaissance culture of manners was Castiglione's *Book of the Courtier* (1528). The book is an exquisite portrait of an Arcadian haven of elegance and grace that never quite existed. It is a guidebook for the aspiring courtier, although book 4 veers into the exhortative idiom of a 'mirror for princes'. Written for an aristocracy in crisis, embattled by the expanding power of the centralized nation-state and the innovations in the technology of warfare which increasingly made its military role irrelevant, the text is a survival manual for the elite. Style, not birth, is the critical factor, it suggests; of crucial importance is the notion of *sprezzatura*, the air of nonchalance that Castiglione urges his peers to display in everything they say and do. Casual ease became the byword for the training of a gentleman in the coming centuries, as exemplified in Locke's *Thoughts Concerning Education* (1693) and Chesterfield's *Letters to His Son* (1774). Locke recommends a graceful carriage that should appear to be 'without care and without thought' and stresses that 'the manner of doing is of more consequence than the thing done'.[42] For Chesterfield, noble identity is defined by the possession of an intangible quality, a *je ne sçais quoi*, that effectively barred entrance to those who were considered lacking in this discipline.[43] Together, the *Courtier* and *De civilitate* epitomize the conflict within the concept of early modern civility with which this book is concerned.

Influenced by Cicero and Quintilian, Castiglione formulates a rhetoric of social life. The rise of civility in the early modern period was closely connected to the Renaissance resurgence of rhetoric.[44] The classical commonplace that rhetoric was the impetus behind civilisation was frequently cited by Renaissance theorists.[45] The roots of the humanist revival of rhetoric lie in thirteenth-century epistolary manuals (the *ars dictaminis*), collections of model letters and rhetorical guidelines, which developed into mirrors for princes, dispensing advice about virtuous conduct to rulers and members of the governing class.[46] Ancient rhetoric, like ancient thought, was rooted in the philosophical notion of a cosmos governed by reason and harmony in which human nature participated, invoked by Cicero in his speaker Crassus's remark that 'all the universe above and below us is a unity and is bound together by a single, natural force and harmony' (3.20).[47] It was a vision that was largely shared by all philosophical schools, even if it was most forcefully articulated in Stoic thought. For ancients, there was a correlation between the ideal self and the larger rational order, reflected in an intrinsic link between external features and one's moral character. One's exterior was thought to denote one's personality: a slovenly demeanour and a careless diction and delivery revealed flaws of the mind. As Seneca puts it, 'Style is the garb of thought'.[48] He devotes Epistle 114 to expanding this notion, castigating a degenerate style of speech

---

42. Locke, *Some Thoughts Concerning Education*, sec. 93.

43. Lord Chesterfield urges his son to acquire 'the pleasing *je ne sçais quoi*, which everybody feels, though nobody can describe'. See his *Letters*, 72.

44. See Peltonen, 'Hypocrisy, Dissimulation, and Education'.

45. See Cicero, *De inventione*, 1.2.2; Quintilian, *Institutio oratoria*, 2.16.9.

46. Skinner, *Foundations of Modern Political Thought*, 1:28–41.

47. Even philosophical schools which rejected this idea, such as Epicureanism, continued to define themselves in relation to it and uphold the value of reason. See Taylor, *Sources of the Self*, 124–26. Also see Kraye, 'Moral Philosophy'.

48. Seneca, *Ep.* 115.2, in *Epistles 93–124*.

that he identifies in Roman society. The classical premise for regulating one's manners and discourse was to shape one's character to align it with the universal rational order. Not only did comportment disclose one's inner self—discipline of the body was a means of moulding the mind. These ideas were adopted wholesale into Christian thought. In Renaissance Europe, Stephen Greenblatt has famously identified an increased propensity towards self-fashioning with an eye to seizing opportunities for self-advancement in every sphere. Rhetorical handbooks as well as courtesy manuals proffered theatrical advice as to how to stage the performance of a desired self.[49]

Renaissance rhetoricians were as concerned with conversational speech (*sermo*) as with oratory in the pulpit and the law courts. One of the most prolific contributors to Renaissance rhetoric was Erasmus. His textbook *De copia* was the most printed rhetoric written in the Renaissance and ran to 168 editions between 1512 and 1580. His epistolary manual, *De conscribendis epistolis*, appeared in 90 editions between 1521 and 1692. Peter Mack argues that Erasmus inaugurated a fundamentally new approach to educational letter writing, shifting the emphasis from following a set of rules to the relationship between writer and addressee. In a manual dedicated largely to behavioural advice, Erasmus underlines the importance of accommodating oneself to the recipient of the letter.[50]

There are close convergences not only between decorous behaviour and rhetoric, but also between rhetoric and acting. Alongside Cicero's work, Quintilian's *Institutio oratoria* was regarded as one of the most important classical texts. Quintilian devotes most of book 11 of the *Institutio oratoria* to discussing the means of achieving eloquence in both speech and body language. *Actio* or delivery, he claims, serves all three goals of rhetoric: to persuade, to please, and to move the audience. Even a mediocre speech delivered effectively will carry more weight than an excellent speech unaccompanied by the appropriate tone of voice or gestures. With meticulous care Quintilian takes the reader through all the elements involved in the deportment of the orator: carriage of the head, neck, shoulders, and arms, expression of the face, gestures of the body, and proper stance. He even gives elaborate instructions as to how the orator should wear the toga. How the orator dresses denotes his standing and should always convey distinction. Quintilian draws frequent analogies to stage practitioners, dissecting the acting styles of famous stage players. At moments his text segues

49. See Greenblatt, *Renaissance Self-Fashioning*.
50. Mack, *History of Renaissance Rhetoric*, 76, 90–96, 245–46.

into an acting manual. He observes that in the course of a speech, 'it is quite proper for the fold [of the toga] to slip, apparently accidentally, off the shoulder', calling attention to the management of dress as a factor in enhancing one's performance. At the end of an oration, disordered clothing contributes a touch of veracity to one's display of passion, he asserts, and adds facetiously, 'Personally, I think that dishevelled hair has some emotional impact'.[51]

It is important to remember that rhetorical training in the early modern age was profoundly theatrical. In a landmark study, *Shakespeare's Schoolroom* (2012), Lynn Enterline points out that humanist schoolmasters reshaped Latin teaching to place emphasis on imitation rather than rule learning. This involved mimicking the schoolmaster's facial expressions and gestures as much as his words, and exercises in which students demonstrated their own skill at delivery. School theatricals were regularly performed to offer further opportunities for the practice of declamation. Grammar schools were laboratories in which a humanist education was intended to engrain the norms of gentlemanly conduct, in the same way as Quintilian's programme of education was meant to mould the future generation of the Roman elite. As Enterline writes, 'Acquiring socially sanctioned habits of speech, movement, and affect in such a disciplinary setting means that a scholar learned to adopt the verbal and corporal behavior of others and also learned to monitor his own performance while imitating those examples'.[52] The popular theatre was indebted to the rhetorical culture absorbed by a host of students who went on to become playwrights, although, as she argues, they frequently set out to undermine many of the ideological precepts drilled into them in the classroom.

A decisive factor in the dissemination of both rhetoric and civility was the print market. Ideas on civility are to be found in works as diverse as books of moral philosophy, treatises on nobility, conversation manuals, educational primers, epistolary guides, and books of table talk. Much of courtesy literature was regarded as ephemera and is rarely mentioned in library or auction catalogues, although a few records of the most prestigious works survive.[53] Peter Burke has meticulously put together a list of readers of Castiglione's *Courtier* before 1700, including those who allude to his book without attribution.[54] The account book of William Cavendish, future Earl of Devonshire and employer

51. Quintilian, *Orator's Education*, 11.3.144, 148.
52. Enterline, *Shakespeare's Schoolroom*, 40.
53. Bryson, *From Courtesy to Civility*, 264.
54. See Burke, *Fortunes of the* Courtier, 163–78.

of Hobbes as tutor for his son, lists binding costs for Guazzo's *Civile Conversation* and notes the purchase of a copy of the *Courtier*.[55] Courtesy books were of interest to aspirants of the merchant and professional class as much as to noblemen. The early modern period saw a fascination with self-help books of every stripe. If religious writings claimed the lion's share of the print market, conduct manuals, together with histories and romances, were among the most frequently printed genres of secular writing in the sixteenth century.[56] As Markku Peltonen points out, the early modern culture of civility was in part a product of the marketplace of print.[57] Admittedly, market share is not the only way of assessing the influence of these texts. Courtesy texts, like other self-help texts, were appropriated, adapted, excerpted, assimilated, or modified in numerous ways, usually without attribution. Widely known texts such as Giovanni Della Casa's *Galateo* (1558) were appended (unattributed) to other writings, often aimed at a less prestigious sector of the market, as was the case with Walter Darell's *A Short discourse of the life of Servingmen* (1578). Another example is Eustache De Refuge's *Traicté de la cour, ou instruction des courtisans* (1616, translated into English in 1622), part of which appeared anonymously under the title *Arcana Aulica: or Walsingham's Manual of Prudential Maxims for the States-Man And Courtier* in 1652. To market the text the publisher insinuates that it had been penned by the Elizabethan statesman Sir Francis Walsingham, a bid to capitalise on the latter's reputation for political sagacity.

The Historical Matrix of Early Modern Civility

As Norbert Elias has shown in the foundational study of the history of manners, *The Civilizing Process* (1939), the notion of civility acquired a particular urgency in the early modern era. While many of his ideas, written under the influence of Freud's *Civilization and Its Discontents* (1930), are no longer in common currency, his important insight that the Renaissance culture of civility evolved in response to the denser web of human relations at court and in metropolitan centres remains invaluable. With the expansion of the nation-state in Europe, the dispersed power bases of feudal nobles were significantly weakened. Power was concentrated at the court of the ruler, where the nobility

---

55. Willes, *In the Shadow of St. Paul's Cathedral*, 55–56.
56. Mack, *Elizabethan Rhetoric*, 135. On the print market, see Halasz, *Marketplace of Print*, and Farmer and Lesser, 'What Is Print Popularity?'
57. Peltonen, *Duel in Early Modern England*, 5.

converged. The centralized states of Europe arrogated a monopoly of violence to themselves, Elias argues, compelling the aristocracy to find means of coexisting in close social spaces without recourse to direct aggression.[58] The fluctuation of status at court made it expedient to defer to all members of court society. But it was the growth of urbanisation which led to an increase in human interdependence on all levels of society and raised the stakes for civility in social intercourse. Self-restraint and the need to avoid offence to others became of vital importance as a means to manage the tensions between various social groups. Manners lubricated relations between all ranks of society, not merely among peers.

At the same time, an aristocracy in crisis was under pressure to find a new self-definition for its role in society. Suave manners became a mark of gentility and served to demonstrate a gentleman's claim to inclusion in the ruling class. Nobility had to be performed and, in a highly volatile social world, needed to be incessantly reiterated.[59] In contrast to earlier generations of the nobility, a premium was laid on education, of which manners were regarded as a part. Affability and a polished social demeanour were also indispensable resources in social advancement. It became imperative to cultivate the art of pleasing and charm those with leverage to help the courtier gain preferment.

In the wake of the dissolution of monasteries, England experienced an explosion in the number of gentry. There was an unprecedented turnover in the sale of land, an index of the rise in social mobility which lasted until the advent of the Civil War. Other factors contributed to the changes in the social fabric too, including the steep demand for administrators in state service, economic growth for those in commerce, and the wide-scale spread of education, at the level of grammar schools as well as the universities and Inns of Court, leading to a sharp increase in graduates vying for the prestigious positions on offer.[60] The definition of a gentleman expanded to include a wide range of individuals, from students to members of the professions. In addition, the sale of titles under James I, gleefully mocked in the theatre, fuelled the inflation in

---

58. For a deeply sceptical view of Elias's theory and its legacy, see Carroll, *Enmity and Violence in Early Modern Europe*, who argues that far from defusing aggression, Renaissance civility and its corollary, a heightened quest for status, served only to exacerbate violence among the aristocracy.

59. See Posner, *Performance of Nobility*.

60. There is a rich vein of historical writing on society in early modern England. See, inter alia, Stone, *Crisis of the Aristocracy*; Wrightson, *English Society*; Thomas, *Ends of Life*; and Withington, *Society in Early Modern England*.

membership of the gentry. The mass medium of the theatre catered to a shared dream of rising in status. Whatever the realities of their lives, it is true that in the metropolis, week for week large numbers of spectators flocked to see plays that dramatized the theme of social aspiration from a seemingly inexhaustible variety of angles.

Treatises of the court such as Castiglione's *Book of the Courtier* may have been written as an attempt to secure the boundaries of an elite club and exclude interlopers; one of the interlocutors in the dialogue, Federico Fregoso, devises the game of defining the ideal courtier around which the book is structured 'in order to put down the many fools who in their presumption and ineptitude think to gain the name of good courtier'.[61] However, once in print, manuals of manners were accessible to a far broader segment of society than their writers might have envisaged and were avidly consumed by a newly literate public hungry for works of self-improvement.[62] In England, the cachet of Italian culture meant that at least until the end of the sixteenth century, these texts were mainly translations from Italian originals, although later on French texts took precedence.[63] (One early homegrown product, *The Courte of Civill Courtesie*, attempts to palm itself off on the reader as the translation of a text 'written by a Noble and grave personage of Italy', one Bengalassa del Mont. Prisacchi Retta. At least one reader swallowed the bait, as is attested by a letter written by Gabriel Harvey in the mid-1570s.)[64] The profusion of translations of classical writings or contemporary works in Italian and French into the vernacular was the fruit of a deeply nationalist project to enrich the culture and improve the mores of the inhabitants of England.[65] In the prefatory letter to his translation of Castiglione's *Cortegiano*, Sir Thomas Hoby, the diplomat and scholar who belonged to the circle around the Cambridge humanist John Cheke, urges his fellow *literati* to undertake the labour of translation to help uplift the nation so that, as he laments, 'we alone of the worlde maye not bee

---

61. Castiglione, *Book of the Courtier*, 1.12. In chapter 1 I draw on the acclaimed Singleton translation in preference to Hoby's version.

62. See Whigham, *Ambition and Privilege*.

63. Alistair Fox describes the upsurge in the number of books translated and adapted from the Italian from the 1560s to the 1590s in *The English Renaissance*, 18–37.

64. R[obson], *The Courte of Civill Courtesie*, A2v. Gabriel Harvey lists it among other well-known courtesy books. See Harvey, *Letter-Book of Gabriel Harvey*, 78–79.

65. On the reception of Italian courtesy books in England, see esp. Javitch, *Poetry and Courtliness in Renaissance England*; Burke, *Fortunes of the Courtier*; Bryson, *From Courtesy to Civility*; Richards, *Rhetoric and Courtliness*; Shrank, 'Masters of Civility'; and Partridge, '"Absolute Castilio"?'

styll counted barbarous in oure tunge, as in time out of minde we have bene in our maners'.⁶⁶ By contrast, George Pettie, who in 1581 is responsible for 'Englishing' *La civil conversatione* (1574) by Stefano Guazzo, defends England as 'the civilest Countrey in the worlde'. In a curiously timeless comment, he blames the bad opinion of the English on the uncouth behaviour of his countrymen abroad. They also slander their homeland, inexplicably reporting that 'our Countrey is barbarous, our maners rude, and our people uncivile'. England, he insists, is as cultured in its manners and lifestyle as every other nation in Europe.⁶⁷ Nonetheless, he is keen to make one of the most influential works on civility available to his compatriots.

While men of letters like Sir Thomas Hoby were fired by the ambition to expand the minds of their fellow countrymen and worried about the stigma of barbarism that clung to both the language and manners of the English, John Keper, the probable translator of Annibale Romei's *Discorsi* (1585), a dialogue set at the court of Ferrara that is closely modelled on Castiglione's *Courtier*, was beset by a different anxiety. In his own epistle to the reader, he acknowledges that making privileged knowledge accessible to all might be a double-edged sword. He cites critical voices who argue that it would be detrimental to the social order to have the 'vulgar sort' enlightened of their ignorance: 'high wisedome, and excellent workes, should be concealed from common sight'.⁶⁸ There is a price to be paid for providing the great unwashed with access to the savoir-faire of the elite—it paves the way for social upstarts to encroach on the preserve of privilege. Manners, he insinuates, have turned into a commodity that can be procured on the marketplace of print. Enabling spectators to ape the conduct of their betters was also one of the accusations levelled at the public stage by social critics, and no doubt contributed powerfully to the appeal of the theatre, where the lifestyle of the elite was retailed to an audience of status seekers in the form of commercial entertainment. Keper articulates the crux at the heart of civility: the conflict between manners as an exclusionary device, intended to distinguish an elitist in-group from outsiders, and manners as a technique of promoting mutuality and communal life. This issue is linked to the question of whether civil behaviour is meant solely to serve the self-promotion of an individual or that of a clique, or whether it contributes to the notion of a shared purpose in society.

---

66. *The courtyer of Count Baldessar Castilio*, B1r.
67. Pettie's Preface to the Readers, *Civile Conversation*, vol. 1, 10–11.
68. Romei, *The Courtiers Academie*, A3r.

The potent brew of ideas that shaped the early modern theatre was also formative for the Renaissance culture of civility. Cicero's *De officiis*, which dominated both the medieval and the early modern eras, remained a vital source of inspiration for thinkers and statemen: with a nod to Pliny, one courtesy writer notes that Lord Burghley 'to his dying day would always carry it about him, either in his bosom or pocket'.[69] By the end of the sixteenth century, however, in the face of the rise of absolutism throughout Europe, Ciceronianism found itself under attack on a number of fronts. Disillusion with early humanism prepared the ground for the rise of Tacitism, with its dark view of political life as based on mendacity and manipulation. The influence of Tacitean ideas, often in conjunction with Neostoicism, was formative in writings by thinkers such as Lipsius and Bacon, but also left its trace on courtesy writings and on the drama of the era. Dissimulation was advocated as the new face of prudence. Court manuals dispense cynical nuggets of advice as to how to navigate the treacherous swamp of court life, often delivered with a disingenuous gloss of disapproval, as in the adage recycled by Eustache de Refuge about the common court practice to 'put out our legge to make a man fall, thereby to binde and obliege him to us, in succouring and lifting him up'.[70] In the theatre, plays such as *Hamlet* and *Sejanus* depict a world of incessant spying and Machiavellian intrigue.

At the same time, the period experienced a resuscitation of Augustianism, in Calvinist culture but also in Counter-Reformation thought. Augustine's stringent denunciation of lying, influenced by Plato's strictures against falsehood in any form, and his scathing exposure of the self-love with which exemplars of classical virtue were riddled were significant for the emergence of the culture of sincerity and the debate about pretence that was staged in the theatre. The question of civil behaviour was by no means uncontested in religious writings. Nevertheless, most divines in the Elizabethan and Jacobean era, whether Puritan in leaning or staunch supporters of the established Church, accepted the importance of a courteous comportment towards others.[71] In his popular guide to a Christian life, *Of Domesticall Duties*, Puritan William Gouge

---

69. Peacham, *The Complete Gentleman*, 57, drawing on the Elder Pliny's tribute to *De officiis* as a volume 'worth having in one's hands every day, nay, even learning by heart', in his *Natural History*, 15. I am grateful to Rhodri Lewis for drawing my attention to this reference.

70. Refuge, *A Treatise of the Court*, V1r.

71. This changed with the appearance of the Quakers, who rejected civility on religious grounds. See Thomas, *In Pursuit of Civility*, 311–18.

grapples with godly objections to civility which point to the rift between manners and morals. He concedes that there is a kernel of truth in arguments that civil conduct is often only a matter of feigning: 'many that have not a sparke of Gods feare in their hearts, are able to carry themselves in their outward behaviour very orderly and mannerly'. Still, he advocates a form of Christian decorum, since 'it beseemeth Christians to *doe all things decently*', and urges parents to teach their children good manners.[72] While stressing the value of deferential manners towards one's superiors, divines such as William Perkins insist that courtesy reflect sincere feelings: 'Right curtesie is with an honest heart', he claims.[73] And the antitheatricalist William Rankins, while lambasting players, who, like flatterers, 'séeme to be that they are not, and are that they séeme not to be', is careful to distinguish between true civility and flattery. Satan, he maintains, uses the 'visarde of humaine [civil] curtesie' to entice us to plays, but in reality, 'flattery and humaine curtesie be two contraries'.[74] On the other side of the religious spectrum, Church of England minister Nehemiah Rogers, friend of Archbishop Laud, emphatically rejects the common belief among 'men of the world' that religion 'makes men clownish [rustic]'. On the contrary, 'God hath his Ethicks, a doctrine of behaviour, in his word', he declares, 'whereby hee teacheth us how to carry our selves wisely and civilly towards all'. Rogers berates those who refuse to greet others and insists that greetings and common salutations are due even to an unbeliever.[75]

Organisation of the Book

In the study of early modern English literature, civility is usually discussed in connection with courtly writings such as Spenser's *Faerie Queene*. A notable exception is *Shakespeare's Comic Commonwealths* by Camille Wells Slights, which looks at Shakespeare's comedies. However, her interest lies in one pole of civility, social interaction in a community, rather than in Renaissance manners.[76]

---

72. Gouge, *Of Domesticall Duties*, 2M1v–2r, emphasis original.
73. *Works of William Perkins*, 2F2r.
74. Rankins, *A Mirrour of Monsters*, D2v–3r, E1v–2r. Like a number of turncoat antitheatrical writers, Rankins was probably a hack writer who tried his hand at writing plays himself. See Hill, '"He Hath Changed His Coppy"'.
75. Rogers, *Christian Curtesie*, E4v–F2r.
76. For an attempt to read *Love's Labour's Lost* in conjunction with Castiglione's *Courtier*, see Ghose, *Shakespeare and Laughter*, 15–51; for a look at *Much Ado About Nothing* through the lens of the culture of civility, see Ghose, *Much Ado About Nothing*.

In this book I look at drama staged at the public theatre as well as in hall playhouses. The focus is on pre-Caroline drama, where the distinctions between the theatrical sites are less decisive than in the period from the 1630s onwards.[77] The role of the theatre as an agent of civility in the Caroline period is patent at a time when plays bear titles such as Shirley's *Love Tricks, or The School of Complement* or Richard Brome's *The New Academy*, both of which exploit the vogue for academies for manners. This book argues that the Elizabethan and Jacobean theatre, too, played a decisive part in the culture of civility. A striking difference between sixteenth-century Italian courtesy books and the English tradition is the sharper focus on the gentlemanly ideal of service to the commonwealth and a marked lack of interest in the discourse of love. While Hoby's translation of the *Courtier*, which grew out of an initial rendering of book 3, the section on the Court Lady, at the request of 'a Gentlewoman of the Courte', was advertised on its title page as 'very necessary and profitable for yonge Gentilmen and Gentlewomen abiding in Court, Palaice or Place', most Elizabethan and Jacobean manuals tend to concentrate on the skills required to forge the image of gentleman.[78] By contrast, the important role of women in the culture of civility is represented in Caroline drama, where it coincided with a renewed interest in Neoplatonism in the late Stuart court under the influence of Queen Henrietta Maria. Nonetheless, the civility of women is reflected in a number of the plays discussed in this book. Female wit in particular plays a central role in the theatre.[79]

The approach taken in the book is not chronological but thematic. Each chapter addresses a different aspect of early modern civility. Reading key courtesy texts alongside a selection of Elizabethan and Jacobean plays provides an insight into how prescriptive norms are translated into the stuff of fiction. What the plays reveal is the slippage between ideal and practice—the contradictions and conflicts that emerge when abstract ethical precepts are set against the variety and complexity of human nature.

The first chapter juxtaposes Castiglione's *Book of the Courtier* with Shakespeare's *Merchant of Venice*. Famous for coining the concept of *sprezzatura* for a performance of nonchalant ease, which became the hallmark of the gentleman in the centuries to come, Castiglione fabricates an ideal society at the

---

77. See Gurr, *Playgoing in Shakespeare's London*, 85–94.
78. *The courtyer*, B1r. Hoby was probably commissioned to translate book 3 of the *Courtier* by Elizabeth, Marchioness of Northampton. See Burke, *Fortunes of the Courtier*, 149.
79. See Withington, 'Tumbled into the Dirt'.

court of Urbino, suffused with laughter, civility, and mutual esteem. The Shakespearean version of Urbino is Belmont, an Arcadian enclave peopled by individuals of style and grace. But in Belmont, as at Urbino, the performance of mutual regard is reserved exclusively for a coterie of cultivated people. Both the *Courtier* and *The Merchant of Venice* are deeply preoccupied with the vexed relation between ethics and aesthetics and the role fictions play in shaping our lives. The play strips away its dazzling veneer of civility to show us a set of careless rich people who retreat back into their money and whose notions of the law ignore the larger connotations of justice and the human bond, a cultural fiction that posits that our interests are inevitably bound up with those of other human beings. The play also reveals unpleasant truths about ourselves as spectators and our craving for a world of glamour that elides the sordid reality on which it is built.

Chapter 2 looks at manners and the early modern market. In a society in the throes of a dream of upward mobility, a variety of treatises and courtesy books discuss the question of how to define a gentleman. Gentlemanly identity, it emerges, is not innate but fluctuates in value and requires constant performance. In Ben Jonson's *Every Man Out of His Humour*, civility is governed by the logic of the market. The motif of ceaseless scrutiny of others reflects a world of ruthless self-interest in which everyone is in competition with one another for enhanced social prestige. In city comedy, teeming with impostors, tricksters, and witty women, personhood is refashioned at will, catering to audience fantasies of re-creating oneself in the metropolis. A phenomenon that represents the radical ambivalence of civility is the duel. Throughout Europe, the Renaissance cult of civility and a fierce struggle for status fuelled a rage for duelling among the elite. Thomas Middleton's *A Fair Quarrel*, cowritten with William Rowley, turns on the themes of honour and the duel and pits a notion of civility as a relationship of mutuality against civility as an obsessive quest for individual self-advancement.

Two works which comment ironically on the Renaissance culture of civility are Philibert de Vienne's *The Philosopher of the Court* (1547) and Della Casa's *Galateo* (1558). In the third chapter, these texts, together with Stefano Guazzo's *Civile Conversation*, are discussed alongside Shakespeare's *Coriolanus*. Philibert's satirical view of Castiglione's *Courtier* is in fact a veiled attack on Ciceronian decorum, which is regarded as opening the way for hypocrisy and falsehood, while Della Casa's work is permeated with anxiety about the close link between civility and lying. *Coriolanus* explores the themes of civility, deceit, and role-playing, portraying a self-righteous protagonist who insists on authentic selfhood and who passionately rejects pretence. The play echoes St Augustine's excoriation of classical ethics as based on a web of lies and his denunciation of classical role models as in thrall to self-delusion. Shakespeare implies that Augustine was right: Coriolanus's dream of radical autonomy is a myth, premised on lying to himself and others. *Coriolanus* does not, however, follow Augustine in advocating an inward turn as a solution to mendacity. On the contrary, it suggests that we are ineluctably social, and that role-playing might be impossible to disentangle from social life. In human interaction, the play intimates, a measure of pretence is inescapable. What is key is the roles we choose to play and the end they serve.

The fourth chapter discusses a number of writings from late sixteenth-century Europe that explore the dark sides of civility: duplicity, mutual surveillance, and sycophancy. A close look at works by political theorists such as Lipsius and Bacon, at a court manual, Lorenzo Ducci's *Ars Aulica*, and at Thomas Wright's treatise *The Passions of the Mind in General* (1604) reveals a widespread concern with concealing one's passions and an intense scrutiny of the self and others for personal gain, or alternatively, for reasons of state. Dramatized in Ben Jonson's tragedy, *Sejanus*, the pervasive culture of spying and paranoia is mirrored in metatheatrical moments in the play. *Sejanus* offers a terrifying vision of a civil society in ruins, in which public discourse is flooded with lies and mutual mistrust flourishes. Influenced not only by Tacitus but also by the anatomy of tyranny in Plato's *Republic* and Aristotle's *Politics*, the play dissects the withering of communal bonds and the eradication of debate—which is precisely the climate that facilitates a repressive regime. Fragments of friendship are all the play offers to shore against the ruins.

The final chapter focuses on wit, civility, and the art of jesting. Wit encapsulates many of the paradoxes of civility. On the one hand, humour is an instrument that can be wielded to exclude members of society. On the other hand, it can serve as a social lubricant and forge a sense of communal cohesion. After a brief survey of classical theories of wit, the chapter looks at the discussion of jesting in Renaissance treatises, in particular Pontano's *De sermone* and Castiglione's *Courtier*. While courtesy manuals promote a skill at sharp-witted repartee as a means to garner social cachet and simultaneously advise their readers to rein in their wit, Castiglione devotes a large section of book 2 to bouts of verbal one-upmanship. Evading conflict, he indicates, might not be conducive to civility—agonistic jesting, a channelised mode of aggression, can cement social bonds too. The theatre, meanwhile, was thronged with witty women as well as urbane men-about-town. Jonson's *Epicene* and Shakespeare's

The Merry Wives of Windsor show how wit can be deployed either as a tool of power or to shore up commonality. Concomitantly, both plays send up the culture of civility itself, mocking a raft of social climbers and the passion for duelling in early modern England. *Epicene* dissects the wits too, whose brilliance masks delusions of grandeur, and unsettles our own complacency in the bargain. Both *Epicene* and *The Merry Wives of Windsor* explore the relationship between the theatre and social performance, probing the idea of whether dissimulation may at times serve an ethical purpose.

Civility and Its Discontents

Civility is not glamorous. It is not the stirring stuff of ideals, as is, for instance, the fight for social justice. It offers little scope for moral purity, so cherished in the current climate. It is not even included in the standard roll call of moral virtues.[80] Civility is a strategic mode of behaviour that is deployed to specific ends. Like verbal rhetoric, the rhetoric of conduct is an art of persuasion—which implies persuading others of our own worth, a goal which is achieved only by conveying our own esteem for them. Like rhetoric, civility can be used for widely divergent purposes—in the interests of self-aggrandisement and to promote narrow group loyalties or to foster the common good. Once again, the notion of contributing to the 'common good' is not an exalted vision as is evoked, for instance, by the term the 'greater good', which conjures up the (somewhat queasy) idea of sacrifice of individual concerns for the benefit of a majority. The 'common good' merely denotes the well-being of all members of a community. What it points to is the idea that we all have a stake in a society of which we are a part, that there is a common endeavour we share. Put mundanely, it would be captured in the phrase 'we're in this together'.[81] Civility is based on the entirely pragmatic assumption that since we have certain needs in common, individual interests are closely allied to the interests of other people; self-serving motives may well be conducive to the common good, as Hobbes has famously argued. In truth, self-serving motives are always at work; even the striving for ideal selves is inevitably tinged by human vanity, as Hume would later point out. At the core of civility is the notion that we are always

---

80. Calhoun, 'Virtue of Civility', 251.
81. The White House, Office of the Press Secretary, 'Remarks by the President at a Campaign Event in Roanoke, Virginia' (13 July 2012), https://obamawhitehouse.archives.gov/the-press-office/2012/07/13/remarks-president-campaign-event-roanoke-virginia.

bound up in relations with other members of society—that we exist only in interaction with one another. What civility does not imply is the evasion of conflict, or timorous acquiescence and self-censorship in the face of those who are most vocal in crying offence over every difference of opinion. In social interaction, conflict is a constant. Civility might in fact pave the way for engagement between antagonists by establishing a baseline mutual respect, however feigned.

Written at a time of seismic change, early modern drama was intensely alert to political and social developments of the time. The sixteenth and seventeenth centuries were a time when repressive religious and political regimes forced persecuted segments of society to disguise their true beliefs. Labelled as 'the age of dissimulation' by historian Perez Zagorin, it saw a virulent debate about lying, feigning, and pretence.[82] Compelled to justify its own medium, the theatre embarked on an intense interrogation of the practice of make-believe.

As this book argues, some plays moot the idea that there might be a continuum rather than a categorical divide between lying and telling the truth—that, as Hannah Arendt once pointed out, lying, deception, and the ability to imagine a different world and change it accordingly all stem from the same source: the human imagination.[83] Instead of insisting on moral absolutes, it might be more helpful to distinguish between the different contexts in which dissimulation is practised and the effect it achieves. In the case of interaction with other members of civil society, different paradigms apply than in our relations to those with whom we share bonds of intimacy. A look at literature, particularly drama as aware of its artifice as early modern drama, is illuminating in exploring the role of fictions in social life and in reasserting the compelling need for shared fictions, beliefs that we jointly agree to endorse as truths. The crux lies in avoiding the morass of a post-truth belief that truth is entirely subjective while admitting that human truths, like human beings, are always defined in relation to each other.

Manners are the minutiae of everyday life, but as Erving Goffman rather fulsomely puts it, 'The gestures which we sometimes call empty are perhaps in fact the fullest things of all.'[84] This may be overstating the case. Civility is a

---

82. See Zagorin, *Ways of Lying*. Also see Andrew Hadfield's masterly *Lying in Early Modern English Culture*.
83. Arendt, 'Lying in Politics', 2.
84. Goffman, 'Nature of Deference and Demeanour', 91.

matter not of noble sentiments but of self-regarding acts which can nonetheless contribute to the common good for the simple reason that they acknowledge a shared realm of experience and mutual interdependence. True reciprocal esteem in the Rawlsian sense might be deeply desirable. But in real life, entire parts of society harbour nothing but disdain, if not revulsion, towards other members of the same community. In its incessant self-awareness, the early modern theatre trains a spotlight on our own inexorable sense of moral certitude and suggests it is based on delusion. It puts forward the idea that dissimulation in the sphere of social life might serve a useful purpose if it promotes debate and a modicum of trust. What the plays intimate is that in the final analysis, the question of how to distinguish the pretence of respect for others from sincere feelings is entirely irrelevant. As they suggest, we are defined by what we do rather than who we are.

1

Castiglione, *The Merchant of Venice*, and the Imperative of Style

IN 1586 Filippo Sassetti, merchant, traveller, and man of letters, picked up a copy of Castiglione's *Libro del Cortegiano* in a small shop in Cochin, on the Malabar Coast of South India.[1] The discovery of Castiglione's book in a port city several thousand miles away from Italy is by no means as fortuitous as it might seem. The Malabar Coast had been a hub of the lucrative spice trade for centuries, and Cochin was the site of the earliest Portuguese settlement in India, founded in 1503, shortly after Vasco da Gama navigated the sea route from Europe to India. As for *Il Cortegiano*, first published by the press of Aldus Manutius in 1528, it was a spectacular success, with around sixty-two editions published in Italy by the early 1600s. A further sixty editions appeared in translations and adaptations, in Spanish, English, German, French, Latin, and Polish.[2]

Together with Erasmus's treatise on manners for children, *De civilitate morum puerilium* (1530), Castiglione's *Il Cortegiano* launched the Renaissance culture of civility. In England, an important agent of civility was the early modern theatre, which appropriated, assimilated, and reinterpreted the ideas about civility circulating in Renaissance Europe. The plays staged in both amphitheatre playhouses and indoor theatres offered paradigms of polished behaviour for spectators eager to emulate elite modes of conduct. Even while mocking the voracious quest for cachet among its viewers, the theatre purveyed urbane manners as a desirable commodity. The followers of fashion watched representations of themselves and modelled themselves on their stage image.

---

1. Sassetti, *Lettere di Filippo Sassetti*, 358. I am indebted to Burke, *Fortunes of the* Courtier, 142, for this reference.
2. See Burke, *Fortunes of the* Courtier, 41, 62.

FIGURE 2. Raphael, *Portrait of Baldassare Castiglione* (ca. 1514–15). Louvre, Paris.

The interrelation between civility, courtesy literature, and the Elizabethan theatre is explicitly laid out in the *Gesta Grayorum*, one of the few surviving scripts of the Christmas revels that took place at the Inns of Court. The Inns of Court served as finishing schools for young gentlemen and aimed to teach their students not only law but social graces. The text has gained considerable attention for its mention of *The Comedy of Errors*, performed in Gray's Inn in 1594, probably by the Lord Chamberlain's Men. As part of the mock ceremonies, the Lord of the Revels, elected by his fellow students and dubbed the 'Prince of Purpoole', founded a new order of knighthood, whose articles were duly proclaimed. They include the following item:

> Every Knight of this Order shall endeavour to add Conference and Experience by Reading; and therefore shall not only read and peruse *Guizo*, the *French* Academy, *Galiatto* the Courtier, *Plutarch*, the *Arcadia*, and the Neoterical [modern] Writers, from time to time; but also frequent the Theatre, and such like places of Experience; and resort to the better sort of Ord'naries [taverns] for Conference [conversation], whereby they may not only become accomplished with Civil Conversations, and able to govern a Table with Discourse; but also sufficient, if need be, to make Epigrams, Emblems, and other Devices appertaining to His Honour's learned Revels.[3]

In a litany of mock rules saturated with references to stylish comportment and fashionable accessories such as toothpicks, lovelocks, and tobacco pipes, the young gentlemen are exhorted to study manuals of courtesy—and frequent the theatre. The titles listed are those of the most famous texts of the genre: Stefano Guazzo's *The Civile Conversation*, Pierre de La Primaudaye's *The French Academie*, Giovanni Della Casa's *Galateo*, and Baldesar Castiglione's *The Book of the Courtier*. Together with learning the codes of elegant discourse and the art of cutting a good figure at salon games and festivities, attending plays is recommended in order to pick up social skills and hone one's style and taste. The vogue for Italianate drama modelled on the plays of Ariosto and his contemporaries, which had dominated the academic drama of the mid-century and of which *The Comedy of Errors* is an exemplar, had by the late sixteenth century been adopted by the professional theatre companies—not only the boys' companies but the adult companies as well.[4] Attending these plays would enable spectators to acquire a taste for sophisticated entertainment.

The theatre was regarded as a space where stylish behaviour was enacted for the consumption and edification of its spectators and as a setting where the carefully cultivated modes of comportment could be put into practice. In the model conversations given in language manuals such as John Florio's *His firste Fruites* (1578) and *Florios Second Frutes* (1591), which doubled as an induction into a stylish lifestyle, young men about town are depicted in their leisurely pursuits: gambling, playing tennis, shopping, gossiping—and watching

---

3. *Gesta Grayorum*, E3r–v.
4. See van Es, *Shakespeare in Company*, 58–60.

plays. Their favourite resorts are St Paul's, the Royal Exchange, the court, fashionable inns, and the theatre.[5] In his satirical courtesy book, *The Guls Horne-booke* (1609), Thomas Dekker advises the aspiring gallant to frequent playhouses 'publique or private' and make a spectacle of himself by sitting on the stage. In a self-mocking marketing gambit, Dekker urges him further to display a copy of his book: 'there draw forth this booke, read alowd, laugh alowd, and play the Antickes'.[6]

Catering to an audience beset with social anxiety, the commercial theatre plied spectators with jokes mocking other aspirants. But the early modern theatre does not just reflect the preoccupation with upward mobility among its audience. At a time when intense political and confessional hostility created a radical rift within society, a number of plays explore civility as a way of living together. They probe the tensions within the notion of civility—as a means of exclusion and a way of shoring up barriers between social groups, or alternatively, as a mode of sociality comprising all parts of a community, based on shared membership of the human community.

This chapter looks at the fraught relationship between the divergent aspects of civility by exploring affinities between Castiglione's *Courtier* and *The Merchant of Venice*. In *The Merchant of Venice*, Shakespeare offers us an alluring vision of a set of people, marked out by style and grace, who seem to personify the Renaissance culture of civility exemplified by Castiglione's court of Urbino. There is no evidence that Shakespeare read *The Book of the Courtier*, although for the eighteenth-century forger William Ireland, the likelihood that he might have done so was compelling enough to warrant fabricating a signature by Shakespeare in a 1603 copy of Castiglione's book.[7] Castiglione conjures up an image not only of the ideal courtier but of an ideal society, based on the performance of mutual respect. By contrast, Shakespeare presents a play in which the dazzling veneer of Venetian civility is revealed to be a facade, serving

---

5. In the dedicatory epistle to his second book, Florio mocks those 'who think they hath learnt a little Italian out of Castilions courtier, or Guazzo his dialogues' (A4v), subtly vaunting the superior access to Italian culture furnished by his own work and providing an insight into the fact that courtesy books were also valued as language primers. On language manuals in Renaissance England, see Wyatt, *Italian Encounter with Tudor England*, and Lawrence, 'Who the Devil Taught Thee So Much Italian?' Also see Coldiron, 'Form[e]s of Transnationhood', who argues that the 1588 edition of the *Courtier* in Italian, French, and English served less as a language manual than as an attempt to stake a claim for English cosmopolitanism.

6. Dekker, *Guls Horne-booke*, E2v, A1v.

7. See Burke, *Fortunes of the* Courtier, 132.

only to further group interests. Both texts also share a concern with fictionality. Preoccupied with the vexed issue of ethics and aesthetics, the *Courtier* is pervaded with self-conscious references to its own fictional status. Shakespeare's play too reflects on the role cultural fictions play in civil society. Many of their ideas are indebted to the theory of civility outlined by Aristotle, Cicero, and Hobbes.

The Classical Foundation of Civility

For the ancients, far from being the trivia of social life, manners bore deeply ethical implications. The notion that manners are virtuous stems from the *Nicomachean Ethics*, where in his list of moral virtues Aristotle explicitly includes three social traits that are 'all concerned with intercourse in word and actions'.[8] These are affability, truthfulness in discourse, and wittiness (4.6–8). Although Aristotle does not assign a name to affability (or to truthfulness, for that matter), his description of the virtue corresponds to what one might term civil behaviour, as humanist scholar Giovanni Pontano points out in his treatise on the virtues of speech, *De sermone*.[9] Aristotle defines friendliness (4.6) as a mean between being obsequious and being surly and contentious. Those who ingratiate themselves with others to gain advantage are flatterers, while those who are always quarrelsome are churlish. Aristotle points out that affability resembles friendship, a linchpin of the good life that he discusses at length later in the treatise. The difference is that cordial behaviour relates to both acquaintances and strangers.

Aristotle's extended anatomy of friendship (books 8 and 9) sets out a far broader view than the narrow concept we associate with friendship today. It also offers noteworthy insights that have a bearing on a study of civility. There are three kinds of friendship, Aristotle declares: the friendship of utility, the friendship of pleasure, and the friendship of virtue. Some associations are mutually beneficial, and some provide mutual pleasure. True friends are those we wish well for their own sake. But as Aristotle elaborates, utility and pleasure play a role in virtuous friendship too. Aristotle asserts that friendship is always self-interested—it is inextricably bound up with self-love (1166a–b). As he goes on to explain, what self-love means is loving the rational part of oneself, and

---

8. Aristotle, *Nicomachean Ethics*, trans. David Ross, 1108a11–12. For an astute discussion of the Aristotelian concept of virtue, see MacIntyre, *After Virtue*, 171–92.

9. Pontano, *Virtues and Vices of Speech*, 1.30.5.

striving to act justly. Accordingly, 'the good man should be a lover of self' (1169a12). Lovers of self aim to live according to rational principles and desire the common good. There are, Aristotle points out, striking parallels between friendship and justice, the paramount virtue that governs relations between all members of a community: as in the *polis*, communities of friendship are based on reciprocal advantage (1159b25). Acting in a way that benefits one's fellows is of benefit to oneself. It is a commonplace that for Aristotle, sociality constitutes human beings. As he writes, one needs friends since 'man is a political creature and one whose nature is to live with others' (1169b18). Less well-known is the concomitant notion that our interests and the interests of the community are closely intertwined—individual flourishing is tied up with the well-being of the community. These thoughts were expanded upon by Stoic thinkers and culminated in the concept of *oikeiosis*, the idea that an affiliation extends from ourselves to humanity as a whole. Hence the individual good is intrinsically connected to the common good. Despite undeniable tensions between the two, as social beings we lead lives that are defined by social relations and inevitably involve membership in the human community. For Stoics, the continuum between our own concerns and those of the human species is grounded in our shared rationality.[10] This theory plays a pivotal role in what became the foundational classical text for ideas of civility, Cicero's *De officiis*.

Cicero's *De officiis*

De officiis is one of the towering texts of the early modern age. For early humanists, the book was a lodestone, inspiring numerous treatises and commentaries from Petrarch to Erasmus. It was one of the earliest texts to appear in print and became a prescribed textbook at Oxford and Cambridge and at grammar school.[11] With regard to civility, two concepts are of note: the idea of decorum and the notion of *personae*.

Although a card-carrying adherent of the school of Academic scepticism, voicing his criticism of Stoicism in works such as *De finibus* and *De divinatione*, Cicero in *De officiis* borrows heavily from a lost treatise by the Stoic philosopher Panaetius, *On the Fitting*. Panaetius, originally from Rhodes, belonged to a

---

10. See Reiss, *Mirages of the Selfe*, 120–38. On Stoicism, also see Sellars, *Lessons in Stoicism* and *Routledge Handbook of the Stoic Tradition*.

11. See Walsh, 'Introduction' to Cicero, *On Obligations*. All citations are taken from the Oxford World's Classics edition.

generation of philosophers who adapted Stoicism to the concerns of the Roman elite and elaborated an ethics that would provide guidance for the active life. In a discussion of the four Platonic virtues of wisdom, justice, courage, and temperance, Panaetius replaces temperance (in the Greek, *sophrosyne*) with 'appropriateness' (*to prepon*), rendered by Cicero as 'decorum', explicitly merging the aesthetic and the ethical by drawing on a term hitherto used to describe appropriate rhetorical style.[12] The postulate to adapt to people and circumstances in order to persuade and please applied to both rhetoric and conduct, Cicero believed. In *De officiis*, his final work, he argues that decorum is a far wider concept than temperance—it is the ruling principle behind all virtues. Cicero distinguishes between two forms of decorum: decorum as a fundamental attribute of all other virtues and decorum in the specific sense of the refined manners befitting a gentleman (1.96). He proceeds to set out a curiously detailed code of elite conduct, presenting a miniature manual of manners nested inside a philosophical treatise.[13]

The essence of decorum, Cicero declares, is to be in harmony with nature, reiterating the fundamental Stoic principle of *homologia*. For the Stoics, nature was synonymous with the rational cosmic order, which also inheres in our rational nature. To achieve this goal, Cicero sets out a few key principles. One is to gain the approval of our peers by means of our graceful behaviour. We should consistently strive for an aesthetic balance and aim for an attractive outer aspect. 'This concept of the fitting is to be observed in every movement and posture of the body' (1.126), he claims. The extremes of either effeminate behaviour or uncouth conduct are to be avoided, as are foppish dress or slovenliness. How a member of the elite walks is of supreme importance: 'We must be careful also not to saunter along too mincingly, ... nor again to hurry along at breakneck speed so that we puff and blow, go red in the face, wear agonized expressions' (1.131). Through continual self-monitoring, we are enjoined 'to take pains to safeguard all that pertains to the image and standing of a gentleman' (1.141).

A second precept is to demonstrate respect towards other people. This implies exercising unceasing restraint and self-control. A virtuous person should

---

12. See Aristotle, *Rhetoric*, 3.7.1 and Isocrates, *Against the Sophists*, 13 as well as Cicero, *De oratore*, 3.210–12. Cicero first uses 'decorum' as a philosophical concept in *Orator*, 20.70–71. On *De officiis*, see Connolly, *State of Speech*, 169–75; Kapust, 'Cicero on *Decorum* and Morality of Rhetoric'; and Kapust, 'Rethinking Rousseau's Tyranny of Orators'.

13. The section on decorum runs from 1.93 to 1.151. I am indebted to Quentin Skinner for drawing my attention to *De officiis* as a classical courtesy manual.

take care not to offend others through immodest behaviour. 'Our stance and walk, our sitting and reclining, our facial expression and our eyes, and the movement of our hands should all preserve that element of propriety' (1.128), Cicero asserts. He disapproves of coarse jokes, indecent exposure, and antics in the forum. In social intercourse, boasting, gibing at others, or monopolising the conversation are to be avoided.

Of further interest is the notion of *personae* that Cicero elaborates in his work, drawing on theatrical imagery to describe the obligations of human life (1.107–20).[14] There are four *personae* or roles that shape our lives. The first consists in the common role we share with the whole of humanity by virtue of our rational faculties, the second role reflects our individual temperaments, the third is shaped by chance or circumstances, and the last is based on the choices we make, selecting professions we wish to devote our lives to or models we wish to emulate. While some of the roles are imposed on us, in the case of others we are free to shape ourselves in accordance with our natural bent and desires. Using the Stoic commonplace of life as a stage as a starting point, Cicero elaborates on the idea of human beings as performers.[15] Decorum is of the essence here, too: to the extent possible, in the same way that an actor chooses a role befitting his talents, we should opt for roles for which we are suited and play them consistently. What Cicero's concept of *personae* ignores is the possibility of tension and friction between the roles we play in disparate aspects of life. Admittedly, the denial of conflict is a blind spot that he shares with Aristotle, influenced by the Platonic notion of an absolute, unified truth.[16] The corollary of this belief was the ideal of a homogenous, integrated self. In Cicero's analogy of life and the theatre, being true to oneself simply meant playing oneself.

De officiis was written in the final months of Cicero's life, under the impression of the tumultuous events at Rome after the assassination of Julius Caesar in March 44 BCE, when the republic was ravaged by a vicious power struggle between antagonistic forces. The question Cicero tackles in this work is whether it is possible to reconcile ethics with expediency, or the honourable and the useful. The conclusion he comes to is breathtakingly simple: there is no contradiction between the *honestum* and the *utile*. 'Whatever is honourable

---

14. See Sherman, 'Of Manners and Morals'.

15. In the *Encheiridion* Epictetus is cited as saying, 'Remember that you are an actor in a play, the character of which is determined by the Playwright' (17).

16. See MacIntyre, *After Virtue*, 184, 190–91.

is also useful' (2.10), he proclaims. Contrary to appearances, the expedient and the virtuous are not opposed to each other, but are indissolubly linked: 'what is useful to the individual is identical with what is useful to the community' (3.27). The rationale for his assertion lies in 'the bond of fellowship which in its widest sense exists between all members of the entire human race' (3.69). Paradoxical though it might appear, our own interests are best served by taking the claims of commonality into account. Cooperation and reciprocity, he argues, are the bulwark of human civilization (2.11–16).

Revered by generations of humanists, for whom *De officiis* was, bar scripture, the ultimate guide to wisdom, in the course of the sixteenth century the Ciceronian logic was increasingly subject to scepticism. Arguably the most drastic critique was articulated by Machiavelli, who severed any intrinsic association between virtue and expediency. In the interests of the state, it might be necessary to set morality aside, he famously argued. Critical was not the practice, but the semblance of virtue.[17] Predictably, Machiavelli's *Prince* set off a wave of outrage. Notwithstanding their differences, there are affinities between Cicero and Machiavelli. Both emphasise the importance of public relations. It is important to remember that for the Romans, virtue was a public affair; *honestas* was closely bound up with status. In book 2 of *De officiis* Cicero proposes a set of techniques that would help his addressee, ostensibly his son Marcus but more broadly his peer group of aspiring young patricians, gain glory, win friends, and influence people. For young patricians embarking on a career in public life, Cicero stresses, it is requisite to gain the approval and trust of the people. To do so, they are advised to cultivate a reputation for virtue and 'civilized and affable manners' (2.32). Astute impression management is of the essence, and he advises his addressees to 'project the image of the good man' (2.39). While conceding the role of self-interest in our lives, Cicero nonetheless insists that it is contingent on the social bond (*vinculum societatis*), based on our common capacity for reason and speech, that ties all human beings to one another.

The legacy of *De officiis* can be traced in a plethora of early modern courtesy manuals, and carried forward to the silver-fork novels of the nineteenth century and the self-help literature of our time. *De officiis* became a primer for patrician conduct for generations of gentlemen. Cicero's theory of decorum laid the foundation for a set of behavioural conventions that buttressed the

---

17. Machiavelli, *The Prince*, chap. 18, 61–63. On Machiavelli's critique of humanism, see Skinner, *Foundations of Modern Political Thought*, 1:128–38.

position of the elite as the model of cultivation and polish. In the process, the radical implications of the idea of decorum as a principle based on shared human fellowship were largely forgotten.

Hobbes and Civility

The tenets of Aristotle and Cicero provide the cornerstone for early modern ideas of civility. There are, however, notable convergences between early modern drama and the insights articulated by Hobbes in his monumental treatise, *Leviathan*, published in 1651 and in a revised Latin edition in 1668, long after the theatres had been closed. *Leviathan* is a vast work, but for a study of civility and the theatre, a few points are particularly pertinent. These relate to theatricality and fictionality.

In his comments on manners, Hobbes brushes away trivialities such as 'how one man should salute another, or pick his teeth before company'. Civility, he avers, consists of 'those qualities of man-kind, that concern their living together in Peace, and Unity', adumbrating a definition of civility in terms of cordial coexistence rather than etiquette.[18] Given that humanity is engaged in 'a perpetuall and restlesse desire of Power after power' (70), 'COMPLEASANCE', the precept '*That every man strive to accommodate himselfe to the rest*', which Hobbes labels as the fifth 'Law of Nature', plays a vital role (106). It is, however, Hobbes's remarks on personhood and on the origins of the commonwealth that have the greatest implications for a conception of civility as based on role-playing and a view of civil society as a fabrication.

Like Machiavelli's, Hobbes's relationship to classical thought was rife with ambivalence. He fulminates against the pernicious influence of the ancients, whose exaltation of liberty has fanned the flames of tumult and rebellion; 'there was never any thing so deerly bought, as these Western parts have bought the learning of the Greek and Latine tongues' (150), he remarks scathingly. To be sure, *Leviathan* is imbued with Ciceronian ideas, from personation to laws of nature—all of which Hobbes radically revises.

In chapter 16, Hobbes distinguishes between two types of persons. A person, he asserts, is he '*whose words or actions are considered, either as his own, or as representing the words or actions of an other man, or of any other thing to whom they are attributed, whether Truly or by Fiction*'. As he elaborates, when the words or actions 'are considered as his owne, then he is called a *Naturall Person*'. When,

---

18. Hobbes, *Leviathan*, 69, emphasis and capitalization original.

however, they are considered as 'representing the words and actions of an other, then he is a *Feigned* or *Artificiall person*' (111). Hobbes notes that the term 'person' is derived from the Latin *persona*, which refers to either the characters impersonated by actors or the masks customarily worn in the Greek theatre and frequently on the Roman stage. His theory of the state is crucially bound up with the question of authorisation. In connection with the agency and responsibility linked to personhood, Hobbes expands the theatrical metaphor by evoking the figure of the playwright. Some artificial persons, he writes, merely carry out the actions and words set down for them by another; 'the Person is the *Actor*; and he that owneth his words and actions, is the AUTHOR: In which case the Actor acteth by Authority' (112).

Hobbes's concept of personhood provides the bedrock for his theory of the state, a person constituted by a community of people with the common purpose of ensuring mutual security and granted the right to act in their name by virtue of an unwritten covenant. What Hobbes does not explain is precisely what type of artificial person the state is. There has been considerable debate about whether the state is to be classified as 'artificial', as Quentin Skinner has argued, or 'fictitious', as David Runciman claims.[19] In the context of civility, what is of interest is the notion of self-representation and, by implication, self-impersonation inherent in Hobbes's theory. Natural persons are able to appoint others to represent their interests, but they are equally capable of representing themselves: 'a *Person*, is the same that an *Actor* is, both on the Stage and in common Conversation; and to *Personate*, is to *Act*, or *Represent* himselfe, or an other; and he that acteth another, is said to bear his Person, or act in his name' (112). Significantly, Hobbes does not distinguish between acting a part onstage and assuming a role in a social context ('in common Conversation'). Nor does he differentiate between assuming a fictitious character and standing in for someone else—both meanings are encompassed by the phrase 'to bear the person of' someone.[20] His theatrical analogy suggests not only that individuals can take on a number of socially recognised roles, representing

---

19. See Skinner, 'Hobbes and the Purely Artificial Person of the State'; Runciman, 'What Kind of Person Is Hobbes's State?'; Martinich, 'Authorization and Representation in Hobbes's *Leviathan*'; and Simondic, 'Hobbes on *Persona*, Personation, and Representation'. On theatricality in Hobbes, also see Vieira, *Elements of Representation in Hobbes*, and Kahn, *Trouble with Literature*, chap. 2, 33–61.

20. *OED*, s.v. 'to bear the person of' in 'bear, v.1', sense P.2.c. See Skinner, 'Hobbes on Representation'.

others, but also that they perform a part on the social stage. What emerges from Hobbes's account is an impression of human beings as social agents who ceaselessly adopt roles in social life at a remove from their inward sense of self. Recent critics have confirmed the idea that for Hobbes, persons are inevitably involved in representation, either of others or themselves. As Lars Vinx points out, 'A person, for Hobbes, is always a relationship (or set of relationships) of representation'—which comprises the capability to impersonate oneself.[21] This is borne out by a passage from Cicero's *De oratore* that Hobbes is fond of adducing.[22] In book 2, Cicero has his speaker, the eminent orator Antonius, describe how he prepares himself before presenting a case in court. After being briefed by his client, Antonius relates, 'I, just by myself, play three roles with complete calmness: my own, that of my adversary, and that of a juror' (2.102). In a one-man show played to an audience of one, himself, Antonius takes on the role of counsel on behalf of his client, the role of his opponent, and the role of a member of the jury. This ploy, Antonius tells us, allows him to grasp the complexity of the case from all its angles. The anecdote intimates that theatricality informs social life. Whether we impersonate others or ourselves, we are always role players. Furthermore, we are capable of playing a range of divergent roles simultaneously.

Hobbes makes it clear that his view of personation extends to imaginary artefacts or a 'meer Figment of the brain' (113). His political theory is constructed around a fiction—but one that has powerful ramifications in the real world. A multitude of human beings living in a condition of nature can make an agreement with one another to transform themselves into a fictitious entity, a commonwealth, 'as if every man should say to every man, *I Authorise and give up my Right of Governing my selfe, to this Man, or to this Assembly of men, on this condition, that thou give up thy Right to him, and Authorise all his Actions in life manner*' (120). As Victoria Kahn points out, by using the term 'as if', Hobbes phrases the act of authorisation as an appeal to the imagination, based on a joint suspension of disbelief; in a recent analysis of the fictionality that for Hobbes constitutes the personality of the state, Sean Fleming affirms that 'fictions remain central to social and political life'.[23] The commonwealth is a fiction in which we mutually agree to believe. The natural condition of humankind,

---

21. Vinx, 'Personality, Authority, and Self-Esteem in Hobbes's *Leviathan*', 140.
22. See Skinner, 'Hobbes and the Purely Artificial Person of the State', 13.
23. Kahn, *Trouble with Literature*, 46; Fleming, 'Two Faces of Personhood', 23. On Hobbes's state as a fictional construct, also see Douglass, 'Body Politic'.

Hobbes declares, drawing on and rewriting Cicero's myth of origins (*Inv.* 1.2.2–3), is a state of unfettered liberty, in which 'every man has a Right to every thing'. Consequently, it is 'a condition of Warre of every one against every one' (91). In his drastic idiom, it was an age in which there was 'no Knowledge of the face of the Earth; no account of Time; no Arts, no Letters; and which is worst of all, continuall feare'. In a time before the conception of civil society, he maintains, life was 'solitary, poore, nasty, brutish, and short' (89). Civil society itself is a fabrication, an artefact created by humankind in imitation of God's creation of the world. In the introduction to *Leviathan*, Hobbes describes human society in terms that rival the divine work of art: 'NATURE (the Art whereby God hath made and governes the World) is by the *Art* of man, as in many other things, so in this also imitated', he writes, 'For by Art is created that great LEVIATHAN called a COMMON-WEALTH, or STATE, (in latine CIVITAS) which is but an Artificiall Man' (9).

More radically than Machiavelli, Hobbes throws overboard classical pieties such as Aristotle's assumption that humankind is innately sociable, or Cicero's belief in the human bond. Self-interest is at the heart of Hobbes's theory; the law of nature is distilled into the imperative of self-preservation. What is notable is how Hobbes's vision is built on the idea of artifice and fictionality. Civil society or the commonwealth—for Hobbes, commensurate with the state—is a contrivance that a community agrees to construct, while outside the state of nature, all of human life consists of social roles. These ideas are at the core of a notion of theatrical civility.

Castiglione and the Aestheticization of Manners

Set in 1507 in the ducal court of Urbino, on the slopes of the Apennines, Castiglione's *Book of the Courtier* recapitulates four evenings of a parlour game played amongst a glittering set of noblemen and ladies, distinguished by their elegant conversation and witty repartee.[24] The game the group selects to play

---

24. For a sample of scholarship on *The Book of the Courtier*, see Woodhouse, *Baldesar Castiglione*; Javitch, *Poetry and Courtliness in Renaissance England*, 18–49; Rebhorn, *Courtly Performances*; Hanning and Rosand, *Castiglione*; Kinney, *Continental Humanist Poetics*, 87–134; Finucci, *The Lady Vanishes*; and Berger, *Absence of Grace*. More recent work on Castiglione includes Richards, 'Assumed Simplicity and the Critique of Nobility'; Burrow, *Imitating Authors*, 183–91; and Ugolini, *The Court and Its Critics*, 13–49. On the reception of the *Courtier*, see esp. Burke, *Fortunes of the* Courtier, and Partridge, '"Absolute Castilio"?' On Castiglione and Shakespeare, see Motta, 'Castiglione e Shakespeare', and 'Il Gentiluomo Innamorato'.

consists in defining the ideal courtier. Written over a period of twenty years, and published only a few months before the author's death in 1529, the book is steeped in nostalgia for an idyllic world of refined bonhomie and cultivated pleasures.

In part a manual of manners, in part a compendium of jokes and a contribution to the *querelle des femmes*, Castiglione's treatise is primarily what J. R. Woodhouse calls a 'handbook for survival' intended for the elite.[25] It was written for his peers at a time of crisis for the Italian aristocracy. The invasion of the peninsula by Charles VIII of France in 1494 had a disastrous effect on the balance of power in Europe. It turned Italy into a battlefield between various states, foremost amongst them France and Spain, and unleashed a struggle for supremacy that lasted well into the nineteenth century. The Wars of Italy had a profound impact on the Italian nobility, whose confidence in their prowess in arms and their role as protectors of the state received a crippling blow. At the same time, the civic humanism that had flourished in *quattrocento* Italy had been formative in disseminating the notion that noble status was no longer a birthright of the highborn, but needed to be earned.[26] The contingency plan for the aristocracy that Castiglione devised was a unique blend of the aesthetic, the ethical, and the expedient. What he proposed was a performance of civility, the incessant display of decorous demeanour and deportment to signal nobility. In an age in which throughout Europe the aristocracy found its position imperilled by the rise of the centralised nation-state and technological developments in warfare, his programme, widely diffused through the medium of print, was adopted by courtiers across the continent.

In England, Castiglione was read in the original, in Latin, and other European languages, and in Sir Thomas Hoby's English translation of 1561. Ten editions of the book, six of Bartholomew Clerke's Latin translation and four of Hoby's English version, appeared in England between 1561 and 1611.[27] Readers were keen to acquire manuals of manners that bore the cachet of Italian (and later French) writers; with the exception of Sir Thomas Elyot's *Boke named the Governour* (1531), no English courtesy books of significance appeared until the seventeenth century. Ironically, what was intended as a method to shore up the position of the aristocracy opened the door for precisely what the code of courtesy had sought to exclude. The handbooks of

---

25. Woodhouse, *Baldesar Castiglione*, 64.
26. See Skinner, *Foundations of Modern Political Thought*, 1:69–112.
27. Burke, *Fortunes of the Courtier*, 65–66.

civility were carefully studied by members of other ranks, avid for access to a status now allegedly less determined by birth than earned by merit.

Castiglione's main debt is to Cicero's *De oratore*, from which he takes the genre of the dialogue and elements of the setting, transposing a leisurely dialogue among a group of Roman statesmen, set in a villa in Tusculum in 91 BCE, into a series of conversations among a handful of courtiers at the ducal palace of Urbino in the first decade of the sixteenth century.[28] Like Cicero, who, in a nod to Plato's *Symposium*, claims that the discussions he describes actually took place in a gathering with historical persons and were related to him in retrospect, Castiglione presents himself as mere transcriber of events. He even borrows the mood of melancholy that permeates Cicero's dialogue, most of whose protagonists had come to a violent end in the rampage of terror unleashed during the civil wars between the factions of Sulla and Marius in the 80s. As Castiglione's readers at the time knew, a similarly tragic fate lay in store for some of the most distinguished noblemen who feature in the *Cortegiano*.

Similarly, there are features in common between Castiglione's treatise and *De officiis*. Castiglione replicates the attention Cicero pays to the mundane acts of everyday life as an index of status. We are judged on the basis of our deportment as well as our words and deeds: 'walking, laughing, looking, or the like', he has one of his interlocutors point out, 'all these outward things often make manifest what is within' (2.28). In book 2, Federico Fregoso stresses the importance of not causing offence through uncouth, rustic behaviour, and admonishes his peers to avoid vile or disorderly habits, or 'certain peasant ways that bespeak the hoe and the plow' (2.38). In conversation, the audience are enjoined to adopt a pleasing manner, and to accommodate themselves to the company they are in. The courtier 'must perceive the differences between one man and another, and change his style and method from day to day, according to the nature of the person with whom he undertakes to converse' (2.17), he asserts. Above all, we must 'govern ourselves always according to a certain decorous mean' (2.41).

For the Renaissance aristocrat, boasting is no longer acceptable. When the representative of old-school values in the text, Gasparo Pallavicino, objects that even among the ancients, men of honour were entitled to proclaim their attainments, Count Ludovico da Canossa, the main speaker in book 1, agrees that it is

---

28. For early moderns, steeped in the classics, the analogies were patent. See Hoby's preface to *The courtyer*, A4r. On Castiglione's engagement with Cicero, see Richards, *Rhetoric and Courtliness*, 43–64; on his debt to Quintilian, see Cox, 'Quintilian in Renaissance Italy'. On the genre of the dialogue in Renaissance Italy, see Cox, *Renaissance Dialogue*.

vital to draw attention to one's accomplishments. However, he advocates an important change in style. Graceful manners involve the artful packaging of one's own worth, deploying finesse, not crass modes of self-advertisement. Self-deprecation and a show of modesty about one's attainments have the paradoxical effect of enhancing one's reputation. By avoiding praising oneself, and calling attention to one's deeds in more subtle a manner, one not only gained approbation for modesty, but reinforced the effect of one's achievements (1.18).

Another astute commentator on the art of self-promotion, Francis Bacon, emphatically agrees with Federico's counsel. In his essay 'Of Vain-Glory', Bacon deplores the custom of boasting and labels it as *passé*. This does not mean that it was no longer necessary to set oneself off to advantage whenever possible. What has changed are the strategies appropriate to this end. 'For excusations, [offering excuses], cessions [making concessions], modesty itself well governed, are but arts of ostentation', he points out.[29] Instead of braggadocio, pliancy in social interaction and adapting to circumstances, both facets of the Ciceronian notion of decorum or 'modesty', as early moderns frequently term it, are more polished instruments to achieve the same end and to boost one's image of noble magnanimity, he opines.[30]

While Castiglione's courtiers reiterate the Ciceronian principles of gaining the approval of one's peers by aiming for a pleasing effect, accommodating oneself to others, and steering clear of offending other members of the group by exercising self-control, the text expends most of its advice on the technique of self-presentation, reshaping rhetorical *ethos* for the purposes of social practice.[31] First impressions are critical: 'the Courtier must take great care to make a good impression at the start and consider how damaging and fatal a thing it is to do otherwise' (2.36), Federico exhorts his audience. To this end, he must stage himself in the most flattering light. An example is engagement in battle. The courtier should discreetly withdraw from the thick of the battle and reserve his daring deeds for the eyes of the most noble spectators available, preferable the prince himself. In this way he ensures that his intrepid performance will not go unnoticed or unrewarded. To illustrate his point, Federico uses an

---

29. Bacon, 'Of Vain-Glory', in *Major Works*, 443–45, 444.
30. *OED*, s.v. 'modesty, n.', I.2.
31. Goffman discusses the techniques of impression management in *The Presentation of the Self in Everyday Life*, 203–30. For the notions of self-presentation and accommodation to others, Goffman later uses the terms 'demeanour' and 'deference'. See his 'Nature of Deference and Demeanour'.

analogy to the theatre, comparing the courtier to the classical actor who 'wished always to be the first to appear on the stage to speak his part' (2.8).

Castiglione's interlocutors present a catalogue of attributes that the ideal courtier should acquire, furnishing copy for the succinct lists and appendices, such as Hoby's 'breef rehersall of the chiefe conditions and qualities in a Courtier' (2Y4r–2Z1v), that would bookend so many future editions of courtesy books. In keeping with the humanist ethos of the treatise, the courtier is no longer defined predominantly by the military vocation but by an all-round regimen of education in letters and practical skills. He should be a perfect horseman and undertake a rigorous training in bodily exercises, including swimming, jumping, running, wrestling, and vaulting on horseback. He should indulge in hunting whenever possible, traditionally seen as preparation for warfare. In addition, he is enjoined to develop his intellectual faculties. The courtier is to study both Latin and Greek, and be skilled in the vernacular, capable of writing both verse and prose. He is expected be an accomplished musician, and trained in drawing and painting. He is to cultivate social skills, and be adept in witty banter and in dancing. What is paramount, however, is that he 'be full of grace in all that he does or says' (1.22). It is not so much what he does that is of interest; what is decisive is the style in which he does it.

Castiglione's achievement lay in elevating the notion of style, not birth, into a prime factor in the definition of the aristocracy. He advanced the idea that what distinguished the nobility from lesser mortals was their refinement in the modes of social behaviour, their demeanour, their gestures, and the way they deported themselves. Elegant style marked out the courtier as superior to the other ranks in society.[32] Cultivating the appearance of being a man of sophistication, tact, and taste would burnish one's reputation and pave the way to preferment. As Cesare Gonzaga puts it pithily in a suave play on words, 'he who has grace finds grace' (1.24). The religious connotations of the term 'grace', alluding to divine benevolence rather than worldly favour, are deftly ignored.

---

32. Pierre Bourdieu draws on Aristotelian ideas of the inculcation of virtue through practice and uses the term *habitus* for the way the refined habits of the elite cement over time to form a characteristic disposition to behave in a certain manner. See Bourdieu, *Outline of a Theory of Practice*, 72–95. On style as a defining factor for Castiglione's courtier, see Lanham, *Motives of Eloquence*, 144–64, and Whigham, *Ambition and Privilege*, 33–35.

The Ethics of *Sprezzatura*

In response to the query as to how precisely this grace is to be acquired, Canossa launches into what is probably the most famous passage in the book. He observes,

> I have found quite a universal rule which in this matter seems to me valid above all others, and in all human affairs whether in word or deed: and that is to avoid affectation in every way possible as though it were some very rough and dangerous reef; and (to pronounce a new word perhaps) to practice in all things a certain *sprezzatura* [nonchalance], so as to conceal all art and make whatever is done or said appear to be without effort and almost without any thought about it. And I believe much grace comes of this: because everyone knows the difficulty of things that are rare and well done ... (1.26)

The key to urbane manners, he claims, is to project an image of sheer effortlessness in all one says or does, however hard one has worked to achieve perfection in any skill. The most egregious aesthetic solecism, on the other hand, is affectation, which reveals the effort it cost to attain any level of perfection in the social arts—and above all, the effort it cost to appear effortless. One's audience of peers would be perfectly aware of the fact that the appearance of insouciance was merely a pretence—and admire the quality of the performance. Eduardo Saccone notes that a display of *sprezzatura* was a crucial signal for members of the same social circle: '*sprezzatura* is the test the courtier must pass in order to be admitted to this club'.[33] Only one's peers would be able to appreciate the work invested in producing the air of nonchalance; they were all involved in precisely the same task.

At times, even one's peers are taken in by the show. For there is a further advantage to mastering the artistry of *sprezzatura*, the Count discloses. It 'brings with it another adornment, which, when it accompanies any human action however small, not only reveals at once how much the person knows who does it, but often causes it to be judged much greater than it actually is'. The reason is that 'it impresses upon the minds of the onlookers the opinion that he who performs well with so much facility must possess even greater skill than this' (1.28). If he were to exert himself, they believe, he would far

---

33. Saccone, 'Grazia, Sprezzatura, Affettazione in the *Courtier*', 60.

exceed his performance. From a mode of setting oneself out in the best possible light, *sprezzatura* segues into nothing less than dissimulation: projecting an image that might have only a tenuous link to the truth.

Pretence is of the essence, Federico stresses. If the courtier wished to advertise his feats, 'he will do it with dissimulation, as if by chance and in passing' (2.8), he declares. While the social performance of the courtier might be presented primarily to courtiers, it is also aimed at other audiences. Federico prescribes the most advantageous style of acting when taking part in a public masque. The courtier's feigning should be wholly transparent and consistently direct attention to his use of artifice, in order 'to show a certain nonchalance in what does not matter' (2.11). To explain what effect he intends the courtier to achieve, Federico provides examples. A young man masquerading as a crone should take care to show off his youthful vigour; a nobleman slipping into the guise of a rustic should arrive mounted on a perfect horse. Underneath the carefully staged display of carelessness, the great unwashed are to be reminded of the identity of the masquerader as a member of the elite, marked out by inherent superiority. Mingling with commoners is simply a useful means to bolster one's reputation for affability and conviviality.

Castiglione's use of the form of the literary dialogue enables him to incorporate—and dismantle—critique of his concept of the perfect courtier in the text itself. When the eternal naysayer in the group, Gaspar Pallavicino, protests, 'This seems to me to be not an art, but an actual deceit', Federico puts forward an eloquent, if specious, defence:

> 'This', said messer Federico, 'is an ornament attending the thing done, rather than deceit; and even if it be deceit, it is not to be censured. . . . if you have a beautiful jewel with no setting, and it passes into the hands of a good goldsmith who with a skillful setting makes it appear far more beautiful, will you say that the goldsmith deceives the eyes of the one who looks at it? Surely he deserves praise for that deceit, because with good judgment and art his masterful hand often adds grace and adornment to ivory or to silver or to a beautiful stone by setting it in fine gold'. (2.40)

Federico does not deny that what he is advocating is a form of deception. However, by having recourse to the imagery of a beautiful artefact further embellished through art, he airbrushes the issue so that the ethical implications virtually disappear. It is of little importance whether the impression created by the social performer reflects the truth or not. What counts is the aesthetically pleasing surface.

With the notion of *sprezzatura* Castiglione ruptures the link between exterior appearance and interior truth posited in classical thought, demolishing the Ciceronian grounds for a decorous deportment. There is, it appears, no intrinsic relationship between prepossessing manners and a virtuous self, between surface and substance. At first sight there seems to be little in common between the cultivated lifestyle described by Castiglione and the ruthless mechanisms of power politics dissected by Machiavelli. And yet there are remarkable correspondences between both writers, both of whom were responding to the catastrophes consuming late Quattrocento Italy—a moment of crisis, memorably dubbed 'the Machiavellian moment' by J. G. A. Pocock, that put paid to the dream of reconstructing the Ciceronian ideal republic.[34] In a discussion of desirable traits a ruler should acquire, Machiavelli encourages him to attain virtue to the extent possible. However, circumstances do not always permit him to do so. More importantly, the ruler needs to cultivate the appearance of virtue. He concludes, 'A ruler, then, need not actually possess all the above-mentioned qualities, but he must certainly seem to' (62). The truth about one's personality or the attributes one possesses is, in the final analysis, immaterial. What counts is the image one projects.

Both Castiglione and Machiavelli underline the priority of appearances over reality and advocate the importance of image management. In the case of *The Prince*, honing one's image is a means towards the final ends in political life: to increase the glory of the prince and to maintain the state. For Castiglione's courtier, at least for the first three books of the *Courtier*, *sprezzatura* is a method of impressing one's peers—and of self-advancement.

Neoplatonic Idealism in the *Courtier*

If in its first three books the *Courtier* sails dangerously close to the reef of ethical egoism, and endorses dissimulation for entirely expedient reasons, the book makes a volte-face in book 4. In yet another moment of internal interrogation, Castiglione has Ottaviano Fregoso, Federico's brother, whose counterpart in real life would proceed to become the Doge of Genoa, dismiss the disquisitions of his predecessors about the qualities of the ideal courtier as 'frivolities and vanities' which serve 'to make spirits effeminate, to corrupt youth, and to lead it to a dissolute life' (4.4). The purpose of acquiring a gamut of attractive attributes, he argues, is solely to equip the courtier to gain the

---

34. See Pocock, *Machiavellian Moment*.

favour of the prince—and thus to guide his master towards the good. By winning the confidence of the prince, the courtier would be able to tell him the truth without needing to fear the consequences of his displeasure; he would be able to dissuade him from evil and lead him 'by the austere path of virtue'. The pleasures laid out for the ruler—music, the discourse of love, witty conversation, verses, displays of physical skill—all serve the end of 'beguiling him with salutary deception' (4.10). Drawing on Plato's notion of a medicinal lie (*Rep.* 389b–c), acceptable only for its curative qualities, Ottaviano deploys the metaphor of a cup of medicine sweetened at the rim to make its contents more palatable. The structure of the *Courtier* enacts a similar shift in focus: after the sparkling banter of the first three books, book 4 is largely devoted to imparting counsel to the sovereign in the style of a mirror for princes.[35]

In book 4, Castiglione attempts to reconcile self-interest with a higher goal—the good of the realm. Polished manners are not merely a way for the courtier to accumulate cultural capital and rise in the world. His true raison d'être is to please his master and steer him towards virtue. Aesthetically pleasing appearances point the way to the world of Ideas; in an idiom resonant of Neoplatonism, Ottaviano proclaims that just as in the sun, the moon, and the stars, an 'image of God is seen in those good princes who love and revere Him and show to the people the splendid light of His justice'. With the guidance of the Courtier, he will become 'a demigod rather than a mortal man' (4.22). The book ends with a long lyrical monologue by the poet Pietro Bembo, who elaborates the Neoplatonic credo of love as a desire for beauty propagated by Ficino in his commentary on the *Symposium*. While the connection to the lofty view of courtiership proclaimed by Ottaviano may seem somewhat tenuous, the underlying rationale linking both discourses is the Neoplatonic ideal of an indissoluble link between the aesthetic and the ethical. What redeems the strategic use of dissimulation in creating aesthetically pleasing impressions, the text implies, is a continuum between the beautiful and the good.

The idealism of Castiglione is usually discussed in relation to the ideal courtier and in book 4, the ideal prince. Less frequently remarked upon is the fact that the text fabricates the image of an ideal society in which laughter, civility, and mutual esteem reign. In reality, court society was as much an arena of cut-throat rivalry as was the larger political canvas delineated by Machiavelli.

---

35. Amedeo Quondam has shown that the shift to the theme of the formation of the prince was present in all drafts of the manuscript. See Quondam, 'On the Genesis of the *Book of the Courtier*'.

The *Courtier* intimates as much: Giuliano de' Medici laughingly mentions the maxim that when one's enemy is up to his waist in water, one should help him out, but when he is up to his chin, one should put one's foot on his head and drown him—only to disavow such tactics for the circle at Urbino (3.70). There are hints at friction between the members of the group. In this connection, the frequent skirmishes between the women and the flamboyantly misogynistic faction might be less significant than appears at first sight. A number of critics have identified the current of anxiety running through *Il Cortegiano* as a fear of the emasculation of the courtier, reduced to the task of seducing the prince to govern wisely. The *querelle des femmes*, they argue, is a cover for ventilating concerns about the relationship between the courtier and the prince.[36] Of greater interest are the submerged resentments and clashes between characters that reflect generational or regional tensions, and perhaps subterranean rivalry.[37] Equally striking are the array of devices used to defuse moments when the animosity between the courtiers erupts to the surface.

An example is the altercation between signor Morello and Federico Fregoso. In response to the supercilious attitude of the older courtier, Federico makes a jab at Morello by referring to men who dye their hair, provoking mirth among the ladies. Before the conflict can escalate, Federico makes a conciliatory move, tempering his critique of the older generation with compliments (2.14–15). When it is Ludovico who sneers at Morello as an aging lover, it is Federico's turn to intervene on his behalf, 'to calm signor Morello and to change the subject', as the narrator remarks (4.56). Potential bitterness is attenuated and aggression is assuaged by performing an elaborate charade of mutual respect, enabling all members of the group to maintain face. Most frequently, the friction that fissures the text is smothered in laughter. It is noteworthy that references to laughing punctuate the dialogue at frequent intervals.[38]

In his dialogue, Castiglione not only describes the mechanisms of civility, but has his courtiers display them in action. The deference and tact that the courtiers of Urbino demonstrate in interaction with one another are not necessarily a sign of sincere regard for one another, but a performance of mutual esteem that is a key component of the cultivated deportment of a gentleman.

---

36. See, for instance, Berger, *Absence of Grace*, 63–115; Kelly-Gadol, 'Did Women Have a Renaissance?'; Quint, 'Courtier, Prince, Lady'; and Trafton, 'Politics and the Praise of Women'.
37. See chapter 5 for a discussion of the tussle of words between the Venetian Bembo and the Florentine Bernardo Bibbiena.
38. See Greene, '*Il Cortegiano* and the Choice of a Game'.

Castiglione represents a world in which self-serving motives might nevertheless be instrumental in fostering communal harmony. The vision of a harmonious community that Castiglione presents is as seductive as is his fantasy of the ideal prince or ideal courtier.

Even so, Castiglione's charming vision of a society of civility and sociability is deeply meretricious. The ostensibly ideal court society is a strictly patrolled community, under siege from a hostile outside world. The community of good fellowship Castiglione creates is an enclosed realm to which only an exclusive handful of members have access. Even if there is rivalry among the courtiers, they share a similar worldview. No one is permitted entry to the world of Urbino who is not a part of the charmed circle. In Urbino, there is no place for outsiders, or for conflicts which are not as smoothly ironed out as are the tensions within the same professional caste, that of the courtier. In *The Merchant of Venice*, by contrast, Shakespeare moves out of the enclave of a circumscribed society into the wider world, in which outsiders encroach on the lives of a privileged clique and in which conflict is an ineluctable feature of life.[39]

Castiglione attempts to recuperate his fascination with aesthetic surfaces for an ethical viewpoint by insinuating that his artful portrait of Urbino is an idealization, not a reflection of reality. As Castiglione claims in his dedicatory letter to Don Michel de Silva, the treatise is an exercise in idealism, aiming to continue the tradition of Plato, Xenophon, and Cicero: 'there is the Idea of the perfect Republic, the perfect King, and the perfect Orator, so likewise there is that of the perfect Courtier' (3). Nonetheless, like the model of an ideal society, the vague Neoplatonic gestures towards the ethical import of alluring manners is profoundly flawed. Beneath its own beguiling surface, the book offers a blueprint for self-promotion and ingratiation—as Castiglione himself insinuates, exploiting the dialogue form to articulate doubts about the idealized version of reality that he offers. The whiff of mendacity hovers over the ideal courtier, while the ideal prince, in a world of increasingly autocratic rulers, is transparently a chimera. One of the interlocutors, Pietro da Napoli, interrupts Federico's discourse on the adulation the Courtier owes his prince with the words, 'it strikes me that you have, in few words, sketched us a noble flatterer' (2.18). Although his critique is smoothly deflected in the text, later critics have been quite as harsh in their verdict. In a spirited defence of Machiavelli, Sydney Anglo lays the blame for the cynicism that invaded court

---

39. On analogies between the *Courtier* and the play, see Berger, '*Sprezzatura* and Embarrassment in *The Merchant of Venice*'.

culture in the sixteenth and seventeenth centuries squarely at the feet of Castiglione, who, he claims, delivered a vindication of the art of sycophancy. The 'general corruption of manners', Anglo states categorically, 'constituted the achievement of Baldassare Castiglione'.[40]

In truth, the book reveals a deep concern with the vexed issue of aesthetics and ethics, style and substance. By using the concept of art that conceals its artfulness for the aesthetics of social performance, Castiglione evokes a rhetorical strategy advocated by Aristotle, Cicero, and Quintilian—as well as a tactic of seduction recommended by Ovid in his *Ars Amatoria*.[41] The *Courtier* itself is devised with meticulous care, its scrupulous craftsmanship concealed under a guise of effortless ease. The book is, however, shot through with self-conscious references to its own artifice. A number of self-referential jokes are slipped into the text: 'we have said enough', Federico announces in the second book, 'to make two books' (2.17), while Ottaviano cites alleged missives from the courtier 'Castiglione', absent on a mission in England (4.38). In a prefatory letter to Don Michel da Silva, Bishop of Viseu, Castiglione compares his book to a painting, and in a graceful, if disingenuous, disclaimer, writes, 'I send you this book as a portrait of the Court of Urbino, not by the hand of Raphael or Michelangelo, but by that of a lowly painter and one who only knows how to draw the main lines, without adorning the truth with pretty colors or making, by perspective art, that which is not seem to be' (4). This is precisely what the book subsequently sets out to do, employing verbal illusionism to create an Arcadian world. And in book 2, Federico explains that the courtier should present his qualities to best advantage and heighten their impact on the spectator 'as good painters who, by their use of shadow, manage to throw the light of objects into relief' (2.7).

There is no question that Castiglione would have been familiar with Leon Battista Alberti's work, *De Pictura* (1435), the first treatise to discuss linear perspective as a device that gave rise to the illusion of depth. But the pleasure

---

40. Anglo, 'Systematic Immorality', 629.

41. The concept of *ars est celare artem* ('it is art to conceal art', possibly a medieval coinage) is usually associated with the comment *si latet, ars prodest*, or 'guile helps when hidden', in the *Ars Amatoria*. See Ovid, *Love Poems*, 2.313. Similar thoughts are expressed by rhetorical writers, e.g., Cicero in his oxymoronic description of the plain rhetorical style as marked by 'careful negligence' (*neglegentia diligens*); Quintilian in his suggestion to avoid the excessive use of figures of speech ('wherever art is put on show, truth seems to be absent'); and Aristotle's advice to writers to 'compose without being noticed' and to 'seem to speak not artificially but naturally'. See Cicero, *Orator*, 23.78; Quintilian, *Orator's Education*, 9.3.102; and Aristotle, *On Rhetoric*, 1404b.

of visual deception is fleeting. Mimetic art, Alberti writes, invariably precipitates a moment of disillusionment, an awareness of the illusory quality of the image.[42] It always calls attention to its status as artefact. Nonetheless, instead of inducing an enduring sense of loss, it might engender reflection on the artwork itself. Castiglione was well aware that his portrayal of a golden world was no more than a fiction. His overriding concern might, however, have been with fashioning an elegy to the memory of his peers and a tribute to the exquisitely cultivated court of his youth. Most importantly, the book is a celebration of the writer's craftsmanship in fabricating the image of an enchanted realm of laughter and reciprocity, one whose appeal reverberates to the present day.

Manners and Money in *The Merchant of Venice*

The Merchant of Venice (1596–97) is a study in civility, in all its facets. The play evokes a world of style and grace, a society of beautiful people distinguished by an inexhaustible store of insouciant charm. Belmont, the epicentre of this world, to which all the fashionable young Venetians gravitate in the course of the play, is Shakespeare's version of Urbino;[43] the very name seems to gesture towards the elegant ducal town located on the slopes of a hill.[44] It is a place suffused with music, poetry, and laughter, redolent of a cultivated lifestyle in which manners and mutual regard hold sway. And yet, what Shakespeare presents in the comedy is a crisis of civility. The play investigates how this society responds when its values are put to the test by the intrusion of outside forces. The play hints at murky depths beneath the shimmering surface of the world it depicts, and exposes the Venetian notion of civility as tailored exclusively to the interests of a select social group. It is also a play about the role of fictions in civil life, the stories that a society tells itself. By highlighting the motif of

---

42. See Ruffini, 'Alberti on the Surface'. Also see Rosand, 'The Portrait, the Courtier, and Death', and Hanning, 'Castiglione's Verbal Portraits'.

43. In what might be a wink at Baldassare Castiglione, Shakespeare includes not just one but two Balthazars in the play, Portia's fictitious lawyer and one of her minions. In *Much Ado About Nothing*, another play concerned with a glittering facade of cultivation that conceals a ruthless obsession with prestige and surveillance, Balthazar is the name given to a court musician memorable only for his exquisitely refined manners.

44. A fantasy location taken from Shakespeare's source story in Ser Giovanni Fiorentino's late fourteenth-century collection of tales, *Il Pecorone* (printed in 1558), it is the only invented place name in Shakespeare, as Stephen Orgel points out. See Orgel, 'Venice at the Globe', 127.

artworks and myths, both Castiglione and Shakespeare draw attention to the fact that the worlds they represent are built around cultural fabrications. But if Castiglione offers his vision of Urbino as an ideal to aspire to, Shakespeare's play works quite differently. The play unmasks its attractive protagonists as careless rich people who retreat 'back into their money or their vast carelessness', as F. Scott Fitzgerald would later put it.[45] It also reveals unpleasant truths about ourselves as spectators, and our own hankering for a world of glamour that elides the sordid reality on which it is built.

Style is what defines the way of life of the characters of the play.[46] Our first impression of Venetian society is one of polished banter and courteous conversation. Lord Bassanio, the highest-ranking member of the company, salutes the two insignificant hangers-on, Solanio and Salerio, with gracious geniality: 'Good signors both, when shall we laugh? Say, when? / You grow exceeding strange. Must it be so?' (1.1.66–67).[47] Antonio has recourse to an elaborately polite falsehood to dismiss them from his company: 'Your worth is very dear in my regard. / I take it your own business calls on you, / And you embrace th'occasion to depart' (62–64). The social performance we witness corresponds perfectly to the metatheatrical image unfurled in the first few lines of the play, in which Salerio compares richly laden, stately ships to 'signors and burghers', to whom smaller vessels pay obeisance in 'pageants of the sea', bowing and curtseying in gestures of deference (10–11). Polite salutations, mutual compliments, and rituals of respect are the common currency of this society, as is badinage and wit. Graziano, the most exuberant member of the clique, cannot resist unleashing a series of wisecracks even as he promises to 'adopt all observance of civility' henceforth (2.3.176). Portia mocks her suitors for their lack of *sprezzatura* in sparkling *aperçus*.

The urbane characters of *The Merchant of Venice* are distinguished by their social graces, their cultured speech, their fondness for lavish spending, and their taste for aesthetic pleasures. In stark opposition to the fashionable Venetians is the towering figure of Shylock. His brusque manner, ruthless business practices, frugality, and violent revulsion towards what he regards as frivolous pleasures mark him out as an outsider. He appears as the epitome of a lack of

---

45. Fitzgerald, *The Great Gatsby*, 184.

46. A recent collection of critical essays is Kaplan, *Merchant of Venice*. Other recent criticism includes Orgel, *Imagining Shakespeare*, 144–62; Gross, *Shylock Is Shakespeare*; Garber, *Shakespeare and Modern Culture*, 124–53; Ryan, *Shakespeare's Comedies*, 104–33; Drakakis, 'Introduction'; Smith, *This Is Shakespeare*, 99–112; and Orgel, 'Venice at the Globe'.

47. All citations from Shakespeare's plays are taken from *The Norton Shakespeare*, 3rd ed.

FIGURE 3. John Massey Wright (1777–1866), scene from *The Merchant of Venice*. Folger Shakespeare Library, Washington, D.C.

civility. Friendship, courtship, music, poetry, and other cultivated pleasures do not seem to play a role in his life. In *The Merchant of Venice* the opposition between Gentile and Jew is not just a clash of cultures: it is a rift along class lines, crystallized in the distinctive taste and deportment that set them apart.[48]

What becomes apparent is that the appealing manners of the *beau monde* are undergirded by wealth, derived from global trading or landed inheritance. They also mask a hardheaded concern with materialistic values. A scene that captures the close nexus between romance, commerce, and dissimulation that marks the play is the casket scene, act 3, scene 2, in which Bassanio makes his choice among the three caskets of gold, silver, and lead and wins the prize, Portia. The beginning of the scene is steeped in music and poetry; Portia and

---

48. See Whigham, 'Ideology and Class Conduct in *Merchant of Venice*'.

Bassanio exchange lyrical declarations of love. Gradually, false notes creep in. Bassanio's love discourse is well-stocked with Petrarchan clichés and demonstrates effortless mastery of the social game of love. 'There may as well be amity and life / 'Tween snow and fire, as treason and my love', he declares in choice Petrarchan antitheses (3.2.30–31). His allusion to treason ironically glances at the undercurrent of deception and betrayal running through the play.

Meanwhile Portia, by far the cleverest and wittiest member of the group, has recourse to a mythical analogy to describe her lover, comparing him to 'young Alcides when he did redeem / The virgin tribute paid by howling Troy / To the sea monster' (3.2.55–57). She is at pains to proclaim that unlike Hercules (another name for Alcides) in the myth she cites, in which the Greek hero rescues the Trojan princess Hesione, Bassanio is inspired by love, not the lure of a reward.[49] In reality, as Portia would have been fully aware, all her suitors, and in particular the impecunious and extravagant Bassanio, are impelled solely by accounts of her vast fortune, which has suitors flock in quest of her hand. As Bassanio puts it, 'the four winds blow in from every coast / Renownèd suitors' (1.2.168–69). Significantly, in his own set piece, in which he inveighs against the value of external impressions, Bassanio reprises the reference to Hercules, reviling fraudulent heroes whose outward appearance belies their lack of true worth: 'How many cowards, whose hearts are all as false / As stairs of sand, wear yet upon their chins / The beards of Hercules' (3.2.83–85).

Before Bassanio launches on his homily, demonstrating how well he has learned to blend Christian values about the vanity of outward show with the lessons on the imperative of style promulgated by Castiglione, another discordant tone is sounded. The song that, on Portia's command, accompanies Bassanio's musings treats of 'fancy', a term for 'love' that bore overtones of the whimsical and capricious.[50] To be precise, the song is a dirge for a transient infatuation that withers in the bud: 'fancy dies / In the cradle where it lies' (68–69). It ends with a doleful call to 'ring fancy's knell' (70). To create a soothing atmosphere for a lover who has to undergo a trial, it is a curious choice. The surprise we might feel at the words of the song gives way to the dawning realisation that Portia is resorting to subterfuge to weigh the scales in Bassanio's favour. The first stanza ends on an insistent rhyme which provides a clue that the right choice is the lead casket: three lines end on the words 'bred',

---

49. For an illuminating discussion of Shakespeare's use of myth in the play, see Bate, *Shakespeare and Ovid*, 151–57, to which I am indebted.

50. *OED*, s.v. 'fancy, n. and adj.', 7.a., 8.b.

'head', and 'nourishèd' (63–65). For the audience, the reference in the song to the site where fancy 'lies' (69) might evoke an additional, less edifying meaning and cast a shadow over our admiration for the witty heroine.

Bassanio's deliberation takes the form of a diatribe on outward display. The world, he laments, is too enamoured of spurious values. From duplicitous pleas in law, whose effect hinges entirely on the gracious delivery of the lawyer, he moves on to a slew of other examples. Winning rhetoric enables divines to dissimulate false beliefs; an engaging appearance enables cowards to dissimulate their lack of martial valour; cosmetics enable women to dissimulate their lack of virtue. These corrupt times, he expostulates, are awash with 'seeming truth' (100). Wheeling out well-worn tropes to castigate women for their seductive appeal, he declaims in orotund tones that 'ornament is but the guilèd shore / To a most dangerous sea' (97–98). Hence, he concludes virtuously, he will reject the allure of gold and silver, and choose the 'meagre lead' casket with its promise of austere frugality.

Nothing that we have previously seen of Bassanio has prepared us for a spiritual rebirth on his part. Nor does the rest of the play bear out this impression. Instead, the suspicion hardens that what we are witnessing is yet another charade, a pretence of virtue that is tailored to produce precisely the effect it achieves—to overcome the hurdles represented by 'the will of a dead father' (1.2.22) and attain the financial reward for which Bassanio hungers.

In act 1 we have seen Bassanio poised to solicit a loan from his munificent friend Antonio, whose alacrity in complying hints at a deep emotional attachment that dare not speak its name. Bassanio admits that his debts are due to an exorbitant lifestyle, his conduct 'something showing a more swelling port' than his means would allow (1.1.124). The solution to his financial problems, he believes, is to make an investment with yet more of his friend's money, using the imagery of archery for what one might regard as a form of venture capital financing: 'when I had lost one shaft, / I shot his fellow of the selfsame flight / The selfsame way, with more advisèd watch, / To find the other forth; and by adventuring both, I oft found both' (140–44).[51] His plan is to stake his chances on wooing the heiress, Portia, who represents ancient, landed wealth. Bassanio concedes it is a high-risk project, given the large number of competitors driven by the same goal. Ironically, the legend on the lead casket, '"Who chooseth me must give and hazard all he hath"' (2.7.16), chimes perfectly with an aristocratic ideology that celebrated risk-taking as the mark of the Aristotelian

---

51. See Smith, *This Is Shakespeare*, 104–6.

virtue of liberality, associated with the gentleman (*EN* 4.1), and that embraced a lifestyle in which gambling for high stakes played as indispensable a part as did conspicuous consumption.[52]

When discussing his plans with Antonio, Bassanio enthuses about Portia's beauty and wealth, employing another mythical analogue. Portia's beauty is elucidated by citing the classical myth of the golden fleece, a symbol of wealth and status:

> her sunny locks
> Hang on her temples like a golden fleece,
> Which makes her seat of Belmont Colchis' strand,
> And many Jasons come in quest of her. (1.2.168–72)

By identifying himself with Jason, Bassanio explicitly equates his suit with a venture undertaken to make his fortune, not a quest for love. The correlation between the Venetian fortune hunters and their mythical forebear is underscored by Graziano, who woos Portia's maid at the same time as Bassanio is courting her mistress. Once both have secured their prize, Graziano boasts gleefully, 'We are the Jasons; we have won the fleece' (3.2.239).

In the light of Bassanio's earlier speeches, his pious exhortation to shun the attractions of lavish living reverberates with irony. In the casket scene, the lines Bassanio utilizes to describe the golden tresses of the heiress are charged with a far more sinister image. He lambastes beautiful women with 'crispèd, snaky golden locks, / Which maketh such wanton gambols with the wind' (3.2.92–93)—before insinuating that their curls are counterfeit. With the relish of a pulpiteer, Bassanio unfurls the macabre vision of a skull whose head of hair now adorns a living woman in the form of a wig.

(There are other, darker connotations that haunt the analogue between Bassanio and Jason—Medea, the sorceress in love with Jason, was a supremely clever woman who stopped at nothing, including murder and mutilation, to assist her lover; Jason betrays Medea, who takes revenge on his new bride. Shakespeare modulates the parallels considerably, but provides glimpses of Portia's ruthless intelligence and jealousy of Bassanio's relationship to Antonio, while the ring plot intimates that fidelity is not a virtue Bassanio is partial to.)[53]

The strains of music and lyricism that introduce the scene give way to muted notes of deceit and duplicity. The scene ends with a brisk discussion of

---

52. Stone, *Crisis of the Aristocracy*, 181–82.
53. Bate regards these connections as tenuous. See Bate, *Shakespeare and Ovid*, 153–54.

bonds, debts, and loans. Portia's parting quip to her fiancé underlines the materialistic underpinnings of the golden world we are witnessing. 'Since you are dear bought, I will love you dear' (311), she remarks acerbically.

Civility in Crisis

A term that resonates through the play is the word 'strange', signifying 'foreign' or 'alien', or 'unfamiliar', with the implication of a lack of civility.[54] In the very first scene Solanio marvels at the diversity of human beings: 'Nature hath framed strange fellows in her time', he muses (1.1.51). Venice, at the time the largest hub of trade with the East, was no doubt swarming with strangers, as is mirrored in the cast of characters in the play. Not only do suitors from all over the world flock to seek Portia's hand in marriage, but the play is dominated by an obdurate outsider, the Jewish moneylender Shylock, whose character radically diverges from that of the stylish Venetians. Solanio claims that he has never encountered 'a passion so confused, / So strange, outrageous, and so variable' (2.8.12–13) as that of Shylock raging against the elopement and robbery of his daughter. Portia wonders at the 'strange nature' of his suit (4.1.175), while the Duke hopes that he will show mercy 'more strange' to him than his 'strange apparent cruelty' (121–22). Defining one's own culture as the epitome of civility in relation to that of barbarous outsiders is a classic strategy, infallibly fuelled by a conviction of cultural and moral superiority. Shylock is relegated to the fringes of all that is savage and uncivil—as the Duke of Venice claims, Antonio's plight would move even 'stubborn Turks and Tartars never trained / To offices of tender courtesy' (4.1.32–33). Shylock is in fact barely human, described by Salerio as a 'creature that did bear the shape of man' (3.2.273) but whose nature is barbaric and brutish. Antonio advises the Duke to abandon his efforts to dissuade Shylock from the course he is set upon. 'You may as well use question with the wolf' (73), he asserts. Addressing Shylock directly, Graziano rages, 'Thy currish spirit / Governed a wolf who hanged for human slaughter' (133–34). The epithet 'dog' is attached to Shylock well before he begins his vicious persecution of Antonio. Straight after the elopement of his daughter, Solanio relates the news of 'the dog Jew' (2.8.14). For his part, Shylock has clearly hoarded in his memory the moments when Antonio treated him with the contempt usually reserved for stray dogs, behaving to him 'as you spurn a stranger cur / Over your threshold' (1.3.112–13).

---

54. *OED*, s.v. 'strange, adj. and n.', 1.a., 7, 11.a.

If on one level *The Merchant of Venice* portrays a society of elegant manners and exquisite taste, on another level it depicts civility in crisis. In the face of the radical alienness of Shylock, the dazzling facade of Venetian civility begins to crumble. References to courtesy run through the play: Bassanio is lauded for bringing 'commends and courteous breath' to Belmont (2.9.89), Portia apologizes for curtailing her 'breathing courtesy' (5.1.141), or words of welcome, to Antonio. Yet what Shylock mocks as 'Christian courtesy' (3.1.41) is increasingly laid bare as a sham. With heavy sarcasm, Shylock reels off a catalogue of the slurs meted out to him by Antonio: '"Fair sir, you spit on me on Wednesday last; / You spurn'd me such a day; another time / You call'd me dog; and for these courtesies / I'll lend you thus much moneys"?' (1.3.119–22). In response, Antonio vows to persist in his callous conduct. Shakespeare rigorously undermines the charm and allure of the cultivated Venetians by displaying their less attractive traits: incivility towards outsiders and an unshakeable belief in their moral rectitude.

In early modern England, the city-state of Venice not only was regarded as the epitome of refinement and high culture but was frequently held up as the model of a commonwealth governed by the principle of justice. Gasparo Contarini's treatise on the Venetian system of government, written in 1549 and translated by Lewes Lewkenor in 1599 with title *Commonwealth and Government of Venice*, was successful in establishing the 'myth of Venice' among political theorists as an ideal republic.[55] The climactic scene of the play is set in a courtroom. Nonetheless, the judicial system itself is not the focus of interest. In a meticulous dissection of the court judgement, Quentin Skinner has shown that Portia's sentence was based on impeccable legal grounds. The decisive argument is not Shylock's violation of the bond by shedding blood, but his transgression against the law penalizing threats to Christian life by aliens.[56]

What is at stake in *The Merchant of Venice* is the larger concept of justice, memorably defined by John Rawls as fairness.[57] It refers to relations between all members of a given society. In Aristotle's view, justice is not just one of the four cardinal virtues, but 'the greatest of virtues' (*EN* 1129b). Cicero defines

---

55. Orgel, 'Venice at the Globe', 126. As Orgel points out, the image of Venice in the theatre, as that of Italy in general, was far more ambiguous, serving as a foil upon which to project England's vices and anxieties.

56. See Skinner, 'Judicial Rhetoric in *The Merchant of Venice*'.

57. See Rawls, *Theory of Justice*.

the essence of justice as good faith (*Off.* 1.23). Injustice, he explains, consists of two kinds: committing an unjust act and failing to prevent injustice to others. Even those who are blameless of inflicting harm are guilty of injustice if they fail to protect other members of society from injury. It is crucial that these precepts apply not only to Roman citizens, but to slaves as well: 'We must remember that justice is to be observed even to the lowliest in society' (1.41). The same is true for foreigners. Cicero says explicitly, 'As for those who argue that we must take sympathetic account of fellow-citizens but not of outsiders, they are destroying the fellowship common to the human race' (3.28). Cicero's belief in our core humanity and the link between all human beings is indebted to the Stoic concept of the divine spark inherent in us all on the basis of our shared rational nature. These thoughts established the notion of human dignity as a fundamental good—and may well have provided inspiration for Kant's postulation of the categorical imperative in his *Groundwork of the Metaphysics of Morals* (1765), based on the affiliation between all members of humanity.[58] In the course of the play, the culture of civility in Venice is exposed as a magnificent edifice constructed, like the city itself, on the shifting waters of injustice.

Ironically, in *The Merchant of Venice*, it is the intransigent, vengeful stranger, bereft of all social graces, who holds up a mirror to Venetian society. When asked what impels him to relentlessly pursue Antonio, Shylock answers with a lengthy speech in which he runs through a list of illogical aversions. 'Some men there are love not a gaping pig', he scoffs, 'Some that are mad if they behold a cat' (4.1.47–48). There is no rational basis for their animosity. The same, he claims, applies to himself: 'So can I give no reason, nor I will not, / More than a lodged hate and a certain loathing / I bear Antonio' (59–61). His words lay bare the irrational nature of the prejudice to which he has been subject throughout the play. The harsh treatment meted out to him is only rationalized retrospectively in terms of his cruel and malicious behaviour towards his victim. In another striking speech, he justifies his callous persecution of Antonio by reminding the Venetians that slavery was a thriving business in Venice. Should he demand that the slave owners release their slaves and treat them as equals, he maintains, they would cry out, '"The slaves are ours"' (98). In analogous manner, he lays claim to Antonio's flesh for the simple reason that, as he

---

58. On Kant's debt to Cicero, see Reich, 'Kant and Greek Ethics (I.)' and 'Kant and Greek Ethics (II.)'; and Nussbaum, 'Kant and Stoic Cosmopolitanism'. Also see Nussbaum's 'Duties of Justice, Duties of Material Aid'.

points out venomously, it is 'dearly bought, 'tis mine, and I will have it' (100). Unerringly, he uncovers the entrenched injustice and the logic of commodification that underpins all human relations in Venice.

The Merchant of Venice turns on written and unwritten bonds, legal contracts and the shared bond of humanity. Portia delivers a landmark speech on the 'quality of mercy', the patrician trait of generosity and moderation towards inferiors: 'It droppeth as the gentle rain from heaven / Upon the place beneath' (4.1.182–84).[59] But it is in the mouth of the outsider Shylock that Shakespeare lays words asserting what Cicero defines as 'the bond of union and association between members of the whole human race' (*Off.* 1.149):

> Hath not a Jew eyes? Hath not a Jew hands, organs, dimensions, sense, affections, passions—fed with the same food, hurt with the same weapons, subject to the same diseases, healed by the same means, warmed and cooled by the same winter and summer as a Christian is? If you prick us do we not bleed? If you tickle us do we not laugh? If you poison us do we not die, and if you wrong us shall we not revenge? If we are like you in the rest, we will resemble you in that. (3.1.49–56)

While Shylock formulates a plea for the dignity of all humankind, Shakespeare inserts another line that slyly mocks the Christian claim to the moral high ground. When Portia, disguised as the lawyer Balthazar, first encounters the litigants, she asks, 'Which is the merchant here and which the Jew?' (4.1.172), a strange query in view of the habitual Jewish garb worn by Shylock (1.3.106). Under the guise of an innocuous question, Portia's words insinuate that however deep the rift between the adversaries, they share an underlying commonality.[60]

The civility practised by the Venetian protagonists of the play, charming and gracious in their intercourse among one another, is directed exclusively at members of the same coterie. They seem to model themselves on the courtiers in the fantasy world of Urbino, a world which is virtually a *hortus conclusus*. Life in a civil society as portrayed in *The Merchant of Venice*, however, always

---

59. The locus classicus for a discussion of clemency, stemming from the late Roman period, is Seneca's *De clementia*. Also see Sir Thomas Elyot, 'That a governour ought to be mercifull and the diversitie of mercye and vayne pitie', in *Critical Edition of Sir Thomas Elyot's* The Boke named the Governour, 132–38.

60. For an incisive reading of this line from a psychoanalytical perspective, see Garber, *Shakespeare and Modern Culture*, 150–53.

involves antagonism between radically opposed segments of the population, all of whom entertain nothing but contempt for the other. The relations between Jews and Gentiles in the play go to the crux of the issue of civility. Elaborating on Kantian ideas, philosopher Stephan Darwall has developed a notion of respect which distinguishes between what he terms 'recognition respect' and 'appraisal respect'.[61] 'Appraisal respect' involves esteem for someone for their qualities or their achievements. 'Recognition respect', on the other hand, is the respect all persons are entitled to by virtue of the office they hold or simply by dint of being human. This variety of respect relates to how we act, not how we feel about people. It would involve behaving as if one possessed a measure of respect for others, irrespective of whether one regarded them with true esteem or not. In other words, it delivers a rationale for dissimulation. Paradoxically, the charade would be grounded in genuine ethical commitment—to the notion of humanity as an end in itself, not merely a means.

According Shylock a semblance of the esteem he craves would not necessarily entail sincere sentiments of regard on the part of the Christians. Nor would it conflict with their self-interest. As both parties are aware, joint commercial interests necessitate cordial relations between Venetians and outsiders, 'Since that the trade and profit of the city / Consisteth of all nations' (3.4.30–31). A facade of mutual respect would cater to the stake all the characters have in the flourishing of Venice. What it would also do is cater to the self-esteem of all characters. In a later age, David Hume would famously argue that vanity was a key ingredient in inspiring virtue. Performing ideal versions of ourselves gratifies our self-regard; vanity impels idealism, at least in part.[62] The idea finds its roots in Aristotle. His claim that self-love and the common good are closely enmeshed is at the core of civility.

It is true that the notion of civility as pertaining to what unites us, not what divides us, is based on a cultural construction: the belief in an alliance between all members of humanity rooted in our shared possession of reason. The concept of *oikeiosis*, the idea that our interests are naturally connected to those of our fellow humans, was first formulated by the fourth-century BCE founder

---

61. Darwall, 'Two Kinds of Respect'.
62. Hume, 'Of the Dignity or Meanness of Human Nature', in *Selected Essays*, 43–48. Kwame Anthony Appiah makes a similar case in his *Honor Code*, where he argues that the desire not just for esteem but for feeling worthy of esteem can be put in the service of humanity. His central claim is that honour, an obsolete term for a perennial concern with status and respect, can play a crucial role in ethics.

of Stoicism Zeno, who regarded it as the basis for justice. It was adopted as a tenet of natural law by Cicero.[63] For Zeno, our self-interest extends in ever widening circles towards other human beings until it creates a link between ourselves and the entire human race. In effect, the concept was one of the earliest formulations of human solidarity and universal commonality.[64] To be sure, the ideal of the human bond is a fiction, a model that a society creates to impose meaning on reality.[65] Fictions are, however, an ineluctable part of human life. We live by fictions, narratives to which a community collectively agrees to subscribe. Shakespeare's play puts forward the idea that while we shape the fictions we believe in, they subsequently shape us.

Ethics and Aesthetics in *The Merchant of Venice*

Not only does *The Merchant of Venice* expose civility in Venice as catering to the desire of a coterie to garner social prestige and shore up their privilege, rather than serving as a conduit of mutual respect among all members of a community. It also comments obliquely on the equation of civility with civilization, invariably defined against other, barbarous outsiders. In a play threaded with allusions to music, poetry, and classical myths, Shakespeare anatomizes the concept of the civilizing effect of art, and the related notion of an intrinsic link between aesthetics and ethics. Neither of these ideas holds up to scrutiny. On the contrary, the play suggests, they are merely fictions that we construct and which subsequently shape our world.

In the famous dialogue between Lorenzo and Jessica in act 5, Lorenzo holds forth on the music of the spheres, and expatiates on the power of music to domesticate wild beasts. His lines echo the paean to music Count Ludovico delivers in the *Courtier*, calling attention to the connection between the music of the spheres and the divine spark in all humans. Here Castiglione draws on Aristotle's views on music as a moral education, conducive both to individual flourishing and to the common good, and melds them with Pythagorean and Platonic ideas of cosmic harmony. Robustly refuting the view that music renders men effeminate, the Count declares that the perfect courtier should be well-versed in music. Music inspires us to virtue, he claims. It tames not only the soul of man, but wild animals too. A lack of musical appreciation is the sign

---

63. On natural law, see White, *Natural Law in English Renaissance Literature*.
64. Ehrenberg, *Civil Society*, 21.
65. See Appiah, *As If*, on the tactical use of fictions in moral and political life.

of a flawed personality: 'he who does not take pleasure in it can be sure that his spirit lacks harmony' (1.47).

In *The Merchant of Venice*, Lorenzo rehearses these thoughts in exquisite verse:

> Therefore the poet
> Did feign that Orpheus drew trees, stones, and floods,
> Since naught so stockish, hard, and full of rage
> But music for the time doth change his nature.
> The man who hath no music in himself,
> Nor is moved with concord of sweet sounds,
> Is fit for treason, stratagems, and spoils;
> The motions of his spirit are dull as night,
> And his affections dark as Erebus.
> Let no such man be trusted! (5.1.79–88)

In a layered allusion, Shakespeare invokes both the classical poet Ovid and the mythical poet and musician Orpheus, whose music had a harmonious effect on nature as well as human beings. By using the word 'feign', a freighted term which bore connotations of both fiction and deception and could mean to fashion either a story or a lie,[66] and with an ironic nod at his own play, Shakespeare reminds us of the entanglement of aesthetics and dissimulation. The play's gesture towards harmony is feigned, too. In enchanting poetry, the lovers recall Neoplatonic ideals of love, music, and cosmic harmony—only to hollow them out. The duet of Lorenzo and Jessica revolves around tales of treachery, cruelty, and betrayal, citing the examples of Cressida, Dido, Medea, and Thisbe before adding their own names to the roll call of blighted lovers.[67]

The idea that poetry was not merely a product of culture but the actual impetus behind civilization reaches back to antiquity. It is evoked in the myth of the orator as the originator of civil society, articulated by Cicero in *De inventione* (1.2.2) and reiterated by Quintilian (2.16.9), and was widely recycled in Renaissance writings, such as Thomas Wilson's *Art of Rhetoric* (1553).[68] In *De oratore* Cicero has his speaker Crassus rehearse the *topos* when he lauds eloquence as the only force that 'could have gathered the scattered members of the human race into one place, or could have led them away from a savage

---

66. *OED*, s.v. 'feign, v.'.
67. See Bate, *Shakespeare and Ovid*, 154–57.
68. See Wilson, *Art of Rhetoric (1560)*, 41–43.

existence in the wilderness to this truly human, communal way of life' (1.33). The orator-poet was frequently identified with Orpheus, as in Horace's *Ars poetica* (391–401). For the ancients, rhetoric and poetics were closely interrelated; both used the techniques of emotional appeal and pleasure in order to sway to the good.[69]

In the Renaissance, the notion of the elevating purpose of art inspired Sidney's paean to the poet in the *Defence of Poesie* as a *vates* or prophet whose art was conducive to virtuous action.[70] Among the most exorbitant claims for the civilizing role of the poet are those vaunted by George Puttenham. In his *Art of English Poesy*, which fulfilled the triple function of a rhetoric, a poetics, and a courtesy book, Puttenham devotes a number of chapters to the civilizing myth, explicitly associated with the poet-orator Orpheus and the founder-poet Amphion, whose song induced stones to erect the city walls of Thebes. Stressing that poetry stemmed from a time 'not, as many erroneously suppose, after, but before any civil society was among men', he celebrates poets as the first priests, prophets, philosophers, astronomers, historiographers, and musicians of the world. Their achievements in the arts and sciences also served the end of establishing a harmonious civil society. Orpheus not only tamed wild animals but 'brought the rude and savage people to a more civil and orderly life'. As the first legislators and statesmen, poets devised 'all expedient means for the establishment of commonwealth', inculcating 'a certain method of good manners', or ethical behaviour, in their peers and encouraging 'virtuous conversation', or exemplary conduct in social interaction.[71] In what is an elaborate bid for royal patronage, Puttenham's inflated claims about the exalted role of the poet are in effect a flagrant exercise in self-marketing.

Lorenzo's eloquent lines about the civilizing force of music end with a warning against those immune to its charms, persons only 'fit for treasons, strategems, and spoils' (5.1.84–85). The play, however, does not bear out the notion that art civilizes us. Works of art are presented as deeply alluring. But there is no sign of their morally uplifting effect on the characters of the play. The most haunting love poetry in the play is articulated by feckless figures like Lorenzo and Bassanio. Music is put to the service of deceit, as in the casket scene, where Portia has Bassanio serenaded with a song whose lines insinuate which choice to make, or in the masque intended as a cover for Jessica's

---

69. See Vickers, 'Rhetoric and Poetics'.
70. Sidney, *Apology for Poetry*, 83.
71. See Puttenham, *Art of English Poesy*, 1.3–4, pp. 96–99.

elopement and robbery of her father. Nor does the play confirm that the possession of aesthetic taste is an index of ethical worth. While Shylock might loathe all forms of festivity, music lovers include playboys and thieves like Lorenzo and Jessica.

By foregrounding aesthetic artefacts and the stories woven around them, Shakespeare invites us to take a closer look at the narrative of the civilizing power of art. The impression evoked is that however seductive the idea, it is, above all, a story we tell ourselves, not a self-evident truth. The play provides no evidence for its veracity. Similarly, despite evoking a world of grace and beauty, *The Merchant of Venice* does not emulate the Neoplatonic idealism that, at least in book 4, serves as ethical scaffolding for Castiglione's Urbino. Instead, it endorses Machiavelli's views about the ethical indeterminacy of rhetoric and applies it to aesthetics. The poetry and music that permeate Belmont, and the beguiling manners of the smart set of the play, say nothing at all about their character. The idea of an intrinsic ethical charge to the aesthetic, the play suggests, is a cultural fiction that we espouse.

What the scenes set at Belmont do, however, is hold up a mirror to our own investment in fictions, as in our stake in the lives of the rich and the beautiful. The rich might not be different from you and me, but the play intimates that this is precisely what we want to believe. We are only too willing to wallow in the romance and surrender to the performance the attractive characters lay on for us, however much we may know the truth of their shallow commitments. The play weaves a spell around us, gratifying our fascination with the glittering and the glamorous of this world, and simultaneously invites us to momentarily step back from the imaginary web it is spinning, exposing to view the illusions to which we are in thrall.

The Merchant of Venice revolves around a set of narcissistic and self-admiring beautiful people who lie and break promises with effortless ease, whose glamour and sophistication conceal the relentlessly acquisitive impetus that fuels this society. For the Christians in Venice, civility is a device of social distinction and a tool of exclusion, not commonality. It relates entirely to safeguarding the interests of a clique of insiders, not to fostering the interests of society as a whole. Neither the Christians nor Shylock harbour a shred of doubt about the moral righteousness of their position. Shakespeare refuses to offer us an outsider who is an innocent victim of ostracism. On the contrary, in Shylock we are faced with a deeply unpleasant, abrasive, and vindictive stranger whose alienness puts our own alleged principles to the test. By foregrounding the operation of fictional constructs in the play, *The Merchant of Venice* probes the part cultural fictions play in facilitating or eroding our sense of commonality—and holds up a mirror to our self-delusion in the bargain. What the play proposes is that we always have a choice of which assumptions we posit as true. If the play hollows out the civilizing myth and unmasks as a chimera the notion that an attractive demeanour or a cultivated way of life correlates with interior worth, it simultaneously puts forward the idea that the belief in a bond that we share might enable the operation of civil society, inexorably fractured by tension.

2

Manners and the Market

IN A COLLOQUY that appeared in 1529, Erasmus fires off a vitriolic salvo at the degenerate nobility of his time. Entitled 'The Knight without a Horse, or Faked Nobility', the piece consists of a dialogue between a wise counsellor, Nestor, and a would-be knight, Harpalus.[1] With disarming frankness, Harpalus confesses that he possesses no claim to a title through either birth or virtue. Nor does he own the means to buy one. Nevertheless, he is consumed by the desire to acquire noble status. The reason is simple: the nobility 'do as they please and get away with it' (887). Nestor obligingly provides a catalogue of advice about the habits of a nobleman. In essence, what he suggests is in order to become a gentleman, all one need do is pass as a gentleman.

The aspiring gentleman should seek out the right company, frequent fashionable haunts, and indulge in the typical pursuits of a gallant: gambling, whoring, drinking heavily, and spending lavishly. Extravagant, stylish clothes are de rigueur, as is acquiring a coat of arms. Erasmus has some fun sending up the obsession of the gentry with heraldry. Nestor and Harpalus launch into an extensive discussion of appropriate armorial bearings, settling for the heads of three slaughtered geese on a field of their own blood, 'bravely spilled', crowned by the head of a drooping dog. To Harpalus's objection, 'That's commonplace', Nestor retorts, 'Add two horns; *that's* not common' (882–83). In order to maintain the illusion of nobility, the counterfeit knight is counselled to hone his skills in acting and bluff his way through the world by virtue of sheer audacity. It is useful to have a supporting cast, a crew of reckless young servingmen decked out in handsome liveries whose task is to spread false rumours about the alleged aristocratic connections of the pretender. Nor is the assistance of the thriving early modern print industry to be neglected. As

---

1. Erasmus, 'The Knight without a Horse, or Faked Nobility', emphasis original.

FIGURE 4. Hans Holbein the Younger, *Portrait of Desiderius Erasmus of Rotterdam with Renaissance Pilaster* (1523). National Gallery, London.

Nestor points out, bribing hack writers to circulate fake credentials of the impostor in cheap print is an exceedingly effective way to diffuse misinformation. Maintaining the exorbitant lifestyle of a nobleman is possible only by living on credit, which, Nestor explains, means exploiting the trust of creditors. Along with play-acting, criminal expertise is indispensable: the recommended accomplishments for the false knight and his band of brothers range from forgery, deceit, fraud, and theft to robbery and violence.

Harpalus asks, what should he do if at long last the swindle is exposed? Nestor's advice is to keep moving. 'Steer clear of little towns where you can't even break wind without people's knowing it' (887), he instructs his interlocutor. He should seek the safety of big cities, where anonymity means freedom, especially the freedom to reinvent oneself. Ingenuity and putting up a brave front often work wonders. A felicitous solution to all financial problems is to marry money, Nestor points out. Tongue in cheek, Nestor warns Harpalus to beware of treacherous writers who exploit the power of print to uncover duplicity.

Penned as a caricature of a fellow humanist, Heinrich Eppendorf, whom Erasmus regarded as a charlatan and braggart, the colloquy is a scathing attack on social upstarts.[2] The corrosive effect of the satire is however double-edged. If the fraud attempts to palm himself off as the real item by mimicking the habits of the nobility, the latter are revealed to be mendacious and debased too. As both medieval and humanist theorists had stressed, the sole justification for the position of the well-born in the social order was their possession of moral values.[3] In Erasmus's depiction of the elite, there is little to distinguish the impostor from the nobleman, the false knight from the true gentleman. In the Renaissance world, Erasmus implies, all gentlemen are pretenders.[4]

---

2. See Craig R. Thompson, 'Introductory Note', in *Collected Works of Erasmus: Colloquies*, 880–81.

3. For a recent discussion of the role virtue played in the humanist programme to reform the European polity, see Hankins, *Virtue Politics*.

4. By the end of the sixteenth century the term 'gentility' had replaced 'nobility' as the holdall term to indicate the difference between those of high birth and commoners. At the same time, 'gentleman' designated the lowest rank of those of gentle birth, while 'nobility' was often reserved for the peerage. See Kelso, *Doctrine of the English Gentleman*, 19–20. The terms were frequently conflated, as in John Selden's *Titles of Honor* (1614): 'That [title] of Gentrie, or the same in another word, Civill Nobility, is, by which, as the first degree above the Multitude, an honoring distinction is made, either by acquisition from the Prince . . . or by Discent from Noble Ancestors. Or indeed you may not amisse comprehend hereditarie Nobilitie in that first kind' (b3v).

Erasmus's satire of the aristocracy had a strong influence on Tudor drama, where the question of true and feigned nobility was urgently debated.[5] It also prefigures many of the themes that characterize city comedy, a genre that emerged at the turn of the century in England. Defined by Brian Gibbons as plays that 'may be distinguished from the other kinds of Jacobean comedy by their critical and satiric design, their urban settings, their exclusion of material appropriate to romance, fairy-tale, sentimental legend or patriotic chronicle', they can be further identified by their mockery of moral didacticism and idealized views of reality.[6] The comedies are thronged with impostors and petty criminals and are preoccupied with conspicuous consumption, incessant role-playing, and the opportunities for creating new personae offered by the metropolis. As in Erasmus's satirical piece, self-referential jokes abound. Strongly influenced by verse satire, in the case of city comedy, stage and print are perhaps more closely bound up with each other than in other types of drama.[7] The generic plot of these plays has been summed up as 'how to get money, and how to spend it; how to get a wife, and how to keep her', but a further question the plays explore is how to define a gentleman.[8]

Renaissance civility, which originated in the Italian city-states and had its roots in ancient Rome, was an urban phenomenon. The close proximity and relative anonymity of people in towns and cities made it imperative to develop codes of coexistence—and spurred a desire for urban legibility. This chapter looks at a number of city comedies by Jonson and Middleton in conjunction with selected courtesy books. Ostensibly concerned to promote the notion of innate nobility, the true raison d'être of the manuals lies in retailing civility as a set of skills that simulate noble status. Both the manuals and the plays acknowledge that gentility is a matter of performance. The plays go further and expose congenital nobility as a myth, mocking any clear distinction between social performers and impostors. In all these texts, civility is above all a

---

5. See Walker, *Plays of Persuasion*. I am indebted to Greg Walker for drawing my attention to the interconnections between interlude literature and city comedy, both shaped by the Inns of Court milieu.

6. Gibbons, *Jacobean City Comedy*, 11. Classic studies are Knights, *Drama and Society in the Age of Jonson*; Bradbrook, 'Anatomy of Knavery'; Leggatt, *Citizen Comedy*; Wells, 'Jacobean City Comedy and the Ideology of the City'; Paster, *Idea of the City*; Leinwand, *City Staged*; Bruster, *Drama and the Market*; and Twyning, 'City Comedy'.

7. See van Es, *Shakespeare in Company*, 205–6.

8. Leggatt, *Citizen Comedy*, 4. For an incisive study of how the theatre affects ideas of gentility in a later period, see Dawson, *Gentility and the Comic Theatre of Late Stuart London*.

relentless pursuit of status. City comedy also presents an anatomy of social spectatorship, foregrounded in self-reflexive insets in the plays. Like their urban audiences, all characters are preoccupied with reading each other. While the comedies highlight the opportunities for self-reinvention offered by urban life—cannily exploited by a host of witty female protagonists—they also uncover the atomisation of society under the pervasive conditions of a market economy. Rowley and Middleton's *A Fair Quarrel*, meanwhile, in an exploration of the issue of honour, juxtaposes both sides of civility: an aggressive quest for aggrandizement and a way of living together premised on reciprocal respect.

Erasmian Manners

Erasmus's treatise *De civilitate morum puerilium* set the cornerstone for the Renaissance idea of civility as a universal mode of behaviour that all members of society could acquire. While granting that propriety is a necessary attribute of those of noble birth, Erasmus propounds the wider humanist definition of nobility as an aristocracy of learning: 'Now everyone who cultivates the mind in liberal studies must be taken to be noble'. Scoffing at the widespread preoccupation with heraldry, Erasmus remarks, 'Let others paint lions, eagles, bulls, and leopards on their escutcheons; those who can display "devices" of the intellect commensurate with their grasp of the liberal arts have a truer nobility'.[9] The treatise is dedicated to a young nobleman, Henry of Burgundy, the eleven-year-old son of Adolph, Prince of Veere, but Erasmus addresses the text to all children, irrespective of rank: 'My purpose is rather to encourage all boys to learn these rules'. Indeed, it might serve as an inducement to commoners when they observe children of illustrious descent 'competing in the same race as themselves' (273). In his *De pueris instituendis* Erasmus had famously declared that human nature was not determined at birth but malleable: 'man is certainly not born, but made man'.[10] In *De civilitate*, he reiterates the idea. No one can choose their parentage, he points out, but each person is free to mould their own personality (289).

Drawing on his formidable learning in classical and medieval educational writings, from the pedagogical principles outlined in book 8 of Aristotle's

---

9. Erasmus, *On Good Manners for Boys*, 274. On *De civilitate* see, inter alia, Elias, *Civilizing Process*, 42–47; Fontaine Verwey, 'First "Book of Etiquette" for Children'; Arditi, *Genealogy of Manners*, 113–21; and Revel, 'Uses of Civility'.

10. Erasmus, *Declamation on the Subject of Early Liberal Education for Children*, 304.

Politics to Plutarch's *Moralia*, Erasmus makes it clear that manners form only one aspect of an educational programme. The aims of pedagogy are to inspire piety, to inculcate knowledge of the liberal arts, to instruct the young in the duties of life, and to teach them good manners. The importance of the latter was based on the classical postulate that external behaviour—comportment, gestures, facial expressions, speech—revealed one's inner nature. However, the self was amenable to training and could be moulded by acquiring decorous habits. As Dilwyn Knox points out, *De civilitate* is of a piece with Erasmus's Christian pedagogy, in which reason and corporeal restraint are key.[11]

It is true, Erasmus admits, that civility might serve a more expedient purpose. 'I do not deny that external decorum is a very crude part of philosophy, but in the present climate of opinion it is very conducive to winning good will and to commending those illustrious gifts of the intellect to the eyes of men' (273), he writes. Pleasing manners, he avers, are not to be disparaged as a means of self-advancement. At the same time, as regards civility, self-interest can be harnessed for the common good. Significantly, Erasmus begins the treatise by referencing St Paul's dictum about being all things to all men (1 Cor. 9:20–22, KJV). St Paul records how in order to spread the Word of Christ, he strategically avails himself of civility, adapting to various groups of unbelievers. In the face of increasingly entrenched positions in the conflict between reformers and the established Church, few concepts resonated so deeply with Erasmus as the notion of Pauline accommodation to others in order to foster commonality in Christ, a concept modelled on the divine accommodation to the finite capacities of human understanding. Throughout his writings, from the early *Enchiridion* (1503) to the programmatic *Ratio verae theologiae* (1519), he reiterates the Pauline injunction to accommodate oneself to others to gain their goodwill. In his *Enchiridion* he urges, 'Adapt yourself to everyone exteriorly, provided that interiorly your resolution remains unshaken. Exteriorly let your friendliness, affability, good nature, and obligingness win over your brother'.[12] Attuning oneself outwardly to other members of society does not imply betraying one's inner beliefs, he claims. Civil behaviour, Erasmus believed, was a way to sway one's interlocutors to the good, which for Erasmus meant re-establishing the unity of faith for which he so fervently hoped. In his *Ratio* Erasmus affectionately describes Paul as a 'chameleon' or 'a sort of polybus', and even compares Christ to Proteus, who accommodates himself to humankind in all its variety for a

---

11. See Knox, 'Erasmus' *De civilitate*', 32.
12. Erasmus, *Handbook of the Christian Soldier*, 104.

higher cause, that of human salvation.[13] For Erasmus, dissembling, if it served an ethical end, was not only acceptable but laudable.

De civilitate reveals the form and pressure of a time in which social environments, at court or in cities, were characterized by increasing density. The treatise consists of observations on seemly behaviour in various situations—in church, at meals, in company, at play, in the bedroom—that signal self-restraint and respect for one's fellows. Written in clear, accessible prose, and although less sparkling in style than Erasmus's earlier works, the text is punctuated by occasional flashes of his trademark irony. 'Some stuff so much at one time into their mouth that their cheeks swell like a pair of bellows. Others open their jaws so widely in chewing that they produce a noise like pigs' (284), Erasmus remarks drily, in images that might have delighted the schoolboys at whom the treatise was aimed. Snorting and heavy breathing are 'for horn-blowers and elephants' (275). In addition to sending up boors, Erasmus offers passing digs at affected courtiers. Erasmus concedes that customs differ in divergent parts of the world and advises readers to accommodate themselves to the societies in which they find themselves. He ends his treatise by qualifying the importance of etiquette, pointing out that those who have not mastered the modes of polished conduct might nonetheless have other virtues, and concludes, 'Nor should what I have said be taken to imply that no one can be a good person without good manners' (289).

Elyot's Governors

The question as to how to define nobility was a pressing concern in the fifteenth and sixteenth centuries, explored in interludes such as Henry Medwall's *Fulgens and Lucres*, based on the humanist dialogue *De vera nobilitate* by Buonaccorso da Montemagno (ca. 1428), and John Heywood and John Rastell's *Gentleness and Nobility* (ca. 1525–27), and remained a locus of debate throughout the early modern period.[14] Together with thinkers such as John Colet, Sir Thomas More, and Roger Ascham, Sir Thomas Elyot was at the vanguard

---

13. See Erasmus, *Erasmus on Literature*, 97, 145, 77. As a number of scholars have pointed out, there are at times startling affinities between Erasmus and Machiavelli. See Kirkpatrick, 'Machiavelli among the Doctors', 130–33; Hoffman, *Rhetoric and Theology*; and Wolfe, 'Cosmopolitanism of the Adages'.

14. See Wakelin, '*Gentleness and Nobility*, John Rastell, c. 1525–27'. Also see Wakelin, *Humanism, Reading and English Literature*.

of the humanist movement in England, tireless in championing education in English society. His *Boke named the Governour* (1531), both a moral essay and an educational treatise, became one of the fundamental works for the English concept of the gentleman, printed eight times in the sixteenth century.[15] Influenced by both Erasmus and Castiglione, Elyot introduces a specifically English angle into the discussion.

Elyot's book begins with a paean to order.[16] He eloquently demands, 'take away order from all thynges, what shulde than remayn?' and promptly supplies the answer: chaos, perpetual conflict. He builds on the medieval concept of the chain of being to argue that all creation was founded on the principle of hierarchy: 'And it may nat be called ordre, except it do contayne in it degrees, high and base, accordynge to the merite or estimation of the thynge that is ordred' (16–17).[17] Since reason is the noblest part of the soul, those who excel in intellectual capabilities should be accorded honour and high rank as their just reward. However, the right to govern is coupled with the responsibility to serve. Unlike all other members of the commonwealth, the governing elite or 'governors', Elyot's term for the English equivalent of guardians in a Platonic ideal state, 'nothinge do acquire, for theyre owne necessities, but do imploye all the powers of theyr wittes and theyr diligence, to the only preservation of other theyr inferiours' (18–19). *The Boke named the Governour* was pivotal in advocating a concept of nobility based on service to the commonwealth, not merely, as in Castiglione's model, to the prince. The ideal of public duty became the hallmark of the English gentry and the premise on which their right to rule was anchored.

Reprising Aristotle's comment that 'nobility means ancient wealth and virtue', Elyot recapitulates the contract theory of the origins of nobility, according to which the formerly egalitarian community of humankind selected a handful of peers for their virtue, whom they ennobled and to whom they voluntarily relinquished their common property (120–23).[18] Adducing a few classical

---

15. Mack, *Elizabethan Rhetoric*, 137.

16. This was, of course, a source for Ulysses's speech on degree in *Troilus and Cressida* in act 2, scene 3. See Muir, *Sources of Shakespeare's Plays*, 151–53.

17. On Elyot, see Arditi, *Genealogy of Manners*, 164–70, and Skinner, *Foundations of Modern Political Thought*, 1:213–41.

18. Aristotle, *Politics*, 1294a22–23. On origin myths of nobility, see Kelso, *Doctrine of the English Gentleman*, 33–36. An alternative theory that locates the origin of nobility in a vicious struggle for power is presented by Jean Bodin in his *Les six livres de la République* (1576). See *The Six Bookes of a Commonweale*, E6r.

examples of men of base origin who evinced true nobility and rose to positions of authority, he stresses that ancient lineage or vast possessions alone do not entitle one to the status of nobility: 'nobilitie is nat after the vulgare opinion of men, but is only the prayse and surname of vertue' (123).

Ideally, Elyot observes, noblemen engender noble children, who emulate the virtues of their forebears, a widespread notion based on Aristotle's remark that 'children of better parents will be better, for good birth means goodness of breed' (*Pol.* 1283a37–38). Elyot takes care to point to virtue as the mainstay of nobility, warning of the degeneration of the aristocracy through error and folly. Nonetheless, he insists, bar a handful of exceptional cases, outstanding ability is to be found among the gentry. It is from their ranks that the governors are to be chosen. The reasons he puts forward extend from the argument that the propertied classes were less susceptible to corruption, that their rule was more likely to be accepted by the populace, to the observation that gentleman were marked by greater courtesy. In addition, the gentry could offer their children a liberal education and thus inculcate them with the virtues requisite for a member of the ruling class (28–29). Virtue might be the only title to rule, but it was the elite who possessed virtue to the greatest degree, he avers. Elyot devotes his book equally to advice about the formation of young gentlemen and to the virtues they should acquire. As a crucial trait of nobility, Elyot cites the Aristotelian virtue of affability. He admonishes his peers to speak courteously to their inferiors, warning them against a display of arrogance: 'they be sore blinded, which do wene [believe] that haulte [haughty] countenance is a comelynesse [appropriate feature] of nobilitie' (124).

As Greg Walker has argued persuasively, Elyot's *Governour* needs to be read in the context of Henrician rule.[19] Addressed to the sovereign, to whom it was dedicated, Elyot's mirror for princes is a bid to steer the fate of the commonwealth by swaying an increasingly autocratic ruler to heed the advice of his counsellors. Elyot's idealized image of the ruling class served a concrete political aim. His ideal of the gentleman was deeply influential on English courtesy literature. The crux that shapes these texts—the question of whether gentility is intrinsic or acquired—is mirrored in the premise of the genre itself. On the one hand, most courtesy texts assert the inherent superiority of the higher-born. On the other hand, the very notion of a manual of manners is based on the idea that civility can be learned—and purveyed as a commodity on the print marketplace.

---

19. See Walker, *Writing Under Tyranny*, 141–80.

What Is a Gentleman?

The early modern age saw an incisive redefinition of the position of the gentry. Throughout Europe their military function dwindled, while the urban business elite, by dint of their expanding wealth, impinged on their power. While courtesy literature might declare that the badge of a gentleman was virtue, best exemplified in those of high birth, in reality gentle status had become a matter of wealth and lifestyle.[20] Social commentators conceded that the category of the gentleman had expanded to include all those who could afford to appear in public as gentlemen. In his 'Description of Britaine', which forms a part of Holinshed's *Chronicles* (1577), William Harrison accords gentle status to 'Whosoever studieth the lawes of the realme, who so abideth in the Universitie, or professeth Physicke [medicine] and the liberall Sciences, or beside his service in the roome [office] of a captaine in the warres, can live ydlely and without manuell labour, and thereto is able and wil beare the port, charge, and countenance of a gentleman'. All members of this group were entitled to be addressed as 'Master'.[21] The emphasis lies on money and manners ('port' referred to lifestyle, 'charge' to expense, and 'countenance' to deportment).[22] The definition Harrison provides is taken virtually verbatim from Sir Thomas Smith's *De Republica Anglorum*, first published posthumously in 1583, some eighteen years after it was written. Smith notes caustically that 'as for gentlemen, they be made good cheape in England' and underscores the importance of self-presentation: 'As for their outward shew, a gentleman (if he wil be so accompted) must go like a gentleman, a yeoman like a yeoman, and a rascall [member of the lowest class of people] like a rascall'.[23] As in Erasmus's satire, the implication is that in order to be accepted as a gentleman, all one needed do was to carry off a convincing performance, furnished with the obligatory commodities as props.

As numerous writers lament, the preserve of the nobility was increasingly being trespassed upon by social climbers who invested their newly gained wealth in a bid to acquire gentle status. In the English treatise *Institucion of a gentleman* (1555; the term 'institution' meant 'education'),[24] the author,

---

20. Wrightson, 'Estates, Degrees, and Sorts', 39. Also see Wrightson, 'Sorts of People'.
21. Harrison, 'Description of Britaine', M1r.
22. *OED*, s.v. 'port, n. 4', 2.a, and 'countenance, n.', 1.
23. Smith, *De Republica Anglorum*, E2r–v.
24. *OED*, s.v. 'institution, n.', 4.

probably Humfrey Braham, bewails the large numbers of upstarts creeping into the strongholds of the gentry. His manual is a self-proclaimed attempt to shore up the position of the gentry and rebuild the house of nobility, threatened by invasion: 'these base sorte of men have easelye entred therin, & at this daye do beare those armes which wer geven unto old gentry'.[25] Admittedly, the nobility themselves are partly to blame, and he attributes their crumbling position to decadence: gentry, he notes sarcastically, is 'sore decayed, & falne to great ruine: whereby suche corruption of maners hath taken place, that almost the name of gentry is quenched, and handycrafte men have obtayned the tytle of honour, though (in dede) of them selves they can chalenge [claim] no greater worthynes then the spade brought unto their late fathers' (*3r–v). The author differentiates between the *gentle gentle*, the *gentle ungentle*, and the *ungentle gentle* (B6v–D3v). The *gentle gentle* are the patterns of excellence who combine gentle birth with learning, arms, and courteous behaviour. The *gentle ungentle* are of noble descent, but have sunk into a pit of iniquity, apparent in their corrupt manners. The *ungentle gentle* are of base origin, but have risen in status on account of their virtue, wit, or industry. The author berates the nouveaux riches who have insinuated themselves into the rank of gentry by buying land, an abuse that, as he points out, has exploded since the Henrician dissolution of the abbeys. For them he reserves the label *unworthy worshipfull* (D3r). Braham emphasises the importance of comportment in upholding social rank: he is 'worshypful [deserving of esteem], which in al worship [distinction] behaveth hymselfe', he declares (G5r).

Half a century later, Henry Peacham published *The Compleat Gentleman* (1622), one of the best-known courtesy books written by an Englishman. The work is dedicated to William Howard, the young son of Thomas, Earl of Arundel and Surrey, whom Peacham served as tutor. Peacham grounds his thoughts on nobility firmly on the premise of a universal, hierarchical order. England, and indeed the entire continent, he declares, is in the grip of a pandemic: 'every undeserving and base peasant aiming at nobility'.[26] He roundly condemns social climbing as a result of wealth: 'the most common and worst of all is in all places the purchasing of arms and honors for money' (26). Yet as the writers of courtesy books knew all too well, and dramatists demonstrated unceasingly, money was the main agent of social mobility. Wealth and nobility were so closely

25. Braham, *Institucion of a gentleman*, *3v.
26. Peacham, *The Complete Gentleman*, 25. On Peacham, see Arditi, *Genealogy of Manners*, 170–75.

entwined that they were virtually impossible to disentangle. In his satirical *Greenes Groats-Worth of witte*, Robert Greene has a new-made gentleman scoff, 'what is gentry if welth be wanting, but bace servile beggerie'.[27] In a set of precepts addressed to his son, circulated during his lifetime as the 'Ten Precepts' (1587), Lord Burghley notes laconically, 'Gentilitie is nothing but ancient Riches', dispensing with the Aristotelian reference to virtue entirely.[28]

How to Become a Gentleman

Resentment at the encroachment of those of low origin on gentlemanly ground was palpable at all levels of the gentry. William Darell's *A Short discourse of the life of Servingmen* (1578) bemoans the plight of second sons, driven out of service by the sons of rich yeomen hoping to become gentlemen by serving in the household of a nobleman. These aspirants often served without wages, a factor that weighed heavily in their favour with impecunious aristocrats. The latter were increasingly under pressure from the high costs of maintaining an adequate style of living in London despite reduced income from their land, a result of the inflation that gripped sixteenth-century Europe. Darell comments sourly on the upstart rivals, 'What profiteth brave [splendid] clothes in any person wanting witt and gouvernement?', hinting ominously that once these bumpkins find themselves in London, they will fall into a cesspool of crime and end their lives on the gallows.[29] In his *A Health to the Gentlemanly profession of Servingmen* (1598), the prolific Gervase Markham rehearses the same themes, censuring the disease of social presumption that has afflicted the nation: 'For the Cobler would be Shoomaker, the Shoomaker a Tanner, the Tanner a Grasier [cattle-grazer]: so that no man resteth contented with his vocation'.[30] His treatise is an elegy for a golden age when noblemen prided themselves on their hospitality. The decay of housekeeping is a motif that runs through social commentary of the time, and gains additional traction from King James's frequent proclamations to the gentry to return to the countryside.[31]

27. Greene, *Greenes Groats-Worth of witte*, B2r.
28. Burghley, *Certaine Preceptes or Directions*, A6v. On Burghley's precepts, see Tromly, 'Masks of Impersonality'.
29. Darell, *A Short discourse of the life of Servingmen*, B1v. On Darell, see Wright, 'Conduct Book for Malvolio'.
30. [Markham], *Health to the Gentlemanly profession of Servingmen*, B1r–v.
31. See Heal, *Hospitality in Early Modern England*. On King James's attempt to revive rural customs, see Marcus, *Politics of Mirth*.

Darell admits that his addressees, servingmen of gentry origin, have gained a bad reputation for their riotous behaviour. To rectify this failing, he recommends a rigorous regimen of good manners: 'For, courtesie is the only badge of a Gentleman and descendeth from nobilite' (C1r). Darell appends Della Casa's *Galateo* to his treatise for his readers to peruse. In his commonplace book, *The Rich Cabinet* (1616), Thomas Gainsford reveals a shrewd grasp of the value of manners as a means of attaining social cachet. 'Curtesie', he writes, 'sheweth, that a Gent: is of good bringing up', and continues, 'curtesy & friendly behaviour is more honor to him that useth it, then to whom it is done'.[32] He too includes Della Casa's treatise as an annexe.

How precisely was one to accrue the cultural capital of courtesy? Darell might piously insist on the virtues of godliness, cleanliness, diligence, and graceful manners. For most would-be gentlemen, it meant pursuing the lifestyle associated with gentility. Wealth alone was not sufficient; it had to be displayed in one's taste for fashionable artefacts and a refined way of living. In this connection, education played a key role. In England, from the middle of the sixteenth century onwards, the practice of sending young noblemen to be trained at great households waned, while sons of noblemen and gentry flocked to the universities, often moving on to the Inns of Court to gain a final coat of polish. For the aristocracy, education did not simply mean learning an assortment of subjects such as logic, grammar, rhetoric, moral philosophy, history, law, cosmography, and geometry, but also attaining accomplishments in the arts and practicing physical exercises that included running, leaping, wrestling, tennis, archery, riding the great horse, hunting, hawking, fencing, and dancing. Increasingly, travel abroad became a desideratum, necessary not only to learn foreign languages but also to nurture aesthetic and even antiquarian sensibilities. Both James Cleland and Henry Peacham, tutors to young noblemen, emphasize the importance of the Grand Tour for their charges. As Cleland puts it, travel is 'the principle & best meanes, whereby a young Noble man, or anie other maie profit his Prince, his Countrie, and himselfe'.[33] While Cleland encourages travel as an indispensable part of the formation of a young gentleman in the service of his nation, for Peacham it is chiefly a means of acquiring individual finesse. In 1634 Peacham expanded his treatise to include the topic of collecting antiquities, claiming that even if collecting itself was reserved for the very rich, every traveller should cultivate a taste in antique

---

32. G[ainsford], *The Rich Cabinet*, D2r.
33. Cleland, *Hero-paideia*, 2I1r.

objects of art in order to be considered refined and, as he implies, to gain access to the circles of the owners of antiquities (117).[34] Peacham's patron and dedicatee of the book, the Earl of Arundel, forged a reputation for himself as a connoisseur of art and put together one of the most magnificent collections in Jacobean England.[35] From the first decade of the seventeenth century onwards, collecting art became the mark of a cosmopolitan personality.[36] Or so the gentry believed—an idea skewered with relish in city comedy. In *The Roaring Girl*, Sir Alexander Wengrave, who shows off his art collection to the audience in a striking metadramatic moment in which his portraits are reflected back by the members of the audience, is exposed not only as a domestic tyrant, but as the most bigoted character in the play.[37]

Despite the rise in stock of travel abroad, reservations about the pernicious influence of European culture, prevalent at least since Roger Ascham's tirade against the 'Englishman Italianated' who travelled to Italy 'only to serve Circe', remained in circulation.[38] Cleland cautions his charge, Sir John Harington, against too long a stay in Italy, seeing that 'the pleasures and diverse allurements to sinne are so frequent' (2K4v). Francis Bacon, while advocating travel as a part of education, warns the young traveller not to 'change his country manners for those of foreign parts'.[39] And in the revised, 1587 version of his 'Description of Britaine', Harrison trains his ire on the fashionable practice of sending young gentlemen to Italy to acquire a veneer of sophistication. This, he warns, will be the ruin of the nation. The young men 'bring home nothing but maere atheisme, infidelitie, vicious conversation [way of life], & ambitious and proud behaviour', he declares, 'wherby it commeth to passe that they returne far worse men than they went out'. He gives examples of cynical and depraved sentiments uttered by Italianate gentlemen, and notes sarcastically, 'This gaie bootie gate these gentlemen by going into Italie'. It is easy to identify

---

34. Chapter 12, 'Of Antiquities', was an addition to the 1634 edition of Peacham's book.
35. See Orgel, 'Devil incarnate', and *Wit's Treasury*, 58–62.
36. See Jardine, *Worldly Goods*, and Levy Peck, *Consuming Splendor*.
37. Dekker and Middleton, *Roaring Girl*, scene 2, 10–32.
38. Ascham, *The Schoolmaster*, 66. Ascham famously turned the Italian proverb deriding Englishmen, '*Inglese italianato è un diavolo incarnato*' ('an Italianate Englishman is a devil incarnate', probably coined in connection with the fourteenth-century English *condottiero*, John Hawkwood), against his countrymen who visited Italy and returned laden with vices, above all papistry. For his part, Florio self-mockingly cites the adage in the address to the reader in his *Second Frutes* (*1r–v).
39. Bacon, 'Of Travel', in *Major Works*, 374–76.

these degenerate specimens: they go around accompanied by comely young pages, 'whose face and countenance shall be such as sheweth the master not be blind in his choice'. Hinting darkly at the usual Italian bogeys, Machiavellianism and sodomy, Harrison breaks off at this point, 'lest I should offend too much'.[40]

In the anonymous dialogue, *Cyvile and uncyvile life* (1579), the dispute between a country and a city gentleman, Vincent and Vallentine, is decided in favour of Vallentine, who argues that a gentleman residing in the city 'is more civil then any Country man can bee'.[41] Rooted in classical tropes, civility was correlated with an urban lifestyle; in Cockeram's 1623 *Dictionarie*, 'urbanitie' and 'civill behaviour' are given as synonyms.[42] London was not only the location of the court, Parliament, and the law courts, but the centre of fashionable life and a flourishing leisure industry. Country gentry flocked to the metropolis, often running up considerable debts in order to afford the high cost of living.[43] By the end of the century, a backlash against urban civility is discernible, particularly in satirical writing. Joseph Hall's diatribe stands for many. Gentility, he announces, no longer has truck with virtue. The exigencies for a gentleman are now quite different:

> If you can follow all fashions, drinke all healths, weare favours [love tokens] and good cloths, consort with Ruffians, companions, swear the biggest Oaths, quarrell easily, fight desperately, game in every inordinate Ordinary, spend your patrimony ere it fall, looke on every man betwixt scorn and anger; use gracefully some gestures of apish complement; talke irreligiously, dally with a Mistris, or (which tearme is plainer) hunt after Harlots, take smoake at a Play-house, and live as if you were made all for sport, you thinke you have doone enough, to merit, both of your blood, and others opinions.[44]

Hall concludes that if these habits be the hallmarks of civility, the rude conduct of the ill-bred is much to be preferred.

40. Harrison, 'An Historicall description of the Iland of Britaine', P2v.
41. *Cyvile and uncyvile life*, N4v.
42. C[ockeram], *The English Dictionarie*, L4r.
43. See Fisher, 'Development of London'.
44. Joseph Hall, Epistle VI, Decade VI, To Master I. B., 'A complaint of the mis-education of our Gentry', E2v–3r. The term 'complement' could refer to observances of civility, including complimentary remarks, as well as more broadly to personal accomplishments. See *OED*, s.v., 'complement, n.', II.7 to 9.

The turning of the tide in courtesy books is manifest in works such as Richard Brathwaite's *English Gentleman* (1630). Brathwaite emphatically favours the country gentleman, who lives 'without the addition of either Taylor, Millener, Seamster or Haberdasher'.[45] His book is the harbinger of the new ideal of the Christian gentleman in seventeenth-century books on manners, one who 'holds idlenesse to bee the very moth of mans time' and labours all day in his vocation (2K4v). Courtesy books aimed at women, as opposed to pious conduct literature, remained rare until the late seventeenth century.[46] However, Brathwaite brought out a companion piece, *The English Gentlewoman* (1631); both texts were subsequently published in a joint volume. Together they exemplify Brathwaite's mission to foster a reformed country gentry who define themselves in opposition to the corrupt mores of courtly life. The ideal gentlewoman, he writes, 'cannot indure this later introduc'd kind of Complement, which consists in Cringies, Congies [bows], or supple Salutes'. Instead of fashionable urban manners, her credo is 'modesty' or scrupulous propriety (2M2r). Happily, he adds, there are still gentlewomen in England who disdain foreign fashions and 'painted Rhetoricke' (2R1v).

Less happily, these paragons have left virtually no trace on city comedy. A genre moulded after classical New Comedy with its focus on the concerns of urban dwellers, city comedy inspired a frisson of excitement with spectators at the novelty of seeing their own quotidian lives displayed onstage.[47] But rather than patterns of gentility to emulate, the plays put on a parade of bungling social aspirants, impostors, and con artists.

Every Man Out of His Humour

Every Man Out of His Humour, Jonson's first 'comical satire', a term he first used on the title page of the first quarto of the play, was an outstanding success as a playtext, running into three editions in 1600 alone.[48] Erasmus's 'Knight without a Horse' was clearly a source for the set piece on how to be a gentleman

---

45. Brathwaite, *English Gentleman and English Gentlewoman*, 2K4r. Also see Ustick, 'Changing Ideals of Aristocratic Character and Conduct'.

46. See Tague, *Women of Quality*, 23. On courtesy literature for women, see Kelso, *Doctrine for the Lady of the Renaissance*; Hull, *Chaste, Silent and Obedient*; Mendelson, 'Civility of Women in Seventeenth-Century England'; and Herbert, *Female Alliances*.

47. See Haynes, *Social Relations of Jonson's Theatre*, 63–64.

48. See Ostovich, 'Introduction', 40. All citations from the play are taken from the Revels Plays edition.

that the jester and parasite, Carlo Buffone, delivers to the upstart country yokel, Sogliardo, who announces, 'I will be a gentleman whatsoever it cost me' (1.2.7–8).[49] Carlo takes him through the steps leading to gentility:

> First, to be an accomplished gentleman, that is, a gentleman of the time, you must give o'er housekeeping in the country and live altogether in the city amongst gallants, where, at your first appearance, 'twere good you turned four or five hundred acres of your best land into two or three trunks of apparel. You may do it without going to a conjurer. And be sure you mix yourself still [always] with such as flourish in the spring of the fashion and are least popular [vulgar]. Study their carriage and behaviour in all. Learn to play at primero and passage [games], and (ever when you lose) ha' two or three peculiar oaths to swear by that no man else swears. But, above all, protest in your play and affirm 'Upon your credit', 'As you are a true gentleman', at every cast. (1.2.41–54)

Lavishly investing in clothes, seeking out the right company, gambling, and swearing are the foundation for gentlemanly behaviour. Further building blocks, as Carlo goes on to explain, are adopting affected mannerisms (such as the use of toothpicks), name-dropping, and, in a reprisal of Erasmus's counsel, forging letters from important people which should be left in the pockets of suits sent for repairs to tailors, a reliable conduit to spread gossip. Carlo also recycles Erasmus's tips about hiring thugs in smart liveries as retainers and managing one's creditors with a mixture of cajoling and bullying. Carlo and his associates (as well as the audience) enjoy a few delicious moments when they hear the description of the coat of arms Sogliardo has ordered for himself: 'a swine without a head, without brain, wit, anything, indeed, ramping to gentility' (3.223–25). It appears to be the exact replica of its bearer. The uplifting heraldic motto is '*Not without mustard*' (244), possibly a sideswipe at the brand-new coat of arms ordered by Jonson's rival, Shakespeare, with the motto *Non sans droict*.[50] Types like Sogliardo furnished rich pickings for satirists, and

---

49. See notes in the Revels Plays edition, 137. On *Every Man Out of His Humour*, see especially the invaluable introductions to the play by Ostovich, 1–95, and by Randall Martin in *The Cambridge Edition of the Works of Ben Jonson*, vol. 1. For a sampling of criticism on the play, see Gibbons, *Jacobean City Comedy*, 50–58; Dutton, *Ben Jonson: To the First Folio*, 34–41; Barton, *Ben Jonson, Dramatist*, 65–73; Cave, *Ben Jonson*, 15–18; Haynes, *Social Relations of Jonson's Theatre*, 43–51; Clare, 'Jonson's "Comical Satires" and the Art of Courtly Compliment'; and Donaldson, *Ben Jonson*, 154–64.

50. See Bednarz, *Shakespeare and the Poets' War*, 24.

he is aptly summed up in the description (or 'character') of 'An Upstart Knight' penned by John Earle: 'He is garded [embellished] with more Gold-lace then all the Gentlemen o'th Country, yet his body makes his clothes still out of fashion. . . . In summe, he is but a clod of his owne earth; or his Land is the Dunghill, and he the Cocke that crowes over it.'[51] All his splendid attire cannot disguise the fact that underneath he is nothing but a country oaf.

As the oath that Carlo impresses on Sogliardo, asserting his status as a 'true gentleman', ironically underlines, the would-be gentleman is a sham, one whose resplendent appearance by no means corresponds to his real self. In an aside to Macilente, the scholarly malcontent of the play, Carlo calls the rustic a 'mere stuffed suit' who 'looks like a musty bottle, new wickered' (1.2.201). In reality, however, his methods do not differ substantially from those of the young men thronging London in pursuit of gentlemanly status. To become a gentleman meant acquiring the habits of the elite company to which one aspired and sharing their leisure activities, their style of speech, and their taste in dress and fashionable accessories. The most important of these, as Carlo points out, is attire. Early modern England was in the throes of a craze for fashion, bemoaned by a slew of social critics. For social critic Philip Stubbes, pride in apparel heads the list of the abuses he anatomizes in England (or 'Ailgna', the anagram he prefers). As he has one of his interlocutors, Philoponus, declare categorically, 'no people in the world, are so curious in new fangles, as they of Ailgna bee.'[52]

Stubbes is particularly galled by the collapse of sumptuary order in contemporary England, with all members of society who can afford to do so donning silks, velvets, satins, damask, and other luxurious materials, which he regards as a threat to the social hierarchy. As he complains, 'now there is suche a confuse mingle mangle of apparell in Ailgna, and suche preposterous excesse thereof, as every one is permitted to flaunt it out, in what apparell he lusteth hymself, or can get by any kinde of meanes. So that it is very harde to know who is noble, who is worshipfull, who is a gentleman, who is not'. The

---

51. Earle, *Micro-cosmographie*, F5v–6r.
52. Stubbes, *The Anatomie of Abuses*, C2v. The largely ineffectual sumptuary laws, flouted throughout the sixteenth century, were finally abandoned in 1604. See Thomas, *Ends of Life*, 137. On the role of fashion in early modern England, see Newman, 'Dressing Up: Sartorial Extravagance in Early Modern London', in *Fashioning Femininity and English Renaissance Drama*, 111–27, and Bailey, '"Monstrous Manner"'. Also see Haynes, *Social Relations of Jonson's Theatre*, 51–68, on whose insights I draw in the following.

dire consequences, he warns grimly, are 'a greate confusion, and a generall disorder in a Christian common wealth' (C3v–4r). To be sure, the scenario of the end of civilization as we know it was wheeled out by moralists as a rhetorical ploy, but it corresponded to a real increase in wealth among the classes that had profited from the economic turbulence of the sixteenth century and from the upheaval in the land market as a result of the dispossession of monasteries. In the rapidly expanding early modern consumer market, luxury items, many of them imported, played a significant role.[53] The theatre was actively involved in promoting the fashion industry. Costumes were the most expensive item of expenditure listed in the impresario Henslowe's diary, and actors paraded the discarded wardrobe of aristocratic owners or their servants, turning the stage into an early modern catwalk for the benefit of a keenly interested public.[54] Spectators, too, came to the theatre to flaunt their attire.

In *Every Man Out of His Humour*, the nonpareil of fashion is the courtier Fastidius Brisk, for his dress as well as his exquisite manners. Fallace, the citizen's wife who dreams of courtly life, swoons over his mannerisms in conversation and at table: 'How daintily he carves! How sweetly he talks and tells news of this lord and of that lady! How cleanly he wipes his spoon at every spoonful of white meat he eats, and what a neat case of pick-tooths he carries about him still!' (4.1.35–39). His stock in trade is court gossip and larding his speech with the names of the great and the good with whom, he insinuates, he is on intimate terms. He is a master of artificial, vacuous speech, punctuated with extravagantly polite gestures (or 'complements'). The embodiment of affectation, a member of the flock of the Osrics and Oswalds that populate early modern drama, he airily explains to Carlo why he eschews the latter's more rawer breath: 'I cannot frame me to your harsh vulgar phrase. 'Tis against my *genius*' (2.1.98–99). His diction is trenchantly anatomized by John Earle in his acerbic 'character' of a 'meere Complementall Man': 'His words are but so many fine phrases set together, which serve equally for all men and are equally to no purpose'.[55] In his *Discoveries* Jonson jotted down Seneca's Epistle 114 on the social ramifications of an affected style of discourse: 'The excess of feasts and apparel are the notes of a sick state, and the wantonness of language, of a sick mind'.[56] Like Seneca,

---

53. See Thirsk, *Economic Policy and Projects*.
54. See Jones and Stallybrass, *Renaissance Clothing*, 175–206, who suggest that Henslowe was also engaged in the trade for secondhand clothes.
55. Earle, *Micro-cosmographie*, E8v–9r.
56. Notes to Jonson, *Discoveries*, 532.

echoing thoughts by Isocrates, Jonson suggests that the decadent lifestyle and speech of individuals is the symptom of a larger crisis in civil society.[57]

At the root of Jonson's satiric vision in this play is the notion of 'humours', famously defined in the induction by the purported playwright Asper, as 'when some one peculiar quality / Doth so possess a man that it doth draw / All his affects, his spirits, and his powers / In their confluxions all to run one way' (Ind. 103–6). All characters in the play are in the grip of specific obsessions.[58] They are in thrall to their private fantasies to such an extent that they have lost touch with social reality; their self-absorbed rituals fail to take the web of social relations in which they are embedded into account. The play exhibits a panoply of posturers engrossed in their solipsistic performances. One of the most interesting studies is that of Puntarvolo. Indubitably a real knight, he is shown performing in a titillating playlet in which he plays a knight errant wooing his own wife. He addresses her in a murky brew of the mock-archaic and the lubricious: 'I have scarce collected my spirits, but lately scattered in the admiration of your form, to which (if the bounties of your mind be any way responsible) I doubt not but my desires shall find a smooth and secure passage' (2.1.322–26). While the parvenues dream of rising through the ranks, Puntarvolo seeks to re-enact a fictitious chivalric past. The gentlemen and would-be gentlemen alike are engaged in the same activity, fabricating their identity in the image of a desired self. Puntarvolo remains entirely oblivious to his wife's abhorrence at being made an object of voyeurism and his own reputation as a laughing stock to the company watching the show. All characters are entangled in solipsistic delusions, blind to the crucial fact that their realities are not solely self-determined but defined in interaction with others.

The Marketplace of Manners

In *Every Man Out of His Humour*, civility is governed by the logic of the market.[59] Gentlemanly identity is not innate but fluctuates in value. This is particularly true of the city, where relative anonymity prevailed, and social identity was something people tinkered with incessantly. In city comedy, personhood is refashioned at will, perhaps catering to audience fantasies of reinventing

---

57. See Vickers, *In Defence of Rhetoric*, 159.
58. See esp. Dutton, *Ben Jonson: Authority*, 115–23.
59. On the market in city comedy, see Hutson, 'Displacement of the Market'. On early modern drama and the market, see Bruster, *Drama and the Market*, and Agnew, *Worlds Apart*.

oneself in the metropolis, fantasies stoked by the burgeoning early modern market economy and the heightened sense of individual agency it engendered. Plays depicting urban life in London might well have gratified the vanity of spectators in finding their everyday practice of role-playing at the centre of interest, while drawing attention to the startling resonances between a fictional world in which everyone is busy watching everyone else and the surveillance—and self-surveillance—that characterise civil society in the metropolis.

This is exemplified in the series of vignettes of social life that structure the play. The pivotal scene, act 3, scene 1, takes place in the middle aisle of St Paul's, a cross between an early modern shopping arcade, a promenade, and a business centre. It was also the preserve of petty criminals and confidence tricksters of every stripe. In the lineup of would-be gentlemen that the play displays, Shift is the crudest variety of impostor, a 'courtesy-man', defined by John Awdeley in his coney-catching pamphlet *The Fraternity of Vagabonds* as someone who 'when he meeteth some handsome young man cleanly apparelled, or some other honest citizen, he maketh humble salutations and low courtesy, and showeth him that he hath a word or two to speak with his mastership'. Once he has engaged his victim in conversation, he launches into a tale of woe, fabricating a history of having been a gentleman servingman in the wars, now fallen on hard times. Crooks of this type are adept at all the gentlemanly forms of behaviour, are 'commonly well apparelled', and 'bear the port of right good gentlemen'.[60] At their best, they are consummate performers of gentility. Shift is emphatically not a master of the craft. None of the other characters are susceptible to his sales pitch, but he finds a willing gull in the naive Sogliardo, who alone takes him for a gentleman.

While the devotee of fashion Fungoso, whose tailor is ensconced behind a pillar, busy copying Brisk's latest suit of clothes, is on a quest to buy gentility by procuring its outer trappings, the other characters are jockeying for status. The scene is a virtuosic choreography of a clutch of characters all vying for prestigious social encounters.[61] Shift is trying to meet potential gulls, Fastidius is eager to ingratiate himself with the knight, Puntarvolo is interested in striking up an acquaintance with the prosperous merchant Deliro, a possible investor in his travel scheme, while Deliro is keen to mix with the gentry and avoid his boorish relatives. They are all busy repackaging themselves as men of taste and cultivation and attempting to market themselves to others.

60. Judges, *Elizabethan Underworld*, 56–57.
61. See Helen Ostovich's masterly reading of this scene in her 'Introduction', 59–68.

While absorbed in promoting themselves, everyone in the play has an eye on everyone else. Throughout the play, the members of the chorus, Cordatus and Mitus (whom Jonson labels the 'Grex' or invited guests of the 'presenter', Asper), carry on a running commentary on what they observe. They are mimicked by the characters onstage. Carlo and Maciliente share their opinions on their fellows in asides to the audience and, increasingly, to each other, until by act 4 they are virtually staging a comic double act, lobbing sardonic remarks back and forth over the heads of the less discerning characters. Act 2, scene 1 consists largely of different groups of characters, the eavesdroppers Carlo, Sogliardo, and Fastidius on the one hand, and the supporting cast of Sordido, the country miser, and his son Fungoso on the other, watching while Puntarvolo runs through his little performance. Earlier in the scene, both Fastidius and Sogliardo try to draw Carlo aside for private conversations in which each comment on the other. In act 4, scene 5, Carlo and Maciliente huddle with Puntarvolo and Fastidius to plan a trick on Sogliardo and Saviolina, the self-styled presiding wit at court, whispering about Sogliardo while the latter remains oblivious.

The metatheatrical gambits revolving around performance, spectatorship, and deciphering visual codes serve to hold up a mirror to the audience, governed as their everyday lives were by the requirement for ceaseless self-presentation as well as meticulous monitoring of other social actors. In a social world in which so much hinged on reputation or 'credit', the fear of having one's social performances exposed might well have struck a chord with the theatre audience, engaged in the same quest for prestige and haunted by the same fears about losing status as were the characters in the play. Watching the responses of others would have offered a guide as to whether one's self-projection was successful or not. Careful scrutiny of the signals sent by one's associates was also necessary to see through the fraudulent claims of others. Early modern literature teems with impostors, be it in coney-catching texts or city comedy. In particular, the genre of 'charactery', mainly associated with Joseph Hall's *Characters of Vertues and Vices* (1608), which first revived Theophrastus' *Characters*, encapsulates the impulse to decode one's fellow citizens on the basis of their traits.[62] In a world in which social roles were felt to be achieved, not given, it was of vital importance to read visual clues.

---

62. The technique of presenting thumbnail descriptions of people was originally a rhetorical exercise for orators in preparation for legal proceedings. The best-known work to adapt the form for the purpose of producing an anatomy of society was *Overbury's Characters* (1614). See Beecher, 'Introduction'.

In its ironic self-awareness, the play does not merely satirize a society of status seekers. It mockingly suggests that we too, Jonson's chosen audience of 'Attentive auditors' who have come to the theatre in order to gratify our 'understanding parts' (Ind. 199–201), are implicated in what we take such pleasure in deriding. We are all performers, in the business of crafting ideal versions of ourselves in the quest for self-advancement and absorbed in incessantly observing one another. While the main thrust of *Every Man Out of His Humour* is to unmask the solipsism and absurd pretensions of an array of fools, the self-consciousness in which the comedy is drenched induces a critical distance which enables us to watch ourselves operate in a social setting. Nonetheless, in a world of role players, one way of furthering a shared stake in society, the play ironically suggests, might be to enter into an implicit agreement with one another to maintain the concept of self that the other has built up.[63]

On occasion, the characters seem to opt for comity rather than for exposing one another's charades, admittedly for entirely self-interested reasons. None of the observers comment on Puntarvolo's erotic skit in his presence, however much they might lampoon it behind his back. When Sogliardo pleads with his new friends to accept the patent swindler Shift into their circle, Puntarvolo responds graciously. 'Sir, for Signor Sogliardo's sake, let it suffice I know you' (4.3.239–40), he says, addressing the dubious hanger-on. In act 2, scene 1, in spite of his previously disparaging remarks, Puntarvolo is the epitome of courtesy to Fastidius, as he is to Sordido and Fungoso, and spares no effort to include them in the company: 'Nay, go not, neighbour Sordido', he insists, 'Stay tonight and help to make our society the fuller' (2.1.533–34). In the following scene Deliro extends a warm welcome to Macilente and defends him to the snobbish Fastidius, disdainful of 'such poor seam-rent fellows' (2.2.283–84). We observe a series of loose alliances among the characters in which they sustain a simulation of cordiality, be it in the hope of future business dealings or in order to engineer a collaborative jest, such as the one played on the lady courtier Saviolina.

It is the righteous crusader, Macilente, bursting with indignation at the degraded mores of his society, who shreds the precarious facade of mutual respect that the characters have at times attempted to establish. Steeped in moral censoriousness, Macilente is ruthless in his mission to expose the pretensions of the poseurs and ensnare the characters in the net of their own delusions. Although he pours vitriol on Carlo for his penchant for backstabbing his

---

63. See Goffman, 'Nature of Deference and Demeanour', 60.

benefactors, describing him as a 'slave' who 'to your back will turn the tail and sting / More deadly than a serpent' (1.2.237–38), he himself has no qualms in betraying his erstwhile ally. The last words Carlo addresses to him before he is silenced are '*Et tu, Brute*' (5.3.259). Jonson reinforces the impression of the human bankruptcy of the social world he portrays by juxtaposing it with the unremitting cordiality among the members of the chorus, Cordatus, Mitis, and Asper—at least until the latter mutates into the self-appointed pillar of moral purity, Macilente.

Manners and the Theatre

Although the play was staged in the new Globe Theatre in 1599, Jonson's target audience were the Inns of Court students, with whom he shared a bond and to whom he dedicated the play in the Folio of 1616. The print history of the quarto as one of the most popular playtexts in the period attests to its success with a reading public with a palate for pungent satirical fare.[64] Jonson was intimately associated with the intellectual circles at the Inns of Court, which included figures like John Donne, John Hoskyns, and John Marston, with whom he was bound in a deeply ambivalent relationship. The legal jokes with which the play is studded, or the reference to the predilection of the men about town, Clove and Orange, for feasting with players ('Characters', 98–99), are characteristic of a type of drama that thrives on in-jokes and self-conscious devices in its caricature of social absurdities. No doubt part of the satire's success lay in its ability to induce audience pleasure at their own performance as superior to that of foppish or fatuous exemplars, like Fastidius or Fungoso, or the daft duo Clove and Orange. At the same time, audience members would have been watching carefully to register which solecisms to avoid in their own quest for style. Inns of Court students were, after all, jostling for preferment in a highly competitive market, hoping for lucrative positions in state or church administration or in noble households.[65]

As Jonson intimates, the theatre, both on stage and in print, was enmeshed in the market of manners that it mocked. It diffused knowledge about a stylish lifestyle at the same time as it held this lifestyle up to ridicule. Paul's Walk was the centre of the market for print, and modish print artefacts belonged among

---

64. See Ostovich, 'Introduction', 28–38.
65. The classic study of the culture of the Inns of Court is Finkelpearl, *John Marston of the Middle Temple*.

the accoutrements of a gentleman. Jonson's play was only one in a chorus of works poking fun at their own investment in the social theatre staged at Paul's Walk. In his parody of a courtesy book, *The Guls Horne-booke*, Dekker devotes an entire chapter to 'How a Gallant should behave himselfe in Powles walkes' (D1r–3v). His instructions resemble nothing so much as tongue-in-cheek stage directions for the aspiring social performer athirst to flaunt his stylish attire: 'in view of all, you may publish your suit in what manner you affect most, either with the slide of your cloake from one shoulder, and then you must (as twere in anger) suddenly snatch at the middle of the inside (if it be taffata at the least) and so by the meanes of your costly lining is betrayed' (D1v). Dekker helps himself to Jonson's episode of Fungoso's tailor spying out fashions and conflates the latest style with the latest print commodity: 'you shall weare your clothes in print with the first edition' (D2v), he promises the reader. Playwrights and satirists are equally unsparing in their jibes about would-be sophisticates who use prestigious works as props to display their erudition and exude a cosmopolitan flair. Of the cipher Clove, Cordatus sneers, 'He will sit you a whole afternoon sometimes in a bookseller's shop reading the Greek, Italian, and Spanish when he understands not a word of either' (3.1.50–51).

As has been extensively observed, the austere moralist Asper and his alter ego Macilente share traits with Jonson. There are also affinities between Macilente and the scurrilous parasite Carlo—affinities which seep into the characterization of Asper and tarnish his image of moral rectitude.[66] The only intelligent characters onstage, Carlo and Macilente are drawn to each other in a natural alliance to send up all the other characters, before Macilente turns on Carlo and betrays him. The canine imagery which runs through the play provides an ironic comment on the analogies between them: Carlo is described as a 'black-mouthed cur' (1.3.234) and Macilente as a 'lean mongrel' (1.2.214); Carlo suggests poisoning Puntarvolo's dog (3.1.62–63) before Macilente actually does so. Carlo is described as a 'feast-hound' whose main pleasure, apart from railing, lies in 'pleasing his palate' and swilling sack ('Characters', 25–29). Carlo is disparaged for debasing his wit to mercenary ends: 'yours be the worst use a man can put his wit to of thousands, to prostitute it at every tavern and ordinary' (1.2.191–93), Macilente chastises him. But as the play reveals, both the cynical parasite Carlo and the moral zealot Macilente are driven by the same imperative—the need to find patrons to bankroll their way of life. Their abrasive censure of other

---

66. Carlo might be based on Charles Chester, a notorious roisterer and hanger-on in the Middle Temple milieu of the time. See Steggle, 'Charles Chester and Ben Jonson'.

status climbers is in fact grounded in the same exigency of self-advancement. Carlo attaches himself like a leech to the propertied Sogliardo in the hope of fleecing him, while Macilente, even if driven by the desire to demolish Deliro's marriage, has no qualms in exploiting his generosity.

Nor, the play signals, is the self-righteous Macilente morally superior to the parasite. Puntarvolo is appalled at Carlo's readiness to slander his benefactor, Sogliardo, exclaiming, 'How dost thou prick the vein of thy friend!' (4.3.100–101). Meanwhile, Mitis is bemused to note how in spite of Deliro's warm hospitality to him, Macilente viciously strips him of his marital delusions, leaving no stone unturned to 'set debate betwixt a man and his wife' (4.2.11). Cordatus explains to Mitis that in truth, Macilente is not impelled by a quest to expose falsehood or by a hunger for justice. Macilente's moral outrage is induced purely by malice or 'envy', a term that for early moderns had a far broader meaning than today.[67] 'For the true condition of envy', Cordatus explains, 'is to have our eyes continually fixed upon another man's prosperity—that is, his chief happiness—and to grieve at that' (1.3.163–67).

It might appear that the playwright Asper, inspired by high-minded passion to 'strip the ragged follies of the time / Naked as at their birth' (Ind. 15–16) and tear down the illusions the characters create for themselves, serves as a mouthpiece for Jonson. If so, Jonson self-mockingly undercuts the moral high ground he seems to occupy.

The Grex, friends of Asper, engage in a stream of commentary about him and his play, implicitly criticising his moral complacency: 'I would like it much better if he were less confident', Mitis remarks (Ind. 219). More importantly, by having Asper double as the envious satirist Macilente, Jonson lays bare the complicity of satirists like himself in the aggressive competition for success and status, be it in the marketplace for print or in the playhouses, where the new style of drama that Jonson was so formative in forging was retailed as a spectacular new product in the early modern market for entertainment.

For his next few comical satires, Jonson shifted to Blackfriars, the theatre site for the boys' companies that re-emerged in 1599.[68] This was the favoured location for city comedy. Using boy actors amplified the parodic effect and added a further salacious layer to the sexual innuendo with which the plays

---

67. *OED*, s.v. 'envy, n.', 1.a.

68. For an incisive account of the difference in style between indoor playhouses and amphitheatres, see van Es, *Shakespeare in Company*, 195–231. Also see Gurr, *Playgoing in Shakespeare's London*, 26–37.

were larded. Unlike *Every Man Out of His Humour*, whose impetus lies in unmasking its raft of would-be gentlemen as impostors, Middleton's city comedies present a troupe of smart, penniless young gallants who outwit their opponents—miserly relatives, grasping merchants, importunate creditors—at every turn and carry off the prize into the bargain.[69] Nonetheless, the plays also glance at notions associated with civility—notions of mutuality, reciprocity, and trust.

Middleton's Witty Fraudsters

In four early comedies by Middleton, *Michaelmas Term, A Mad World, My Masters, A Trick to Catch the Old One*, and *Your Five Gallants*, all staged by the Children of St Paul's around 1606, the plots turn on how to make one's fortune in early modern London. Drawing on Plautine and Terentian comedy, with their stock cast of young wastrels and miserly parents, clever courtesans and crafty slaves, as well as on contemporary genres such as prodigal plays and coney-catching pamphlets, Middleton portrays a world populated by sharks, pimps, citizens, whores, and impoverished gentlemen. Gentlemen down on their luck and prostitutes are celebrated in the plays if they possess a vital quality: wit.[70] Wit in city comedies came to stand specifically for a set of traits that were indispensable in urban life—resourcefulness, audacity, a knack for improvisation, and a capacity to use language in a dexterous manner.[71] These were skills that law students were anxious to whet during their sojourn in London, and perhaps part of the appeal of city comedy lay in its providing coterie

---

69. On Middleton's city comedies, see the titles listed in note 6 of this chapter. Also useful are Covatta, *Thomas Middleton's City Comedies*; Heinemann, *Puritanism and Theatre*; Chakravorty, *Society and Politics*; and Jowett, 'Thomas Middleton'. Also see Ghose, 'Middleton and the Culture of Courtesy'.

70. A term that originally denoted both mental capacity and the faculties of perception, as in the expression the 'five wits', which comprised cogitation or instinct, memory, fantasy, imagination, and common sense, 'wit' in the late sixteenth century increasingly acquired the connotations of imaginative dexterity and ingenuity. By the end of the sixteenth century these five separate internal senses were increasingly collapsed into a single function, usually called 'imagination'. 'Wit' additionally began to take on the meaning of a capacity to express things in a brilliant and amusing way, the predominant meaning today. See Park, 'Organic Soul'.

71. See Salingar, '"Wit" in Jacobean Comedy', in *Dramatic Form in Shakespeare and the Jacobeans*, 140–52; Withington, 'Sociable Self' and 'Tumbled into the Dirt'; Zucker, *Places of Wit in Early Modern English Comedy*; and Munro, 'Matter of Wit and the Early Modern Stage'.

audiences with a series of role models whose recipe for success they might emulate, at least in fantasy. Wit is, as it were, *sprezzatura* in an urban setting.

The plays are suffused with the uncertainties of how to adapt to city life without losing face. In *Michaelmas Term*, the fraudster Shortyard takes the country gentleman Easy in hand, allegedly to show him the ropes with regard to urban mores. He warns Easy, 'There's a kind of bold grace expected throughout all the parts of a gentleman' and explains, 'a man must not so much as spit but within line and fashion' (2.1.105–8).[72] Not just impersonators of gentility, but real gentlemen too are under continual pressure to demonstrate their quality by means of external signs—deportment, manners, style. Shortyard even coaches Easy which jokes to find funny. When another gallant, Rearage, delivers a mock-sententious adage, Shortyard instructs the neophyte, 'Laugh at him, Master Easy' (141), simultaneously cueing audience laughter. What might trigger a sense of unease is the effortlessness with which the confidence man himself slips into the role of a gentleman. Easy is duped by him to such an extent that he sings his praises: 'So full of nimble wit, various discourse, pregnant apprehension, and uncommon entertainment; he might keep company with any lord for his grace' (3.2.13–15). Without the help of the citizen's wife, Thomasina, who is enamoured of him, the scam to which Easy succumbs would never have been uncovered. Not only the gullible Easy, the other gallants are hoodwinked by the swindler too. If that quintessential quality of true nobility, grace, is so easy to counterfeit, the play implicitly asks, how can we know the gentleman from the fraud? At a closer look, the differences between the two threaten to collapse. This is, of course, precisely the concern that haunts the discourse of civility, evoked in episodes such the gulling of Saviolina in *Every Man Out of His Humour*, which echoes a jest in Castiglione's *Courtier* (2.85). The court lady loses face resoundingly after boasting she has 'deciphered' the country boor Sogliardo, who, she asserts, is a gentleman impersonating a clown—instead of precisely the contrary (5.2.95).

Your Five Gallants revolves around a competition between a string of fraudsters for the prize of the hand of a wealthy heiress.[73] Pretenders to the status of gentleman, they are a motley band of petty criminals, ranging from a pimp

---

72. All citations from the plays are taken from Taylor and Lavagnino, *Thomas Middleton: The Collected Works*. On *Michaelmas Term*, also see Leggatt, 'Middleton, *Michaelmas Term*', and the introduction to the play by Theodore B. Leinwand in *The Collected Works*, 334–36.

73. On *Your Five Gallants*, see the introduction to the play by Ralph Alan Cohen in *The Collected Works*, 594–97.

to a broker who runs a pawnshop, a cardsharp, a thief, and a gigolo. The quality they aspire to is 'impudence'—a darker variety of wit.[74] Frip, the broker-gallant, declares, 'Since impudence gains more respect than virtue, / And coin than blood—which few can now deny—/ Who're your chief gallants, then, but such as I?' (1.1.328–30). At a time when social hierarchies are crumbling, the question of whether virtue or birth defines the gentleman is irrelevant, he opines. Prestige and wealth are attainable by means of sheer audacity. His chief competitor, Fitzgrave, a true-born gentleman, complains bitterly that counterfeits have swamped society: 'The brightness of true gentry is scarce seen' (3.1.180). While the play seems to set up a firm opposition between true gentlemen and impostors, in truth Fitzgrave imitates many of the actions of the frauds, insinuating himself into their company under false pretences. Reinventing oneself at will emerges as a trait shared by the gentleman of wit and his double.

Much of the pleasure the play elicits lies in its witty, self-aware games. Quips about young Templars, students at the Inner and Middle Temples, and casual allusions to familiar locales such as the Mermaid and Mitre taverns add to its attraction, while metatheatrical insets reinforce the sense of social spectatorship which pervades the play. In the final act, Fitzgrave assembles a band of true gallants to expose the crooks by means of a masque he has inveigled them into performing, in which the gentlemen act as torch bearers. The Latin mottos on the shields, which the swindlers are too ignorant to decipher, reveal their true professions. But the heightened artifice of the scene, staged as a play-within-the-play with fifteen players onstage, serves to only confirm the sense of a world awash with status seekers with little to distinguish between them. Nor does the crooks' ignorance of Latin identify them decisively—several of the gentlemen-gallants require a translation too. In an exchange between two of the gentlemen, one asks, 'Are these our gallants?' and the second echoes his remark in the form of a chiasmus: 'Are our gallants these?' (5.1.74–75). The ironic question, ostensibly referring to the onstage masquerade of the confidence tricksters, not only confuses true and false gallants, but also gestures towards the theatrical reality of an interchangeable set of actors who mirror equally indistinguishable spectators, further eroding any sharply defined distinction between gentlemen and counterfeits.

---

74. Chakravorty describes impudence in the play as 'a black version of *sprezzatura*' (*Society and Politics*, 62).

Metatheatrical games are central to *A Mad World, My Masters* too.[75] Richard Follywit, an impecunious young prodigal, invests his wit in devising parts for himself in which he flaunts his acting skills. After slipping into the role of a lord in order to camouflage a robbery on his wealthy uncle, Sir Bounteous Progress, Follywit next cross-dresses as the courtesan of his uncle, and finally disguises himself as a travelling actor. In act 5, in a dazzling agglomeration of self-conscious jokes, the ironies spiral vertiginously. The boy actor playing Follywit appears in three additional roles, the prologue, a player, and a character in the play-within-the-play. The play is brimful with intertextual witticisms: the young prodigal echoes Falstaff's lament about how Hal has corrupted his mores; the constable, first cousin to Dogberry, complains he has been called an ass; and the parodic opening line of the prologue, 'We sing of wandering knights, what them betide' (5.2.18), is a facetious wink to an audience steeped in classical and contemporary epics such as Spenser's *Faerie Queene* and Ariosto's *Orlando Furioso*, translated by John Harington in 1590. The title of the play-within-the-play, *The Slip*, is a multilayer pun, comprising a play on some of the manifold meanings of 'slip' as 'counterfeit coin', 'escape', 'mistake', and 'young adult', the latter possibly a playful reference to the boy actors.[76] The term also referred to an offshoot or descendent, suggesting parallels between the criminal nephew and his uncle, not merely in their sharing a partiality for theatrical japes and the same taste in women. Meanwhile, the onstage audience is at a loss to distinguish between the (fictional) reality and the fiction they are watching.

The genial old country knight, who at first sight appears as the embodiment of old-time hospitality, is exposed as yet another spurious example of gentility. He is careful to dispense his bounty mainly to those above him in the social hierarchy. 'There's not one knight i'th' shire able to entertain a lord i'th' cue, or a lady i'th' nick, like me', he boasts, the bawdy connotations of the terms 'cue' and 'nick', which refer to male and female genitals respectively, hinting at his willingness to go to any lengths to please the upper nobility. In a wicked play on both Castiglione's *grazia* and the meanings of 'slip', Middleton has the knight declare portentously, 'There's a kind of grace belongs to't, a kind of art which naturally slips from me, I know not on't, I promise you, 'tis gone before I'm aware on't' (2.1.58–62). Unwittingly, he admits that the ostensible natural

---

75. On *A Mad World, My Masters*, also see the introduction to the play by Peter Saccio in *The Collected Works*, 414–17.

76. *OED*, s.v. 'slip, n. 2 and n. 4'.

grace of a nobleman eludes his grasp. As his nephew observes, his behaviour is typical of his sort: 'most of your rich men ... always feast those mouths that are least needy, / And give them more that have too much already' (3.3.23–26). The young prodigal might be a thief and liar, but the debauched old knight lives by exploiting the weak, and is a usurer to boot. In the interests of maintaining prestige, the knight is not above play-acting, either. In another play on the term 'slip', Sir Bounteous declares, 'Well, things must slip and sleep. I will dissemble it / Because my credit shall not lose her lustre' (4.3.54–55).

The supreme performers in the plays, and the true winners in the contests of wit, are the courtesans.[77] In Middleton's plays, there is little of the blend of prurient fascination and moral outrage with which John Marston depicts the whore Franceschina in *The Dutch Courtesan*. Instead, prostitutes are portrayed with a quantum of ironic amusement. Both gentlemen in *A Man World, My Masters* are tricked by the whore and her mother, who show themselves to be consummate actors and impresarios of themselves. The courtesan stages a series of miniature plays of her own devising, in which she acts as an invalid to enable the tormented Penitent to meet the married woman he desires, maintains her role as kept mistress to Sir Bounteous, and poses as bashful virgin to Follywit, which enables her to entrap a gentleman heir as husband. In these plays financial security, the ultimate prize, is achieved by all the whores. Costumes are an indispensable part of their self-marketing strategies. As social commentators point out, in early modern England clothes made the woman as much as the man. Philip Stubbes fulminates against the propensity of women from all ranks to don luxurious apparel, 'whereby it commeth to passe, that one can scarsly know, who is a noble woman, who is an honourable, or worshipfull woman, from them of the meaner sorte' (F7v). More dispassionate observers confirm Stubbes's impression of the instability of the social order. Appearances, Florio explains, are an unreliable index to social rank: 'You shal see a woman wyfe unto a marchant, cladde so sumtuously, that she wil seem a Lady, a wife of a Shoomaker, that wyl seeme a Gentlewoman'.[78] In *Michaelmas Term*, the Country Wench, pranked out in lavish attire to which the finishing touches are being applied onstage, metamorphoses into a gentlewoman before our eyes. In the meantime the pander, Hellgill, waxes eloquent about the transfiguring power of clothes. 'What base birth does not raiment make glorious? And what glorious births do not rags make infamous?' (3.1.2–4), he

---

77. On female wit and civility, see Withington's illuminating piece, 'Tumbled into the Dirt'.
78. Florio, *His firste Fruites*, E1r–v.

declaims, breezily dismissing categories such as pedigree or virtue. Surface, not substance, is the measure of all value. The parodic point is sharpened by foregrounding the theatrical context in which costume was key in transforming a troupe of boy actors into both courtesans and their clients. The Country Wench soon mutates into a canny businesswoman, defending her profession by drawing analogies to other business practices: 'Do not all trades live by their ware, and yet called honest livers? . . . Is not wholesale the chiefest merchandise?' (4.2.11–14). The comic innuendo on words such as 'ware' and 'wholesale' (both quibbles on female genitals) contributes its mite to sweeping aside any possible didactic impetus in the play.

Trust

A Trick to Catch the Old One differs from the other plays by staging a partnership between two confidence artists, the witty prodigal, Witgood, and the courtesan, Jane.[79] They jointly set about swindling the usurers, Lucre and Hoard, and snaring the reward, which in the case of Witgood consists of repossessing his land and marrying an heiress, and in the case of Jane, of marrying the lecherous old usurer who courts her while she is in the guise of a rich widow. Jane is distinct from the other courtesans in one further respect: she evinces a modicum of consideration for her future husband, Hoard, and commits herself to being faithful to her marriage vows. Once she has secured marital status, she tries to rein in Witgood, who is plotting to exploit Hoard even further. Instead, she offers to maintain the facade of respectability of her newlywed husband. In the face of Witgood's cynicism, she stresses her belief in the importance of keeping faith: 'For where I once vow, I am ever true' (4.4.152). This sets her apart from both the smart young gallants and the canny courtesans of the other plays. If city comedy holds up a parodic mirror to a society in which we are all, to a greater or lesser extent, pretenders, a reciprocal acceptance of one another's performance might point the way to how to live together amicably in civil society. But in a fictional universe in which radical individualism holds sway, good faith and trust are commodities in short supply.

City comedies portray a world of ruthless self-interest where in a scramble for social prestige, everyone is in competition with one another. Carlo's lessons

---

79. On *A Trick to Catch the Old One*, also see the introduction to the play by Valerie Wayne in *The Collected Works*, 373–76.

to Sogliardo on how to be a gentleman include the following advice: 'now you are a gentleman, you must carry a more exalted presence, change your mood and habit to a more austere form, be exceeding proud, stand upon your gentility, and scorn every man. . . . Love no man. Trust no man. Speak ill of no man to his face, nor well of any man to his back. Salute fairly on the front, and wish 'em hanged upon the turn. Spread yourself upon his bosom publicly, whose heart you would eat in private. These be principles' (3.1.260–71). Carlo mockingly insinuates that status is achieved only by pursuing a course of aggressive egotism. To be successful, social climbers must steer clear of all close human ties and be prepared to betray others whenever necessary. On no account must they have faith in the goodwill of other humans.

Critics have commented on the frequent use in city comedies of the term 'credit', a word that originally meant reputation, but increasingly acquired its present meaning of trust in a customer's integrity in financial dealings.[80] *A Trick to Catch the Old One* harvests comic capital from the term 'trust'. Witgood has been cheated of his estate by his uncle, who, in his eagerness to further what he thinks is an alluring marriage prospect for a relative, is willing to return it to him 'in trust' (4.2.56), that is, under his temporary guardianship, in the hope that it will be tamely handed back after the wedding by the nephew he once duped. This is precisely the scenario that Witgood has been hoping to engineer. The frequent puns on 'cozen', that is, 'deceive', and 'cousin', a generic expression for a relative, underline the lesson Witgood has learned: not to have faith in family bonds. Or any other human bonds, for that matter. The witty young heroes of city comedy forge shifting alliances with various accomplices, but they are quintessential loners, wary of placing trust in anyone but themselves. Even Witgood and Jane are bound in a business partnership, not in an intimate friendship. To be sure, tricksters, to whom the smart young protagonists are close kin, are by definition solipsistic figures, reaping pleasure from intrigue and subterfuge. Nonetheless, by depicting a roster of urban protagonists for whom human attachments of any kind are an irrelevancy, the plays also comment on the market conditions that shape them.

A number of plays ironically point up the alienation that identifies their characters. Friends, Carlo maintains, are vastly overrated. 'Is there any such

---

80. On the role of credit in early modern England, see Muldrew, *Economy of Obligation*. On the link between credit and early modern drama, see Sullivan, *Rhetoric of Credit*; Waswo, 'Crises of Credit'; Donaldson, *Ben Jonson*, 345–46; and Kolb, *Fictions of Credit in the Age of Shakespeare*.

foolish thing i' the world?', he scoffs, and goes on to declare, 'the title of a friend, it's a vain idle thing, only venerable among fools. You shall no have one that has any opinion of wit affect it' (4.3.102, 109–11). In *Your Five Gallants*, the gallants lecture the neophyte in their circle, Master Bowser, who is actually Fitzgrave in disguise, that he must learn to forgo human ties. The country gentleman, Bungler, preens himself on never acknowledging a debt to others. He recounts how once, robbed of all his clothes and money, he was helped by a poor shepherd. The same shepherd approached him later for help, but Bungler refused to recognize him. His viciousness is a source of pride, '''Tis a gift giv'n to some above others', he boasts (2.4.107–8). Both Carlo and Bungler are caricatures of degraded specimens of humanity. But the prodigal gallants too, endowed as they are with savvy, audacity, and boundless energy, are too caught up in the competitive hustle of urban life and the business of forging ahead to cultivate close human relationships of any kind. Their wit marks them out as models to emulate for spectators in pursuit of social distinction and the dividends it earns, but the plays make it clear that the cost involved is impoverishment in terms of social relations.

Despite the cult of friendship that was celebrated in early modern England, inspired by classical sources such as the praise of friendship in the *Nicomachean Ethics*, in Cicero's *Laelius de amicitia*, and in Plutarch's *Moralia*, the literature of civility often expresses deep reservations about relationships of trust.[81] Predictably, court manuals stress the importance of keeping secrets to oneself and urge the courtier to beware of trusting his peers, all of whom are in the same race for preferment.[82] In his *Treatise of the Court*, de Refuge laconically states, 'In Court there are no great friends, nor small enemies' (S3v). The ever pragmatic Burghley counsels his son to 'Beware of suretishippe for your best friend' (B1r) and to 'Trust no man with your credit' (B2r), while Peacham suggests, 'hold friendship and acquaintance with few . . . but endear yourself to none' (146). More idealistic manuals take a similar stance. In his *Youths Instruction* (1616), William Martyn, while citing Cicero and Plutarch in praise of friendship, urges his son, a student at Oxford, not to reveal secrets to his friend, however close they might be. 'Now though your friend be more then a principal part, or member of your selfe, yet do I counsel you to retaine your

---

81. On early modern friendship, see Thomas, 'Friendship and Sociability', chap. 6 in *Ends of Life*, 187–225.

82. Much of this advice rehearses standard prudential counsel, as set out in Albertano da Brescia's thirteenth-century *De arte loquendi et tacendi*, frequently reprinted during the Renaissance. See Mack, *History of Renaissance Rhetoric*, 54.

chiefest secrets of choicest importance to your self', he writes.⁸³ Admittedly, it is difficult to find a friend who is both honest and faithful; indeed, 'it is almost impossible' (H2v). In these circumstances, being on one's own might be preferable: 'It is far better to be solitary, and alone, then to be sorted with wicked company' (F4v). And the ideal English gentleman is exhorted by Brathwaite not to confide secrets to his friend too hastily. He warns, 'wee ought not to give our *friend* power over us' (X2r). Baltasar Gracián, finally, whose *Pocket Oracle and Art of Prudence* (1647) was a digest of the ideas on civility of the preceding century, writes, 'Confidences between friends are especially dangerous', and concludes pithily: 'Secrets: don't listen to them or tell them'.⁸⁴

Civility and the Duel

In *A Fair Quarrel*, a tragicomedy cowritten with William Rowley about a decade after his city comedies, Middleton revisits some of his earlier themes. The keynote is set by the term 'honour' rather than 'credit', and appropriately, the tone is more elevated than in the comedies. Probably written between 1615 and 1617, and first staged at the Red Bull by Prince Charles's Men, the play reveals the changes in mores that have taken place in the ten years since the city comedies.⁸⁵ The comic subplot, presumably by Rowley, deals with the craze for 'roaring' which had invaded London, while the main plot registers the debate about duelling in Jacobean England.⁸⁶ Markku Peltonen has argued that rather than a remnant of the medieval concept of honour, the duel was linked to the early modern culture of civility.⁸⁷ It was imported into England from the courts of Renaissance Italy and regarded as a method of boosting civility by channelling violence into a ritualized practice with sophisticated rules.

---

83. Martyn, *Youths Instruction*, H2r.
84. Gracián, *Pocket Oracle and Art of Prudence*, no. 237, p. 90.
85. See the introduction to the play by Suzanne Gossett in *The Collected Works*, 1209–12.
86. A number of plays mock the variety of gallant termed 'roaring boys', pugnacious roisterers who roamed the streets of London. As Anna Bryson points out, anticivility is simply another mode of fashionable behaviour and serves the same strategic ends, to define social identity and set off a clique from others within the same social class. The belligerence of the roisters was usually directed at other members of gallant society, e.g., men of wit or Inns of Court men. See Bryson, *From Courtesy to Civility*, 243–75.
87. See Peltonen, *Duel in Early Modern England*, 17–79. Also see Kelso, *Doctrine of the English Gentleman*, 99–106; James, 'English Politics and the Concept of Honour'; Thomas, *Ends of Life*, 156–59; Skinner, 'Hobbes and the Social Control of Unsociability'; and Carroll, 'Violence, Civil Society and European Civilization'.

FIGURE 5. Title page of *A Fair Quarrel* (1622) by Thomas Middleton and William Rowley. Boston Public Library.

Lauded in a number of treatises, the duel was defended as an indispensable means of safeguarding honour.

The Renaissance code of honour drew its justification from classical thought and was rooted in the Aristotelian concept of magnanimity (*EN* 4.3). Proponents of the duel argued that the law of honour was a form of natural law; civil law was disdained as relevant only for commoners, not the nobility. What was conveniently overlooked was the marked preference for due process of law in the writings of Roman political theorists like Cicero. The duelling code was the expression of an individualistic concept of honour—it was not concerned with defending the reputation of a clan or group. It was symptomatic of a society engaged in a fierce competition for prestige.[88]

There was by no means a consensus that duels were mandatory to protect one's reputation. In *Hero-paideia* James Cleland reminds the young nobleman that his life belongs to his sovereign and the state, and that he has no right to risk it unduly. As for insults to honour, 'It is a too grosse opinion to thinke that anie Noble mans honor dependeth upon an other mans word: for properlie no man can be deprived of his honor, but by himselfe, in flying from vertue to embrace vice' (Gg2). True honour, he insists, is a matter of inner worth, not of public reputation. Nicolas Faret explicitly denounces as 'one of the most insupportable abuses which hath crept into our age, to imagine, as they doe, that true and heroique valour doth only consist in fighting'.[89] In his *Courtiers Academie*, Annibale Romei takes such a decisive stance against duels that in his preface the translator, John Keper, anxious to appeal to all segments of the market, hastens to defend him against possible accusations of 'savouring too much of feare, and pusillanimitie' in his pacific approach towards quarrels of honour (A4r). In Romei's treatise, the speaker Signior Gualinguo strongly condemns individual combat (S1r–Y2). Honour cannot be impugned on the basis of a challenge, he asserts. On the contrary, it is the slanderer who stands exposed as dishonourable. The real disgrace is to transgress the laws of human sociality: 'honour is lost by failing in justice' (Y2v), he declares. As some early modern writers note perceptively, the question is how we define the ideal of honour, in individual terms, as enhanced status, or as reciprocal respect based on self-esteem. As Kwame Anthony Appiah has argued recently, respect and pride are goods that have never ceased to play a crucial role in social life. If mobilized in the service of humanity, honour is in fact an integral part of the ethical life.[90]

For the Stuart dynasty with its absolutist pretensions, duels were regarded as a serious threat to the social order—and to the prince's authority. After a series of notorious duels, James I had his attorney general, Sir Francis Bacon, put together a formal *Charge* or injunction addressed to the Star Chamber in

---

88. See Peltonen, *Duel in Early Modern England*, 72–77.
89. Faret, *Honest man*, C4v.
90. See Appiah, *Honor Code*, esp. chap. 1, 'The Duel Dies', 1–51.

1614, firmly asserting the king's authority over all civil affairs. Bacon lambasted the practice of duelling as an 'illusion and apparition of honour; against religion, against law, against moral virtue'. As he writes scathingly, the very idea 'gives the law an affront, as if there were two laws, one a kind of gown-law, and the other a law of reputation', in which 'some French and Italian pamphlets' had precedence over statutes.[91] Duels, unknown to the ancients, are crimes not against individuals, he declares, but against the civil order. Similar sentiments are echoed by Middleton in his pamphlet, *The Peacemaker; or Great Britain's Blessing* (1618), licensed for publication with royal approval and widely regarded as written by the king himself. Middleton excoriates the surge in duels, lamenting that 'now the compounding of quarrels is grown to a trade', aided and abetted by unscrupulous lawyers. Like Bacon, he pillories the dangerous fiction that spurs the passion for duels among young gentlemen—'the false and erroneous imagination of honour and credit'. In their folly, they succumb to an illusory conception of honour, one defined by external reputation rather than inner virtue.[92] The two treatises marked a radical shift in royal policy, dismissing any grounds whatsoever for duelling.

A Fair Quarrel sets up an opposition between a delusionary concept of honour and that of sociability, juxtaposing individualistic notions of prestige with the idea of mutual respect. The vastly contrived plot turns on a quarrel between Captain Ager and his friend and superior officer, the Colonel, who insults his honour by calling him the son of a whore. Thirsting to take up the challenge, Ager hesitates only long enough to assure himself that the accusation is indeed a lie. Not that he has any reason to suspect the virtue of his mother, a model of rectitude. However, as he helpfully points out, 'she's but woman, / Whose frailty let in death to all mankind' (2.1.28–29). No woman, however virtuous, can ever escape the taint of her sex, he maintains. The flagrant absurdities of the ideology of honour, which in the case of a woman referred primarily to her chastity, are manifested in a series of convoluted plot twists. Lady Ager lies in order to save the life of her son, only to be rewarded with his fury at having been robbed of a chance to defend his honour. Fortunately, the Colonel obliges by adding a second insult (cowardice) to his injury. Ager leaps at the opportunity to prove his manhood, crowing, 'Now I have a cause!' (3.1.114). A duel ensues; the Colonel is duly felled. When Ager learns

---

91. See Bacon's 'Charge Touching Duels', in *Major Works*, 305–13, 305–6.
92. Thomas Middleton, *The Peacemaker; or, Great Britain's Blessing*, in *The Collected Works*, 1306–19, 1314–15.

the truth about her unimpeached virtue from his mother, he responds with alacrity—by issuing yet another challenge to the Colonel.

Unlike the slick, street-smart city comedies, which would have played havoc with the pomposity of all the men of honour, and although the myth of honour is exposed as ludicrously threadbare, *A Fair Quarrel* allows its protagonists to retain their dignity. A notable moment offers a glimpse of social relations built on a different set of values altogether: mutual respect and trust. When the Captain faces the Colonel at the appointed hour, his first resolve is to reach a reconciliation. 'I come with mildness, / Peace, constant amity, and calm forgiveness' (3.1.70–71), he announces. He admits that he will lose face in the eyes of society, and that others have sought vengeance with even less cause. However, he recalls the ties that once bound them together:

> But when I call to memory our long friendship
> Methinks it cannot be too great a wrong
> That then I should not pardon. Why should a man,
> For a poor hasty syllable or two,
> (And vented only in forgetful fury),
> Chain all the hopes and riches of his soul
> To the revenge of that, die lost for ever? (79–85)

Against the imperative of maintaining status at all costs, the play pits the ideal of amicableness and sociability. The idea is hastily quenched by the 'friends' of both parties, who egg on each side and gloat when blood is drawn. When the Colonel collapses, one of the 'friends' declares sonorously, ''Tis right and fair, and he that breathes against it, / He breathes against the justice of a man, / And man to cut him off, 'tis no injustice', and thanks the Captain for redeeming the cause of nobility (161–63). Taking a man's life is not unjust; on the contrary, opposition to a duel of honour would be a transgression against justice, he asserts.

These lofty sentiments are held up to ridicule in the play, as is the righteous insistence of the high-born men on ferreting out slights to their honour. True nobility is demonstrated only by the female protagonists. Lady Ager flouts public opinion and the opprobrium inevitably entailed by a breach of chastity in the hope of saving her son; the Physician's sister, Anne, offers to help the pregnant Jane deliver her child in secret; and the Colonel's sister keeps her word, however reluctantly, to offer her hand to the enemy of her brother. They all evince a far greater sense of generosity and magnanimity than do the men of honour. In its subplot, the play also presents a merciless parody of the cult of honour.

In a nod to Jonson's *Alchemist*, the fatuous country gentleman Chough and his valet Tristram receive lessons in how to quarrel in the 'roaring school', run as a joke by the military men. They inform the clowns that quarrelling is a sport, like wrestling, in which a round always ends in companionable sociality: 'Then there must be wine ready to make all friends, for that's the end of roaring, 'tis valiant but harmless' (4.1.64–66). In place of the jargon of duelling, the clowns are furnished with a lexicon of bizarre insults like 'centaur' or 'bronsterops', which they promptly put into practice by staging a jousting match with a trio of lowlifes, a pander, bawd, and a whore, who indulge them with amused contempt. Duelling, like the inane performance of flyting put on by the clowns, is merely another puerile game, the play implies. The difference is that one ends fatally.

A Fair Quarrel concludes in a reconciliation of the erstwhile friends; the Colonel declaims, 'Fair be that quarrel makes such happy friends' (5.1.448). The pat dénouement serves only to emphasise the wish fulfilment with which the plot is liberally doused. As the play implicitly concedes, in social relations true mutual regard might be desirable, but in the face of the antagonism pervasive in human relations, this might be a precarious foundation on which to build a civil society. The charade of civility that the clowns are taught might be preferable. As Chough declares, 'I like it the better because no blood comes on it' (4.1.68–69). And in a self-referential joke, the bawd urges everyone to attend 'the new play'—to learn 'better manners' (4.4.17–18).

3

Theatricality and Lies in *Coriolanus*

GABRIEL HARVEY, ever a reliable barometer of the currents of social climbing in Elizabethan England, reports on the frustration of his fellow scholars with the curriculum on offer at Cambridge.[1] In a draft letter, probably written in the mid-1570s, he describes the rigorous reading programme those aspiring to a career at Court or its environs set themselves to redress their deficits in worldly skills: 'And nowe of late forsoothe to help countenaunce owte [bear out] the matter they have gotten Philibertes Philosopher of the Courte, the Italian Archebysshopies brave Galateo, Castiglioes fine Cortegiano, Bengalassoes Civil Instructions to his Nephewe Seignore Princisca Ganzar, Guatzoes newe Discourses of curteous behavior, Jovios and Russellis Emblemes in Italian, Paradines in French, Plutarch in Frenche, Frontines Stratagemes, Polyenes Stratagemes, Polonica Apodemica, Guigiandine [Guicciardini], Philippe de Comines, and I know not how many owtlandishe braveryes [foreign displays] besides of the same stampe.'[2] Despite his supercilious tone, Harvey pored over these works as avidly as the next man; he owned no fewer than three, copiously annotated copies of Castiglione's *Courtier*, in Italian, English, and Latin.[3] While his letter continues with an inventory of books of political theory, among them the works of Jean Bodin and Niccolo Machiavelli, the first few items refer to fashionable courtesy books of the time, including Giovanni

---

1. In one of the less charitable assessments of Harvey, Neil Rhodes describes him as 'a living travesty of Castiglione's ideal to which he absurdly aspired'. See Rhodes, *Power of Eloquence*, 58.

2. 'A pleasaunt and merry-conceited letter to himself just before his master's commencement', letter to John Young, in Harvey, *Letter-Book of Gabriel Harvey*, 78–79.

3. On Harvey's marginalia in the *Courtier*, see Ruutz-Rees, 'Some Notes of Gabriel Harvey's in Hoby's Translation of Castiglione's *Courtier* (1561)'; Moore, *Gabriel Harvey's Marginalia*; Stern, *Gabriel Harvey*; and Stamatakis, '"With diligent studie, but sportingly"'.

FIGURE 6. Jacopo Pontormo, *Monsignor della Casa* (1541–44). National Gallery of Art, Washington, D.C.

Della Casa's *Galateo*, first published in 1558 and Englished by Robert Peterson in 1576, and Stefano Guazzo's *Civil conversatione*, which appeared in 1574 and was translated into English by George Pettie and Bartholomew Young between 1581 and 1586. Less well-known is the first title Harvey mentions, Philibert de Vienne's *Philosophe de court*, published in Lyon in 1547; an English version translated by George North appeared in 1575. Unlike most of the better-known courtesy books in the sixteenth century, Philibert's text was published in French, not Italian. More noteworthy is the fact that *The Philosopher of the Court* is an acerbic spoof on courtesy books. Whether or not Harvey and his peers grasped the import of Philibert's satire is a moot point.

In this chapter I read Shakespeare's *Coriolanus* together with a number of the treatises Harvey mentions, Philibert de Vienne's *Philosopher of the Court*, Della Casa's *Galateo*, and Guazzo's *Civile Conversation*. A keyword that threads a number of these texts is 'grace', which comprises connotations as varied as Castiglione's ideal of ineffable charm, Ciceronian decorum, and the theological doctrine of grace.[4] Philibert's satire of court manners equates Ciceronian decorum with dissimulation and expediency, and unmasks the flimsy foundation on which Cicero's ethics is based. *Galateo*, on the other hand, is a distorting mirror of the *Courtier*. Instead of offering an exquisite portrait of civility in practice, it bombards the reader with a barrage of nauseating images to underline its warnings against offensive conduct. While paying tribute to the classical notions of grace and harmony, Della Casa is preoccupied with the mendacity that pervades early modern society, in particular with regard to those with no claim to a place in the sun. Guazzo's *Civile Conversation* attempts to meld civility with sincerity, but the text exposes the ideal of reconciling the social and inner self as beset with tension.

In *Coriolanus* (1608) Shakespeare tests the theoretical precepts about lying and dissimulation propounded in the courtesy texts against the life of a historical protagonist—only to reveal the fractures that emerge when human reality is judged in terms of rigid moral norms. His play is centred on a self-righteous protagonist who abhors civility as a tissue of lies and insists on radical self-sufficiency. Despite his self-definition as a Roman patriot, little sense of a common purpose with other Romans, be they patricians or plebeians, spurs the protagonist. Coriolanus regards himself as self-created; his success derives solely from his own merits. Rejecting any notion of shared standards of truth, he insists on being true to himself. The play, I suggest, echoes Augustine's denunciation of classical ethics—without following Augustine in his advocacy of introspection as the road to authentic selfhood.[5] Instead, it demonstrates

---

4. *OED*, s.v. 'grace, n.'.

5. I use the terms 'authenticity' and 'sincerity' interchangeably in the sense of a truthful correspondence between inner feelings and outer expression, although the former came into circulation only in the twentieth century. Admittedly, this elides the nuances between religious

that Coriolanus's self is ineluctably social, governed by relations with those he repudiates. Role-playing, it suggests, is impossible to disentangle from social life; pretence is woven into the very fabric of civil society. Coriolanus's claims to authenticity, it emerges, are founded on a fiction.

Philibert de Vienne's *Philosopher of the Court*

As the French Renaissance scholar C. A. Mayer was the first to note, Philibert's treatise is written in the style of the Lucianic mock encomium, ironically showering praise on contemptible aspects of contemporary life.[6] In Lucian's paean to the parasite, *De Parasitu*, the resourcefulness of the parasite in living on his wits and his expertise in flattery, scandal, and intrigue are lauded as the virtues of a consummate artist. Similarly, Philibert mockingly presents a degenerate code of courtly manners as the true philosophy, the ultimate truth about how we should live in the world. His work belongs in the long tradition of anti-court satire that reaches back to antiquity, but which saw a flowering in sixteenth-century France, often in the form of paradoxical literature, modelled on Erasmus's *Praise of Folly*.[7] Under the sway of the queen, Catherine of Medici, France experienced an influx of Italian courtiers. Resentment at their increasing influence was articulated in a wave of satirical works that took aim at the alleged decadence, duplicity, and atheism that permeated Italian courtly mores and specifically Castiglione's *Courtier*. In a nod to Bertrand de La Broderie's *L'Amye de court* (1542) or 'the lover of the court', a satire that lampoons Castiglione's ideal court lady, Philibert's text is addressed to a disdainful Lady, 'a lover of vertue'.[8] Philibert places a signpost pointing to the satirical thrust of his treatise at the very beginning of the text, where he writes that in describing the new philosophy, he has borrowed the method of the mocking philosopher Democrites (B5v).

---

authenticity and the Sartrean variety with its emphasis on truth to one's choices in life. The classic work on sincerity remains Lionel Trilling's *Sincerity and Authenticity*. For an attempt to recuperate authenticity for an ethical standpoint, see Taylor, *Ethics of Authenticity*.

6. See Mayer, 'L'Honnête Homme'. On Philibert de Vienne, also see Porter, 'Philibert de Vienne'; Smith, *Anti-Courtier Trend*, 138–47; Javitch, 'The Philosopher of the Court'; Scaglione, *Knights at Court*, 288–90; Richards, *Rhetoric and Courtliness*, 8–10; Peltonen, *Duel in Early Modern England*, 19–21; Anglo, 'Systematic Immorality'; and Snyder, *Dissimulation and the Culture of Secrecy*, 80–81.

7. See Roberts, 'Too Paradoxical for Paradoxes'.

8. Vienne, *The Philosopher of the Court*, B1r. See Smith, 'Introduction', 32.

In his prologue, the narrator claims that it is no longer relevant to study the wisdom of the ancients. What now counts as philosophy is the study of courtly life. He defines this new philosophy as comprising 'A certaine & sound judgement, howe to live according to the good grace and fashion of the Court' (C5r). In order to gain mastery in this discipline, the manners and customs of the court need to be rigorously analysed. What might previously have been dismissed as trivia now must be regarded as serious research, centred on questions such as 'What doe theye? What saye they? What manner of lyving is there nowe among them? What sortes of apparell, what sportes [diversions], what fashyons newlye forged?' It is equally important to be *au courant* with court gossip: 'who is beste welcome, most regarded, and in greatest estimation? who is most brave [finely dressed]? who is the trimmest [most elegant] dauncer, the pleasantest devyser [the most skilful in organising entertainments], and the beste vawter [vaulter]? what authors are moste alowed, what bookes reade they, what songs carryeth the brute [are the subject of general conversation]? And a thowsande other lyke demaundes' (C8r). If the end of moral philosophy is to achieve virtue, in this branch of philosophy, virtue is elucidated as 'a manner of lyving according to the manner of the Courte' (C7r). Instead of living in accordance with Nature, as the ancients recommend, all one need do to lead an unimpeachable life is to follow the customs of the court.

Philibert divides the treatise into separate sections, each of which treats the four cardinal virtues that Plato lists in *The Republic*. He adds a final category, 'de la bonne grace'.[9] Courtly wisdom consists in mastery of a range of musical instruments and a gamut of modish dances, and in excelling at parlour games. Any other form of knowledge, the narrator scoffs, is vastly overrated. To seek knowledge for its own sake is a sign of pedantry which, he counsels, must be avoided at all costs. It is far more important to pick up scraps of knowledge, 'chopt up in hotchpotch togither', in order to cut a good figure in conversation (D5v). At court, dilettantism is regarded as a supreme virtue.

In the section on justice, Philibert, about whom little is known apart from his profession of parliamentary lawyer, launches into a disquisition on legal and moral justice only to conclude that neither have any bearing on the life of a courtier; it is perfectly acceptable to cheat and deceive others so long as one remains undetected. In his treatment of liberality, magnanimity, and

---

9. The *accent circonflexe* was introduced only in the eighteenth century. I am grateful to Claude Bourqui for this information.

temperance, Philibert rehearses well-worn classical axioms, only to put them in the service of his courtly philosophy. Increasingly, it becomes apparent that the ultimate goal of pursuing virtue is to acquire social prestige for the courtier: 'the summe of our science, and the ende of our vertue hir selfe, is the glorie and reputation of anye man: and he which desireth, and seeketh it, is worthily accounted wise' (E8v).

Courtly Grace

In the final segment of the treatise Philibert turns to an overriding principle distilled from courtly civility. It is the principle of 'good grace, which Cicero in his Offices calleth *Decorum generale*' (H5v). But what precisely does this imply? While attractive appearances and the winning impression we make on others are assets, the decisive virtue in this philosophy is to be pliant and accommodating to one's peers in order to gain their recognition and enhance our prestige. 'Grace', in other words, means expediency. What it entails is dissimulating our real thoughts and feelings. This is the secret of courtly success.

In a series of mock-casuistic manoeuvres, Philibert discusses the vexed question of dissimulation. The narrator concedes that the ancients disapprove of dissembling one's true nature. But the courtier immersed in accommodating himself to his peers is not involved in duplicity. Pleasing others is his raison d'être. Citing classical sources such as the Ovidian concept of art that dissembles art and roping in Socrates as 'the greatest dissembler in the worlde', Philibert puts forward the tongue-in-cheek argument that in the case of the true courtier, guile is far from reprehensible. 'For such dissembling', Philibert declares, 'is not euill, and in it is neyther deceyte nor fraude: but all good fayth, as it were done not of purpose to shewe our selues otherwise than we be: but to the ende to please the worlde' (H7v). Ingratiating oneself with all and sundry is the right course to chart at court. Those who continue to behave in a frank and natural manner are 'beastes and ydiotes' (H8v), and are welcome to join Timon the Misanthrope. The court emerges as a theatre of marionettes, with puppet courtiers 'plyant like waxe, redie to receyue any honest or frendly impression'. As he elucidates, 'For if it be needefull to laughe, hee reioyceth: If to be sad, he lowreth [looks mournful]: If to be angry, he frowneth: If to feede, he eateth: If to faste, he pyneth [starves]. And to conclude, he is ready to doe whatsoeuer it be, according to the humors and complexions of his felowship and Courtly companie, althoughe his affections are cleane contrary' (J5r). In sum, adapting to society means incessant dissimulation.

There is one nation that has achieved a rare excellence in the art of courtiership, which Philibert holds up as a role model to his peers. The masters of courtly manners are the Italians, he claims: 'they seeme to vs the beste for Courtly grace in the worlde' (J6r). His mocking remarks tap into the simmering Italophobic rancour among the French elite in the mid-sixteenth century.

The Philosopher of the Court and Classical Ethics

In a widely cited article, Daniel Javitch asserts that neither the translator, George North, nor his readership understood the satirical intention of the book.[10] He pins the reason on 'the myth of the perfect courtier' (117) which was prevalent in Elizabethan England in the 1570s and 1580s. Even texts that castigate abuses of court life, such as Roger Ascham's *Scholemaster* (1570) or Edmund Spenser's *Mother Hubberds Tale* (published in 1591, but written at least a decade earlier), reveal an underlying faith in the courtly system, he argues, which continued until the 1590s, when disillusionment set in. Nor did the English share the French hostility towards Italian culture, which, despite the taint of papacy, continued to radiate an air of elegance and sophistication (120–22).

Javitch's argument is persuasive, even if not all the evidence he adduces is equally convincing. He points out that North translates a line in which Philibert explicitly announces his satirical aim—claiming in writing the treatise, 'je n'ay pu que je n'aye fait le Democrite, & usé de facities'—as 'I have played *Democrates*, & applyed the whole too a pleasant [humorous] conclusion' (B5v). Javitch contends that the replacement of Democritus, the laughing philosopher, with Democrates, an otherwise unknown Presocratic thinker, was a sign of misinterpretation on the part of the translator which had the effect of obscuring the reference (110). However, the names of the two philosophers were frequently confused, and are both accepted as relating to Democritus.[11] The fact that *The Philosopher of the Court* appears in Harvey's list of recommended reading is not necessarily proof that the satire was misunderstood, as Javitch believes (115). Early moderns were utilitarian readers, and selectively plundered works for

---

10. See Javitch, '*The Philosopher of the Court*'. There has been a renewed interest in George North ever since a recent study claimed that his unpublished work, 'A Brief Discourse of Rebellion and Rebels', is a source for Shakespeare. See McCarthy and Schlueter, *Brief Discourse of Rebellion and Rebels by George North*.

11. See the authoritative Diels and Kranz, *Die Fragmente der Vorsokratiker*, 45A.

ideas they could use for their own purposes. To a certain extent this is, of course, true of all readers. It is worth recalling, however, that in the Elizabethan age, the translation of prestigious foreign works was regarded as a national project, a matter of cultural transmission of high-end goods to a society racked with a sense of inferiority.

The ironic thrust of the treatise is flagged up in the second edition. It contains an additional poem by 'Le Petit Angevin', the sobriquet of the poet Jean Maugin, which explicitly drew attention to its comic matter in the lines, 'I only wanted to warn you / In a word and without lying / That you will find matter for laughter here / Far more than I could say'.[12] As Pauline Smith has shown, North used this edition, although he did not translate the poem, nor the dedicatory sonnets by Maurice Scève and O. B. which were included in the first edition.[13] This suggests that North may well have decided to ignore the satirical pointers and considered the text useful as a source of information about court norms for his readership.

Admittedly, Philibert's own argument is obscured by the twofold objective of his satire. He announces that he will adopt the voice of the ancients in order to expose the new philosophy, 'to the end the world may know theyr double follie and ignorance' (B8v). But Philibert does not just present a scathing portrait of the degraded manners at court, characterised by sycophancy, banality, and amorality. His aim is far more drastic: he sets out to demolish the very foundation of classical civility. His treatise is not an excoriation of the way Castiglione has debased Cicero. It is a veiled attack on Ciceronian ethics from a Christian perspective.[14] In an age rife with religious tension, his insistent use of the term 'grace' would have served as a reminder that courtly grace, be it in the sense of elegant manners or seemliness, was a travesty of the only grace that counted: divine beneficence. It might be worth noting that Calvin's *Institutes* (1536), in which grace plays so pivotal a role, appeared in a French translation in 1541, only a few years before Philibert's own book.

---

12. 'Seulement vous avertiray, / Et d'un seul mot ne mentiray / Que vous y trouverez à rire / Trop plus que ne pourrois rescrire'. Vienne, *Le Philosophe de Court*, 178, my translation. I am grateful to Didier Maillat for his help.

13. See Smith, 'Introduction', 38–39.

14. This seems to me to have been insufficiently acknowledged. Pauline Smith muses whether the satire of Castiglione might implicate *De officiis* and suggests that Cicero's text might itself bear the seeds of its debasement in Castiglione's treatise. See Smith, 'Introduction', 35–36. Javitch notes that the book is remarkable for its 'defiance, even rejection, of classical authority', but does not comment further. See Javitch, 'The Philosopher of the Court', 98.

As Philibert spares no effort to point out, the rationale behind the imperative to dissemble is to boost our social status: 'this is an rare [splendid] meane to wynee and drawe to us the good willes of all men, whereof commeth honor and reputation' (H7v). We accommodate ourselves to others in society in order to win the esteem of our peers. Alongside 'grace', an emphasis on the opinion of others threads the text. In the more serious parts of the text that bookend the satire, Philibert repeatedly draws an analogy between Christianity and pagan culture. A target that he singles out for censure is the classical concept of honour, which Aristotle defines as a reward for virtue (*EN* 1123b). While the ancients might claim that virtue was the greatest good, in reality, they were driven by a craving for renown, both for themselves and their descendants, he declares.

From a Christian viewpoint, there is a deep flaw at the heart of ancient virtue: the idea that the honour and approval that we seek are based on human judgement, not on divine wisdom. The leading tenets of classical ethics, above all the belief that the supreme good consists in living in accordance with virtue, or as Plato and the Stoics insist, in harmony with the rational order of the universe, are premised on the notion that by nature human beings strive towards the good. For Plato, knowledge of the truth is the decisive factor; Aristotle, by contrast, highlights the role of choice in virtuous conduct: vice and virtue are in our power, he asserts (*EN* 1111b–1115a). For the ancient philosophers, we are responsible for our own flourishing. For Christian thinkers, however, our fallen nature does not permit us to achieve virtue. Without the help of divine grace, we have no access to the truth. The fallacy of classical ethical thinking, they believe, is to ground our notions of what constitutes virtuous conduct on the opinion of humankind, and to claim self-sufficiency in the human quest for virtue.[15]

In his conclusion, Philibert lays his cards on the table. The philosophers of antiquity, with their faith in our proclivity for the good, succeed only in inflating human pride. 'Wherfore I affirme that true Philosophie is the despising and contemning of Philosophie and his foundation, which is this second nature, that God hath not made. For by the faulte of man it is become so

---

15. Michael Frede notes that the notion of a free will was first adumbrated by the Stoics, in particular the second-century CE philosopher Epictetus, and made into a pivotal tenet of Christianity by Augustine. However, the latter contends that due to original sin, our will is flawed, perverted by our pride; without divine grace we are unable to choose the good. See Frede, *A Free Will*.

corrupted' (J7r–v). No longer is Philibert alluding solely to the specious 'philosophy of the court'—his indictment encompasses all of pagan philosophy in its sweep, which fails to take the fallen condition of humanity into consideration. A quest for true wisdom would mean jettisoning classical philosophy altogether. Accordingly, the very notion of decorum, of behaviour framed to reflect the harmony and order of the universe, is misguided.

Philibert's dismantling of classical ideals is clearly influenced by the similar critique of the ancients articulated by St Augustine. In *City of God* Augustine sets out to unmask the ideals of the ancients as inherently fallacious, and skewers the self-infatuation that animates the allegedly heroic deeds of the ancients.[16] There is always a hidden self-regard and hunger for approbation at the root of their apparently virtuous deeds, even in the acts of role models such as Cato and Lucretia, he argues.[17] They are consumed by greed for praise and glory: 'glory they most ardently loved. For its sake they chose to live and for its sake they did not hesitate to die'.[18] Augustine reveals pagan culture to be riddled with deceit. The exemplars of classical heroism are motivated not by virtue, as they claim, but by their overwhelming appetite for fame. Classical ideals are inextricably bound up with dissimulation: the ancients were incessantly lying about their true motives, both to others and to themselves.

In his indictment of classical culture, Philibert goes further than Augustine, who, for all his criticism, continued to revere Cicero as an authority. In a number of sideswipes he castigates Cicero for his preoccupation with glory. He admits that in his discussion of magnanimity in *De officiis*, Cicero attempts to bridle the desire for glory by asserting that only deeds that serve the common good would qualify. Still, as Philibert is quick to point out, Cicero does not deny that great deeds are often impelled by a quest for fame. This he attributes to the Roman orator's own thirst for glory. 'I believe Cicero then thought of him selfe, for supposing that some knew him very covetous of honour, and yet would seeme noble minded and vertuous, he would not altegither separat this desire of glory from magnanimity' (C1v), he remarks caustically. He insinuates that Cicero too was dissembling his true motives: 'truelye I beleeve, if other testimonie might have bin had of *Ciceros* conscience (whome I name so oft for

---

16. See Hundert, 'Augustine and the Sources of the Divided Self'. Also see Taylor, *Sources of the Self*, 127–42. On the important role of Augustianism in Renaissance England, see Ettenhuber, *Donne's Augustine*.

17. Augustine, *City of God*, vol. 1, bk. 1.19, bk. 1.23–24.

18. Augustine, *City of God*, vol. 2, bk. 5.12.

the excellencie of the man) than by his owne writings: we should find, that in truth honor made him attempt and execute many things, especially he above all the other Romaines; which it appeareth he could not altogither so covertly conceale' (C8v–D1r).¹⁹ Disingenuously lacing his critique with praise, Philibert notes that everything that Cicero undertook was driven by the desire for acclamation.

Perhaps Philibert's radical critique of Ciceronian civility triggered a sense of unease with early modern readers in England, for whom the status of *De officiis* as a guide to ethical living was unrivalled. At all events, the translation of his text was never reprinted.

Della Casa's *Galateo*

In contrast to *The Philosopher of the Court*, *Galateo*, written by the poet and humanist scholar Giovanni Della Casa, Archbishop of Benevento, is one of the most popular courtesy texts of all time. It has remained in print for the past four centuries in Italy, where the term has become a catchword for good manners.²⁰ Within the first forty years after its publication in 1558, it appeared thirty-nine times, in French, English, Latin, Spanish, and German. A bilingual edition (Italian and French) appeared in 1583, a four-language edition (with Latin and Spanish) in 1598, and a five-language edition (with the addition of German) in 1609. It was used as a textbook in Lutheran, Calvinist, and Jesuit schools.²¹ Translated into English by Robert Peterson in 1576, it appeared in a number of new versions in early modern England, for instance in William Style's translation from the Spanish entitled *Galateo Espagnol, or the Spanish Gallant* (1640), Nathaniel Walker's *The Refin'd Courtier, or A Correction of Several Indecencies crept into Civil Conversation* (1663), and Josiah Dare's adaptation, *Counsellor Manners his Last Legacy to his Son* (1673).²² An index of the

---

19. Montaigne, whose *Essays* are in continual dialogue with Cicero, shares these sentiments: 'that fellow was so raging mad with a passion for glory that, if he had dared, he would readily have fallen into the extreme which others fell into: that even Virtue herself is only desirable for the honour which ever attends her'. See Michel de Montaigne, 'On Glory', in *The Complete Essays*, 2.16, p. 705.

20. I am grateful to Manfred Pfister for pointing this out to me.

21. See Santosuosso, 'Books, Readers, and Critics', 105–6.

22. Recent English translations are *Galateo or The Book of Manners*, trans. Pine-Coffin; *Galateo*, ed. and trans. Eisenbichler and Bartlett; and *Galateo, or, The Rules of Polite Behaviour*, ed. and trans. Rusnak.

role it played in the history of manners is its appropriation and adaptation, with or without attribution, by a wide variety of manuals that rolled off the press throughout Europe in the early modern era. It was appended to texts such as Thomas Gainsford's commonplace book, *The Rich Cabinet* (1616), and Walter Darell's *A Short discourse of the life of Servingmen* (1578). A digest of its main precepts that appeared in a Jesuit manual, *Bienséance de la conversation entre les hommes* (1595), was published with the title *Youths Behaviour* in 1640; attributed to a precocious eight-year old, Francis Hawkins, it was reprinted eleven times between 1640 and 1684. The precepts were copied out by the fourteen-year-old George Washington and became known as *Washington's Rules of Civility*.[23] A new translation into English by M. F. Rusnak was brought out by the University of Chicago Press in 2013 in a stylish, handy version.[24]

In a book replete with references to artists and writers, and that generously strews in examples from the fictions of Dante and Boccaccio, the narrator draws an analogy between his book of rules and the theories of art delineated by a sculptor he calls 'Chiarissimo'.[25] This is a coded reference to the Greek sculptor Polycleitus, whose name means 'very clear'.[26] The quip on the sculptor's name, mocking the ignorance of the narrator, is one of the many inside jokes that peppers the text. It is a typical example of the narratorial style that Della Casa adopts in this work: the device of an elderly 'idiota' or uneducated narrator exhorting a young relative to adopt the regime of manners that he lays out for him. The narrator writes ruefully that while the famous sculptor translated his aesthetic rules into a work of art that exemplified his theories in concrete form, he himself is too rough-hewn—and too old—to be able to practice what he preaches. But he hopes that his precepts will be of use to the young addressee of the book and help mould him into a paragon of manners.

The narrator expatiates on his overarching analogy between manners and the arts. 'But you must understand with all this, that, Men be very desirous of bewtifull things, well proportioned and comely', he reminds his readers. Conversely, men dislike things that are 'fowle and ill shapen' (O3v). He rehearses

---

23. *Washington's Rules of Civility and Decent Behavior in Company and Conversation*. See Santosuosso, 'Books, Readers, and Critics', 110.

24. For a magisterial analysis of *Galateo*, see Berger, *Absence of Grace*. Also see Elias, *Civilizing Process*, 64–66; Santosuosso, 'Giovanni Della Casa'; Eisenbichler and Bartlett, 'Introduction'; Scaglione, *Knights at Court*, 253–56; Arditi, *Genealogy of Manners*, 116–21; and Hadfield, *Lying in Early Modern English Culture*, 207–13.

25. Della Casa, *Galateo* of Maister John Della Casa, Archebishop of Benevento, N3v–4v.

26. See notes to Della Casa, *Galateo*, ed. Eisenbichler and Bartlett, 77.

classical ideas about aesthetic decorum as grounded in the convergence between beauty and harmony, citing the well-worn example of the artist Zeuxis and his solution to the conundrum of creating the ideal female shape by combining elements from different models. Human minds take pleasure and delight in symmetry, he stresses, and elaborates, 'It is not inoughe for a man, to doe things that be good: but hee must also have a care, hee doe them with a good grace. And a good grace is nothing els, but suche a maner of light (as I may call it) as shineth in the aptnes of things set in good order and wel disposed, one with another: and perfectly knit and united together' (P1v). Grace is a concomitant of order and proportion, he explains. Without due regard to balance and measure, even that which is good will not be beautiful, and beauty itself will not be pleasing. In all aspects of life, be they ever so trivial, it is necessary to aim for grace and harmony.

Galateo and the Tradition of Grobianism

What is striking for a reader of *Galateo* is the fact that there is very little sense of grace in the rest of the book. Della Casa offers quite a different vision of social life from the beguiling image of Urbino that Castiglione conjures up. Although at the outset the narrator declares that he wishes to discuss 'what manner of Countenance and grace, behoveth a man to use, that hee may be able in Communication and familiar acquaintance with men, to shewe him selfe pleasant, courteous, and gentle' (B1v), he expends little effort on advising his readers how to acquire stylish manners. Instead, the text parades an exhausting inventory of the revolting habits of his peers. These are described in so graphic a manner that one might speak of an aesthetics of disgust. The effect is often hilarious.

Thus the narrator describes individuals who 'in yauning, braye and crye out like Asses', or who 'in coffyng or neesing, make suche noyse, that they make a man deafe to here them', spraying everyone near them in the face (B4r). He admonishes his addressee that 'when thou hast blowne thy nose, use not to open thy handkercheif, to glare uppon thy snot, as if thou hadst pearles and Rubies fallen from thy braynes' (B4v). He also advises against sniffing at one's food or drink 'because it may chaunce that there might fall some droppe from his nose, that wold make a man to loath it' (C1r).

In a brilliant set piece that revels in the idiom of the grotesque, Della Casa veers into pure caricature. After discussing the cultivated set of people who regularly enjoyed the hospitality of the eminent and learned Bishop Gian Matteo Giberti, he writes,

Now what shal we thinke this Bishop, his modest and honest company about him would say, if they sawe these whome wee see other while, (like swine with their snouts in the washe, all begroined) never lyft up their heads nor looke up, and muche lesse keepe their hands from the meate, and with both their cheeks blowne (as if they should sound a trumpet, or blowe the fyer) not eate but ravon: whoe, besmearing their hands, almost up to their elbowes, so bedawbe the napkins, that the cloathes in the places of easement, be other while cleaner. (C2v–3r)

Deliberately ratcheting up the revulsion factor by inducing an association between table habits and toilet habits, Della Casa proceeds relentlessly: 'And to mend these slovenly maners, be not ashamed, many tymes with these filthy napkyns, to wype away the sweat that trickleth and falleth downe their browes, their face and their necke (they be such greedy guts in their feeding) and otherwhile to, (when it comes uppon them) spare not to snot their sniveld nose uppon them' (C3r).

At moments like this the text verges on undiluted social satire. The book creates the image of a world peopled by louts, greedy for wealth and status; the tropes of gluttony with which the text is pervaded figure the materialistic impulse that governs their life. While rehearsing precepts on corporeal control set out in medieval manuals, especially the twelfth-century treatise *Urbanus Magnus* by Daniel of Beccles,[27] Della Casa is also drawing on the vibrant if minor tradition of Grobianism, a variety of satirical conduct writing that ironically counsels its readers to embrace bad manners and describes them in a glut of monstrous details. The most famous example is the neo-Latin poem *Grobianus* by German humanist scholar Friedrich Dedekind, a first version of which appeared in 1549.[28] Influenced by the satirical allegory *Das Narrenschiff* (*The Ship of Fools*) by Sebastian Brandt, published in 1494, which introduced the figure of St Grobianus, the patron saint of boors, and the legendary folk hero Ulenspiegel of early sixteenth-century chapbook literature, Dedekind's poem belongs to a body of writing that includes Rabelais's *Gargantua and Pantagruel* (1534). It was translated into English and appeared under the title *The Schoole of Slovenrie: or, Cato turnd wrong side outward* in 1605. Thomas Dekker's *Guls Horne-booke* is a variant of *Grobianus* adapted to early modern London.

---

27. See Thomas, *In Pursuit of Civility*, 22.
28. On Grobianism, see Correll, *End of Conduct*.

Lying and Social Pretence

Before writing *Galateo*, Della Casa wrote a book of manners in Latin entitled *De officiis inter potentiores et tenuiores amicos*, which was published in 1546. It was translated into English by Henry Stubbe only in 1665 with the title *The Arts of Grandeur and Submission*. The text is of interest chiefly for the light it sheds on Della Casa's views on social relations. While advocating restraint, accommodation, and prudence, the text is imbued with resentment at the newly rich and powerful who owe their rise to the vagaries of fortune. Those of noble lineage frequently find themselves reduced to a state of dependency towards their former inferiors, constrained '*to revere, court* and *complement* such as before were *their creatures*'.[29] *Galateo* too depicts an urban landscape where social status is in flux and where a well-dressed cobbler or barber might be mistaken for someone of a higher station in life (G2r). It was advisable to be polite to everyone one encountered, since rank was often elusive.

In *Galateo*, the narrator labels social pretenders as liars. Lies are not only spoken untruths, the narrator asserts. Men may lie through their actions, 'as some you shall see, that being of meane, or rather base condition and calling, use suche a solemnitie in all their doings, and marche so stately, and speake with suche a prerogative, or rather discourse lyke Parleament men, setteling them selves, as it were, in a place of Judgement, proudly prying about them like Peacockes' (F2v). In these lines the English translator, Robert Peterson, apparently felt called upon to insert a topical reference to members of Parliament of the lower sort who were usurping a status which was not merely unwarranted, but fraudulent. 'Ceremonies', the elaborate formalities that, like a disease, have invaded all spheres of life in Italy, meet with the narrator's derision too. He declares that ceremonies are not merely lies, but also 'Treacheries and Treasons', barbarous customs imported from Spain and imposed upon a humiliated and impoverished Italian nation, rich only 'in vayne woords' and 'superfluous titles' (G1v). He pours vitriol on the artificial rites that now dominate social encounters, with people 'bending, and bowing their bodyes, in token of reverence one to another, uncovering their heads, using highe titles and Styles of honour, and kissing their hands as if they were hollye things' (G1r). In contemporary society even persons of low origin are treated with effusive civility. These empty shows consist in 'semblance without effect',

---

29. Della Casa, *Arts of Grandeur and Submission*, B5r, emphasis original.

appearances without substance (G2r). Nonetheless, he advises grudgingly, since it is 'the fault of our tyme, wee are bounde to followe it' (G2v). We need to adapt to the usages of the time. The narrator calls this 'a sufferable leesing' (H3r) or a permissible lie. It is those who are overly lavish in observances of deference in order to pander to others who are truly reprehensible.

Della Casa's vision of social interaction is one in which it is essential to avoid offence and to demonstrate respect to other members of society, however much one might despise them in reality: 'we honour them to their face, whome we reverence not in deede, but otherwhile contemne' (G1v). But social climbers with their ostentatious manners are denounced for their duplicity. Despite his tribute to the classical ideal of grace, Della Casa's narrator is under no illusion as to the ethical worth of what he is discussing. Manners, he concedes, might be considered frivolous, and of far lesser value than the classical virtues. However, as he observes drily, they play a great role in everyday life, whereas the noble virtues are seldom pressed into service. Furthermore, as far as furthering one's career is concerned, people who possessed true virtue were frequently outstripped by those who possessed no noble traits other than suave manners, 'which hath byn suche a helpe & advauncement unto them, that they have gotten greate preferments [promotion]' (B2r).

Despite Della Casa's invocation of Ciceronian grace and decorum, in the world of *Galateo*, civility has become perverted from an ethical ideal into a tool of careerism. Della Casa's choice of an uneducated narrator who flaunts his own ignorance, and in a garbled version of the *Symposium*, jauntily refers to 'a goodman of that time, Socrates, by name' who indulged in a drinking bout with 'another good man, Aristophanes' (Q2v), no doubt serves to raise a few chuckles with the learned readership of the book. But it also undercuts the life narrative of the humanist scholar Della Casa; in the quest for self-advancement, education seems to have become gratuitous. The text is tinged with bitterness at the triviality of what it nonetheless advocates. It is striking that in his references to grace, Della Casa largely avoids the term *gratia* (an older spelling of *grazia*), preferring more mundane synonyms like *leggiadria*.[30] It appears the Archbishop of Benevento wished to evade not only the resonances of Castiglione's Neoplatonic vision but also the religious implications of the term, increasingly insistent at the time he was writing.

30. I am indebted to Edoardo Simonato and Uberto Motta for explaining the implications involved to me.

Guazzo's *Civile Conversation*

John Jeffries Martin identifies a new phase in Renaissance formations of identity: the sincere self, a mode of personhood that involved revealing one's true feelings.[31] Martin detects features of the sincere self in writers like Montaigne, with his emphasis on self-expression, and Stefano Guazzo, whose conduct manual, *Civil conversatione* (1574), played quite as vital a role in the Renaissance culture of civility as did Della Casa's *Galateo*. The title of the treatise was pivotal in bringing the term 'civil conversation' (or 'conduct in social interaction') into wide currency.[32] Unlike the *Courtier*, the *Civile Conversation* outlines model relationships among a wide range of participants and between different estates, for, as one of the interlocutors of the dialogue points out, 'it is our hap to come in companie, somtime with the young, sometime with the olde, assoone with Gentlemen, assoone with the baser sorte, nowe and then with Princes, nowe and then with private persons, one while with the learned, another while with the ignoraunt, nowe with our owne Countriemen, then with strangers'.[33] In a brief discussion, the focus will be on the traces of the culture of sincerity discernible in the book.

The cult of sincerity was decisively influenced by the Calvinist movement and the major revival of Augustinianism in the Reformation. Augustine did not dismantle the classical doctrine of an order based on reason and concord that governed the universe—this was, in Charles Taylor's influential account of the emergence of modern identity, the achievement of Descartes.[34] Nevertheless, Augustine introduced a decisive new element: a turn to the interior of the human self. In Augustine's version of the Platonic model, the Ideas are transmuted into the thoughts of God. God is to be found not only in the outside world, but deep within the self, in the image of God within the soul of each human being. The way to God involves a journey of self-discovery, a delving into the soul in order to reintegrate our fragmented personality, torn between conflicting desires, and achieve a unified self. Only a unitary, collected self is capable of finding the way to God. Another major distinction

---

31. Martin, *Myths of Renaissance Individualism*, 102–22.

32. Lievsay, *Stefano Guazzo*, 34. Lievsay's is the most extensive study of the treatise. On Guazzo, also see Javitch, 'Rival Arts of Conduct in Elizabethan England'; Scaglione, *Knights at Court*, 257–62; Bryson, *From Courtesy to Civility*, 54–57, 78–79; Richards, *Rhetoric and Courtliness*, 16–17, 22–42; and Hadfield, *Lying in Early Modern English Culture*, 215–20.

33. Guazzo, *Civile Conversation of M. Steeven Guazzo*, vol. 1, 2.168.

34. In the following I draw on Taylor's account in *Sources of the Self*, 127–42.

from the classical model lay in the value Augustine accorded to emotions. For Augustine, the heart was of central importance. Articulating one's emotions was not a sign of a lack of rational control over the passions, but could be regarded as a laudable expression of inward truth. The key virtue in social interaction, he claims, is charity, in which the love between God and man is reduplicated in our love for our fellow humans.

Elements of the culture of sincerity are apparent in Guazzo's treatise. The text recounts the alleged conversations between the younger brother of the author, William (or in the original, Guglielmo), afflicted by melancholia, and his neighbour, the physician Anniball Magnocavalli, over the course of four days. The dialogue covers a wide variety of topics that touch upon relationships between members of a civil society. In their discussion of recommended modes of discourse, Anniball proclaims that 'the purity of speech' required 'the puritie and sinceritie of manners' (2.147). He stresses the importance of gracious conduct, accommodation to others, affability, and courteous words in social interaction. But an elegant veneer alone would not fulfil the norms he sets up. Adducing Socrates, he urges his interlocutor to 'indevour, to bee such a one in deede, as hee desireth to seeme to bee in showe' (2.148). Like Cicero (*Off.* 2.43), Anniball follows Socrates in dismissing any thought of accepting a discrepancy between seeming and being. Instead, he counsels William, he should strive for a correlation between feeling and expression, between inward truth and outward appearance. The crucial point is to be sincere: true to oneself.

In a notable passage, Guazzo goes to the heart of the conundrum of sincerity. Modes of comportment, William announces in a sudden fit of petulance, are merely empty rituals. He demands that elegant manners and all 'ceremonies' or conventional forms of courtesy be thrown overboard. They are nothing but an expression of 'curious vanitie', a fastidious and futile exercise. Instead, he lauds straightforward behaviour as an index of sincerity: 'when you see one goe plainely to woorke both in woordes and jesture, you say by and by, that he is a good honest meaning man' (2.164). Frankness of speech and a forthright manner are the mark of a man of honour and integrity, he asserts.[35]

William mocks elaborate gestures of deference, in particular those sedulously displayed by social upstarts, which, he points out, serve only to expose

---

35. In this period, the term 'honest', originally relating to honour, increasingly acquired the meaning of 'truthful' and 'sincere'. See *OED*, s.v. 'honest, adj.', 4.b, where Pettie's translation of Guazzo is cited as an example. On the permutations of the term 'honest', see William Empson's fine essay, 'Honest in *Othello*'.

the arrivistes as ridiculous and betray their origins: 'coveting to bee courtlike, they become plaine cartlike' (2.165). Anniball begs to disagree. Even those who show contempt for manners have a secret hankering for them, he claims. For manners are a sign of respect, something every human being desires. By refusing to go through the motions of civility, one laid oneself open to the suspicion not only of being rustic or ill-bred, but of harbouring disdain towards others: 'a clowne, a rudesby, or a contemner of others'. Those who claim to set no store by manners are performing a charade to cover their yearning for tokens of esteem. As he astutely points out, a claim to authenticity is itself a performance: 'For their very saying so, is a certaine kind of Ceremonie and behaviour, whereby they goe about to cover their ambition' (2.165–66). He concludes that conventional observances of civility are much to be recommended—they garner good will and embellish one's reputation as a man of cultivation.

When William inquires what exactly polite comportment would involve, Anniball finds himself mired in contradictions. Manners should be deployed 'in such sort, that he which useth them, bewray thereby the affection of his heart, that the inward love may bee knowne, as well as the outwarde honour is seene, other wise ceremonies are loathsome unto us, and shew that the hearte is faigned', he explains (2.166). Only sincere gestures of respect are valid, he argues, those that correspond to the true feelings of the social agent. All simulated expressions of regard are to be repudiated. After arguing persuasively in favour of the pragmatic value of civil manners irrespective of their truth, he doubles back on his words to advocate a stance of sincerity. How this paradox is to be resolved is a question the text evades.

Throughout the treatise, a defence of civil manners rubs up uneasily against the discourse of sincerity. Religious connotations play into the dispute about civility as opposed to sincerity too. In defence of the value of appearances, Anniball draws an analogy to religious rituals which serve a purpose to promote faith among the uneducated. Sacred rituals, he writes, if 'voide of supersition', are 'not displeasant in Gods sight, and stirre up to devotion the mindes of the ignorant people, *whiche are not come to the perfect knoweledge of Gods worde*' (2.166, emphasis added). The qualification (reproduced in italics) does not, however, stem from Guazzo. It is an insertion by his English translator, George Pettie, and betrays reservations about a full-scale endorsement of religious spectacle.[36] The use of sacred observances was precisely the crux upon which disagreement between Reformers and the established Church would continue to turn. The

---

36. See Lievsay, *Stefano Guazzo*, 60.

Platonic tension between surface and substance, seeming and being, appearances and reality, was transposed into the conflict in Christianity between idolatry, theatricality, illusion, and lying on the one hand and inner truth on the other, a conflict that is crystallised in the dissension about civility and sincerity in the early modern period.

Although Guazzo was not a Protestant, his treatise, infused with a spirit of piety and directed at provincial bourgeoisie rather than at courtiers, was uniquely amenable to a Protestant worldview, and its popularity in Europe made it one of the leading treatises of courtesy in England, alongside Castiglione's *Courtier*, Erasmus's *De civilitate*, and Della Casa's *Galateo*. George Pettie's translation of 1581, although largely based on the 1579 French version by Gabriel Chappuys, seamlessly interpolates a two-page paean to Queen Elizabeth and Protestantism, 'the very high road to heaven' (2.202), into the second book.

Plutarch, Coriolanus, and Civility

The problem with Caius Martius Coriolanus, Plutarch implies, is his lack of civility. Plutarch tells us that while Martius's forceful personality led to success in a number of notable endeavours, his violent temper and obstinate nature made him a disagreeable and uncongenial associate. He was admired for his indifference to pleasure and riches and his capacity for unstinting labour, all of which earned him praise for possessing the virtues of temperance and fortitude. But his rudeness and arrogance were considered offensive by his fellow citizens. These traits might be attributed to shortcomings in his education. The most important effect of the Muses, the Greek philosopher and moralist reminds us, is to refine human nature and induce moderation. However, as he notes laconically, in early Rome, virtue was synonymous with martial valour; the term *virtus* (or '*manly valour*') was considered identical with the designation of virtue in general.[37]

Plutarch's work is suffused with the conviction that what the Romans lacked was a generous dose of Greek education, or *paideia*.[38] Sir Thomas

---

37. See Plutarch, *Caius Marcius Coriolanus*, trans. Bernadotte Perrin, Loeb Classical Library, 119–21, emphasis original.

38. See Russell, *Plutarch*, 132. On Shakespeare and Plutarch, see the essays in 'Shakespeare's Plutarch', ed. Mary Ann McGrail, special issue of *Poetica* 48 (1997), esp. Pelling, 'Shaping of Coriolanus', and Denton, 'Plutarch, Shakespeare, Roman Politics and Renaissance Translation'.

FIGURE 7. 'As if a man were author of himself / And knew no other kin'. Soma Orlai Petrich, *Coriolanus* (1869). Mihály Munkácsy Museum, Békéscsaba.

North based his translation of the *Parallel Lives*, the first part of which appeared in 1579, on the French version by the scholar Jacques Amyot, whose own translation was published in 1559. Both writers, inspired by humanist ideals, are far more emphatic in their references to civility. Amyot is somewhat expansive in transmitting Plutarch's words, often spelling out what he thinks Plutarch should have said. Thus he helpfully explains that by referring to the Muses, Plutarch means the humanities (*'c'est-à-dire de la connaissance des bonnes lettres'*), and adds that without the civilising influence of education, humans are uncouth and wild.[39] North usually follows Amyot and faithfully reproduces the additional elucidation to men as being 'rude and rough of nature'. However, his version differs from Amyot's in a few nuances. Where Amyot speaks of the effect of the Muses as refining human nature (*'adoucissent leur nature'*), remaining close to Plutarch, North speaks of learning explicitly

---

Also see Marshall, 'Shakespeare: Crossing the Rubicon'; Braden, 'Plutarch, Shakespeare and the Alpha Males'; and Burrow, *Shakespeare and Classical Antiquity*, 226–39.

39. Plutarque, *Vie de Coriolan*, trans. Amyot, 472. The phrase he inserts alludes to human nature, *'qui était auparavant sauvage et farouche'*. I am indebted to Plutarch scholar Thomas Schmidt for his help in collating the different versions of the text.

as a means to teach men 'to be civil and courteous'. North renders Amyot's description of Coriolanus's character as unsociable and unaccommodating ('*mal accointable et mal propre pour vivre et converser entre les hommes*') with three terms, as 'churlish, uncivil, and altogether unfit for any man's conversation'.[40] And in the comparison between Alcibiades and Coriolanus that sums up the two *Lives*, both Amyot and North highlight civility as a significant difference between the generals. While Plutarch merely speaks of Alcibiades's ability to 'treat in a friendly manner those who met him' as opposed to Coriolanus's 'arrogant pride', Amyot succeeds in inserting three references to '*grace*' in as many lines, while North opts for a string of synonymous collocations: Martius, he explains, lacks affability, while Alcibiades 'had a trim entertainment [excellent manners], and a very good grace', and 'could fashion himself in all companies'.[41]

The heightened emphasis on civility in the Renaissance versions of Plutarch might have inspired Shakespeare to give prominence to Coriolanus's rejection of civility in his own play. In *Coriolanus*, Plutarch's thoughts about the deficiencies in Martius's upbringing are articulated by the smooth operator, Menenius. He excuses Coriolanus's rudeness to the tribunes on the grounds of his being 'ill-schooled / In bolted language; meal and bran together / He throws without distinction' (3.1.312–14). Using a culinary metaphor relating to the sifting of grain after grinding (to 'bolt' means to sift), Menenius claims that in interaction with others, Coriolanus is incapable of applying the rules of decorum. He uses the same mode of speech in every social situation. But Shakespeare adds a note that is missing in Plutarch, one that reflects the new ideal of sincerity. Menenius describes Coriolanus as the epitome of sincerity: 'His heart's his mouth: / What his breast forges, that his tongue must vent' (250–51). According to Menenius, Coriolanus's words serve as a direct conduit to his inner feelings.[42]

---

40. Plutarch, *Life of Caius Martius Coriolanus*, trans. North, 137–38.

41. See Plutarch, *Comparison of Alcibiades and Coriolanus*, trans. Bernadotte Perrin, Loeb Classical Library, 225; *Alcibiades et Coriolanus*, trans. Amyot, 521, and *Comparison of Alcibiades with Coriolanus*, trans. North, 181.

42. Important criticism on *Coriolanus* includes, inter alia, Miola, *Shakespeare's Rome*, 164–205; Miles, *Shakespeare and the Constant Romans*, 149–68; Coppélia Kahn, *Roman Shakespeare*, 144–59; Shrank, 'Civility and the City in *Coriolanus*'; Chernaik, *Myth of Rome*, 165–95; Kerrigan, 'Coriolanus Fidiussed'; Holland, 'Introduction'; Skinner, 'Rhetorical Redescription and Its Uses in Shakespeare'; and Lewis, 'A Kind of Nothing', in *Shakespeare's Tragic Art*.

Civility and Flattery

In *Coriolanus* Shakespeare explores the implications of a radical repudiation of civility.[43] The often contradictory strands of classical and Christian thought that formed the early modern age are ironically refracted in a protagonist who models himself on the ideal of the Aristotelian magnanimous man whose predominant concern is honour, but who abjures civility in an idiom reminiscent of the Augustinian castigation of lying. Traces of the debate on civility in the writings of Philibert, Della Casa, and Guazzo are visible in the play. Like Philibert in his satire of courtly manners, Coriolanus equates civility with flattery and deceit, riding roughshod over Aristotle's careful distinction between the social virtue of friendliness and its perversion in obsequiousness (*EN* 4.6). To Coriolanus's mind, affability and simulating regard for other members of society are forms of lying. Like Della Casa, Coriolanus denounces a world overrun by social upstarts. And like Guazzo, he yearns for an authentic self, whose inner feeling correlates truthfully with his outward expression.

In Renaissance Europe, the model of warrior aristocracy Coriolanus cleaves to was being consigned to history. Coriolanus represents the old guard who considered the emergent culture of civility an assault on their aristocratic privilege. Along with cowardly commoners, Martius's special ire is reserved for the new type of nobleman: the courtier. 'When drums and trumpets shall / I'th' field prove flatterers, let courts and cities be / Made all of false-faced soothing [flattery]', he declaims, deploring an age 'when steel grows / Soft as the parasite's silk' (1.9.42–45) and martial virtues are discarded for courtly flattery. While ostensibly canvassing election votes, he spews his disdain for the new order. To the citizens he remarks sardonically, 'I will, sir, flatter my sworn brother, the people, to earn a dearer estimation of them; 'tis a condition they account gentle'. The commons are so ignorant and degraded that they mistake blandishments for a sign of nobility. He adds, 'since the wisdom of their choice is rather to have my hat than my heart, I will practice the insinuating nod and be off to them most counterfeitly' (2.3.89–94). The people prefer a pretence of courtesy to a profession of honesty, he observes contemptuously.

---

43. For a reading that explores the link between civil and civic and draws analogies to the civic politics of Jacobean England, see Cathy Shrank's incisive essay, 'Civility and the City in *Coriolanus*'. Shrank reads the uncivil language of the professional soldier Martius as symptomatic of his antipathy towards the civic community.

Coriolanus's refusal to cultivate the fashionable codes of courtesy is not a merely a matter of differing styles of aristocratic conduct. Incensed by the call of the tribune Sicinus for greater civility on his part, who demands, 'you must enquire your way, / Which you are out of, with a gentler spirit' (3.1.52–53), Coriolanus explodes with anger, training his fury on his fellow patricians. He warns them of the dire consequences of their affable conduct, which he regards as identical to flattery: 'in soothing them, / We nourish gainst our Senate the cockle / Of rebellion, insolence, sedition' (66–68). Civility towards the plebeians will lead to social upheaval and oust the patricians from their position at the apex of the Roman state, he declares categorically, and compares the appeasement policy of his peers to a perverted form of husbandry in which the Senate has wilfully sown the weeds (or 'cockle') of insurgency in the polity. The Senate's 'courtesy' (129) to the people, as he terms their acquiescence to the people's demands for corn, will be seized upon as a sign of cowardice, and will undermine their authority. The result will be a political catastrophe:

> Thus we debase
> The nature of our seats and make the rabble
> Call our cares 'fears', which will in time
> Break ope the locks o'th' Senate and bring in
> The crows to peck the eagles. (3.1.132–36)

In Hitchcockian imagery, Coriolanus describes the outcome of the Senate's strategy of accommodation as the inversion of the political order. The regime of eagles, the symbol not only of Rome but of the aristocracy, will be overthrown by the rule of the common crow.

The senators do not heed his advice. Accordingly, once he has been banished, Coriolanus no longer bestows the epithet of eagle on his fellow patricians. To the Volscians, he cryptically describes Rome as the 'city of kites and crows' (4.5.41), bracketing patricians together with plebeians in the category of scavenger birds. In his eyes, he is the last exemplar of the Roman nobility. Among the final words in the play that he utters is the boast, 'like an eagle in a dovecote, I / Fluttered your Volscians in Corioles. / Alone I did it' (5.6.112–14). There is one eagle left in the world; the Volscians are his prey. The double syntax reinforces the singularity on which he insists.

In the play, the only representative of civility is the seasoned senator Menenius. Far from a model of virtue, he is known more for his congenial presence at dinner parties than for his political record as a senator: 'you are well understood to be a perfecter giber for the table than a necessary bencher in the Capitol' (2.1.73–75), the tribune Brutus sneers. Menenius wholeheartedly agrees. 'I am known to be a humorous patrician, and one that loves a cup of hot wine with not a drop of allaying Tiber in't' (43–45), he admits cheerfully, and goes on to list his other failings. He acknowledges that in his judicial function, he is reputed to be overly hasty in drawing conclusions, happy to curtail the procedure by accepting the first version of a dispute brought before him; he is short-tempered, and fond of revelling. And yet, he is the only character in the play to display civility in practice, remaining in dialogue with the people as well as the tribunes throughout the play.

In the first scene of the play we see him deliver a paternalistic version of the fable of the belly, manipulating the commons by means of his trademark breezy affability.[44] Although he clearly expresses his disapproval of the uprising, sarcastically calling it 'this most wise rebellion' and comparing the citizens to rats (1.1.149, 153), they accept him as 'one that hath always loved the people', or at least, someone who is 'honest enough', as the First Citizen grudgingly concedes (44–46). Similarly, while he mocks the tribunes for being proud, he remains on civil terms with them.

As the antagonism between Coriolanus and the plebeians escalates, Menenius attempts to defuse the tension by calling for calm and restraint: 'On both sides more respect', he urges (3.1.177). He remonstrates both with Coriolanus, imploring him to rein in his fury, and with the tribunes, entreating them to impute the general's lack of manners to his profession as soldier: 'Consider this: he has been bred i'th' wars / Since 'a could draw a sword' (3.1.311–12). To his peers, he vents his frustration. 'What the vengeance, / Could he not speak 'em fair?' (255–56), he demands rhetorically, exasperated at the obduracy of his protégé. Throughout the conflict, he appeals for more civil discourse: 'Speak fair', he pleads to Coriolanus, and admonishes him, 'Only fair speech' (3.2.70, 96).[45] Coriolanus brusquely dismisses his request: 'I would not buy / Their mercy at the price of one fair word' (3.3.86–87), he proclaims. Even after the banishment, Menenius continues to regret Coriolanus's unwillingness to seek a compromise with his opponents, remarking wistfully, 'He could have temporized' (4.6.18), wishing he had negotiated or temporarily adapted himself to the circumstances, if only to gain time.[46]

---

44. On the fable of the belly, see esp. Barton, 'Livy, Machiavelli, and Shakespeare's *Coriolanus*'.
45. 'To speak fair' could mean 'civilly'. See *OED*, s.v. 'fair, adv.', 2.a.
46. *OED*, s.v. 'temporize, v.', 1.a; 3; 4.a.

Menenius is not an admirable character. He lacks the towering personality of Coriolanus and Volumnia, or the stern charisma of Aufidius. Nor does he possess the charm and grace of the stylish Venetians in *The Merchant of Venice*. He appears as a somewhat oleaginous figure, adept at adapting himself to the company he is in. He is at a loss to comprehend the implacable anger of Coriolanus, attributing it to a lack of dinner: 'He was not taken well; he had not dined' (5.1.49). He attempts to wheedle his way into the Volscian camp with an embarrassing mixture of self-puffery and adulation of their general. Significantly, the issue of lying, so crucial for Coriolanus, is merely a game for him. He quips that in the same way as in the past he occasionally overshot the mark in a game of bowls, his exuberant praise of Coriolanus has often legitimized untruths: 'sometimes, / Like to a bowl upon a subtle ground, / I have tumbled past the throw, and in his praise / Have almost stamped the leasing [lie]' (5.2.19–22). The Volscian guards, shaped in the image of their inexorable leader, whom they laud in Senecan idiom as a 'rock, the oak not to be wind-shaken' (104),[47] have only contempt for the easygoing, pliant senator. They humiliate him, and quibbling on his admission of being a 'liar' (30), toss sexual taunts at him, before Coriolanus delivers the coup de grâce.

Coriolanus and Lies

The foundation on which Coriolanus's sense of self is anchored is an unequivocal rejection of pretence. He sees himself as the only authentic character in the play, whose innate honour is demonstrated in his truth to himself. He spurns civility as a denial of selfhood, demanding of his mother, 'Why did you wish me milder? Would you have me / False to my nature?' (3.2.14–15). Gracious, conciliatory behaviour to the commons would erode the constancy that defines his self-image. If flattery is a form of lying to others, what agitates Coriolanus to an equal extent is the thought of lying to himself. In this regard the play attests to the influence of Augustinian thought on lying. Consistent with his focus on free will, Augustine is concerned above all with the effect of feigning on the individual and less on others in society.

Lying, for Augustine, is holding one opinion in one's mind and giving expression to another. In his treatise *De mendacio*, he defines lying as 'a false

---

47. See Seneca, 'De Constantia Sapientis'.

statement made with the desire to deceive'.[48] Augustine sets up an eightfold taxonomy of lying, graduated according to the degree of sinfulness involved, which was further simplified by Jerome, followed by Aquinas. Lies against God or lies that harmed others were bracketed as 'malicious' lies by Jerome, lies merely to please others as 'humorous' lies, and lies that benefited others as 'useful' lies.[49] In *Contra mendacium*, written twenty years later, Augustine rehearses his main precepts. Addressing his correspondent Consentius, Augustine condemns clandestine activity for the purposes of surveillance, even against a heretical group, the Priscillianists. Lies for a higher end are sins too, he stresses, and compromise our soul. While he concedes that not all lies are mortal sins, he leaves no doubt about his views that all lying is reprehensible. 'There is no lie which is not contrary to truth', he reiterates.[50] Aquinas points out that lying encompasses deceptive actions as well as false words: 'deception is a lie consisting in the signification of outward acts'. As he stresses, lying, deception, and hypocrisy are 'the direct opposite to truth'. Following Augustine, he claims that citing lies by biblical prophets in support of the argument that some lies were admissible was unacceptable: 'it would put an end to the certainty of faith, which rests on the authoritativeness of Sacred Scripture'.[51]

Coriolanus is shot through with the vocabulary of civility, theatricality, and lying. The web of allusions is most dense in act 3, scene 2, when Volumnia sets out to teach her son a lesson in play-acting. It is not the case that Coriolanus rejects the notion of role-playing per se. Coriolanus is perfectly willing to take on board the Ciceronian notion of *personae*, which implied finding an appropriate role which would be fused with one's selfhood. Rather than demand that he belie his true nature by accommodating himself to the plebians, Coriolanus declares to his mother, she should acknowledge that his actions are perfectly in character: 'say I play / The man I am' (3.2.14–16). As becomes apparent in the play, the fallacy of the Ciceronian model is that it elides the idea that we are contradictory beings, torn by conflicting impulses. It opens the way for a person as self-deluded as Coriolanus to succumb to his image of himself.

Volumnia will have none of this exalted notion of roles. Her view of role-playing involves adapting to the circumstances one is in and adjusting to one's

---

48. Augustine, *Lying*, 54, 60. On lying, see Zagorin, *Ways of Lying*, and Hadfield, *Lying in Early Modern English Culture*.
49. Aquinas, *Summa theologiae*, 2a2ae, q. 110, a. 2.
50. Augustine, *Against Lying*, 129.
51. Aquinas, *Summa theologiae*, 2a2ae, q. 111, a. 1, a. 3.

interlocutors. 'You might have been enough the man you are / With striving less to be so', she retorts (19–20). A less intransigent insistence on being true to himself would not have jeopardised his selfhood; on the contrary, it would have secured the position of consul that is his due. Volumnia shrugs off her son's notion of acting a single role for life, and pointedly steers the discussion into the realm of drama. Like a stage director, she proceeds to give her son detailed acting instructions. She urges him to 'speak / To th' people, not by your own instruction, / Nor by th' matter which your heart prompts you, / But with such words that are but roted in / Your tongue' (3.2.52–56). Like an actor, he needs to learn his part, not say what he feels. She gives him graphic instructions how to play the part persuasively. 'Go to them with this bonnet in thy hand, / And thus far having stretched it—here be with them, / Thy knee bussing the stones' (73–75), she begins. Step by step, she takes him through a routine of the most effective gestures to use, helping herself liberally to the advice on delivery (or *actio*) expounded in rhetoric manuals—as she reminds him, 'in such business / Action is eloquence' (75–76). She admits that the role is new and challenging, but encourages him to exert himself to the utmost, dangling the promise of her applause as a reward: 'To have my praise for this, perform a part / Thou hast not done before' (108–9). Cominius seconds her, promising theatrical support: 'we'll prompt you' (107).

In this scene, the language of acting merges with the language of civility or social rhetoric. The gestures Volumnia describes are typical acts of courteous behaviour. With withering sarcasm, she alleges that instead of bearing in mind the larger consequences of his intransigent behaviour, he is keen to show the plebeians 'How you can frown than spend a fawn upon 'em' (67); 'fawn' refers to an obsequious observance of courtesy.[52] Urging him to appeal to their indulgence on the grounds of being a soldier who lacks experience in 'the soft way', she advises him to promise to turn over a new leaf and henceforth to 'frame' himself to them, accommodating himself to their desires (80–86). She appeals to his experience of tactics in the field of warfare, where sometimes goals are achieved through prudent strategy (or 'policy') rather than force. He himself has admitted that 'Honor and policy, like unsevered friends, / I' th' war do grow together', she reminds him (42–43). She herself would use dissimulation in the interests of herself or her family, she declares (62–64). The entire scene is punctuated with remonstrances directed to Coriolanus by Menenius and Cominius to speak 'fair' and 'mildly' to the crowd, both synonyms for

---

52. *OED*, s.v. 'fawn, n. 2'.

courteous speech (70, 96, 139, 144).[53] Coriolanus ironically turns their plea into a theatrical cue which he mockingly parrots. 'The word is "mildly"', he sneers, 'Well, mildly be it, then, mildly' (142, 145).

Coriolanus does not give in without a struggle. The role is too difficult for him, he protests, adopting Volumnia's language of stagecraft even as he rejects it: 'You have put me now to such a part which never / I shall discharge to th' life' (105–6). In lines whose fragmented metre reveal his agitation, he demands, 'Must I / With my base tongue give to my noble heart / A lie that it must bear?' (99–101). The antithesis between false speech and true feeling is drawn from the early modern discourse of sincerity, but the opposition he sets up between baseness and nobility betrays his own preoccupation with social status. In his lexicon, lying to please is indissolubly linked to low social rank. For Coriolanus, the thought of trying to beguile or charm is equivalent to sinking to the level of an itinerant entertainer, a 'mountebank' (132) or a 'harlot' (112), which could mean a vagabond or a prostitute. In a final attempt to resist the browbeating of Volumnia, he declares, 'I will not do't, / Lest I surcease to honour mine own truth / And by my body's action teach my mind / A most inherent baseness' (121–24). Once again, he sets off the truth of his noble selfhood ('mine own truth'), against the lies of the low-born, this time eliding the latter with corporeality while his nobility is identified with the mind or soul.

'Author of Himself'

Coriolanus is the play of a man who dreams of self-creation: 'As if a man were author of himself / And knew no other kin' (5.3.36–37). Coriolanus regards himself as autonomous, moulder of his own reality. What the play displays, however, is a protagonist whose identity is inescapably social. Far from self-created, he is the product of an aristocratic culture and the warrior ethos on which he was weaned. His personality has been forged by his mother, whose towering pride and anger he mirrors. And far from self-sufficient, his self-definition depends entirely on the opinion of others.

As the First Citizen shrewdly notes, the dependence of Martius on his mother runs so deep that his glorious achievements are merely an attempt to win her approval: 'he did it to please his mother' (1.1.32–33). The First Citizen is in fact citing Plutarch, who notes that for Martius, love of honour was in

---

53. *OED*, s.v. 'mild, adj., adv., and n. 1', 1.d and 1.e.

reality adulation of his mother. If other warriors were spurred by the quest for glory, Martius was propelled by the desire to give his mother pleasure. 'And as for other, the only respect that made them valiant, was that they hoped for honour: but touching Martius, the only thing that made him to love honour, was the joy he saw his mother did take of him', Plutarch observes.[54] Volumnia herself is quick to remind her son that he is her creature: 'Thy valiantness was mine: thou suck'st it from me' (3.2.128).

Apart from his mother, Martius is bound in a curious, symbiotic relationship to his arch-foe Aufidius and to the plebeians whom he loathes. Martius divulges his true thoughts when he speaks of Aufidius, who figures as his double in the play. He remarks to the senators that he is consumed with desire for his rival's high qualities. 'I sin in envying his nobility', he confesses, 'And were I anything but what I am, / I would wish me only he' (1.1.221–23). His sentiments disclose a peculiarly self-absorbed obsession with his counterpart. Martius proceeds to offer a glimpse into his entangled feelings about the *pas de deux* the two protagonists perform in the play. He reveals that his dreams consist of a hothouse world populated only by the two men. 'Were half the world by th'ears and he / Upon my party, I'd revolt to make / Only my wars with him. He is a lion / That I am proud to hunt' (224–27), he declares. In a few remarkable words, whose treasonous import the senator fails to grasp, Martius proleptically sketches a scenario of his betraying Rome to join the enemy camp. To be sure, Martius speaks of deserting his side in order to maintain his rivalry with Aufidius, not to join forces with him, as he does later in the play. Nonetheless, it becomes clear that he regards the wars between Rome and its enemies as a deeply personal affair. He would abandon the affairs of 'half the world' in order to pursue a personal quest for glory, he states. The glory he strives for is to defeat his alter ego Aufidius in single combat, in a conflict between two noble creatures, as in the contest between hunter and lion, the king of beasts. What impels Martius is not *pietas* towards Rome but an intensely solipsistic concern with individual honour.

Aufidius, whom Shakespeare derives largely from Plutarch's comparison between the Greek and the Roman generals, Alcibiades and Coriolanus, is far cannier than his counterpart, particularly in manipulating public opinion. What he shares is Martius's vision of heroic individualism. The parallels between the two antagonists are striking. When they meet face to face, Aufidius claims, 'We hate alike: / Not Afric owns a serpent I abhor / More than thy

---

54. Plutarch, *Life of Caius Martius Coriolanus*, trans. North, 140.

fame and envy' (1.8.2–4). Rather than patriotic motives, what goads both warriors to exert themselves in battle is resentment of the glory the other has accumulated. In fiery rhetoric, Aufidius declares that he would go so far as to transgress the laws of hospitality to wreak his revenge on Coriolanus. 'Where I find him, were it / At home ... even there / Against the hospitable canon, would I / Wash my fierce hand in 's heart' (1.10.23–26), he vows. When they meet in Aufidius's home, however, he welcomes him as a soulmate. His words are charged with latent eroticism:

> Thou has beat me out
> Twelve several times, and I have nightly since
> Dreamt of encounters twixt thyself and me—
> We have been down together in my sleep,
> Unbuckling helms, fisting each other's throat—
> And waked half dead with nothing. (4.5.120–25)

The love-hate relationship between Coriolanus and Aufidius is characteristic of the agonistic rivalry of aristocratic culture, in which noblemen sought to define themselves by excelling each other in manly pursuits.[55] Within this class, the boundary between aggressive competition and idealisation of an adversary, between antagonism and bonding, was porous. The play suggests similarities between Coriolanus and Aufidius not only with regard to their overweening ambition, and the cycle of fury, injured pride, and vengefulness in which both are caught, but also in their scorn for their fellow countrymen. As Cominius relates, after the Volscian defeat Aufidius showers his compatriots with curses for their flawed martial performance and sullenly retreats to his home town (3.1.9–11). 'I would I were a Roman, for I cannot, / Being Volsce, be that I am' (1.10.3–4), Aufidius declares in disgust, hinting at a desire to betray his country that he, unlike Coriolanus, never carries out.

While both warriors set themselves off sharply from the common people, they require the latter as a negative foil to reinforce their own worth. Coriolanus goes as far as to deny their identity as fellow Romans. 'I would they were barbarians', he rages, while his fellow peers barely succeed in restraining him from massacring the plebeians, and avers that to all intents and purposes, they are interchangeable with barbarians, 'though in Rome littered' (3.1.232–32). He spews a barrage of abuse at the plebeians, describing them as 'rats', 'curs', 'geese', 'hares', and 'minnows' (1.1.240, 159, 163, 162, and 3.1.86). In addition to

---

55. See Rebhorn, 'Crisis of the Aristocracy in *Julius Caesar*'.

the lexicon of animals, the play abounds in the idiom of disease: Martius calls the commoners 'scabs' (1.1.157), 'a herd of boils and plagues' (1.4.32), and 'measles' (3.1.76) infecting the body politic of Rome. Little enrages Martius more than the plebeians' lack of gratitude towards their betters. 'Who deserves greatness / Deserves [earns] your hate' (1.1.167–68), he fumes. While campaigning for votes, he voices a similar grievance: 'Better it is to die, better to starve, / Than crave the hire which first we do deserve' (2.3.106–7). He revolts inwardly at the thought that he has to earn what should be his just recompense. And to Aufidius he remarks bitterly, 'the drops of blood / Shed for my thankless country are requited / But with that surname' (4.5.68–70). Of the honour owed him for his services, all that remains is his title. One of the cornerstones of the culture of honour was the concept of trustworthiness. Martius pours scorn on the plebeians for their lack of fidelity: 'Trust ye? / With every minute you do change a mind' (1.1.172–73). Ironically, despite priding himself on his constancy, breaking faith is a trait he shares with them.

Coriolanus and the Renaissance Culture of Honour

In the *Nicomachean Ethics* Aristotle describes *megalopsychia*, or 'greatness of soul', as it is often rendered, as a virtue concerned predominantly with honour; if not the highest good (which Aristotle identifies as *eudaimonia* or well-being), it far exceeds pleasure or wealth as the greatest of the external goods.[56] The great-souled man scorns the goods other men strive for, such as wealth, power, good fortune, but also disregards danger and hardship. As a reward for his virtue, he expects approbation from others. However, he even regards honour with a certain nonchalant disdain. He will accept it as his just deserts, but honour 'from casual people and on trifling grounds he will utterly despise' (1124a10–11). Leading a self-determined life, the proud man possesses 'a character that suffices to itself', the source of virtue residing in himself (1125a12).

The Renaissance age of courtesy might have seen the erosion of the military role of the nobility, but the idea of honour remained of pre-eminent importance

---

56. *Megalopsychia* is discussed in book 4.3 as the mean between vanity on the one hand and undue humility or pusillanimity on the other. In the Oxford World's Classics edition, cited here, David Ross renders *megalopsychia* as 'pride'; Terence Irwin uses the term 'magnanimity', while in the Loeb edition H. Rackham uses 'greatness of soul'. See *Nicomachean Ethics*, trans. Terence Irwin, and *Nicomachean Ethics*, trans. H. Rackham. On Coriolanus as an exemplar of magnanimity, see Holloway, 'Shakespeare's Coriolanus and Aristotle's Great-Souled Man'. Also see Ghose, 'Pride'.

for the early modern gentleman. Honour was defined as a deeply individual affair, an inner sense of worth that, it was claimed, was the sole possession of the higher-born. It was seen as an irrefutable caste mark that distinguished the gentleman from the commoner; in reality, a good reputation was valued at every level of society, although the terms used, for instance 'credit' or 'good name', often differed.[57] The term 'honour' itself epitomises the tensions that mark aristocratic selfhood. On the one hand, honour refers to the esteem or glory conferred on a person; on the other, it refers to an inherent inward quality which entitled a person to these very signs of deference.[58] In truth, as Aristotle acknowledges, honour is contingent on those who bestow it rather than those who earn it. Those who crave honour are dependent on the vagaries of people's opinions, however much they might claim to despise them. Aristotle draws attention to the profound insecurity of people under the sway of the culture of honour: 'men seem to pursue honour in order that they may be assured of their merit', he writes (*EN* 1095b25–28). He points out that we seek the esteem of others to demonstrate our value to ourselves: if we are being honoured, we feel we must be worthy of esteem. Honour, Keith Thomas remarks, needed to be constantly reasserted.[59] Plutarch notes perceptively that in the case of Coriolanus, contempt for the plebeians is merely a cover for his hunger for their acclamation. 'For to take a repulse and denial of honour so inwardly to the heart, cometh of no other cause, but that he did too earnestly desire it', he observes.[60] Although Coriolanus strives to emulate the Aristotelian great-souled man, in the play, the fiction of Coriolanus's self-sufficiency fragments under pressure.

The fissures in his ideal of sovereign selfhood are encapsulated in the motif of names that runs through the play. In early modern England, the term 'name' referred crucially to one's reputation, not merely the designation by which one was known. For Coriolanus, names are wholly self-generated, and can be discarded at will. What he ignores is that appellations are always tied up with social relationships. An episode that illustrates Shakespeare's use of names to unsettle his protagonist's vision of autonomy is Coriolanus's lapse of memory after the

---

57. Keith Thomas, chap. 5, 'Honour and Reputation', in *Ends of Life*, 147–86, 163. On Renaissance honour, see Watson, *Shakespeare and the Renaissance Concept of Honour*; James, 'English Politics and the Concept of Honour'; and Peltonen, *Duel in Early Modern England*.

58. *OED*, s.v. 'honour, n.', 1.a and 2.a.

59. Thomas, 'Honour and Reputation', 157.

60. Plutarch, *Comparison of Alcibiades with Coriolanus*, trans. North, 183.

battle of Corioles (1.9). Much has been made of the fact that in a play in which Shakespeare remains close to his source, he inserts two changes to the account of this incident in Plutarch: in the *Life of Coriolanus*, the prisoner whose life Martius requests his commander, Cominius, to spare is an old, wealthy friend, whereas in the play Coriolanus speaks of a poor man; and in Plutarch, where the anecdote is embedded in the larger context of Martius's refusal of the offer by Cominius of a larger share in the spoils of war as corroboration of his lack of greed, there is no mention of Martius's moment of forgetfulness.[61]

Shakespeare's *Coriolanus* does indeed embody many virtues of the great-souled man. His disdain for personal profit and his bravery in battle are patent. What he conspicuously lacks are the constraints with which Cicero, in his own exposition of magnanimity, attempts to rein in the lust for glory that marks his contemporaries: a concern for justice and the common good, and decorum, that is, treating others with a modicum of respect and exerting oneself not to cause offence (*Off.* 1.62–64, 1.88).[62] Civility, Cicero insists, is an indispensable component of magnanimity. Indeed, 'the more exalted we are, the more humble should be our behaviour' (*Off.* 1.90), he maintains.

Paradoxically, it is at a moment when Coriolanus displays a quintessentially noble trait such as generosity, not merely to his peers but to those of low rank, that his flaws become most apparent. Coriolanus fails to grasp the import of social identity. His insistence on autonomy elides the fact that he is as bound up in a social framework as is everyone else. In the same way as one's inward sense of honour is linked to public recognition, a person's identity hinges on their relations to others, which includes the appellations by which they are known. Coriolanus's inability to name the prisoner will have fatal consequences that he is unable to avert, despite his desire to save the man. Shakespeare's changes to Plutarch heighten the poignancy of the episode. In a way, Coriolanus's momentary slip of memory epitomises his tragedy: he believes that he is fully self-determined, but control of the repercussions of his actions eludes him. For all his merits, he forgets that identity is a social affair, not something forged in the furnace of one's mind, but shaped in interaction with other human beings.

---

61. Plutarch, *Comparison of Alcibiades with Coriolanus*, trans. North, 146. For a recent discussion of the episode, see Smith, *This Is Shakespeare*, 273–82. On the significance of names in the play, also see Lucking, '"The Price of One Fair Word"'. Lucking reads the motif of names in the play as an analogue of Coriolanus's quest for absolute meanings.

62. See Kapust, 'Rethinking Rousseau's Tyranny of Orators', 188–90.

The theme of names is underscored in the exchange between Coriolanus and Aufidius after Coriolanus deserts Rome and enters the house of the Volscian general. Aufidius does not recognise him, and assails him with a volley of questions about his identity with which Shakespeare, once again, embellishes the account in Plutarch: 'Thy name?'; 'What's thy name?'; 'What is thy name?'; 'Say, what's thy name?'; 'What's thy name?'; 'I know thee not. Thy name?' (4.5.52–63). Yet again, Coriolanus fails to realize the implications of Aufidius's inability to place him without a name. Once he switches allegiances, in a bid to reinvent himself, he rejects all former designations, biding his time until he can coin a new honorific for himself. Cominius reports that he 'forbade all names. / He was a kind of nothing, titleless, / Till he had forged himself a name o'th' fire / Of burning Rome' (5.1.12–14). For Coriolanus, creating and discarding names is purely a matter of personal choice.

It is Volumnia who reminds her son that his reputation is not something he is free to shape at will. Should he conquer Rome, she warns, 'the benefit / Which thou shalt thereby reap is such a name / Whose repetition will be dogged with curses'. Chronicles will record that 'his name remains / To th'ensuing age abhorred' (5.3.142–48). His legacy in Roman history will be determined not by his self-image but by the way others regard him. The lesson is driven home by Aufidius in his own betrayal of Coriolanus. Reverting to calling him 'Martius', he denies him his cognomen, calling it a 'stol'n name' (5.6.88). He strips Coriolanus of the reputation he took a lifetime to acquire—before demolishing his honour with the accusation of being a traitor.

Breaking Faith

Keeping faith, whether with oneself or others, was regarded as the most crucial component of aristocratic honour.[63] It was grounded in the notion that, as Cicero put it, 'The foundation of justice is good faith, in other words truthfully abiding by our words and agreements' (*Off.* 1.23). For Cicero, mutual trust constitutes the bedrock of civil society. In his discussion of justice in book III of *The Governour*, Elyot distinguishes between 'faythe', which relates to 'belevynge the preceptes and promyse of God', 'credence', pertaining to promises or covenants, 'truste' in relations 'Betwene persones of equall astate or condition', and 'loyaltie' for the fidelity owed by subjects to the sovereign. All

---

63. See Thomas, *Ends of Life*, 156. On the role of *fides* in the play, see Kerrigan's important essay, 'Coriolanus Fidiussed'.

terms denote varieties of a quality that is indispensable for a gentleman: trustworthiness (189–90). The word of a gentleman was considered as equivalent to a bond; the corollary was the notion that a gentleman could not lie—a notion that was far more capacious than is adumbrated in the Augustinian definition of a lie as a statement intended to deceive.[64] The most devastating slur that could be cast on the honour of a gentleman was to hurl the allegation that one's opponent was a liar, someone guilty of a betrayal of trust or a breach of faith. 'I do hate thee / Worse than a promise-breaker', Coriolanus snarls at Aufidius, who returns the compliment, comparing him to a serpent, a symbol of treachery (1.8.1–3). Accusing Coriolanus of being a traitor or false to his allegiance triggers precisely the response of unbridled fury that his opponents intend. For his part, Coriolanus reacts by denouncing his enemies for lying. He reviles Sicinus for his 'lying tongue' (3.3.70), while he slurs Aufidius as a 'Measureless liar', appealing to the Volscian lords to 'give this cur the lie' (5.6.105, 109). By contrast, Coriolanus prides himself on his firm adherence to the truth.

What we see in the play, however, is a man who ceaselessly breaks promises and betrays his allegiance. When he goes into exile, he promises his loved ones, 'you shall / Hear from me still [always], and never of me aught / But what is like me formerly' (4.1.51–53). Nothing could be further from the truth. Not only does he sever all bonds to family and friends, but he radically reverses his loyalties. In one of his rare moments of introspection Coriolanus admits as much. When he enters Antium he reflects, 'O world, thy slippery turns!' and goes on to cite examples of dramatic swerves of fidelity among former friends and foes, only to concede, 'So with me' (4.4.12, 22). In this respect too, it appears, Coriolanus is no different from the rest of humanity.

The society portrayed in the play is one in which lying and betrayal are rampant. The citizens and tribunes lie when they indict Coriolanus of treason, the nobles betray his trust, the Volscians are disloyal to their former idol, Aufidius, whom they desert to serve Coriolanus. Faced with the threat of invasion, the Roman citizens immediately switch loyalties, turning on the tribunes in fury. Coriolanus rejects and humiliates his former mentor, Menenius. When his mother and wife appear in the Volscian camp, Coriolanus demands, 'Shall I be tempted to infringe my vow / In the same time 'tis made? I will not' (5.3.20–21)—before promptly doing so.

The theme of betrayal is ironically parodied in the cameo appearance of the Roman spying for the enemy, a minor traitor who mirrors the acts of his

---

64. Kelso, *Doctrine of the English Gentleman*, 78.

betters. The play depicts a world riddled with spies: in act 1, scene 2, the Volscians complain of spies having revealed their secret plans to their enemies, and the messenger during the battle of Corioles blames his delay on the spies whom he has had to circumvent (1.6.18–21). At the end of play, Coriolanus is betrayed by the very man who welcomed him warmly into his own home and shared his glory with him.

Against the notion of inward truth, the play sets the idea of keeping faith to others. Shakespeare's *Coriolanus* portrays a protagonist who passionately rejects the lies of civility in order to be true to himself. Montaigne remarks trenchantly that we tend to take bitter offence at the accusation of lying the more it applies to ourselves. Breaking one's word, he notes, following Cicero, 'breaks all intercourse and loosens the bonds of our polity'.[65] It is tantamount to betraying human society. Coriolanus, however, does not only betray his family, his friends, and his nation. He also breaks faith with himself, betraying the foundation on which his selfhood is built. As a Roman warrior whose article of faith it was 'that his country's dearer than himself' (1.6.72), a traitor is an object of deep revulsion; as a patrician, whose self-definition is enmeshed with the notion of keeping his word, breaking faith is a stain on his honour. Aufidius ponders the question where the source of Coriolanus's propensity towards self-destruction might lie. As a possible fatal flaw he considers pride, or defect of judgement. Finally, he muses whether the answer might lie in Martius's personality: his nature 'Not to be other than one thing, not moving / From th' casque [helmet] to the cushion' (5.1.42). Coriolanus, Aufidius reflects, clings to a unitary notion of inner truth. He refuses to adapt to the circumstances he finds himself in, and applies the same rigorous yardstick to the realm of war as to that of politics. His concept of identity is one that is unwavering and changeless, shaped by moral absolutes. Volumnia, no less relentless than her son in pursuit of her goals, rebukes her son, 'You are too absolute' (3.2.39), before reminding him that even warriors need to reconcile their exacting demands with the exigencies of a specific situation.

Coriolanus's model of selfhood does not merely imply a categorical denial of theatricality. It also entails an unrelenting belief in one's autonomy and one's own merits. When asked by a plebeian what motivated him to stand for office, the answer is a brusque 'Mine own desert' (2.3.60). His achievements, Coriolanus believes, are solely due to his own efforts. These entitle him to appropriate recompense. He emphatically repudiates the idea that we are indebted to

---

65. Montaigne, 'On giving the lie', in *The Complete Essays*, 2.18, pp. 753–58, 756–57.

a community which enables our achievement, or that we evolve in interaction with others, and are embedded in a network of social relations.[66]

The play suggests that Augustine was right: the vision of radical autonomy is a myth, grounded in fraudulence and self-deceit. The play does not, however, follow Augustine in advocating an inward turn as a solution to mendacity. Coriolanus's inner truth is a fabrication built on self-delusion. Authenticity is revealed to be an ideal riven with contradictions; pretence, the play suggests, might be an ineluctable element in social interaction. Civility may be a form of duplicity, but social life is inevitably embroiled in role-playing.

In a brief moment of insight, Coriolanus seems to realise that his adherence to sincerity is no more than a performance. When he capitulates to his mother's pleas and reneges on his vow to take revenge on Rome, he notes wryly, 'Like a dull actor now / I have forgot my part and I am out, / Even to a full disgrace' (5.3.40–42). He reconciles himself to his mother's view of human life as a matter of playing divergent roles, and acknowledges that his own performance is badly flawed. An addition that Shakespeare makes to his source is to insert Coriolanus's comment that 'the gods look down, and this unnatural scene / They laugh at' (184–85). The mocking, metatheatrical remark, which gestures at the *theatrum mundi* topos, intimates a fleeting awareness on his part that theatricality is an inevitable part of human interaction.[67]

A World Elsewhere

In a play suffused with animal imagery, one set of images brilliantly captures the essence of the protagonist. Butterflies weave their way through the language of the play. Young Martius is described as chasing a butterfly and in his rage, tearing it to pieces (1.3.56–61). Cominius reiterates the image of boys pursuing butterflies (4.6.93), and Menenius uses the comparison between grubs and butterflies to point up the change in Coriolanus. He juxtaposes this image with that of a dragon: 'This Martius is grown from man to dragon' (5.4.10–12). A dragon is how Coriolanus would like to see himself: 'I go alone / Like to a lonely dragon' (4.1.29–30), and how Aufidius sees him when he describes how he 'Fights dragon-like' (4.7.23). The image of butterflies hints at a

---

66. In the twentieth century, the term 'possessive individualism' was coined by C. B. Macpherson for precisely the same phenomenon. See Macpherson, *Political Theory of Possessive Individualism*.

67. Also see Righter, *Shakespeare and the Idea of the Play*, 171.

world elsewhere, away from the harsh world of the play, a world of grace, beauty, poetry, and imaginative freedom. It also gestures towards a paradigm of mutating and multifarious identity quite different from the inflexible notion Coriolanus espouses. By contrast, the image of a dragon, always a solitary creature, figures the singularity and rigorous antisociality of the protagonist. In subtle deviations from his source, Shakespeare takes care to highlight the isolation of his protagonist. In Plutarch, Martius enters Corioles with a tiny handful of men; in Shakespeare, 'Alone he entered / The mortal gate of th' city' (2.2.7–8), as Cominius marvels. In Plutarch, he goes into exile with a few friends; in Shakespeare, alone (4.1).[68] The image of a dragon also chimes with a certain archaic quality in Coriolanus's self-conception, his sense of belatedness as the representative of an ideology that was no longer relevant. Perhaps most significantly, dragons are mythical creatures, entirely imaginary constructs. Coriolanus's inexorable vision of a unified, authentic identity is rooted in a fiction. Repudiating the world of human bonds, Coriolanus chooses a fabricated reality, one he has created himself.

68. Plutarch, *Life of Caius Martius Coriolanus*, trans. North, 144, 159.

4

Sejanus and the Degradation of Civility

BEN JONSON'S *Sejanus* explores the dark sides of civility: duplicity, social surveillance, and opportunism. It depicts a society eviscerated of a common purpose, rife with self-serving and mutual suspicion, in which all forms of debate are stifled. The play offers a terrifying vision of the civil fabric in shreds. Jonson's dissection of a state under tyrannical rule is, however, far more sweeping in its implications. Jonson sets out to demonstrate that when civil society falls apart, repressive regimes thrive.

In this play, typical elements of civility are perverted into instruments that undermine, rather than foster, social bonds. Decorum, or prudence, its close cousin, correlates with expediency to further personal gain or alternatively, reasons of state. Winning the approval of others takes the form of pervasive flattery. Dissimulation is used purely for the purposes of self-advancement or as a tool of power. Observation of others is debased into a culture of surveillance and mutual spying. Mocked in early modern comedy as a feature of social climbing in which all members of society are scrutinizing one another's performances and attempting to read status signifiers, in this tragedy, monitoring others mutates into a strategy of power to sow distrust and hollow out any sense of community.

The late sixteenth and early seventeenth centuries saw a spate of writings concerned with the management of the passions, intense scrutiny of the self and others, and dissimulation. These strategies are recommended in political life as well as civil society. The texts surveyed in this chapter include writings by political theorists, a treatise on the passions, and an exemplary if little known court manual. In none of them is accommodation to others promoted to ease living together in the same society, nor is social play-acting proposed

FIGURE 8. Paul van Somer I, *Portrait of Francis Bacon* (1617). Lazienki Palace, Warsaw.

to feign mutual respect rather than sycophancy. Careful observation of others as well as self-scrutiny, recommended by Cicero to enable us to avoid inappropriate behaviour to the extent possible (*Off*. 1.146), is endorsed solely as a means of political or social control. In these texts, the idea that gauging the effect of our words and gestures on our interlocutors might help us adapt our behaviour in order to signal regard for others is dismissed as irrelevant.

The atmosphere of secrecy and uncertainty in fin-de-siècle England, a correlative of the climate of religious persecution and state paranoia, is captured in a plethora of late Elizabethan and Jacobean tragedies. Suppression of one's thoughts and feelings was not simply a means of rising in the world. An emphasis on self-preservation gradually takes priority over the self-promotion that was such a crucial feature of books such as Castiglione's *Courtier*. A number of texts from this period reveal remarkable parallels to the claustrophobic world of plays such as *Sejanus* and *Hamlet*, permeated by secrecy, rumour, and eavesdropping.

The Culture of Observation and Dissimulation

One of the claims Norbert Elias puts forward in his *State Formation and Civilization* is that the tendency towards self-observation and observation of others in the absolutist courts of Europe was the result of a more disengaged relation to oneself and others.[1] He attributes this development to the new exigencies in elite circles, in which a class of arrivistes competed with old aristocracy for positions of power and influence which were increasingly concentrated on the court. While conceding that Elias has indeed identified a movement that was prevalent in court society, other scholars have enriched his analysis considerably and expanded the scope of his survey to include larger segments of society. Katharine Eisaman Maus, Elizabeth Hanson, and John Jeffries Martin point out that while a preoccupation with a hidden self was not an invention of the Renaissance, the necessity for heightened self-monitoring and suspicion of others was a result of intense insecurity and political oppression of those of oppositional views, in particular of dissenting faiths.[2] The imperative to hide one's beliefs was such a widespread phenomenon throughout early modern Europe that Perez Zagorin has dubbed the period 'the age of dissimulation'.[3]

In a study of the theme of dissimulation in a range of texts, including courtesy manuals and political treatises, Jon Snyder contends that the sixteenth and seventeenth centuries saw the emergence of dissimulation as the main component of prudence.[4] In classical thought, prudence is the faculty of

---

1. Elias, *Civilizing Process*, 475–92.
2. See Maus, *Inwardness and Theater in the English Renaissance*; Hanson, *Discovering the Subject in Renaissance England*; and Martin, *Myths of Renaissance Individualism*.
3. Zagorin, *Ways of Lying*, 905.
4. Snyder, *Dissimulation and the Culture of Secrecy*. I am indebted to his work in the following.

judgement which enables us to act in a fitting manner. The facility to determine the most appropriate action to take in the social and political arena is informed by the same set of rules that applies in the case of rhetoric or art—to adopt the most suitable means in the given circumstances. Aristotle stresses the fact that prudence or practical wisdom (*phronesis*), the knowledge of how to act in a manner befitting specific situations, is indispensable in leading a virtuous life. Practical wisdom, or right reason, is a necessary condition of virtue; conversely, all virtues involve the operation of practical wisdom (*EN* 1144b). For Cicero, practical wisdom is closely linked to decorum (*Off.* 1.143). In the course of the sixteenth century, however, prudence increasingly became congruent with expediency (or 'policy', as early moderns termed it). In Bacon's discussion of prudence, he distinguishes between wisdom in general and wisdom in promoting one's own fortune.[5] Prudence, he notes dispassionately, is the science of rising in life. For Jesuit scholar Baltasar Gracián, whose *Pocket Oracle and Art of Prudence* (1647) became one of the most popular guidebooks to behaviour in the seventeenth century, 'The most practical kind of wisdom is dissimulation'.[6]

Snyder traces the influence of an amalgam of movements such as Pyrrhonic scepticism, Neostoicism, and Tacitism on the texts of civil and political discourse that appeared in increasing numbers in this period, many of them reason-of-state treatises. The move towards an endorsement of dissimulation, however hedged about with reservations, signals a shift in late humanism from Ciceronianism to Tacitism, one which included a replacement of Cicero with Seneca as the most important classical sage and that precipitated a change in literary style from Cicero's eloquence to Senecan terseness.[7] Cicero's elaborate periodic style was superseded by a vogue for the aphoristic and paradoxical brevity that characterised the prose style of Seneca and which was emulated by writers such as Lipsius, Bacon, and Montaigne. More importantly, Tacitism involved an absorption with the work of the Roman historian Tacitus and his

---

5. See Bacon, 'On Civil Knowledge', *The Advancement of Learning* book 2, in *Major Works*, 265–68. On prudence in the Renaissance, see Kahn, *Rhetoric, Prudence, and Skepticism in the Renaissance*.

6. Gracián, *Pocket Oracle and Art of Prudence*, no. 98, p. 36.

7. On the conjunction of Stoicism, Tacitism, and scepticism in late humanism, see Tuck, *Philosophy and Government*, 31–64. On the influence of Stoicism and Tacitism in seventeenth-century England, see Salmon, 'Stoicism and Roman Example'; Smuts, 'Court-Centred Politics'; and Worden, 'Ben Jonson among the Historians'. Also see Burke, 'Tacitism', and 'Tacitism, Scepticism, and Reason of State'.

coolly analytical account of imperial rule from Tiberius to Domitian. Tacitus's scrutiny of the hidden motivation impelling the key players in Roman power politics was regarded as a more palatable version of Machiavellian theory, in part because his work was imbued with classical prestige, and in part because his writings steered clear of an explicit recommendation of political amorality. In oppositional circles in England which espoused republicanism, he was read as a critic of imperial rule. In Lipsius's influential reading, Tacitus was seen as espousing Stoicism and was linked to Seneca. In the late sixteenth century, the surge in interest in Tacitism and Stoicism was associated with a widespread scepticism and disillusionment with civic humanism, in which Ciceronian principles had been an article of faith. An age of political turmoil and virulent religious strife, infiltrated by duplicity and treachery, saw a rapid erosion of belief in the values of Ciceronian republicanism. In this regard, the conditions in which Stoicism had flourished in the early Roman Empire and those that saw its resurrection in the late sixteenth century were remarkably similar.

The saying *qui nescit dissimulare nescit regnare* (he who does not know how to dissimulate does not know how to rule), attributed to Louis XI, became axiomatic, while the strategies of self-examination and vigilant scrutiny of others were advocated as mandatory for life in the public sphere. Actors in social interaction not only were engaged in a ceaseless round of performance, but doubled as spectators, of others as well as of themselves. In matters of state policy, dissimulation was increasingly justified on the grounds of reason of state, the idea that in the interests of the state, any means were justified. While hard-boiled theorists like Machiavelli and Guicciardini, his friend and fellow thinker who originally coined the expression 'reasons of states' (*ragioni degli stati*), made no distinction between simulation and dissimulation, in his *Della Ragion di Stato* (1589), Counter-Reformation thinker Giovanni Botero argued strenuously for a clear divide between immoral policies such as flagrant falsehood and those acceptable for a Christian ruler, which included concealing one's motives and dissimulating one's intentions if necessary for the well-being of the polity. Dissimulation of the truth was tantamount to a form of prudence; the prince was counselled to rein in his passions and hide his true feelings. The key biblical verse used to sanction this position was Christ's injunction to the Apostles to 'be therefore wise as serpents, and harmless as doves' (Matt. 10:16, KJV). In a world in which guile and deceit reigned, it was advisable to temper innocence with prudence. It is true that in St Augustine's exhortations on the sinfulness of all forms of lying, withholding the truth was excepted. As he puts it in *Against Lying*, 'it is not a lie when truth is passed over in silence, but when falsehood is brought forth in speech'.[8] St Aquinas even allows that 'one may, however, prudently mask the truth'.[9]

This position was not restricted to Catholic thinkers. The leading Puritan cleric William Perkins stresses that 'Wise and godly silence is as excellent a vertue as holy speech'. He recommends secrecy to both the individual and the Magistrate, and urges, 'That which thou wouldest not have knowen, tell no man'.[10] Similarly, in a treatise entitled *The Dove and the Serpent* (1614), the Anglican divine Daniel Tuvill sanctions secrecy and dissimulation in public affairs, taking care to qualify his remarks by distinguishing between courts abroad, riddled with feigning and flattery, and the 'honest and religious' courtiers of England. He regards the few exceptions as bad apples corrupted by the teachings of Machiavelli.[11] Increasingly, dissimulation was regarded as the exemplary prudent course of action in both civil and political life.

Neostoicism and Tacitism

The ramifications of two important, related currents in this period, Neostoicism and Tacitism, are discernible in courtesy literature as well as drama.[12] Both movements were launched into broad debate by the Flemish humanist scholar Justus Lipsius, whose first edition of Tacitus's *Opera omnia* appeared in 1574. His *De constantia* (1584) attempts to meld Stoicism with Christian thought and provides the cornerstone for the Neostoicist movement, while his late years were devoted to editing Seneca. Lipsius's achievement was to recuperate the Stoic notion of constancy and highlight its affinities with the Augustinian ideal of a unitary self, which corresponded to the uniformity of the divine. In this way Lipsius and other Neostoic thinkers deflected attention from Augustine's corrosive attacks on Stoicism as pandering to human pride and the delusion of self-sufficiency.[13] In the Neostoic reading, constancy is a doctrine of fortitude and stability, not, as with Cicero, a matter of a steadfast

---

8. Augustine, *Against Lying*, 152. Also see his *Lying*, 85–86.

9. Aquinas, *Summa theologiae*, 2a2ae, q. 110, a. 3.

10. Perkins, *Direction for the Government*, D8r, E1v, E2v.

11. T[uvill], *Dove and the Serpent*, E3v–4r. The treatise largely regurgitates Francis Bacon's ideas in *The Advancement of Learning*.

12. A brilliant discussion of the influence of Tacitean thought on Shakespeare is Rhodri Lewis's *Hamlet and the Vision of Darkness*.

13. See Augustine, *City of God*, vol. 6, bk. 19.4.

adherence to our mutual obligations and consistency in playing the appropriate roles in life.[14]

Constancy, particularly in its Senecan variety, implied the repression of emotion. This, of course, provided the template for dissimulation. What is of interest here is Lipsius's work on political doctrine, *Politicorum sive civilis doctrinae libri sex*, which appeared in 1589 and was widely translated. Reprinted over fifty times between 1589 and 1760, it became one of the foundational works of political theory in the era.[15]

Lipsius begins his book in classic Ciceronian manner, asserting that 'I can not be induced to beleeve, anie can possibly be a good Citizen, except likewise he be an honest man'.[16] The *honestum* and the *utile* are indissolubly bound up together: acting virtuously is the most expedient course of action to adopt. He announces that his discussion will focus on virtue and prudence in civil life, and presents piety as the principal element in virtue. From book 2 onwards, the focus is on the sovereign and the importance of prudence in government. In Lipsius's conservative brand of Stoicism, which lays emphasis on political quietism rather than on the concept of *oikeiosis*, the notion that our interests are always tied up with the common good, it is in the interests of the commonwealth to allow only one state religion (book 4.2–4). Cicero is increasingly displaced by Tacitus; the text is peppered with citations from the *Annals*. As Victoria Kahn points out, Tacitus is merely a screen for the thinker whose precepts shadow the book: Machiavelli.[17]

In book 4 Lipsius's refutation of Cicero is most apparent. In chapter 13 Lipsius engages with the question: is deception an acceptable strategy for the ruler? Much as he would prefer to deny it, he claims, he has little choice in the matter: we live in a fallen world, not in the pristine Republic of Plato. Who are the people among whom we live? '[C]raftie and malicious persons, who seem *to be made of fraude, deceipt, and lying*' (Q1r). In these circumstance, he

---

14. See Miles, *Shakespeare and the Constant Romans*, 63–82.

15. On Lipsius, see the wealth of information in Waszink, 'Introduction'. Also see Oestreich, 'Main Political Work of Lipsius'; Snyder, *Dissimulation and the Culture of Secrecy*, 124–29; Brooke, *Philosophic Pride*, 12–36; and Lagrée, 'Justus Lipsius and Neostoicism'. On the reception of Lipsius in England, see Salmon, 'Stoicism and Roman Example', and McCrea, *Constant Minds*.

16. Lipsius, *Six Bookes of Politickes or Civil Doctrine*, B1r, emphasis original.

17. Kahn, 'Machiavelli's Afterlife and Reputation to the Eighteenth Century', 248–49. For Christopher Brooke, the text is both 'a critical response to as well as a partial appropriation of Machiavellian political theory'. See his *Philosophic Pride*, 27. Martin Dzelzainis states that Tacitus is cited 547 times. See his 'Bacon's "Of Simulation and Dissimulation"', 331.

argues for what he terms 'mixed prudence' (P8v), and draws an analogy to wine adulterated with water: 'a fewe drops of deceit' (Q1v) do not dilute the prudent policy substantially. Dissembling for a good end is acceptable; if exercised for the public good and the benefit of the prince, strategies usually regarded as unethical are transposed into honourable policies. Sometimes dissimulation is a virtue.

In two pages, Lipsius contrives to strew four references to foxes and lions, glossing his sources as Persius, Erasmus, and Plutarch. Only at the end of this section does he show his hand, urging the judicious reader to forbear to 'strictly condemne the Italian *fault-writer*, (who poore soule is layde at of all hands)'. In William Jones' translation, which, while largely faithful to the original, omits Lipsius's preface in which he acknowledges Machiavelli's sharp intellect only to distance himself from his views, the only explicit mention of the diabolical Italian is in the marginal note, which says, 'Some kind of persons rage too much against Machiavelli' (Q1v). Lipsius's adroit manoeuvring failed to prevent his work from being placed on the 1590 Index. Ever the Machiavellian, he came to an agreement with Vatican censors to drop the passage in order to have the book removed from the Index. In the third edition of 1596, the lines disappeared. Nonetheless, the substance of his argument remained unchanged.[18]

Having established that subterfuge put into practice for the good of the Prince and the state is legitimate, Lipsius proceeds to set out a graduation of deceit. 'Light deceipt' he correlates with distrust and dissimulation, 'middle deceipt' refers to the use of corruption and guile, and 'great deceipt' denotes treachery and injustice. 'The first sort of deceipt I persuade, the second I tollerate, and the third I condemne' (Q2r), he declares. The Prince is warned to believe nothing and no one and to be constantly on his guard. At court he is surrounded by dissemblers and liars. No one can be trusted; as for friendship, 'in *Princes pallaces* this word friendship is but vaine, and a thing of nothing' (Q2v). At the same time, Lipsius avers, the prince must himself engage in dissimulation. Not only must he conceal his suspicions about his courtiers; he must enact a charade of trust precisely to those he distrusts most. In support Lipsius adduces not only the well-worn adage about a ruler who does not know how to dissemble as unfit to rule, but also an endlessly cited passage from Tacitus: 'Tiberius prized none of what he considered to be his virtues as highly as he did his ability to dissemble'.[19]

---

18. See Waszink, 'Introduction', 165–89; Brooke, *Philosophic Pride*, 19–20.
19. Tacitus, *The Annals*, 4.71.

The Prince, Lipsius sums up, must be adept at play-acting. The ruler is encouraged to simultaneously veil his true thoughts and project the impression of a frank and open personality. Using theatrical imagery, Lipsius addresses the Prince directly and urges him to 'play thy part comely, and with a good grace, *for they which use to dissemble but a little, and in those things which are not seene and discovered, do appeare gratious*' (Q3v). Somewhat disingenuously, Lipsius adapts Aristotle's description of the social virtue of truthfulness, the mean between boasting and ironically understating one's qualities (*EN* 4.7), to his own ends. Aristotle lauds ironic understatement as being far preferable to boasting. Lipsius draws on Aristotle's allusion to *eirôneia* (or 'dissimulation') to make a slightly different point: dissimulation is effective only if it is not detected. 'Learne this once in all kind of dissimulation', he instructs the reader, '*Deceipt is no deceipt, if it be not cunningly* [skilfully] *handled*' (Q3v).

As regards the second degree of deceit, which includes bribery and lying, he refers to Cicero in support of the former and St Augustine, who grants that some lies are less culpable than others, in support of the latter. Once again, the decisive factor is whether these acts serve to benefit the state. The third mode of deceit, treachery and breaking oaths, includes dubious deeds at which Lipsius only hints. With reluctance, he concedes that they might be permissible in certain circumstances such as self-defence. The critical element is necessity, he asserts, rehearsing Machiavelli's key rule. The Prince, he argues, 'should alwaies follow that which were most necessarie to be effected, not that which is honest in speech' (R2r). Lipsius ends book 4 on a sombre note, admonishing the rulers of Europe to fear God's will, and suggesting that the troubles that afflict the continent might be divine retribution for corrupt and unjust policies.

Baconian Civil Philosophy

Lipsius insists that his advocacy of 'mixed prudence', or prudence leavened with deceit, is restricted to the prince, not a recommendation for private individuals (Q3r). Nonetheless, his ideas were applied to civil society. One of the thinkers for whom his ideas were formative was Francis Bacon. In book II of *The Advancement of Learning* (1605), Bacon rounds off his discussion of philosophy with a section devoted to 'civil knowledge'.[20] This he subdivides into three parts, 'Conversation', which treats social intercourse, 'Negotiation', which

---

20. Bacon, *Major Works*, 265–88. I am indebted to Vickers's notes throughout.

refers to dealings with other people and public life, and 'Government' or state policy, respectively.

First he briskly treats social behaviour or manners. Social rhetoric is a critical part of rhetoric, he points out, and advises the reader not to ignore the impact of gestures and deportment. Inappropriate facial expression can undermine one's speech, however eloquent one's words. At the same time, he warns against posturing, which creates the impression of transposing the manners of the stage into real life. He has little time for those who lavish too much attention on social accomplishments or are too absorbed with *puntos* (formalities) and etiquette, or with accommodating every whim of others. A fastidious obsession with courtesy is an impediment to real civic engagement. Conversely, those who have gained a reputation for deeds rather than merely pleasing manners have no need to exert themselves to comply with every fashion. He concludes by drawing an analogy between manners and apparel. Behaviour, he states, is like 'a garment of the mind'. Accordingly, 'it ought to be made in fashion; it ought not to be too curious [fastidious]' (266). One's comportment ought to be suited to the times, and display one's personality in the best light while concealing one's weaknesses, but not be too precious, or restrict one's scope of action. For Bacon, manners are an attractive veneer, but are not of substance. He rehearses this advice elsewhere, in the essay 'Of Ceremonies and Respects' and, very briefly, in his 'Short Notes for Civil Conversation'.[21]

Bacon refers the reader to the extensive courtesy literature in circulation, wherein these issues have been 'elegantly handled' (266). Where the heart of his argument lies is in adumbrating a science of how to rise in life, a field of study that has not received the rigorous attention that is its due, he claims. 'For there is a wisdom of counsel, and again there is a wisdom of pressing a man's own fortune' (271), he asserts. While the former is fully accepted, the latter discipline has been largely neglected in scholarship, a desideratum that he sets out to redress. Each man is the architect of their own fortune, Bacon points out, drawing on a well-known classical adage. He allows that knowledge of how to forge a career for oneself might not be the ultimate end of human life. Nonetheless, it is a subject deserving of dispassionate attention. His cool, clinical approach is clearly indebted to Machiavelli, whom he frequently cites and to whom he famously pays tribute earlier in the book: 'So that we are much beholden to Machiavel and others, that write what men do

---

21. Bacon, *Major Works*, 441–42, and *Works of Francis Bacon*, vol. 7, 109–11, respectively.

and not what they ought to do. For it is not possible to join serpentine wisdom with the columbine innocency, except men know exactly all the conditions of the serpent; his baseness and going upon his belly, his volubility [gliding motion] and lubricity, his envy and sting, and the rest; that is, all forms and natures of evil' (254). Referencing Matthew 10:16, Bacon aims to apply a scientific approach to prudence, suggesting that moral axioms have little effect unless they are buttressed by rational analysis. His avowed aim is to demonstrate the inductive method in action, for 'it hath much greater life for practice when the discourse attendeth upon the example, than when the example attendeth upon the discourse' (271). A scientific approach would imply drawing general principles from specific examples, not developing a theory first and then adducing proof to support it. It is the former method, he states admiringly, at which Machiavelli excels, particularly in his *Discorsi*.

The first precept, Bacon announces, is to obtain information about the hidden operation of other people's minds. Attentive observation would allow one to penetrate the facade of outward appearances. The reader is enjoined to distrust the apparent truth of a person, be it their appearance, their actions, or their words, and instead to scrupulously scrutinize 'the private and subtle motions and labours of the countenance and gesture' (274). The goal is to ferret out the secret passions that motivate one's object of study. A particularly useful method is to use counter-dissimulation to unearth the truth, Bacon states, citing the Spanish proverb, 'Tell a lie and find a truth' (275).

The second precept is to attentively observe oneself, and know one's own strengths and weaknesses. In addition, it is advisable to set oneself out to advantage, displaying one's virtues and concealing one's defects. Echoing Machiavelli, Bacon insists that the key skill is to be able to adapt to circumstances: 'nothing is more politic [expedient] than to make the wheels of our mind concentric and voluble [capable of revolving] with the wheels of fortune', he contends (280).

Bacon sums up by conceding that the Politic man that he has described is an ideal rather than a reality. Thus he sees himself as continuing in the tradition of Cicero's *Orator*, Machiavelli's *Prince*, or Castiglione's *Courtier* (284). What follows is a somewhat perfunctory moralistic rebuttal of Machiavelli's claim that the impression of virtue alone suffices. Instead, as Bacon piously reminds the reader, the first priority should be to seek the kingdom of God (Matt. 6:33).

In an essay entitled 'Of Simulation and Dissimulation', Bacon develops some of the ideas he has set out in *The Advancement of Learning*, focusing on the issue of deceit.[22] A man of peerless discernment, he admits, knows when to tell the truth, when to partially tell the truth, when not to reveal the truth, and to whom. But for lesser mortals, it is advisable to resort to secrecy and dissimulation. He distinguishes between secrecy, when one conceals one's thoughts, dissimulation, when one hides one's truth by means of feigning, and simulation, when one pretends to be what one is not.

Secrecy is much to be recommended, since it enables one to gain access to useful information: people who are believed to be discreet are frequently chosen for confidences. Bacon points to the dangers of betraying one's thoughts in one's facial expression; as he admits, 'he that will be secret must be a dissembler in some degree' (350). Secrecy inevitably leads to dissimulation. In addition, people do not let others maintain an impartial position, but beleaguer them to take a stance. Simulation, however, is less commendable. Those who pretend to be otherwise than they are tend to make a habit of play-acting in every situation. From a prudential viewpoint, it is simply too dangerous.

The advantages of employing these three techniques are undeniable. They allow one to take one's adversaries by surprise, depriving them of the time to plot their counter-strategies. Second, they permit one to change one's opinion without losing face. Third, they enable one to delve into the minds of others. Bacon reiterates the maxim he cites in *The Advancement of Learning* about using lies to smoke out the truth. He grants that there is a price to be paid for these strategies of surveillance. These are roundabout means for achieving one's aims; they might deprive one of potential allies, who are left in doubt about one's views. Mendacity forfeits trust. The ceaseless practice of duplicity leaves one isolated, 'and makes a man walk almost alone to his own ends' (351).

Nonetheless, Bacon winds up by commending all three mutations of dissembling, although in varying degrees. Secrecy should be cultivated as a habit, dissimulation, when useful, and simulation, when necessary. In a piece of rhetorical legerdemain, Bacon's chief counsel is to 'have openness in fame and opinion' (351). Precisely when the reader might expect a resounding endorsement of honesty, he qualifies his remarks by calling for a facade of frankness as the shrewdest public relations ploy in the toolbox. For all the reservations about Machiavellian 'evil arts' articulated in *Advancement* (284), he follows the Florentine to the letter. Feigned honesty is the best policy, he maintains.

---

22. Bacon, *Major Works*, 349–51. See Dzelzainis, 'Bacon's "Of Simulation and Dissimulation"' for a somewhat different reading.

Thomas Wright's *The Passions of the Mind*

Not only in works on civility and political philosophy was the importance of monitoring the self and others recommended. Botero's thought had a decisive influence on Jesuit scholar Thomas Wright, whose *Passions of the Mind* (1604) was the definitive treatment of the emotions in early modern England published in English.[23] Wright's work of moral philosophy is written in the *nosce te ipsum* ('know thyself') tradition, arguing that the goal of knowledge of the passions is self-awareness (1.1.172–81). Only by knowing the passions to which one was susceptible would one be able to discipline them and harness them for an ethical life. His view of the passions is shaped by Thomistic thought, which, based on Aristotle, emphasizes the positive uses to which emotions could be put.

At the same time, he is keenly aware of the pragmatic value of bridling the affects in social intercourse. By exercising self-restraint, the gentleman 'winneth a gracious carriage of himself and rendereth his conversation most grateful [agreeable] to men' (147–48), acquiring a reputation for refined deportment and pleasing manners. Unlike Botero, at no point does Wright explicitly endorse dissimulation. Nevertheless, he maintains, it is important to use prudence in our engagement with the passions. He distinguishes between the use of 'prudence' and 'policy' (3.3.12–17), or between the management of the self and interaction with others. He stresses that it is imperative 'to conceal as much as thou canst thy inclinations, or that passion thou knowest thyself most prone to follow, and this for two causes: first, for credit; secondarily, for many inconveniences that may thereby ensue' (3.3.63–67). Revealing one's weaknesses would be detrimental to one's standing. Furthermore, he contends, it was not wise to lay open to the world what affects one might be swayed by, knowledge which would be seized upon by one's enemies for their own ends.

But how was one to conceal one's passions? Wright admits this is a difficult question. One way to do so would be to repress one's feelings in public, where they would be observed by others. This would gain one the reputation of being a person in command of their affects. Another method would be 'to dispraise before others that passion thou art most addicted unto, for by so doing thou shalst make men believe indeed that thou abhorrest much that vice' (3.3.146–49).

---

23. Wright, *Passions of the Mind in General*. References are to book, chapter, and lines. On Wright, see Sullivan, 'Passions of Thomas Wright'.

He proposes that one feign a distance to precisely the feelings by which one is most moved. One might, if so inclined, label such conduct dissimulation.

As regards 'policy in passion', he lists a number of rules for judicious social interaction. One of them is to pretend to share the preferences and tastes of one's superior and associate: 'if thou wilt please thy master or friend thou must apparel thyself with his affections, and love where he loveth and hate where he hateth' (3.4.39–42). This, he claims, is a form not of flattery but of charity, and fosters love of humankind. Crucial is to uncover what passions others are moved by. Wright devotes a section of book 4 to helping the reader in this task. He concedes that 'we cannot enter into a man's heart and view the passions or inclinations which there reside and lie hidden' (4.1A.29–31). We need to use our powers of observation to unearth this vital information, focusing on men's words and their deeds.

It is not sufficient to simply draw conclusions about what really motivates people from what they articulate in speech. People are adept at hiding their true thoughts and inclinations. Hence, he advises, 'we must sound out a little further, and wade something deeper into a certain secret survey of men's speeches to see if we may discover some more hidden passions; and this either in the manner or matter of speech' (4.1A.76–80). What follows is an early modern digest of psychology, in which Wright describes a range of ways in which people reveal their inward feelings in speech and gesture. He discusses people who talk volubly or slowly or affectedly, or those who tend to entertain their peers with jests at the expense of others. He strongly recommends reticence, 'because in conversation, when men either would conceal their own affectations or discover others', prudence and policy require a space of silence' (4.1A.132–35). Interlocutors who are overly argumentative or captious, or conversely, who are lavish with compliments, are dissected in the same methodical manner as those who are indiscreet. He warns against people who inveigle their way into one's confidence by allegedly sharing secrets, a technique that in reality they employ with a great many people, or who pretend friendship only the better to betray one. Similarly, he notes, there are some who poison one's mind against one's companions, claiming they have revealed one's secrets, only to lure one to turn informer oneself.

The impression that emerges from Wright's text is that the public sphere is fraught with danger, awash with betrayal and backstabbing, in which the best policy would be to seal one's lips on all occasions. Although he acknowledges that everyone has a friend to whom they can entrust their secrets, in recounting an anecdote about three students who betray their promises of loyalty, he breaks into the first person to conclude dolefully, 'Who that knew these men would scarcely have believed that any such errors could by them have been committed; but by this experience ... I got occasion to suspect falsehood in fellowship, to try ere I trusted, and finally, thought none more secret than a man to himself' (4.1B.230–35).

The treatise continues with a catalogue of external actions that reveal the truth about one's fellow beings by analogy to the gestures of stage players. People inadvertently uncover their real feelings and intentions while indulging in apparently innocuous activities such as playing, feasting, and drinking, and in their deportment, in what they wear, and in how they express themselves in writing.[24] Painstaking observation of the behaviour of others enables one to identify parallels in one's own conduct and allows one to know oneself better. Detecting the inner workings of the minds of one's peers is also a precondition for being able to cater to their passions and inclinations. The whiff of a society obsessed with mutual surveillance filters through the carefully maintained scholarly facade of the work. It points to the cloud of suspicion that in Elizabethan England surrounded a Catholic priest like Thomas Wright at all times, despite his strident loyalism (the book was probably written while he was under house arrest).[25] This oppressive mood is captured in Ben Jonson's *Sejanus*, written in 1602–3.[26] Wright has been named as the priest who guided Jonson in his conversion to the Catholic faith, and whom Jonson offered to bring before the Privy Council to assist in the investigations into the Gunpowder Plot.[27] A commendatory poem by the dramatist, albeit somewhat desultory, graces the treatise, as does one by H. H. (probably Hugh Holland, a recusant poet and member of Jonson's clique), who also extolled Jonson's play when it appeared in 1605.

Lorenzo Ducci's *Ars Aulica or The Courtiers Arte*

A treatise that distils the brew of scepticism and Tacitism swilling around fin-de-siècle Europe is Lorenzo Ducci's breviary for the calculating courtier, *Arte aulica* (1601), Englished by Edward Blount in 1607 and published under

---

24. He also includes a cryptic remark, as elsewhere in the treatise, about the passions involved in censoring books (4.2.588ff.). Possibly the first edition of the book (1601) was a censored version of the expanded 1604 version. See Newbold, 'Textual Introduction' to Wright, *Passions of the Mind in General*, 56–60.

25. See Newbold, 'General Introduction' to Wright, *Passions of the Mind in General*, 12.

26. On the early modern culture of espionage, see Archer, *Sovereignty and Intelligence*.

27. See Stroud, 'Ben Jonson and Father Thomas Wright'; Teague, 'Jonson and the Gunpowder Plot'; and Donaldson, *Ben Jonson*, 138–43, 223.

the title *Ars Aulica or The Courtiers Arte*. Ducci, a private secretary in the employ of Cardinal Gian Franceso Biandrate di San Giorgio Aldobrandini at the papal court of Ferrara, exemplifies the increasingly marginal role the courtier played in the formulation of state policy.[28] There is little in the text that evokes Castiglione's idealistic views about the courtier guiding the Prince towards the path of virtue. Instead, as Ducci states with unvarnished pragmatism, what motivates the courtier is self-interest. As he announces at the beginning of the manual, 'the end for which the *Courtier* voluntarilie submits his necke unto the yoke of servitude, is his owne profit'.[29] To achieve this end, he is constrained to direct his energies towards the profit of the Prince. Sweeping aside any academic distinction between simulation and dissimulation, Ducci's text is soaked in references to Tacitus, in particular the history of Sejanus. Far from pontificating about court corruption, Ducci holds up the erstwhile court favourite as a role model to emulate, while the aspects of his fall serve as a cautionary tale about the pitfalls to be avoided in climbing the greasy pole.

Ducci's treatise deliberately seems to highlight the distance travelled by Renaissance courtiers since the Arcadian gathering in Urbino. A case in point is his conspicuous omission of any reference to *sprezzatura* or *grazia*. '[T]he favour of the Court', Ducci writes pointedly, 'is not gotten by the opinion of vertue, but by the use and exercise thereof to the Princes profit' (E8r). It is not self-display and elegant performance that matter, but gratifying every desire of the Prince. 'This chiefly consisteth in manifesting an exact diligence with a desire to spare no paines fully to give him satisfaction', he explains (E8r–v). Nonetheless, in a glance at Castiglione's *Courtier*, he warns us to take care 'to shunne a most dangerous rocke, that is, *curious and open affectation*' (E8v).[30] The danger of trying too hard to please is that it plants a suspicion in the Prince's mind that in his demonstrations of love, the courtier might be dissimulating. In addition, he would become a laughing stock to other courtiers for being 'like an inamoured lover in the service of his Lord' (E9r). Like Lipsius, Ducci stresses that dissimulation should be dissimulated. Despite the echoes of the Ovidian dictum, *ars est celare artum* ('it is art to conceal art'), from which Castiglione derives his notion of *sprezzatura*, the divergences from

---

28. On Ducci, see Snyder, *Dissimulation and the Culture of Secrecy*, 90–97, and Anglo, 'Systematic Immorality', 607–14. On Blount, see Taylor, 'Blount [Blunt] Edward'.

29. Ducci, *Ars Aulica or The Courtiers Arte*, B5r.

30. Castiglione famously advises the courtier to 'avoid affectation in every way possible as though it were some very rough and dangerous reef' (*Courtier*, 1.26).

the *Cortegiano* are striking. From a vade mecum on graceful behaviour, however suffused with ambiguity, the courtier's manual has atrophied into a set of guidelines for sycophancy.

If dexterously executed, devoted service will please the Prince and might yield a rich dividend. Ducci advises us not to wait for the master's command, but to burrow one's way into his mind to gauge what his wishes might be. Indeed, he recommends additional, voluntary service, attending on the Prince in order to catch his eye and find opportunities for discourse with him. It is imperative to study his nature, habits, passions, and moods in order to accommodate oneself to him. But the courtier is emphatically not a puppet. Ducci draws a sardonic analogy between the courtier and an artisan. Like every other craftsman, the professional courtier needs to be thoroughly conversant with his material to be able to produce good work. But how is one to appraise the Prince's true nature, given that he too dissembles? Ducci recommends careful scrutiny; even the greatest secrets are divulged to 'prying eies' (F3r). Rigorous surveillance of the Prince will uncover the secrets of his true personality, Ducci assures the reader. However cunning a dissembler, it is impossible for the ruler to keep up his guard at all times, and a circumspect and wise courtier will sooner or later penetrate his cover. Two well-tried methods are to stir up the passions of the Prince, which inevitably entails a slipping of his mask, or to gain his confidence. Sejanus is cited admiringly for his artful manipulation of Tiberius.

Courtiers are not the only ones attempting to fathom others' minds. Life at court is a zero-sum game in which everyone is watching everyone else and trying to fathom the truth behind the performance. In a cat-and-mouse strategy, princes too are busy trying to plumb the depths of the courtier's mind. They might try to solicit the help of courtiers for highly dubious enterprises, and to this end devise ways to test or trick him. How is the courtier to know when he is being sounded out by his ruler? Once again, Ducci recommends careful observation of his character to detect possible clues. The court was a world of fierce competition, with other courtiers waiting in the wings for the opportune moment to bring one to fall. As important as observing the prince was to keep all other courtiers under surveillance, for instance, by means of informers who insinuated themselves into the confidence of one's enemies. Amassing information about what they did and even thought in private might be useful to help undermine their position.

In dealing with one's detractors, Ducci suggests a number of options. The courtier should try to win them over, or to insinuate himself into their favour.

He should attempt to block their access to the Prince. As a last resort, he might need to arrange for their downfall. In an ironic deployment of the figure of *occultatio*, Ducci hints at sinister deeds that he dare not name: 'I will not speak of badde offices: since these as inhumane & not fitting any woorthy or honourable man ought to bee banished the very thoughts of every good and Christian Courtier'. Furthermore, he adds, they are too dangerous (N2r-v). Ducci makes it clear that the courtier must keep his tracks covered at all times and delegate unsavoury tasks to others.

Blount's translation of Ducci's text does not seem to have met with great demand and was not reprinted. His thoughts, however, were widely circulated, repackaged in the form of another treatise, Eustache de Refuge's *Traicté de la cour, ou instructions des courtisans*, published in 1616 and translated by John Reynolds in 1622 with the title *A Treatise of the Court or Instructions for Courtiers*. This work was immensely popular, both in France and in England, as its colourful history in print for a century after its first publication reveals. Over thirty editions appeared in French, English, Italian, German, Dutch, and Latin, supplanting Castiglione's *Courtier* in popularity.[31] Book 2, imparting practical advice as to how to gain favour, maintain favour, and avoid a fall from favour, appeared separately as *Arcana Aulica: or Walsingham's Manual of Prudential Maxims for the States-Man And Courtier* in 1652, named after the translator, Edward Walsingham, but slyly capitalising on the nimbus surrounding the Elizabethan statesman Francis Walsingham, credited with creating the English secret service. The book was reprinted in 1655; it appeared in an expanded version in 1694 and continued to be published at regular intervals in the eighteenth century. A second version of book 2 was published under the title *The Accomplish'd Courtier* in 1658 and 1660, while selections from the book entitled *The Art of Complaisance or the Means to oblige in Conversation* appeared in 1673 and 1677. In a paradoxical feedback loop, the *Arcana Aulica* was retranslated into French, touted as Walsingham's book of secret wisdom. *Le secret des cours, ou le journal de Walsingham, Sécretaire d'Etat sous la Reine Elisabeth* was published in 1695 and *Maximes politiques de Walsingham* in 1717. The precepts about the imperative to dissimulate, the necessity to assiduously observe those one served as well

---

31. See Cooper, 'Introduction', to whom I am indebted in the following. Cooper promotes his new translation as a management guide written by 'the first European management guru' (23). On De Refuge, also see Snyder, *Dissimulation and the Culture of Secrecy*, 98–99, and Anglo, 'Systematic Immorality', 614–22.

as one's peers, and the expediency of concealing one's feelings in order to prise out those of others became common currency in discussions of both political and civil life. In these texts, the historical example of the rise and fall of Sejanus is often held up as a case study.

Sejanus His Fall and the Early Modern Court

The culture of dissimulation and surveillance that early modern treatises describe is dramatized in Jonson's Roman tragedy *Sejanus His Fall*, starring the protagonists Sejanus and Tiberius.[32] To heighten the echoes to Tacitus, the play adopts a spare, Tacitean idiom. In this play Jonson lays bare the mechanisms of tyrannical power as built on the foundations of fear, flattery, falsehood, and a network of spies. *Sejanus* presents a society deeply infiltrated with timeservers and rumour-mongers, scrambling to turn informer on each other, eager to curry favour with those in authority or in the ascendant. To highlight parallels to the contemporary world, even as he cloaks them in meticulous historicity, Jonson steeps the play in self-reflexive devices which create a mirror effect, implicating us in the onstage world of incessant observation and deception. Nor does the play, with a self-ironic nod, spare artists from its sweeping indictment of a degraded civil society, unmasking their entanglement in structures of power.

But Jonson makes an even more radical point. Drawing on Aristotle's analysis of tyranny, *Sejanus* shows how when social bonds wither, a repressive regime flourishes. The play portrays an atomised society in which the bonds of collective life have ruptured and any sense of a common purpose has eroded, while individuals are jostling with one another to aggrandize their personal advantage at all costs. Aristotle defines tyranny as a form of government in which the ruler pursues their own private interest, not the common good (*Pol.* 1311a11–15). To prosper, it requires the attenuation of solidarity and a climate of mutual mistrust and suspicion. As Philip Ayres points out, the play is not the tragedy of an individual, but the tragedy of Rome.[33] The tragic fate it depicts is the death of civil society. The play presents shreds of friendship as the only buffer, however fragile, against an authoritarian state.

First performed in 1603, *Sejanus* reflects the milieu during the final years of the Elizabethan reign, rife with spying, treason, denunciation, and

---

32. On court manuals and the culture of espionage in *Sejanus*, see Hutson, 'Civility and Virility in Ben Jonson'.

33. Ayres, 'Introduction', 24. All citations are from the Revels Plays edition of the play.

ÆLIUS SEJANUS, *Gunsteling van Keyser* TIBERIUS, *Gewurgt, en aan de Gemonische Trappen deerlyk Mishandelt.*

FIGURE 9. Jan Luyken, *Sejanus, Favourite of Emperor Tiberius, Strangled, and at the Gemonian Stairs, Miserably Abused* (1698). Rijksmuseum, Amsterdam.

political unrest. Peter Lake identifies two strains of Neostoicism in England at the time—a 'monarchical republicanism' endorsed by the queen's counsellors, the circle associated with Secretary of State Robert Cecil, Elizabeth's principal adviser, and the enthusiasm for Tacitism cultivated by the oppositional clique around the Earl of Essex. He aligns Jonson with the latter.[34] The play also registers the paranoia of the times and a surge in censorship, marked by the trial of the historian Sir John Hayward over his *First part of the life and raigne of King Henrie the IIII* (1599), dedicated to Essex, and the Bishops' Ban of 1599, directed at satires, epigrams, histories, and plays. The *Quarto* appeared in 1605; on 7 November 1605, two days after the Gunpowder Plot, Jonson, who had attended a dinner hosted by one of the plotters, Robert Catesby, only a few weeks before the attempted coup, was summoned before the Privy Council to defend himself against the charge of 'popery and treason'. A rich critical discussion has grown around the parallels between the play and contemporary politics in England, in particular the persecution of the Catholic community, a member of which Jonson remained until 1610.[35] Although it remains moot whether the play alludes to the Essex Rebellion in 1601 or the show trial of Sir Walter Raleigh in 1605, and draws analogies between Tiberius and Elizabeth or James I, there is no doubt that it portrays a state under a reign of terror, sustained by untrammelled self-serving.

The opening passage of the play depicts a world familiar from the more cynical court manuals circulating in fin-de-siècle Europe. One of the members of the oppositional faction of the Germanicans, Sabinus, defines the outsider status of his companions and himself. In doing so he delivers a blistering censure of contemporary mores:

> No, Silius, we are no good engineers;
> We want the fine arts, and their thriving use
> Should make us graced, or favoured of the times.
> We have no shift of faces, no cleft tongues,
> No soft and glutinous bodies, that can stick,
> Like snails, on painted walls; or, on our breasts,
> Creep up, to fall from that proud height to which
> We did by slavery, not by service, climb. (1.4–11)

With heavy sarcasm, Sabinus proceeds to describe the 'fine arts' of courtiership, mastery of which enables one to gain favour with the powerful. These

---

34. See Lake, 'From *Leicester His Commonwealth* to *Sejanus His Fall*'. Also see Cain, 'Introduction to *Sejanus*'.

35. For a sampling of the debate, see Wikander, '"Queasy to Be Touched"'; Evans, '*Sejanus*'; and Lake, 'From *Leicester His Commonwealth* to *Sejanus His Fall*'. On *Sejanus*, also see Barton, *Ben Jonson*, 92–105; Maus, *Ben Jonson and the Roman Frame of Mind*, 31–39; Donaldson, *Ben Jonson*, 175–92; and Lenthe, 'Ben Jonson's Antagonistic Style'. I am particularly indebted to Schindler, *Religious Dissimulation*, 128–59.

skills consist of dissimulation, lying, treachery, and sycophancy. The term 'shift', whose connotations include a plot device and a change of clothes, glances at the theatricality of the courtier, as does the word 'enginer', a word which alludes to both plots and stage machinery.[36] In a fascinatingly repellent image, one that reveals Jonson's penchant for the grotesque, the Roman nobility are compared to slugs, soft, slimy, and spineless creatures that slowly move upwards, oozing adulation along the way.[37] The allusion to 'cleft tongues' refers to the centrality of flattery in a tyrannical regime, a theme that runs through the play and that is echoed in Sejanus's mocking description of the serpent that emerges from his statue with a 'A tongue / Forkèd as flattery' (5.38–39). The lines gesture obliquely towards the biblical serpent, who plummeted from its once elevated status as angel in the same way as the Roman senators have sunk from exemplars of free men to their current debased condition, where advancement is only possible through 'slavery'. Sabinus goes on to hint at other, darker arts—crime, blackmail—to conclude in a punning nod to the early modern centres of power, 'We stand not in the lines that do advance / To that so courted point' (18–19). He and his companions, he notes bitterly, lack the talent to forge a career for themselves as grovelling courtiers.

The Germanicans, who operate as choric commentators for the greater part of the play, continue to paint a sombre picture of the type of courtier whose fortunes soar in a time of tyranny. His core competencies are to lie,

> Flatter, and swear, forswear, deprave, inform,
> Smile, and betray; make guilty men; then beg
> The forfeit lives, to get the livings; cut
> Men's throats with whisp'rings; sell to gaping suitors
> The empty smoke that flies about the palace;
> Laugh when their patron laughs; sweat when he sweats;
> Be hot and cold with him; change every mood
> Habit, and garb, as often as he varies;
> Observe him, as his watch observes his clock ... (28–36)

In savage Juvenalian mode, Jonson presents a devastating image of life at court, implicitly conflating Rome with London. Through the mouthpiece of Silius, who will pay a heavy price for his opposition to the rule of Tiberius, he excoriates the culture of servility, venality, and duplicity that characterises the regime of

---

36. *OED*, s.v. 'shift, n.' and 'engine, n.'.
37. Anne Barton describes Jonson's 'taste for the grotesque' in *Ben Jonson*, 96.

ancient Rome and, by implication, that of contemporary England. Lickspittles are engaged in ceaseless observation of powerful people, the better to fawn on them, aping their every move; in the meantime, they hawk chimerical promises of advancement ('smoke') to their own clients. More chillingly, Jonson describes a society in which informers prosper, profiting from the generous rewards for betrayal offered in Rome as in early modern England. His harsh imagery brackets informers with murderers: they 'cut / Men's throats with whisperings' (30–31).

Surveillance and Spying

The motif of spying runs through the play. Much of the action consists of different groups of characters onstage monitoring others. In act 1 we see the Germanicans watching and commenting on Satrius and Natta, clients of Sejanus, who in turn exchange whispers about Cordus. Cordus and his friends pass remarks on Sejanus, who, for his part, has them firmly under observation: 'I note 'em well' (1.177). When warned by his friends that he is under scrutiny, Arruntius recklessly taunts the spies: 'You, sir, I would, do you look!' before his friends succeed in restraining him (258–60). Throughout the play, the opposing factions keep each other's movements under surveillance, culminating in the Senate scene in act 5, in which Arruntius and Lepidus present a running commentary on the time-servers fawning on Sejanus while the senators make it clear that they are keeping a sharp eye on the outsiders. One of the senators reads the isolated position of the friends in the senate house as an ominous sign that they have been singled out for disfavour, and helpfully advises the others to avoid the taint of their company: 'Let 'em alone, they will be marked anon' (5.501).

In act 2 Silius warns Agrippina how her household has been infiltrated:

And every second guest your tables take
Is a fee'd spy, t'observe who goes, who comes,
What conference you have, with whom, where, when;
What the discourse is, what the looks, the thoughts
Of every person there ... (2.444–48)

Even the domestic sphere is not immune to penetration by spies, as Jonson was later to lament in his poem, 'Inviting a Friend to Supper'.[38] As Christopher Ricks has pointed out, allusions to eyes and ears pervade the play.[39] Agrippina

---

38. Jonson, 'Inviting a Friend to Supper'.
39. Ricks, '*Sejanus* and Dismemberment'.

responds defiantly to the warning by her friend, deploying the imagery of corporal fragmentation, one of the many images of dismemberment in the play that foreshadows the fate of Sejanus, torn limb from limb by a mob in near-cannibalistic fury:

> Were all Tiberius' body stuck with eyes,
> And every wall and hanging in my house
> Transparent, as this lawn [fine linen] I wear, or air;
> Yea, had Sejanus both his ears as long
> As to my inmost closet, I would hate
> To whisper any thought, or change an act ... (450–55)

Silius is proven right by the ensuing events. Ironically, it is he who falls victim to the spies at Agrippina's table. At his trial, his fate is sealed when evidence is brought against him that was gleaned at a dinner conversation at Agrippina's. In *Sejanus*, being monitored paves the way for death, as Sabinus's equation of spies with birds of prey makes clear. He denounces a society in which citizens are made 'The prey to greedy vultures and vile spies / That first transfix us with their murdering eyes' (4.140–41). Ironies spark in the eavesdropping scene, during which these words are spoken. If the entire play is a hall of mirrors, where observers and observed reflect each other, in this scene Jonson expands the orbit of surveillance to take in the audience. We watch how an agent provocateur, Latiaris, leads his kinsman Sabinus into a trap while two senators eavesdrop from above, ready to rush in and accuse him of treason as soon as he utters incriminating words. At the same time, the self-reflexive ruse serves to train a spotlight on the audience.[40] We too are under observation by the play—as is the poet himself.

Despite displaying little enthusiasm for the theatre in his treatise on the passions, Thomas Wright advises attending stage plays in order to watch and learn about our fellow human beings. Skilful actors have honed their art in careful observation, and hold up a mirror to society: 'this the best may be marked in stage-players who act excellently, for as the perfection of their exercise consisteth in imitation of others, so they that imitate best act best' (5.3.238–41). In *Sejanus*, it is Jonson who takes a close look at the society he lives in, and what he sees is not a pleasant sight. When they reveal themselves, the senators who spy on Sabinus are greeted by him with scathing sarcasm: 'So white! So full of years! / ... my most reverend monsters' (4.221–22). These

---

40. On self-reflexivity in the play, see Marotti, 'Self-Reflexive Art'.

venerable members of the political elite gratuitously engage in betrayal of one of their own class in the vague hope of being rewarded by Sejanus. They lie to themselves, insisting that they are serving the state. 'To be a spy for traitors / Is honorable vigilance', Rufus, one of the senators, puts it piously (223–24). Jonson is pillorying a world in which mutual trust has eroded and which is perforated with informers and undercover agents, a view he shares with the Catholic priest Thomas Wright. In a recent study of the figure of the informer in early modern drama, Bill Angus argues that scenarios of eavesdropping in early modern drama do not merely capture the pervasive climate of eavesdropping and spying. They also reveal the paranoia of playwrights about the malicious misconstruing of their words by members of the audience—and evoke an uneasy resemblance to writers themselves, in the business of observing others and at times, of intelligence gathering. The toadying spies in the play reflect the audience's own image back to itself—and possibly that of Jonson himself and his fellow authors too, anxious to curry favour with those in authority.[41]

Tyranny and the Decay of Civil Society

Jonson's enduring interest in Neostoicism is attested by his assiduously annotated copies of Lipsius's *Opera* and his *Sixe Bookes of Politickes or Civil Doctrine* as well the excerpts from the classics appropriated from Lipsius in Jonson's *Discoveries*. Even if his copies, as do most entries in the *Discoveries*, postdate the play, some critics discern an affinity for Stoic political thought earlier in his career, one that is reflected in the play.[42] What is undoubtedly the case is that Jonson's play reprises the Stoic concern with sociability and reaffirms the belief that our interests are connected to those of our fellow humans. *Sejanus* demonstrates the vital importance of a civil community for a political system that governs in the common interest, not solely in the interest of those in power.

Jonson's main source for the play is Tacitus, to whose *Annals* he adheres punctiliously, his notes often borrowed wholesale if unacknowledged from the

---

41. See Angus, *Metadrama and the Informer in Shakespeare and Jonson*, esp. 115–35.
42. See esp. Evans, *Jonson, Lipsius, and the Politics of Renaissance Stoicism*. On Jonson's sympathies with Stoicism, also see Maus, *Ben Jonson and the Roman Frame of Mind*. On Jonson and Lipsius, see further Boughner, 'Jonson's Use of Lipsius in *Sejanus*'; Salmon, 'Stoicism and Roman Example'; McCrea, *Constant Minds*, 138–70. For a more sceptical view, see Schindler, *Religious Dissimulation*, 143–48.

edition by Lipsius. It is patent that the giants on whose shoulders the Roman historian stands are Plato and Aristotle. Writing at a time of crisis in the Athenian democracy, when demagogues were on the rise, Plato's main concern is with the psychopathology of the tyrant.[43] Socrates explains that democracy mutates into despotic rule when an ambitious leader panders to the desires of the people for uncurbed liberty and fosters class war. Once in power, he increasingly avails himself of brutal repression in order to retain control, reducing the people to servitude and purging men of courage or vision. The only people to whom he can resort are newly made men whom he has helped to create. The tyrant himself is under the sway of immoral and bestial lusts. He is tyrannized by his own passions. Freed from any restraint, he resorts to a range of crimes to be able to indulge his desires while keeping up a fraudulent front of probity. His companions are upstart followers who take over the country, while towards him they are subservient parasites. The tyrant has no friends; his only relationships are those of a master to slaves. He himself is slave to his desires, which he can never fully satisfy. Ravaged by the fear of being deposed, Plato notes, the tyrannical personality is compelled to control others although he cannot control himself.

The parallels to Jonson's portrait of Tiberius are manifest. Tiberius is described as a ruler secretly ruled by his passions. A model of modesty and self-restraint in public, he seems 'to shun / The strokes and stripes of flatterers, which within / Are lechery unto him, and so feed / His brutish sense with their afflicting sound' (1.412–15). In one of Jonson's trademark pungent images, flattery is correlated with Tiberius's deviant sexual proclivities, desires to which he is secretly addicted. His hunger for acclamation is gratified by a swarm of toadies, the most adept of whom is Sejanus, who, Arruntius remarks contemptuously, began his meteoric rise to power as a prostitute to the decadent epicure Apicius (212–16). At the same time, Jonson portrays Tiberius as haunted with fear. As Lepidus astutely comments, 'his fear / Would ne'er be masked, albe his vices were' (4.477–78).

The close correspondence between Jonson's depiction of Tiberius and Plato's description of the tyrant is underscored by the wolf imagery that traverses the play. Sejanus remarks, 'wolves do change their hair, but not their hearts' (2.273); Silius speaks of Roman society as 'a world of wolf-turned men' (3.251); and Arruntius comments on Tiberius with the words, 'Excellent

---

43. See Arruzza, *Wolf in the City*. On tyranny and the tyrannical character, see Plato's *Republic*, bks. 8 and 9, 562a–587b, in Plato, *Complete Works*.

wolf! / Now he is full, he howls' (347–48). He laments the state of civic society and pronounces the 'Roman race most wretched that should live / Between so slow jaws' (486–87).[44] Lepidus espouses Stoicism and passive endurance: 'Not tempting the wolves' jaws' (4.298). A favourite image of Jonson's,[45] it echoes the analogy between the tyrant and the wolf in Plato's *Republic*. Plato briefly alludes to the rumours about cannibalistic rites carried out at the shrine of Zeus Lykaeus in Arcadia, where allegedly a morsel of human flesh was intermingled with the animal sacrifice. The man who tasted it turned wolf. Tyrants too, Plato asserts, 'change from man to wolf' (565d–566a), mutating from protector of the masses against the greed of the oligarchy to the epitome of greed, unbridled appetite, and savagery. The wolf motif, a Renaissance commonplace, chimes with the Hobbesian description of human society without civility as one in which 'Man to Man is an arrant wolf'.[46]

Aristotle, on the other hand, introduces a radically different angle into the analysis of tyranny. His interest lies in the type of society that nurtures an autocratic regime.[47] Aristotle points out that for tyranny to thrive, any sense of community must be debilitated. It is imperative to corrode the bonds of mutuality that tie humans in a community to each other. He alleges that the tyrant must take care to destroy the trust citizens have in one another and foster a climate of fear and suspicion. This is achieved by creating a dense network of spies, informers, and agent provocateurs, who seek to foment friction and set friends against each other. Tyrants always aim for three goals: to break the spirit of their subjects, to curtail opportunities for political action, and to sow the seeds of mutual distrust. What is disastrous for a tyrant, Aristotle claims, is if citizens 'are faithful to one another and to the other citizens, and do not inform against one another nor against the others' (1314a8).

Aristotle agrees with Plato that tyrannical rule reduces the people to the condition of abject slavery. Tyranny is the ultimate perversion of the principle

---

44. The phrase, from Suetonius, could also allude to the myth of the titan Chronos devouring his own offspring. See Marotti, 'Self-Reflexive Art', 218.

45. See Donaldson, *Ben Jonson*, 175. He uses the phrase 'the wolf's black jaw' in 'An Ode to Himself', line 36. The resonances with Shakespeare's 'universal wolf' (*Troilus and Cressida*, 1.3.120) are compelling. Both plays were written at around the same time, and Shakespeare's satire has often been seen as commenting on the Poets' War. See Bednarz, *Shakespeare and the Poets' War*.

46. Hobbes, 'Epistle Dedicatory', in *On the Citizen*, 3.

47. The critical section is *Politics*, bk. 5.9. Also see Boesche, 'Aristotle's "Science" of Tyranny'.

of government, whereby a state is ruled solely in the private interest of the ruler (1293b28, 1295a19–23). Like Plato, Aristotle sees the tyrant as impelled by a hunger for pleasure, wealth, and absolute power (1311a3–20). Aristotle too draws attention to the central role of flattery in degenerate political systems: the demagogue flatters the people, and as a tyrant, he himself craves flattery. As Aristotle points out, tyrants always fear those they rule. To maintain control, tyrants need to destroy the most outstanding citizens, free-spirited men of pride, and to undermine friendship in all human relations.

Tyranny and Friendship

For Aristotle, friendship has far wider implications than the term evokes today, and develops out of the virtue of affability (akin to civility) that ideally frames relations between all members of society: a state, he argues, is a partnership of citizens defined by affability (*Pol.* 1295b24). In the *Nicomachean Ethics*, he draws an analogy between the concept of friendship and the political community (8.9–11). He equates the different types of friendship he has identified—associations of utility, those of shared pleasure, and those of trust and affection—with particular types of community. These separate communities are, however, all part of the political community, and further the common advantage of all members of the state. Friendship, he asserts, holds states together—relationships of reciprocity exist in every type of government (1155a20). But not all political orders are defined by friendship in equal measure. Under tyranny, he contends, expanding on Plato's insight, friendship barely exists. A society in which members live in isolation from each other, entirely absorbed in private concerns to the detriment of any sense of common purpose, is the ideal environment for oppressive rule.

Early moderns had a similarly capacious concept of friendship, although the term 'friend' covered a variety of additional significations: it could denote 'relation', 'lover', or 'patron'.[48] In practice, as Keith Thomas reminds us, the vast majority of early modern friendships were instrumental relationships and were part of networks of support.[49] At the same time, an enthusiasm for the ideal of friendship took hold of the popular imagination, celebrated in an outpouring of poems, plays, and writings of every kind. It was fuelled by classical texts such as Cicero's *Laelius de amicitia*. Cicero follows Aristotle in insisting

---

48. *OED*, s.v. 'friend, n.'.
49. Thomas, 'Friendship and Sociability', 190–91.

that friendship exists only amongst free men—in the life of tyrants, 'friendship has no place'.[50] As Aristotle had stressed, tyrannical rule is the form of government which is most inimical to free-born men (*Pol.* 1295a19–23). For Cicero, friendship is characterised by frank speech. By contrast, flattery is the hallmark of tyranny (*Lael.* 24.89). Similarly, Plutarch defines frankness as 'the language of friendship'.[51] This theme is further developed by Horace. In his satires and epistles, Horace, who prided himself on his candid relationship with his patron Maecenas, whom he regarded as a friend, emphasizes the importance of truthful speech (*parrhesia*) among friends, insinuating that even in a tyrannical regime, free speech survives in social relations.[52]

In the play, we see how the small circle of dissenting Romans who mistrust Tiberius and his favourite engage in a free exchange of thought amongst each other, in full awareness that their words, if reported, would cost them their lives. Not that they always agree: Aruntius contemptuously dismisses Drusus, son of Tiberius, as a 'riotous youth' (1.107), while Sabinus and Silius protest that there are hopeful signs that he will mature with age; Cordus sings the praises of Alexander the Great, while Sabinus disparages the Macedonian general as 'voluptuous, rash, / Giddy, and drunken' (145–46). More fundamentally, they radically differ from one another as to how to respond to the regime of terror to which they are subjected. When Lepidus pleads for Stoic endurance, 'the plain and passive fortitude / To suffer, and be silent', Arruntius explodes in frustration and anger. He fiercely demands, 'May I think, / And not be racked? What danger is't to dream? / Talk in one's sleep? Or cough?' (4.294–95, 304–6). Tyrannical rule seeps into the most intimate moments of everyday life and sabotages any semblance of normality, he maintains. Nonetheless, the relationship of the friends is built on profound trust. Each of them is secure in the knowledge that none of the group will betray the other.

Against the claustrophobic climate of spying and denunciation that permeates the play, Jonson throws into relief the attentiveness with which the friends guard each other from any dangerous misstep. When the impetuous Arruntius erupts in an outburst of rage about Sejanus, Sabinus warns him, 'You'are observed, Arruntius' (1.258) and demands that he curb his tongue. Twice in the

---

50. Cicero, *Laelius de amicitia*, 15.53.

51. Plutarch, 'How to Tell a Flatterer from a Friend', 51C.

52. See James, *Ovid and the Liberty of Speech*, 150. On Horace's independence from Maecenas, see his *Epistle* 1.7.

same scene, unable to bear the grovelling of the senators and Tiberius's announcement that Sejanus's statue will be erected in Pompey's theatre, Arruntius is on the verge of confronting the tyrant. Only his friends restrain him from plunging headlong into danger, taking him to task for his rashness. Sabinus admonishes him that 'It is not safe t'enforce a sovereign's ear' (433) while Silius berates him sharply for his lack of restraint (547). The quiescent political views of Lepidus are vehemently opposed by Arruntius—the former rejects resistance of Tiberius on the grounds that 'he is our prince', while Arruntius retorts, 'He is our monster' (4.372–73). Nonetheless, Lepidus takes care to prevent Arruntius from betraying himself in the presence of acolytes of Sejanus. The group of Romans who exchange views with one another is not limited to the Germanicans, but includes senators such as Lepidus and the independent-minded Gallus. At the end of the play, they even lend a sympathetic ear to Terentius, loyal supporter of Sejanus, when he describes the gruesome fate meted out to the fallen favourite and his children, whose mutilation figures the dismemberment of the body politic.[53] What unites all members of this circle is despair at the disintegration of civil society in Rome.

Dissimulation as a Tool of Power

In his ironic catalogue of advice for a tyrant, doubtless a model for Machiavelli's own subversion of the mirror for princes genre, Aristotle also discusses the importance of dissimulation (*Pol.* 1314a30ff.). An effective device to retain power is to scrupulously cultivate the appearance of a legitimate ruler who pursues the good of his subjects, not merely his own. He proposes that in all actions, the tyrant should 'cleverly play the part of royalty' (1314a40). The tyrant should attempt to moderate his desires; if this is not possible, he must at all events avoid revealing his habits to his subjects.[54] In addition to advocating image management in the interests of maintaining power, Aristotle sets out a number of other points that Machiavelli would incorporate into his own recommendations, including the importance of sedulously husbanding

---

53. Ricks, '*Sejanus* and Dismemberment', 301. Also see Smith, '"[P]lain and Passive Fortitude"'.

54. Cf. Machiavelli, *The Prince*, chap. 15: 'because circumstances do not permit living a completely virtuous life, one must be sufficiently prudent to know how to avoid becoming notorious for those vices that would destroy one's power' (55).

resources and maintaining the facade of being devout. When keen to inflict punishment, the tyrant is enjoined to utilize others as a front. When exalting an individual to a position of power, it is advisable to raise two or more so that they keep watch on one another. This is precisely the strategy pursued by Tiberius, who plays out two favourites, Sejanus and Macro, against each other.

Jonson's Tiberius seems to have fully absorbed Aristotle's counsel. Analogously, the writings of early modern political theorists promoting dissimulation as a vital tool of power have left an indelible trace on the play. Tiberius is a master of dissembling. Even Arruntius, who makes a meticulous study of him, confesses he is unable to 'understand this Sphinx' (3.65), while Cordus caustically applauds his performance of servility towards the Senate: 'Rarely dissembled!' (1.395). His close observation of others empowers him to control them by simultaneously exploiting their anxieties and gratifying their vanity. His command of the twin arts of instilling fear and using flattery is displayed most effectively in his public appearances. His addresses to the senators are masterly set pieces of manipulative rhetoric. In his first speech he proclaims himself 'their creature' and declares, 'there can be nothing in their thought / Shall want to please us, that hath pleasèd them' (1.439, 449–50). He proceeds to deliver an oration that displays his finesse in setting out both sides of the question, simultaneously disavowing the intention to have himself and his family worshipped as gods and defending the practice, artfully citing Augustus in support of his claims. His rhetoric is so finely calibrated that the political import is veiled in a mist of mellifluous sound, as Arruntius recognises, refusing to stay to 'hear more cunning, and fine words, / With their sound flattered, ere their sense be meant' (506–7). Flattering the senators is simply part of a performance that Tiberius stages for public consumption. In reality, there is no question of soliciting their views or attempting to persuade them to adopt a course of action. Nonetheless, he nourishes their delusion that they are still participants in the political arena. As the senators know only too well, they are merely spectators in a play in which the roles of director, playwright, and star are fused in the person of the ruler.

This is most apparent in act 3, where Tiberius begs the senators to indulge his wish to retire from office, pleading that the 'burden is too heavy' (3.113). Sejanus promptly speaks in the Senate's name to refuse his request, declaring rhapsodically that should Tiberius no longer rule, 'Rome, whose blood, / Whose nerves, whose life, whose very frame relies / On Caesar's strength' would collapse into 'general ruin' (128–31). Sejanus's show of servility is applauded on cue by the other senators, who launch into a eulogy of the tyrant's 'modesty', 'wisdom', 'meekness', 'piety', and 'bounty' (142–47). The entire charade is acerbically commented on by Arruntius, who mockingly applauds the performance with the words, 'Well acted, Caesar' (105). Tiberius delivers a gushing speech of thanks, declaring, 'if the Senate still command me serve, / I must be glad to practise my obedience' (139–40). His obsequious words are ironically undercut by the two show trials that are staged immediately afterwards. Arruntius continues his commentary in the idiom of the theatre: 'The curtain's drawing' (154).

A notable expansion on his sources, Jonson's masterpiece in the play is Tiberius's letter to the Senate in act 5, denouncing his erstwhile favourite, Sejanus. A dark parody of arguing *in utramque partem*, his epistolary oration oscillates between raising Sejanus to the peaks of praise and dropping him into the troughs of damnation, allowing Tiberius to flaunt his consummate control of audience reaction even in his absence. In a spectacular visual metaphor of audience manipulation, Jonson has the audience of spineless and cowed senators furtively shift away from Sejanus with every twist in the emperor's argument. The truth of his claims is irrelevant. Like a puppet-player, Tiberius operates the emotional strings of his audience, pitching them from one emotion to the next and playing on their hopes and fears.

Sejanus, Rhetoric, and Art

In *Sejanus* Jonson delineates a civil society in ruins. In conjunction with the degeneration of social rhetoric, the play presents an image of the debasement of rhetoric, eviscerated of its function to provide a conduit for debate and collective deliberation.[55] The play encapsulates the debate about rhetoric that loomed over the early modern period—one that revisited Platonic attacks on rhetoric as bound up with flattery and falsehood.[56] The late sixteenth-century wave of scepticism had spilled over to encompass the Ciceronian vision of rhetoric, hollowing out the lofty ethical claims the early humanists had promulgated. In the play the most skilful practitioners of the art are Tiberius

---

55. See Loxley, *Complete Critical Guide to Ben Jonson*, 57–65.

56. Cf. Plato's *Gorgias* and *Phaedrus*. On the crisis of rhetoric, see Kahn, *Rhetoric, Prudence, and Skepticism in the Renaissance*. Also see Rhodes, *Power of Eloquence*, 58–63, and Rebhorn, *Emperor of Men's Minds*, 197–258.

and Afer. Afer, a distinguished orator and teacher of Quintilian, who cites him admiringly, is described by Arruntius as follows:

> One that hath phrases, figures, and fine flowers
> To strew his rhetoric with, and doth make haste
> To get him note, or name, by any offer
> Where blood or gain be objects; steeps his words,
> When he would kill, in artificial tears—
> The crocodile of Tiber! (2.419–24)

The play adopts Tacitus's unflattering portrayal of the famous orator as a person 'in a hurry to gain celebrity by any deed'.[57] In his hands rhetoric, far from a civilising tool, is an instrument of death. In his exorbitant desire for fame he has no scruples in accepting assignments that hinge on corruption or the destruction of others. By analogy with the false tears of a crocodile, his command of elegant figures of speech serves as a hypocritical cover for his murderous acts. For this orator, emotional display is nothing but a charade.

Afer's chief victim is Silius, whom he accuses of treason on a trumped-up charge. In return, Silius pours scorn on Afer's 'mercenary tongue and art' (3.177). He speaks of Afer's style of rhetoric as consisting of 'unkind handling, / Furious enforcing, most unjust presuming, / Malicious and manifold applying, / Foul wresting, and impossible construction' (3.226–29). With bitter irony, Silius points out that as a master practitioner of the art, Afer's expertise lies in the abuse of rhetoric. His use of rhetoric as a forensic instrument aims not to uncover the truth but to pervert the course of justice for material gain. In the trial, the clinching piece of evidence put forward against Silius is Afer's own testimony, who Jonson, in a rare addition to his sources, brands as a spy who betrays those into whose convivial company he has inveigled himself.[58] In his final words, Silius refers to Afer's 'bloodying tongue' (3.328), retrieving the wolf motif to stigmatize rhetoric as a savage weapon.

In *Sejanus*, Jonson portrays a perversion of rhetoric. In the Rome of Tiberius, rather than serving as a vehicle for the interchange of opinions, rhetoric is a tool of tyrants and their willing executioners. The precepts about the elevated achievements of rhetoric, stemming from Cicero and Quintilian, that had played such a decisive role in shaping humanism, are exposed as spurious.[59]

---

57. Tacitus, *The Annals*, 4.52.
58. Hutson, 'Civility and Virility in Ben Jonson', 6–7.
59. The classic study is Vickers, *In Defence of Rhetoric*.

Eloquence is severed from wisdom and truth; the moving of emotions does not persuade to the good. There is no sense of the skilled orator being a *vir bonus*, a man of virtue, as Quintilian had postulated (*Inst.* 12.1–44). Instead, elevated thoughts are expressed by speakers such as Tiberius and Afer who have no intention of enacting the sentiments they proclaim. The image of the orator presented in the play harks back to Plato's devastating depiction of the sophist Gorgias as cynical and self-serving, a master of specious reasoning. Arruntius denounces the divide between the form of Tiberius's honeyed words and their content, deploring 'the space / Beween the breast and lips' (3.96–97) and the fact that his words are 'merely but lip-good' (1.410). The imagery of mutilation that suffuses the play relates not only to eyes and ears, but to tongues as well. Nero, son of Germanicus, fantasizes about a fitting treatment for informers: to 'rip forth their tongues, sear out their eyes' (2.477).

Both Tiberius and Afer are consummate artists in their own right, virtuosos of words and emotions.[60] Their arts aim at manipulating people for the purposes of power, gratifying their own pleasure and profit, not that of their audience. Plato's disdain for rhetoric is of a piece with his hostility towards art. By appealing to emotions, tragedy in particular catered to the tyrant, enslaved by his own passions. Plato's discussion of tyranny includes an attack on dramatists. He pours scorn on playwrights who curry favour with tyrants, singling out Euripides for special opprobrium (*Rep.* 568a–d). The tragedian, Socrates remarks sardonically, believes that he is acting as counsellor to the tyrant while in reality he is merely a cat's paw. The self-delusion to which artists are in thrall only confirms Plato's deep suspicion of the arts and his claim that poets exert a pernicious influence on the state.

There is no doubt that *Sejanus* shows a world in which rhetoric is used to disseminate lies and serves to debilitate rather than shore up civil society. And yet, this is not the whole story. For all his disillusionment about the abuse of rhetoric, Jonson does not replicate Plato's pessimism about playwrights. If the play delivers a stinging rebuke to writers who ingratiate themselves with authoritarian regimes, it also offers a vindication of the role of art in dark times. Not all artists, the play suggests, pander to tyrants. In a self-conscious ploy, Jonson has the historian Cremutius Cordus make a powerful cameo appearance in the play. He is first introduced in the discussion between Tiberius and

---

60. See McDonald, 'Jonsonian Comedy and the Value of *Sejanus*'.

Sejanus, who describe him as a troublemaker, who, like Jonson himself, while ostensibly writing about the past, castigates his own society:

> who, under colour
> Of praising those, doth tax the present state,
> Censures the men, the actions, leaves no trick,
> No practice unexamined, parallels
> The times, the governments; a professed champion
> For the old liberty—(2.307–12)

Accordingly, at his show trial Cordus is accused of sedition, the prize exhibit being his annals where, as Afer asserts, 'By oblique glance of his licentious pen' (3.404) he attacks Tiberius. In response, Cordus draws attention to previous rulers who respected the works of historians unfavourable to themselves, and points to the plethora of opposing views in circulation in the past. In effect, Cordus delivers a moving plea in defence of the freedom of speech and expression. His final lines articulate fervent hopes for the enduring legacy of art. 'Posterity pays every man his honour' (456), he avers, and alleges that with time, he too will be remembered.

The uneasiness of an authoritarian establishment in the face of the power of art is captured by Jonson in the barrage of attacks hurled by the sycophantic senators: 'give order that his books be burnt', Cotta howls, 'Let 'em be burnt', Latiaris urges, and Gallus insists, 'All sought, and burnt, today' (465, 469). Jonson has Arruntius respond with withering scorn: 'O how ridiculous / Appears the Senate's brainless diligence, / Who think they can, with present power, extinguish / The memory of all succeeding times!' (471–74). Jonson is reprising the exultant remarks of Cordus, reported in Tacitus's *Annals* (4.35), about the work of the historian surviving the senators' edict. As Sabinus points out, the legacy of art is only enhanced by persecution: 'the punishment / Of wit doth make th'authority increase'. On the writers themselves, it confers 'an eternal name' (475–76, 480).

As both detractors and supporters of rhetoric well knew, rhetoric could be pressed into service by tyrants or their opponents. It could be used to exploit emotions or to appeal to both emotion and judgement, using persuasion for the common good; it could be utilized to occlude an exchange of views or to facilitate debate. Jonson's play is imbued with the awareness that in human communication, there is no escape from rhetoric. Jonson, like Shakespeare, had absorbed Machiavelli's insights about the ethical indeterminacy of rhetoric—and, by implication, art. What is decisive is the end to which they are deployed and the effect they achieve.

Sejanus depicts the fragmentation of a social order in which rhetoric as a medium for collective reasoning has atrophied. It offers a searing indictment of the way in which those with a rapacious appetite for power seize control, and the way sleazy enablers pave their way to supremacy. The play issues a trenchant warning to the audience that the decay of civil society enables a tyrannical regime to flourish. By exposing the workings of tyranny, Jonson implies that like the historian Cordus, he too is using his art to shore up the values of a shared citizenship and to foster bonds to those who share his vision of a common project, not the 'rude multitude' (5.818), of whom he consistently despaired, but a community of 'understander[s]'.[61] In his poem, 'Inviting a Friend to Supper', he wistfully conjures up a society built on a foundation of reciprocal faith and trust, in which ideas circulate freely and members are not constrained to hold their tongue for fear of informers amongst them: 'Nor shall our cups make any guilty men, / But at our parting we will be as when / We innocently met'.[62]

Coda

After *Sejanus*, booed off the stage at its initial performance, Jonson abandoned tragedy, with the exception of *Catiline*, written in 1611. Instead, he focused on comedies that excoriate society from different angles. One of the most striking, if minor, scenes in *Sejanus* is a miniature comic masterpiece, one that would be plundered in his later satirical drama, such as *Epicene*. In act 2, Livia, probably seated in front of the mirror, is discussing cosmetics with her physician, Eudemus, who doubles as a pimp. Sejanus, her new lover, bustles in and out self-importantly, busy planning the murder of her husband, Drusus. While the men around her are plotting murder and mayhem, Livia remains single-mindedly focused on her appearance. Sejanus is worried that she might be afraid of Drusus, whom she has just agreed to have poisoned. But as she assures him, this is not the case. Neither fear nor love seem to play a significant role in her life. In between dispensing beauty tips, Eudemus is at pains to make her appreciate her good fortune in having a lover who is a rising star on the political firmament. Livia remains unimpressed. In despair, Eudemus appeals to her vanity. Exchanging lovers has had a positive effect on her looks, he claims. 'This change came timely, lady', he urges, 'restoring your complexion'

---

61. Jonson, 'To the Reader', in *The Alchemist*, line 1.
62. Jonson, 'Inviting a Friend to Supper', lines 37–39.

(2.134–35). This plea too fails to elicit more than a perfunctory response. Livia remains engrossed in the most interesting object in her life: herself.

While the scene is a virulent attack on some of Jonson's favourite *bêtes noires*, decadence and amorality, it also comments on the theme of tyranny and recapitulates Aristotle's insights. A not insignificant role in the withering of the bonds of communality, *Sejanus* suggests, is played by solipsism. The vision of a common good cannot survive in a fractured society in which individuals do little else than nurture their narcissism and pursue their private concerns, immersed in a bubble of self-absorption. The play suggests that in a world peopled by Afer, Livia, and their ilk, civility is at a premium.

5

Wit and the Art of Jesting

MANY OF THE paradoxes of civility are encapsulated in the practice of jesting. On the one hand, wit can be wielded as a weapon to devastate one's opponents and exacerbate conflict. Aggressive humour is a powerful instrument that can be used to humiliate and exclude certain members or groups within society. It can serve to strengthen the bonds that connect members of a coterie and reinforce social factionalism. On the other hand, humour can be pressed into service as a social lubricant, defusing social tension and creating a larger community that includes divergent segments of society, welded together through the shared pleasure of laughter. Verbal adroitness confers a considerable degree of social cachet, fuelling the desire to hone one's wit, either to taunt and debase others, or alternatively, to further social cohesion. At its best, humour itself has the potential to unsettle our certainties, allowing us, for a brief moment, to gain an insight into the contradictions in our own views and destabilizing our boundless moral complacency.

A fascination with wit was pervasive in the Renaissance. It was one of the offshoots of the Renaissance love affair with rhetoric. After a brief survey of the discourse on wit in classical treatises, this chapter looks at jesting in Renaissance courtesy manuals, focusing on Pontano's *De sermone* and book 2 of Castiglione's *Courtier*. Classical rhetorics commend wit as an indispensable rhetorical tool and a social asset. What is less well-known is that classical discussions of *sermo*, or conversational speech, also underline the importance of being able to take a joke. While advocating the art of jesting as a useful skill, Renaissance prescriptive writings on civility, particularly those intended for courtiers, warn their readers about the dangers of antagonising others in a society in which power dynamics are often opaque and continually shifting, and draw increasingly close cordons around hostile jeering. Pontano and Castiglione moot a number of more perceptive thoughts. They concede that in

FIGURE 10. A witty woman. Andrea del Sarto, *Portrait of a Lady with a Book* (ca. 1528). Uffizi Gallery, Florence.

communal life, friction is inevitable. Not eliding but managing conflict in the form of an agonistic game might be a way to ensure civility in social interaction. Jokes, they suggest, are communicative acts. As in the case of every other mode of rhetoric, key is the work the jokes do in a specific situation. Both texts also highlight the fact that humour thrives on dissimulation—in the form of benign deception, wordplay, or irony.

The theatre, meanwhile, depicts a world teeming with witty men and women who show off their ingenuity and verbal dexterity in a never-ending series of battles of wits. A glut of comedies catered to the pleasure of spectators in sharp quips, quick-fire repartee, double entendre, and imaginative feats, ironically offering models to emulate in the cut and thrust of the urban world. Two plays that scrutinize the practice of jesting even while spurring audience laughter are Jonson's *Epicene, or The Silent Woman* and Shakespeare's *Merry Wives of Windsor*. Both plays feature witty protagonists who use the art of jesting as an instrument of social correction, mocking deviants from societal values—and garnering added prestige in the bargain. Concomitantly, both send up the culture of civility itself, poking fun at a panoply of social climbers and pointing up the absurdities of the rage for duelling and the passion for taking umbrage on which it was based. *Epicene* dissects the wits too, uncovering their delusions of superiority—which, the play insinuates, might mirror our own. If *Epicene* displays wit brandished as a tool of power, *The Merry Wives of Windsor* shows jesting used to foster social bonds. Both plays, however, use laughter to forge a community in the auditorium. By means of a string of metadramatic set pieces, both plays explore the relationship between the theatre and theatricality in social life. They reflect on the link between wit and dissimulation, probing the idea whether deception might serve an ethical purpose.

Classical Theories of Wit

In contrast to Plato, who in the *Philebus* (48a–50b) disparages humour as inevitably bound up with malice, and in the *Republic* (606c2–10) condemns comedy for pandering to our lower passions, allowing them to gain control over the rational part of our soul, Aristotle recuperates wittiness (*eutrapelia*) as a virtue—even as he cements the connection between wit and class.[1] In the *Nicomachean Ethics* (4.8), he explicitly defines the mean between vulgar buffoonery and an uncouth lack of humour as the tasteful wit of the well-bred gentleman. The buffoon will go to any lengths to gratify his craving for laughter, be it at the price of affronting others or at the expense of his own dignity,

---

1. Plato, *Complete Works*. It must be said that throughout the dialogues, Plato presents Socrates as a witty, ironic, but courteous conversationalist. On classical laughter, see Skinner, 'Hobbes and the Classical Theory of Laughter'; Halliwell, *Greek Laughter*; and Beard, *Laughter in Ancient Rome*. A recent, useful collection of essays is Destrée and Trivigno, *Laughter, Humor, and Comedy in Ancient Philosophy*.

while the boor is wholly deficient in the social skill of wit.[2] Aristotle's discussion of comic rhetorical devices in the *Poetics* is lost, but in his remarks on style in the *Rhetoric*, he recommends witty, urbane speech, or *asteia* (3.10). He endorses humour as a rhetorical tool to subvert the arguments of opponents and briefly points out that mocking irony is more befitting of a gentleman than buffoonery (1419b7).[3] Aristotle concedes that an undercurrent of aggression runs through much of humour. In his anatomy of the young, who are very partial to wit, he defines wittiness as 'cultured insolence' (1389b15). The notion of irony as associated with good breeding is discussed in greater depth in his treatment of another social virtue, truthfulness with regard to one's own qualities, which he opposes to boastfulness (*EN* 4.7). Rather than unvarnished speech, Aristotle lauds understatement and irony as the traits of a man of refinement, referencing Socrates as a paragon of the virtue.

The emphasis Cicero and Quintilian lay on an urbane, ironic style of speech harks back to Aristotle. In the excursus on wit in *De oratore*, Cicero advances humour as a valuable resource for the ideal orator. Wit is indispensable to score points against the opponent, to contribute to a relaxed atmosphere, and to show 'the orator himself to be refined, to be educated, to be well bred' (2.236). Cicero's speaker in this section, Gaius Julius Caesar Strabo, exhorts his listeners to avoid the gross buffoonery and mimicry associated with lower-status persons such as the buffoon or *scurra*—either a professional entertainer or a social parasite—and the actors who performed in mimes, at the time a vulgar type of drama (2.237–39). He also advocates repartee as a particularly sophisticated type of wit (2.230). In his programmatic prologue, Cicero declares, 'it is essential to possess a certain esprit and humour, the culture that befits a gentleman, and an ability to be quick and concise in rebuttal as well as attack, combined with refinement, grace, and urbanity' (1.17).[4] Quintilian

2. Also see Walker, 'Aristotle on Wittiness'.

3. *Asteismus* is dubbed 'the Civil Jest' by Puttenham, 'a mirth very full of civility and such as the most civil men do use', without 'any gall or offense'. See Puttenham, *Art of English Poesy*, 3.18.275. Peacham describes it as 'a wittie jesting in civill maner', which is 'more meete for private companie, then publike orations'. See Peacham, *Garden of Eloquence*, G1r–v.

4. Also see 1.159: 'from all types of urbanity we must take bits of witticism and humor that we can sprinkle, like a little salt, throughout all of our speech'. Cicero himself was keen to hone his image as a wit. Unfortunately, this flattering view was not shared by all his peers. Macrobius mentions the disparaging epithet, 'the consular wag', attached to him by his enemies, and even Quintilian wistfully muses that a more discriminating selection of the witticisms attributed to Cicero in the three volumes of his jests (now lost) would not have been amiss. See Macrobius,

expands on these ideas in the *Institutio oratoria* (6.3), reiterating Cicero's argument that for humour to be effective, it is of primary importance to take account of the persons, the occasion, and the circumstances involved (*De or.* 2.221, 2.229; *Inst.* 6.3.28). Like Cicero, Quintilian observes that humour is equally suited to a conversational context as to the forum (*De or.* 2.271; *Inst.* 6.3.14). In *De officiis*, Cicero deplores the fact that while extensive handbooks on rhetoric abound, there are few rules for sociable converse (or *sermo*).[5] Citing the witty, ironic style of Socrates as a paradigm to emulate, he proceeds to set out some guidelines. None of the participants should dominate the conversation, or boast about themselves, or indulge in malicious wisecracks. Strong emotions of any kind should be avoided, and aggression mitigated. Highlighting the performative dimension of social interaction, Cicero sums up, 'Above all we should demonstrate our apparent respect and affection for those with whom we are to converse' (1.136).

Cicero's ideas on *sermo* were elaborated on by Plutarch in his *Quaestiones convivales*, which, together with the fifth-century *Saturnalia*, Macrobius's compendium of table talk, was formative for Renaissance compilations of jests. As in the rhetorical tradition, the aim is urbane wittiness, in which boorish aggression and coarse obscenity have been banished. Drawing on an anecdote in Xenophon's *Cyropaedia*, whose depiction of the court of Persian king Cyrus as the pattern of civility played an important part in shaping Castiglione's vision of Urbino,[6] Plutarch has one of his interlocutors assert that tactful jesting is an essential element in the art of conversation. Particularly praiseworthy are those 'whose very jokes offered pleasure and gratification to those who were the butts' (629F).[7] The *Quaestiones convivales*, modelled as it was on the genre of the symposium, makes it clear that it is imperative to maintain cordial relations with all participants of the company. The observance of good taste in jesting is the mark of a gentleman, Plutarch claims, conceding that it requires exceptional skill to be able to joke without offending one's interlocutor.

What is equally important is to be able to take a joke. Plutarch counsels self-mockery or including oneself when teasing others (634D). This is a

---

Saturnalia, 2.1.12, and Quintilian, *Institutio oratoria*, 6.3.5. Also see Guérin, 'Laughter, Social Norms, and Ethics in Cicero's Works', 127–28.

5. On *sermo*, see Kennerly, '*Sermo* and Sociality in Cicero's *De Officiis*'; Burke, *Art of Conversation*; Burke, 'A Civil Tongue'; Miller, *Conversation*; and Randall, *Concept of Conversation*.

6. Burke, *Fortunes of the Courtier*, 10.

7. Plutarch, *Moralia*, vol. 8. The section on jesting is question 1 in book 2.

noteworthy departure from the rhetorical tradition, where Quintilian strongly advises that 'To make a joke against oneself is normally a matter for the professional jester (*scurra*), and is at any rate not to be approved in an orator' (6.3.82). But Quintilian too acknowledges that 'It is sometimes a good joke to speak about yourself' (6.3.95), echoing Cicero's inclusion of self-disparaging humour in his statement that laughter is provoked by 'mocking other people's character or giving a humorous hint of our own' (2.289). Aristotle makes it clear that sociability entails an ability to laugh at oneself. In a discussion of affability in the *Rhetoric*, he underlines the importance of being able to both make and take jokes in good sport (1381a33–35). In Macrobius's *Saturnalia*, Plutarch's injunctions to avoid offence are recycled; at the same time, Augustus is extolled by one of the interlocutors for his unfailing courtesy in tolerating jokes rather than for his talent in making them.[8] These thoughts shaped Renaissance ideas on civility. The English manual *The Courte of Civill Courtesie* (1577) advises its readers, when mocked, 'either with wit turne it to some merrie conceit', or to join in the laughter at one's expense (F1r). Hobbes, for whom the eighth 'Law of Nature' to facilitate peaceful coexistence consists of refraining from contumely (or insolent abuse), simultaneously dismisses those who are quick to take umbrage as pusillanimous (*Leviathan* 107, 213). In his *Pocket Oracle*, Gracián neatly reverses the impetus behind jesting. 'Take a joke, but don't make someone the butt of one', he advises. Taking a joke 'is a form of politeness' and demonstrates one's cultivation.[9] Incivility, it appears, consists equally in offending and in a determination to ferret out offence.

Pontano's Man of Wit

Giovanni Pontano, a well-known poet who founded the Academy in Naples that later bore his name, achieved a considerable reputation as a man of letters. His mirror for princes, *De principe liber* (1468), was written for his charge, Alfonso, Duke of Calabria and son of Alfonso the Magnanimous, ruler of Aragon and Naples and legendary as a cynosure of wit. Pontano's theory of humour, delineated in the treatise *De sermone* (*On Speech*), published posthumously in 1509, derives largely from Cicero's *De oratore* and Quintilian's *Institutio oratoria*. Rather than in oratory, Pontano sets out to discuss the virtues and vices in 'common speech' and 'civil intercourse' (1.3.2). His interest lies in wittiness,

---

8. Macrobius, *Saturnalia*, 2.4.19.
9. Gracián, *Pocket Oracle and Art of Prudence*, no. 241, p. 91.

which he claims is a 'moral and civic virtue' (5.2.3), not merely an oratorical one. Urbane wit, Pontano asserts, is the badge of the Renaissance gentleman. If Castiglione aims to present the perfect courtier, Pontano's ideal is what he terms the *vir facetus*: the man of wit.[10]

Pontano's point of departure is the triad of qualities that Aristotle labels as virtues of social intercourse: affability, truthfulness relating to one's achievements, and wittiness (*EN* 4.6–8). Pontano devotes the greater part of his treatise to the third, insisting that like all virtues, wit is a skill that can be trained. Pontano's text also offers a cornucopia of jests, no doubt assiduously accumulated over years and invaluable for readers to plunder.

For Pontano, as for Cicero and Quintilian, the effect of humour depends entirely on contextual criteria: 'what is fitting and how much, in what way, at what time, likewise at what place, with whom' (3.6.4). Dissimulation, he notes, is a key strategy in jokes. Cicero advocates witty anecdotes, either fabricated or if true, 'spiced with little lies' (*De or.* 2.241) and praises the 'elegant and witty' art of irony (or *dissimulatio*) at which Socrates excelled.[11] Quintilian commends simulation and dissimulation, in particular irony, as 'the greatest sources of laughter'; the former consists in 'faking an opinion of one's own' while the latter amounts to 'pretending not to understand what others mean' (*Inst.* 6.3.85).[12] Pontano makes every effort to condemn falsehood, feigning, and deception which aim to sow hatred and hostility and undermine harmony in a civil community (2.8.2). However, he exempts Socratic dissimulation, a form of self-deprecation that he terms 'honorable' and accounts a virtue (6.3.3).[13] Indeed, Pontano admits that dissimulation is an inextricable part of social life. Sometimes, he maintains, 'prudence, in accordance with the place, time, business, duties, dangers, and the role that we bear, both requires and also advises us now to simulate, now on the contrary to dissimulate, now to hide the truth, now to feign and maintain things that are by no means true'. He concludes, 'Sometimes feigning must be imputed a virtue' (2.17.9). Critical is the end it serves.

---

10. On Pontano, see Luck, 'Vir Facetus'; Bowen, 'Renaissance Collections of *facetiae*'; and Pigman, 'Introduction'.

11. Cicero identifies the Greek term *eirōneia* with *dissimulatio* in *De or.* 2.269.

12. Quintilian, who prefers the term *ironia*, delivers a more technical disquisition on irony as a trope or figure of speech in *Inst.* 8.6.54–58 and as a figure of thought in *Inst.* 9.2.44–53. In both cases irony is defined more narrowly than in Cicero as saying the opposite of what one means (*Inst.* 9.2.50).

13. In his condemnation of all forms of lying, St Augustine exempted jocose lies since, although frivolous, they did not intend to deceive. See Augustine, *Lying*, 54.

Pontano emphatically rejects wit that 'is annoying and odious and tends to quarreling and contention' (4.6.1), or jests which are 'abounding with bile', or 'obscene, buffoonish, very bitter, or rustic, rude, unseasoned, not worthy of the city' (4.11.18). This does not mean that the distinction he sets up between acceptable and unacceptable humour would chime with our own more squeamish age. For Pontano, as for the ancients, the governing factor is social status. Pungent witticisms and barbs are applauded if they avoid any taint of rusticity and steer clear of the antics of parasites and mimes. His compilation of jests brims with risqué and aggressive jokes.[14] Not all contemporaries would approve of his taste. In the *Ciceronianus* (1528), while Erasmus has his interlocutors acknowledge Pontano as 'a great man with many exceptional gifts of mind', they grouch that his light verse 'would have been thought of more highly if he had avoided obscenity'. As for his prose, sometimes 'it's difficult to say whether he's a Christian or not'.[15]

Sharp retorts, Pontano avers, produce 'admiration and delight' (4.1.5). An example he recommends (borrowed from Poggio Braccolini's *Facetiae*, the first Renaissance jestbook) is the following:

> A Florentine traveler, extremely fat as well as sharp-witted, journeying through the city of Siena, happened to be leaving by the gate that leads to Rome, and his raised mantle showed a very large and swollen paunch. And thereupon the guards of the gate said, joking and laughing, 'This little man is clever because he placed his bag in front, not in back'. Then he, beaming for all he was worth, said, 'Would you walk safely with your property through this territory of thieves and assassins in any other way?' (4.3.9)

Pontano enthuses, 'What could be more charming and witty than that?' (4.3.10). The virulent enmity between the Sienese and Florentines, reaching back to the thirteenth century, meant that violence frequently lurked beneath the surface of any encounter between the citizens of the two city-states. Crucial for Pontano is the idea that in a situation charged with tension, wit can be deployed in a verbal duel that by eliciting a shared pleasure in competitive wit, however reluctantly acknowledged, compels the antagonists to remain within the bounds of civil interaction. For Pontano, jokes are a form of play (5.2.9).

---

14. Freud would later distinguish between jokes which aim solely to delight and 'tendentious' humour, which comprises aggressive and obscene jokes. See Freud, *Jokes and Their Relation to the Unconscious*, 107–46.

15. Erasmus, *Ciceronianus*, 436.

Ideally, in combative wit, antagonism is transposed into agonism, predicated on a baseline respect of the other if only as co-combatant.

Castiglione's Laughing Courtier

Castiglione's Urbino reverberates with laughter. References to laughing courtiers thread the conversation, while book 2 is largely devoted to a discussion of the art of jesting. The ideal courtier, Federico Fregoso explains, 'should know how to sweeten and refresh the minds of his hearers, and move them discreetly to gaiety and laughter with amusing witticisms and pleasantries' (2.41). In this society, a talent for quips and sparkling banter is a vital means of acquiring social distinction. The style of humour in which the courtier indulges defines him as a man of cultivation, in the same way as his comportment, his speech, and the clothes he wears. No longer acceptable, Federico maintains, are the loutish japes courtiers used to enjoy: 'They often push one another downstairs, deal each other blows with sticks and bricks, throw fistfuls of dust in one another's eyes, cause their horses to roll one on the other in ditches or downhill; then at table they throw soups, gravies, jellies, and every kind of thing in one another's face; and then they laugh' (2.36). Bernado Bibbiena, famous for his wit, takes over from Federico and reiterates his warning to steer clear of buffoonish behaviour or slapstick. He also admonishes his fellow courtiers to avoid 'jibes that are too cutting' (2.49); jokes should be strictly regulated by the norms of decorum, and be adapted to the persons, place, and situation involved. Those too wretched to be laughed at, those too malevolent to merit laughter, and those too powerful to be made the target of derision should be precluded from humour. Civil jesting, he contends, is a way of providing recreation and pleasure, not a continuation of war by other means.

Virtually all Castiglione's comments on humour, and a generous handful of his jokes, derive from *De oratore*, including the distinction between humorous narrative and sharp, clever one-liners (*De or.* 2.218), although Castiglione has Bibbiena add a third category, practical jokes.[16] The references to laughter strewn throughout the *Courtier* contribute significantly towards the mood of playful relaxation and bonhomie. In the enchanted enclave of Urbino, friction and hostility seem to be relegated to the harsh realities of the outside world. Book

---

16. Mary Beard points out that Cicero's distinction between the terms *cavillatio, dicacitas,* and *facetiae* (in the later *Orator*) is often contradictory. See her *Laughter in Ancient Rome*, 113–15.

194   CHAPTER 5

2 does not merely offer a fireworks of jokes, which made it a favourite section of the book for a range of contemporary readers, including the Italian poets Vittoria Colonna and Gian Giorgio Trissino, the scholars Vincenzo Maggi and Antonio Riccoboni, and Gabriel Harvey and Ben Jonson.[17] It also demonstrates how jesting might work in social interaction. By no means are the jokes as benign as Bibbiena would have them. One example of a skirmish of wit which reveals the hidden fault lines of aggression that run through the text is an exchange of jokes between the Florentine Bibbiena and the Viennese Pietro Bembo.[18]

Bibbiena has been delegated the task of discussing jokes. He is interrupted by Bembo. 'And why do you not tell the one about your friend the Florentine commander, who was besieged in Castellina by the Duke of Calabria?', he asks, before immediately relating the joke himself, a jibe at Bibbiena's fellow Tuscans for their ineptitude in warfare (2.52). Bernado laughs and threatens to tell jokes about Bembo's own countrymen, the Venetians, rivals of the Florentine Republic. Instead, he delivers a joke about the Sienese. Bembo persists. 'I am speaking of the Florentines, not the Sienese', he says. He is goaded on by the presiding court lady, the spirited and sharp-tongued Emilia Pia. With relish, Bembo narrates a second amusing anecdote about Tuscan practices during war, depicting the obtuseness of Florentine statesmen and their willingness to exploit their allies, in this case the city-states of Prato and Pistoia. Signora Emilia turns to Bibbiena and taunts him, 'Messer Bernado, will you allow messer Pietro to ridicule the Florentines in this manner without taking your revenge?' (2.52). Bibbiena remains courteous, but at this point a joke is interposed by Cesare Gonzaga from Mantua, another member of the coterie at Urbino:

> I heard a delightful blunder uttered by a Brescian who went to Venice this year for the Feast of the Ascension, and in my presence was telling his

---

17. Burke, *Fortunes of the Courtier*, 152. Jonson praises the 'pithy sayings, similitudes, and conceits . . . such as are in *The Courtier*, and the second book of Cicero, *De oratore*'. See Jonson, *Discoveries*, 576. In his copy of Thomas Wilson's *Art of Rhetoric*, Harvey notes, 'One of mie best for the art of jesting: next Tullie, Quintilian, the Courtier'; qtd. in Stern, *Gabriel Harvey*, 160.

18. For an insightful analysis, see Cavallo, 'Joking Matters'. On the section on jokes in Castiglione, also see Grudin, 'Renaissance Laughter'; Woodhouse, *Baldesar Castiglione*, 101–8; Rebhorn, *Courtly Performances*, 138–42; and Finucci, *The Lady Vanishes*, 77–103. For an analysis of the difference in jesting between *Il Cortegiano* and *De oratore*, see Javitch, *Poetry and Courtliness*, 34–37.

companions about the fine things he had seen there.... And when one of his companions asked him which kind of music he liked best of what he had heard, he said: 'It was all good; but I noted especially a man playing on a strange trumpet which with every move he would shove down his throat more than two palms' length, and then suddenly he would draw it out, then shove it down again; you never saw a greater marvel!'

Then everyone laughed ... (2.53)

By shifting the butt of the jests to a bumpkin from Brescia who has never seen a trombone, a relatively recently invented instrument, Cesare successfully diverts the attention of the group from the latent hostility between the Florentine and the Venetian to a target that unites all participants of the gathering in shared mirth. Making jokes about those outside a group is a well-worn device to create social cohesion.[19] With his reference to a musician who seems to be swallowing his instrument while continuing to emit a stream of harmonious sounds, Cesare obliquely pays tribute to the elegance and agility with which Bernardo has absorbed the insults of his fellow courtier into the flow of his cultivated conversation. Castiglione's anecdote demonstrates how jests in civil conversation might be used not only as a source of cultural capital, but also as weapons in a verbal joust that paradoxically can serve to cement group cohesion. Studies of the culture of aggressive wit in convivial societies such as those associated with the Inns of Court have shown that combative wittiness can shore up social bonds, ministering as it does both to the pleasure in competition and the pleasure in laughter.[20] As Shaftesbury would later put it, 'We polish one another, and rub off our Corners and rough Sides by a sort of *amicable Collision*'.[21] The antagonism between members of the group is transmuted into agonism, in which opponents are accorded respect not for their personality, but in their capacity as agonistic combatant. Simultaneously, wit can serve as a means to defuse tension by enabling both parties to save face, forging a temporary sense of interconnection that includes all members of a given community.[22]

---

19. See Davies, *Jokes and Their Relation to Society*.

20. See O'Callaghan, *English Wits*, and Magnusson, 'Scoff Power in *Love's Labour's Lost* and the Inns of Court'.

21. Cooper, '*Sensus Communis*', 39, emphasis original.

22. See Lombardini, 'Civic Laughter'. On the association of wit with civility, also see Withington, *Society in Early Modern England*, 186–201.

Jesting in the Renaissance

The Renaissance was deeply interested in the phenomenon of wit and laughter. A spirit of *serio ludere* flourished, a mode of thought yoking play with philosophical reflection. It stoked a vogue for paradox and Lucianic satire—rediscovered at the beginning of the fifteenth century—which was enthusiastically cultivated by humanists such as Erasmus and Sir Thomas More.[23] In a major shift from the long tradition of hostility towards levity expressed by ecclesiastical authorities, Erasmus was formative in revalorizing humour as an important source of recreation, drawing on the justification for relaxation furnished in the *Nicomachean Ethics*. While pleasure is not the *summum bonum*, Aristotle had declared, amusement fortifies us in the quest for the good life (1176b33–35). Following in the line of Petrarch, Erasmus compiled a store of ancient wit in his *Apophthegmata*, first published in 1531, which became an early modern bestseller. Erasmus and More were avid collectors of jokes, which they relished as a means to explore paradox, wordplay, the indeterminacy of language, and fallacious reasoning.[24]

Concurrently, early modern society was awash with hostile laughter. Jacob Burkhardt describes sixteenth-century Italy as 'a school for scandal' in which venomous jokes were pervasive.[25] In early modern England, explosive urbanisation and political and religious conflict inspired a vast outpouring of vitriol and libel. Divines were vocal in their disapproval of jeering. In his manual for right speech, William Perkins writes approvingly of decorous, urbane humour, 'whereby men in seemly maner use pleasantnes [humour] in talk', but castigates 'jesting which standeth in quippes, tauntes, and girdes [jeers], which serveth onely for the offence of some, with the delight of others'.[26] Observers of early modern society such as Thomas Wright present an image of social life in which callous laughter and derision are rampant. He writes, 'Certain men entertain their company with scoffing, nipping, gibing, and quipping; they think to have won a great victory if in descoursing some other's defect they can make the company laugh merrily. They will seem to make much of you,

---

23. The classic study is Colie, *Paradoxia Epidemica*.
24. See Prescott, 'Humanism in the Tudor Jestbook'.
25. Burckhardt, *Civilization of the Renaissance in Italy*, 110–19, 114.
26. Perkins, *Direction for the Government*, C8v, D1v. As Adrian Streete has argued persuasively, the early modern theatre absorbed and reflected the debates about laughter. See Streete, 'Polemical Laughter'.

but to the embracements of scorpions follow stinging tails' (4.1A.261–66). He warns against those who 'so quip and nip that they principally pretend to discredit or shame those persons at whom they jest' (272–73)—whose aim is to devastate others by means of humiliation.

Perhaps in response, most later manuals of civility do not share Castiglione's exuberant espousal of jesting. The narrator in Della Casa's *Galateo* (1558) declares categorically, 'I doe not allow, that a man should scorne or scoffe at any man, what so ever he be: no not his very enimy' (J3v). Derision, he argues, is a sign of contempt and disdain, and in all one's actions one should strive to convey the impression that one respects one's peers. In marked contrast to Cicero, he strongly disapproves of jokes about physical defects: 'they that scoffe at any man, that is deformed, ill shapen, leane, litle, or a dwarfe, are much to be blamed for it'. Indeed, he considers them 'unworthy to beare the name of an honest gentleman' (J4r). Della Casa counsels his readers to aim for toothless humour. Echoing a passage in *Decameron*, the narrator advises, 'Jestes must bite the hearer like a sheepe, but not like a dogge. For if it pinche, as the byte of a dogge: it shalbe no more a Jeste but a wronge' (K2r). He agrees that a skill at jesting is a social asset. But if one lacks talent, it is best to desist.

In Stefano Guazzo's dialogue, *The Civile Conversation* (1574), Anniball expresses his distaste for the 'mockers and flouters, who without any comely grace, deride every man, and more easily persuade them selves that they are pleasant and mery conceited fellowes, then perceive them selves to be ignorant and undiscreete fooles' (1.72). Jeering is the mark of a lack of breeding. Conversely, tasteful jesting coupled with good humour are invaluable in cultivated company: 'a certaine wittie and readie pleasantnesse delighteth wonderfully the hearers . . . no lesse in jesting merrily with others, then in taking jest patiently of others' (2.158–59). As in Plutarch's *Moralia*, Guazzo emphasizes the importance of being able to take a joke in good grace. The reason he puts forward is less ethical than pragmatic: 'wee must not mocke at other mens imperfections, least others likewise laugh at ours' (160).

Other courtesy books strike a similar note, oscillating between proposing witty speech as a desirable accomplishment and warning readers of the risks involved. William Martyn in *Youths Instruction* (1612) commends jesting 'so that it be prettie & witty, not bitter, not scorning' but admonishes his son to 'avoid foolish iesting & peeuish scoffing' (O3v). In *The Compleat Gentleman* (1622), Henry Peacham approves of seasoning one's conversation 'with conceits of wit and pleasant invention, as ingenious epigrams, emblem, anagrams, merry tales, witty questions and answers, mistakings', enumerating the favourite forms of dinner table entertainment in cultivated company (155). Like Castiglione, he reminds the reader that humour is an index of one's social persona, adducing Ecclesiasticus 19:30: 'by gait, laughter and apparel a man is known what he is' (198). In court manuals, injunctions about the bounds of humour become increasingly punctilious. In his *Treatise of the Court or Instructions for Courtiers* (1616), Eustache de Refuge grants that 'Pleasant jests and Replyes make also a part of Affabilitie'. Yet he advises readers to suppress any impulse to make scurrilous jokes or deliver jibes and bitter quips. When mocked, he counsels them to respond 'with a grave silence' or with a smile (C3r). In *L'honneste-homme ou, L'art de plaire à la cour* (1630), translated by Edward Grimeston with the title *The honest man: or, The art to please in court* (1632), Nicolas Faret distinguishes between wit and jesting, foreshadowing the distinction between 'raillery' and 'jesting' that took hold in English in the second half of seventeenth century. Amusing words or witticisms not only please one's audience, but embellish one's reputation: they 'make him that speakes them be regarded with extraordinary admiration' (P3v), he writes. But he expressly warns against the dangers of jesting. However entertaining, the social price exacted by jokes is high. Jests are always tainted by a tincture of anger or contempt, and 'never so milde in the beginning, but they leave some bitternesse in the minde, which is not so easily pulled out' (O12v). He also acutely analyses the element of gamesmanship involved: 'it seemes that it is a law in this sport, to the end that the liberty of biting to the quick may be more insolent, that the first which is discontented to loose the party' (P1r–v). Faret concludes that it is a dangerous pastime, one that inevitably entails losing a friend or gaining an enemy.

Meanwhile, no doubt in part due to the towering influence of Ciceronian rhetoric, witty jesting became a desirable resource. Social aspirants sedulously collected jokes and bon mots; on the print marketplace, jestbooks, handbooks, and conversational manuals provided a trove of wit for the upwardly mobile customer.[27] The jestbook began its career in print in 1477 as a compendium of amusing stories or *Facetiae*, tales that the scholar and papal secretary

---

27. The term 'jest', derived from the Old French *geste*, which originally denoted an exploit or a tale of exploits, took on the meaning of a humorous story in the early sixteenth century. On Renaissance jokes, see Bowen, *Humour and Humanism in the Renaissance*; Manley, 'London in Jest'; Munro, 'Jestbooks'; and Smyth, '"Divines into Dry Vines"'. On jesting in the Renaissance, see Holcomb, *Mirth Making*, and Ghose, 'Jesting, Nostalgia, and Agonistic Play'. A foundational work remains Thomas, 'The Place of Laughter in Tudor and Stuart England'.

Poggio Bracciolini swapped with colleagues and friends at the Vatican and that furnished diversion for other humanists. A genre that straddled oral and literate culture, the seventeenth-century jestbook developed into a popular print commodity, often compiled by hack writers who also wrote for the theatre. Amusing stories remained popular, but became shorter; the stock of sharp quips and one-liners took a steep rise. Books of table talk such as *The Schoolemaster, or Teacher of Table Philosophie* (1576) offered a vast selection of jokes, and handbooks such as *A Helpe to Discourse, Or, A Miscelany of Merriment* (1619) included jokes among a welter of encyclopaedic information, riddles, and epigrams. They retailed wit to an audience who appreciated the value of nimble ripostes and improvisation in metropolitan life. Playwrights and satirists regularly poke fun at the throng of gallants swarming to the theatre and jotting down jokes and quips in their commonplace books to reuse elsewhere. In his *Guls Horne-booke*, Dekker scoffs at punters who pilfer wit from the theatre in the hope of gaining social cachet, mockingly urging his readers to 'hoard up the finest play-scraps you can get, upon which your leane wit may most favoury feed, for want of other stuffe' (E4v). In a feedback loop, the theatre recycled comic matter from social life to lure an urban audience to its comedies—and duly charge them. This is brilliantly captured in *The Fair Maid of the Exchange* (1607), attributed to Thomas Heywood. One of the main protagonists, the Cripple, impresario of the plot intrigues, describes how a writer garners material for plays: by eavesdropping on gallants in a tavern, collecting their jests to 'put them into a play, / And tire them too with payment, to behold / What I have filch'd from them'.[28]

Jesting in *Epicene*

The lighthearted atmosphere at Urbino is sustained by carefully suppressing all mention of the grim truths that close in on the idyll from the outside. Occasionally, these truths encroach on the text, and require a conscious effort on the part of the courtiers to banish them to the borders of their cultivated preserve. In book 1, Count Ludovico alludes to the painful memory of the ignominy of the Italians in the recent wars, only to relegate it to silence (1.43), while in book 2 Federico notes that Italy has become the quarry of all nations, adding bitterly, 'little more is left to prey upon, and yet they do not leave off preying' (2.26)—before plunging back into a discussion of fashion. The laughter with

28. Heywood, *Fair Maid of the Exchange*, 50.

which the dialogue rings also serves to keep at bay the hostile reality in which the text is set.

In *Epicene*, as in the *Courtier*, jesting plays an important role in evading the darkness surrounding the self-absorbed world which is the focus of the play. The plot of *Epicene* takes place almost entirely in the Strand, the West End location that by the early seventeenth century had become the most desirable address in the city. Set in contemporary London during a plague epidemic and probably first performed by the Children of Her Majesty's Revels in early 1610 when the theatres reopened, the play is traversed by reminders of the fatal disease. Knowledge of the plague diffuses into the text mainly in the form of jokes: the plot turns on the elaborate confidence trick played on a misanthrope who hates noise—at a time when the bells are tolling incessantly for the dead. In Jonson's play, however, the blithe denial of the reality within which the fictive world is embedded differs significantly from the disavowal of foreign threat by the courtiers in Urbino in their attempt to safeguard their fragile idyll. Jonson scatters reminders of mortality throughout *Epicene* in order to foreground the lack of self-awareness that characterises all protagonists of the play, wits and dupes alike—and glances at the spectators too.[29]

Wit is the stock in trade of the trio of gallants who dominate *Epicene*. Exemplars of the stylish men about town who increasingly populated fashionable London, and role models for the men of mode of Restoration comedy, Truewit, Clerimont, and Dauphine epitomise the urbane art of jesting that is cardinal to the culture of civility. The wits are in their element when mocking others, whether behind their back or to their face. Truewit, the wittiest of the clique, excels in brilliant set pieces built on irony and paradox, as in his mock encomia in praise of cosmetics or artifice, which present Ovidian precepts suffused with a Juvenalian spirit.[30] But he is peerless when baiting the misanthropic Morose, Dauphine's uncle and their main target. His savage satire of marriage begins with the remark, 'your friends do wonder, sir, the Thames

---

29. Useful criticism of the play includes Kay, 'Jonson's Urbane Gallants'; Barton, *Ben Jonson*, 120–35; Salingar, 'Farce and Fashion in *The Silent Woman*', in *Dramatic Form in Shakespeare and the Jacobeans*, 175–88; Ayers, 'Dreams of the City'; Newman, 'City Talk: Femininity and Commodification in Jonson's *Epicoene*', in *Fashioning Femininity and English Renaissance Drama*, 131–43; Haynes, *Social Relations of Jonson's Theatre*, 90–98; Dutton, 'Introduction'; Zucker, 'Social Logic of Ben Jonson's *Epicoene*'; and Bevington, 'Introduction to *Epicene, or The Silent Woman*'. All references to the play are taken from the Revels Plays edition and are given in parentheses.

30. See Barish, 'Ovid, Juvenal and *The Silent Woman*'.

being so near, wherein you may drown so handsomely; or London Bridge at a low fall with a fine leap, to hurry you down the stream' (2.2.20–23), and continues with a list of methods of suicide which he claims concerned friends of Morose urge on him in preference to what he insists is the living death of wedlock. Adept at twisting the knife in the wound, Truewit later pretends to misunderstand Morose's ire at being tricked as excessive lust for his wife, and rebukes him for trying to have the doors barricaded. 'Would you go to bed so presently, sir, afore noon? A man of your head and hair should owe more to that reverend ceremony, and not mount the marriage-bed like a town bull', he lectures him mock-sanctimoniously (3.5.41–44). Equally nimble in shifting ground, he diverts the blame for the marriage to Cutbeard the barber, and lures Morose into joining him in a bizarre round of flyting, cursing the culprit's trade:

> MOROSE: Let his warming-pan be ever cold.
> TRUEWIT: (A perpetual frost underneath it, sir.)
> MOROSE: Let him never hope to see fire again.
> TRUEWIT: (But in hell, sir.)
> MOROSE: His chairs be always empty, his scissors rust, and his combs mould in their cases. . . . Or for want of bread—
> TRUEWIT: Eat ear-wax, sir. I'll help you. Or, draw his own teeth and add them to the lute-string. (76–90)

Truewit plays a cat-and-mouse game with his victim, goading him into an increasingly surreal crescendo of imprecations against Cutbeard until the realisation dawns on Morose that he is being sent up. Although the play sets up an opposition between the common tastes of Captain Otter, a regular of the Bear Garden, and the sophisticated lifestyle of the smart set, the imagery of animal baiting lurks just beneath the surface of the witty idiom of the play.[31]

Sometimes the wits stage a double act or team effort in making sport of other members of the society portrayed in the play, none of whom live up to the standards of effortless style and taste that they represent. Dauphine and Clerimont embark on a mission to poke fun at Sir John Daw, who counts himself as a wit but is a caricature of philistinism and intellectual grandstanding. At the mention of classical giants such as Seneca and Plutarch, Daw exclaims, 'Grave asses! . . . I do utter as good things every hour, if they were collected and observed, as either of 'em' (2.3.48–51). Accordingly, the wits set

---

31. See Haynes, *Social Relations of Jonson's Theatre*, 97.

him up, with Dauphine asking him innocently whom he considers great authors. '*Syntagma juris civilis, Corpus juris civilis, Corpus juris canonici*, the King of Spain's Bible' is the fatuous reply. Not only are none of these authors, but the first two titles are simply Greek and Latin terms for the same canonical legal text, a joke that would be particularly relished by spectators from the Inns of Court. Dauphine continues in mock-innocuous vein, 'What was that *Syntagma*, sir?' Daw responds in all seriousness, mimicked by the wits:

> DAW: A civil lawyer, a Spaniard.
> DAUPHINE: Sure, *Corpus* was a Dutchman.
> CLERIMONT: Ay, both the *Corpuses*, I knew 'em: they were very corpulent authors. (2.3.78–86)

Daw is too inane to realise that he is being lampooned, which only heightens the hilarity of the two young men—and the audience, who are invited to share in the pleasures of coney-catching: as Dauphine promises, the wits bag the gulls as 'in a purse-net', used to catch conies or rabbits (3.3.94). The trio preside over the play, parading a series of fools, social misfits, and arrivistes in front of us for our delectation. La Foole, for instance, is ridiculed for his social ineptitude and posturing. As Clerimont reports, 'He will salute a judge upon the bench and a bishop in the pulpit, a lawyer when he is pleading at the bar, and a lady when she is dancing in a masque, and put her out. He does give plays and suppers, and invites his guests to 'em aloud out of his window as they ride by in coaches' (1.3.31–36). In his eagerness to ingratiate himself with those he considers important, he stands condemned for affectation, a mortal sin in the canon of the *Courtier*. The Collegiates, on the other hand, a travesty of the members of salons run by bluestockings such as the Countess of Bedford, one of Jonson's patrons, are lambasted for their woefully inadequate literary judgement, in a scathing comment on the power they wield.[32] Truewit explains that they 'cry down or up what they like or dislike in a brain or a fashion, with most masculine or rather hermaphroditical authority' (1.1.77–79). The brief discussion of literature as a cure for Morose's alleged madness lays bare their crass ignorance and appalling taste. When Sir John proposes Aristotle's *Ethics*, Mavis retorts dismissively, 'Say you so, Sir John? I think you are deceived: you took it upon trust' (4.4.94–95), while Lady Haughty recommends Thomas Becon's tract *The Sycke Mans Salve* (1561) and Robert Greene's

---

32. For a discussion of Jonson's ambivalent relationship to his female patrons, see Dutton, 'Introduction', 21–24.

Groats-Worth of witte (1592), both low-end market print commodities Jonson's audience, patrons of the fashionable indoor Whitefriars Theatre (Prol. 24), would mock as antiquated. 'A very cheap cure' (105), Truewit remarks sardonically, punning on both the quality and the price.

The wits do not just indulge in witticisms and wisecracks at the expense of the other characters. They also unleash a series of practical jokes on them. These range from organizing a charivari to Morose's house, provoking Daw and La Foole into a fight, turning the Otters on each other, to initiating mock divorce proceedings in the course of which Morose is compelled to declare himself impotent and is exposed as a cuckold. The star architect of the jests is Truewit, but the overarching device that the plot is structured around, the hoax of the silent woman, is designed by Dauphine. The protagonists are driven by the desire to devise ever more spectacular pranks: Truewit is keen to turn the entertainment orchestrated for Morose's wedding day into 'a jest to posterity' (2.6.27). However, it is not just the pleasure of playing witty games that impels them to outdo each other in concocting extravagant stunts or brilliant quips. The three leisured gentlemen are engaged in burnishing their self-created reputation as models of urbanity. Witty young men are on a constant quest for aristocratic patronage, the lack of which Truewit points to in his comment on the 'common disease' of the times: 'we complain that great men will not look upon us nor be at leisure to give our affairs such dispatch as we expect' (1.1.56–58). It is worth noting that whatever they might say about the Collegiates in private, they are careful not to ridicule them in public, perhaps hopeful that aristocratic favour might lead to preferment. Dauphine's own motive for the exploit of the silent woman is of course a hard-headed economic one, as the end of the play reveals.[33]

Nor are the wits alone preoccupied with raising their status or anxious not to tarnish their social standing. All characters of the play are driven by aspiration. The gallants are successful in prodding Daw and La Foole into making fools of themselves by playing on their fears of losing face by permitting the other to publicly snub them. Both Daw and La Foole are concerned to preserve the pose of being *bons vivants* and men of the world, which is why they fall into Clerimont's trap and pretend to have been lovers of Epicene. The Collegiates, too, are keen to gain distinction as intellectuals and femmes fatales. In this society, even drones like Otter and barbers like Cutbeard make a bid for higher-class credentials by showing off their smattering of Latin.

33. I am indebted to Zucker's astute analysis of the economic underpinnings of the gallants' wit.

The dream of upward mobility is personified by Mistress Otter, the cousin of La Foole who has become rich through the trade in china, a luxury commodity much in demand in high society. She is inordinately proud of rubbing shoulders with the elite, and oblivious of the sneering undertone to Truewit's backhanded compliment that 'she is the only authentic courtier that is not naturally bred one, in the city' (3.2.28–29). For the wits, her pretensions to a class code to which she has no real claim are a source of endless jocularity. In response to her simpering remark, 'I am the servant of the court and courtiers, sir', Truewit insists with faux ingenuousness, 'They are rather your idolaters' (34–35), a comment dripping with irony which, once again, is appreciated only by his peers.

A votary of the cult of civility, she labours to improve the manners of her wastrel husband, shirking no effort to do so: 'I'll ha' you chained up with your bull-dogs and bear-dogs, if you be not civil the sooner', she threatens (3.1.1–2). His lament is that she refuses to countenance his drinking games on the grounds that 'they are no *decorum* among ladies' (3.3.121). She, on other hand, is intent on demonstrating her mastery of refined speech, bandying about affected terms such as 'obnoxious' or 'difficil' (3.2.3). Dauphine flatters her with an equivocal tribute whose mocking implications are intended for the benefit of his friends: 'What an excellent choice phrase this lady expresses in!' (26).

If the gallants have exuberant fun at the expense of social climbers, there are moments when the satire appears to cut close to the bone. The wits only gently twit Mistress Otter when she relates her nightmares about London, confessing wistfully, 'anything I do but dream o' the city' (3.2.65). All her dreams involve scenarios of social opprobrium in which her possessions, luxury items such as sumptuous clothes, are irreparably damaged. The mishaps inevitably take place in public and involve setbacks to her societal aspirations. However risible Mistress Otter's anxieties appear to be, they tap into the fear of a fall in status the wits share—and that might resonate with the audience. Although aimed at Daw, Truewit's remark to Lady Haughty is prescient: 'That falls out often, madam, that he that thinks himself the master-wit is the master fool' (3.6.48–49). At the end of the play, he too is forced to cede his role as star wit to Dauphine.

Epicene as a Satire of Civility

Epicene does not merely skewer the self-importance of an array of social pretenders. The play is a satire of the culture of civility to which Jonson's England was in thrall. The play levels its dispassionate gaze on the gallants too, paragons of civility. The wits are virtuosic dramatists who revel in staging playlets to subject their victims to humiliation. By presenting several of their pranks as metadramatic insets, Jonson creates an ironic distance to his witty protagonists and their japes, however brilliantly orchestrated. We do not simply watch all characters, gulls as well as wits, with a measure of critical detachment. In addition, we find ourselves under scrutiny as spectators. It becomes gradually clear that the wits are in the grip of hubristic delusions of grandeur—which, the play insinuates, we might share. By exposing the charade of the marital life of the Otters, by pitting Daw and La Foole against each other in a fabricated assault on their honour, and by shredding the facade of Morose's marriage, the wits aim to annihilate their victims. It becomes equally apparent that their dazzling wit is not necessarily a sign of intellectual perspicuity. Not only are they as fervently in pursuit of prestige as their victims. In their zeal to demolish the gulls, they do not hesitate to resort to the assumptions that underpin the frenzy for duelling in early modern society—assumptions that were increasingly being called into question.

Throughout the play, the undertow of rivalry among the wits threatens to sabotage their camaraderie. At times they train their cutting jibes on each other. When Truewit expresses his low opinion of Daw, Clerimont baits him by proclaiming, 'They say he is a very good scholar', an assertion he repeats thrice (1.2.71–81). His remarks seem to have the sole purpose of needling his friend, who takes pride in his own scholarship. On another occasion, Truewit and Clerimont are witness to an attempt by Daw and La Foole to belittle Dauphine in front of the Collegiates. Although indignant at the presumption of the two fops, the wits cannot resist goading Dauphine with a luridly embellished report. Dauphine, predictably enraged, rounds viciously on Truewit, who has promised to devise a plan for revenge, snapping, 'Ay, you have many plots!' (4.5.20). The gentlemen are not above lashing out at each other in spite. Dauphine accuses Truewit of gamesmanship and attempting to upstage his companions, attacking him with the words, 'This is thy extreme vanity now; thou thinkst thou wert undone if every jest thou mak'st were not published' (4.5.237–38). The lack of trust among the friends is striking. Dauphine's final coup finds his confidants entirely unprepared.

In *Epicene* Jonson showcases the allure of the Ovidian gentlemen about town the play helped to shape, even while casting a cold eye on their failings. Their poise and casual ease comprise insouciant cruelty, as Dauphine's gratuitous degradation of his uncle after he has achieved his goal of securing his inheritance makes apparent. Even Truewit is taken aback at the lengths to which Dauphine is prepared to take a jest. When Dauphine suggests accepting

Daw's cowardly offer of a limb to appease what he thinks is a raging adversary, Truewit exclaims, 'How! Maim a man for ever for a jest?' (4.5.127). Conversely, whatever sympathies the dénouement might inspire for Morose, his boorish repudiation of civility is satirized too. Despite his court connections, Morose rejects manners as a superfluous frivolity. He refuses to waste time welcoming the supposed legal experts engaged to help him get a divorce. 'Salute 'em? I had rather do anything than wear out time so unfruitfully', he sneers, and complains, 'I wonder how these common forms, as "God save you" and "You are welcome", are come to be a habit in our lives! Or "I am glad to see you!" when I cannot see what the profit can be of these words, so long as it is no whit better with him whose affairs are sad and grievous that he hears this salutation' (5.3.25–31). His intransigence recalls that of the Puritan divines who spurn the culture of civility.[34] Nonetheless, consumed by envy at the prospect of his nephew's knighthood, he insists that his wife, although preferably mute, should conform to courtly manners. Nor does the play offer the slightest indication of a wish on his part to escape London, the centre of fashionable life, by moving to the country. Morose mirrors the ambivalence towards civility that marks the play.

An alternative, albeit parodic, take on civility is offered in the performance of reconciliation put on by the two cowardly knights, Daw and La Foole, after they have been gulled by the wits in the play-within-the-play that the latter stage for the ladies' benefit. Warned of the alleged violent propensities of the other, they maintain a front of impeccable courtesy when they meet, pretending to be unaware of the recent disgrace they have suffered, as they believe, at the other's hands. Their dancelike ceremony of etiquette involves their putting on a show of amicable unity, speaking with one voice. 'Sir John Daw and I are both beholden to you', La Foole declares to Clerimont, echoed by Daw asserting, 'Sir Amorous and I are your servants, sir' (5.1.5–8). They lavish compliments on each other, and defer to the other in exaggerated politeness:

DAW: Why-a-do you speak, Sir Amorous.
LA FOOLE: No, do you, Sir John Daw.
DAW: I' faith, you shall.
LA FOOLE: I' faith, you shall. (5.1.56–59)

Their cosy collegiality culminates in the fantasy that they have jointly indulged in sexual adventures, claiming they have been 'In the great bed at Ware together at our time' (61). Their boast to have enjoyed the sexual favours of

---

34. See Thomas, *In Pursuit of Civility*, 306–10.

Epicene seals their fate, provoking their final unmasking. Admittedly, in the light of the cynicism towards women articulated by the wits throughout the play, the spurt of zeal displayed by the latter to rescue the honour of all ladies from the slander of 'common moths' (5.4.235) such as the two fops appears somewhat spurious.

The entire vignette is outrageously funny, holding up the fops and their stylized social rituals to ridicule. Nevertheless, a brief glance at Jonson's source for this episode, the 'combat of the cowards' in *Arcadia,* is revealing.[35] In Sidney's version, two craven characters, the clown Dametas and the treacherous Clinias, are persuaded to engage in a farcical duel. But there are subtle differences. Both Dametas and Clinias issue bombastic challenges to the other, something the pacific fops in *Epicene* never do. While Dametas crows over what he believes was his victory, Clinias is eaten up by a sense of dishonour, and turns against his lord, Amphialus, whose role in inciting him to fight his rival he deeply resents and whom he plots to have poisoned.

Unlike Clinias, in whom deep rancour festers after having been shamed in public, La Foole and Daw attempt to save face, both their own and that of their antagonist. For all their absurdity, the charade of reciprocal respect acted out by La Foole and Daw and the care they take not to expose each other's fictions contributes towards defusing the conflict, while the witty jests engineered by the gallants thrive on aggression. Truewit announces their gulling as a 'tragicomedy between the Guelphs and the Ghibellines' (4.5.30). But there is little in common between the timorous Daw and La Foole and the violent factions whose incessant strife was a bane to civil life in medieval Italy. It is true that in their civil behaviour, the effete knights are impelled by cowardice, not commonality. And there is no question that the play scoffs at the fatuous knights for their affectation. At the same time, the humour of the exploit cuts both ways. Significantly, the gulls reproach the wits with a plaintive appeal to their own honour: 'Is this gentleman-like, sir?' (5.4.91). Staged as a miniature play, the episode invites the audience to look somewhat more critically at its own pieties, such as the myth of honour and a righteous insistence on being affronted. In the case of La Foole and Daw, the play makes it clear that there is no slur on their honour that they need to redress. The conflict is entirely concocted. Ironically, they respond precisely as the Stoic philosopher Epictetus

---

35. Sidney, *Countess of Pembroke's Arcadia,* bk. 3, chap. 13, 509–16, 516. Richard Dutton attributes the identification of the source to Emrys Jones, 'The First West Comedy'. See Dutton, 'Introduction', 29–30.

would advise, who in the *Encheiridion* points out that it is not possible to be offended without one's consent.[36]

The last joke in the play is a jest played by Jonson on the audience. In the final moments of the play, immediately after Morose has signed away a third of his estate to Dauphine and instated his nephew as sole heir, the latter announces his uncle's 'release' (5.4.198) from the bondage of marriage and removes Epicene's wig. The climactic revelation that the only silent woman onstage is a boy has usually been analysed in terms of the gender politics of the play and its performance practice.[37] What has been less frequently noted is the fact that not only is Epicene uncased, but Otter and Cutbeard are stripped of their disguise onstage as well. With the dismantling of theatrical illusion in the final scene, *Epicene* does not merely reveal gender identity to be a performance. Spectators in the early seventeenth century were used to games with boy actors dressing up as girls dressing up as boys. Jonson's self-reflexive joke is far more audacious. He breaks the frame of the theatrical experience itself, stripping away its artifice and exposing its mechanisms. If the other jokes in the play, the pranks, hoaxes, and deceptions, involve elaborate bluffs or fictions, this jest drastically disrupts audience expectations by breaching the convention that actors onstage, even in cross-dressing scenarios, are always in character. For a fleeting moment, as the player playing Epicene appears to step out of his role, the distinction between actor and audience dissolves. Jonson's joke upends our assumptions about the clear-cut divide between reality and fiction. And yet, the unmasking of Epicene onstage is an intrinsic part of the show. There is no escape from the framework of the performance.[38] At a deeper level, Jonson's joke unsettles our complacencies about role-playing and what we call authentic identity.

Epicene draws attention to the theatricality inherent in all social life. Thomas Greene has famously argued that Jonson's entire corpus reflects a yearning for stable selfhood.[39] Nonetheless, the play suggests that role-playing is an inescapable element of our existence. Epicene may be a boy playing a girl, Cutbeard a barber playing a lawyer, and Otter a loafer playing a priest. But everyone else in the play is acting a part, too, playing a role in the charade called social

---

36. Epictetus, *The Encheiridion*, 20.

37. See, for instance, Rose, 'Sexual Disguise and Social Mobility in Jacobean City Comedy', in *Expense of Spirit*, 43–92; Levine, 'Theatre as Other: Jonson's *Epicoene*', in *Men in Women's Clothing*, 73–88; and Swann, 'Refashioning Society in Ben Jonson's *Epicoene*'.

38. See Goffman, *Frame Analysis*, 345–77.

39. See Greene's seminal article 'Ben Jonson and the Centered Self'.

life. The unmasking of three of the players onstage reminds us of the vertiginous multitude of roles each individual plays in their own life. By drawing attention to its patent fictionality, the play suggests that we too are bound up in the fabrications we devise for ourselves.

Witty Women

Apart from *The Courtier*, few sixteenth-century courtesy books specifically address the skills of the lady. However, it is clear that the texts were considered to be as relevant to gentlewomen as to gentlemen. In his dedicatory epistle Hoby promotes the *Courtier* as addressed not only to princes and courtiers, but 'to Ladyes and Gentlewomen, a mirrour to decke and trimme themselves with vertuous condicions, comely behaviours and honest entertainment toward al men' (A3v). And the patrician Annibale Guasco, in the manual penned in 1586 for his eleven-year-old daughter, Lavinia, who had been appointed lady-in-waiting at the court of Turin, exhorts her to study the works of Castiglione, Della Casa, and Guazzo carefully. He also encourages her to cultivate the art of jesting, 'a delightful and noble thing and proof of a ready wit'.[40]

In book 3 of the *Courtier*, the ideal Court Lady is described as the counterpart of the Courtier. Her task is to please and gain the ear of her mistress (3.4). Accordingly, it is essential that she cultivate her wit, in the sense of both nurturing her intellect and honing her skill at quips and repartee. Her education should be on par with that of the Courtier—the Magnifico has no doubt that 'women can understand all the things men can understand, and that the intellect of a woman can penetrate wherever a man's can' (3.12). He stresses that women too should be able to converse and jest in a refined manner: 'in her talk, her laughter, her play, her jesting, in short in everything, she will be most graceful and will converse appropriately with every person in whose company she may happen to be, using witticisms and pleasantries that are becoming to her' (3.9). It is true that the Magnifico is at pains to curb any predilection the Court Lady might have for risqué humour. He insists that his paragon of virtue should not 'utter unseemly words or enter into any immodest and unbridled familiarity'; if others indulge in scurrilous talk, she ought to display 'a light blush of shame' (3.5). There is little sense in the text that the ladies present pay the slightest attention to his advice—certainly not the bold and quick-witted Emilia Pia, appointed by the Duchess of Urbino to lead the discussions.

---

40. Guasco, *Discourse to Lady Lavinia His Daughter*, 85, 88.

Cesare Gonazago goes so far as to attribute the entire culture of civility to the influence of women. He gushes, 'Who learns to dance gracefully for any reason except to please women? Who devotes himself to the sweetness of music for any other reason? Who attempts to compose verses, at least in the vernacular, unless to express sentiments inspired by women?' (3.52). A more grudging version of the same sentiment is put forward by James Cleland, who in his *Hero-paidea* (1612) encourages his noble charge to frequent the company of ladies 'as profitable to forme your Civil behaviour', even as he expresses reservations about ladies of 'alluring behaviour' (2H4r).

Not all writers of manuals would agree with Messer Cesare. Some are adamant that civility in women is tantamount to chastity. Giovanni Michele Bruto's treatise, *The necessarie, fit, and convenient education of a yong gentlewoman* (1598), written in 1555 and translated into English and French in a trilingual edition, is addressed to a Genoese merchant, Silvestre Cataneo, and discusses the education of his daughter, Marietta Catanea.[41] Bruto strongly disapproves of educating women in the liberal arts. He pours scorn on ancient female philosophers and women famed for their wit, such as Damo, Diotima, Aspasia, and Thargelia, and declares that they deserve 'an opinion of light & uncivill women' (F4v). Female chastity, the quintessence of honour for women, he insists, is more important than learning: 'we account honestie & true vertue to bee more comely and a better ornament, than the report and light renowne of great science and knowledge by her attained unto' (F8r). Erudition would merely gain a young gentlewoman 'light renowne', a reputation of little value. The English translator underscores the equation between learning and licentiousness by repeating the term 'light', whose connotations range from shallow and frivolous to dissolute, and in the first case, coupling it with 'uncivill'.

Bruto argues for sober speech, or preferably silence, rehearsing the commonplace that Nature has enclosed our tongues within two rows of teeth while the ears are open. The same truism is wheeled out by Richard Brathwaite in his *English Gentlewoman* (1631), who opines, 'Silence in a Woman is a moving Rhetoricke, winning most, when in words it wooeth least' (2T1v). He does, however, admire female models of civility whose jests are 'savoury, yet without saltnesse', and whose responses are 'milde without tartnesse' (2Q2v).

Meanwhile, the inexorable rise of the court lady began to leave its trace on courtesy literature. Nicolas Faret reserves the final part of his treatise, *The honest*

---

41. Bruto, *The necessarie, fit, and convenient education*; Thomas Salter's *A Mirrhor mete for all Mothers, Matrones, and Maidens, intituled the Mirrhor of Modestie* (1579) is an adaptation of Bruto's book.

man: or, *The art to please in court* (1632), for advice to the aspirant gentleman as to how to conduct himself in female company. It is here, he points out, that 'all the rules of pleasing should bee put in practice' (R4v). He expounds on the importance of creating just the right impression through gesture, voice, and, above all, dress, in addition to devoting oneself to the 'thousand observations and petty services which are to bee done' (R8r) in order to charm the ladies at court, whose favour opens doors to social advancement (Q8v–95). The Augustinian deacon Giovanni Bruto was fighting a rearguard action. His fellow divine, the Franciscan monk Jacques du Bosc, who produced a counterpart to Nicolas Faret's *L'honneste-homme* (1630) entitled *L'Honneste femme* (1632), translated as *The Compleat Woman* in 1639, refuses to accept a divide between wit and virtue. He expects the virtuous woman to be socially accomplished. He also advocates learning for women. Reading, he writes, is indispensable in cultivating a woman's mind and equipping her for social life: 'It is *Reading* which makes Conversation more sweet'.[42] His views hark back to the approval of female education articulated by humanists such as Juan Luis Vives, tutor to the future Queen Mary, in his popular manual, *The Instruction of a Christian Woman* (1524), which appeared in an English translation by Richard Hyrde in 1529.

While courtesy books largely ignored witty women, and conduct manuals focussed doggedly on domestic duties, other genres were poised to fill the gap. Paradoxically, a genre that presents a raft of nimble-witted women is the jestbook. Cuckoldry and lascivious women are, of course, a staple of the genre. But the ambiguity inherent in all humorous discourse could work against the grain of the joke. Take, for instance, a classic example of a cuckoldry joke: 'A Man, going with his Wife by a deepe river side, began to talke of Cuckolds, and withall he wisht that every Cuckold were cast into the river; to whom his wife replyes: husband, I pray you learne to swimme.'[43] It is true that the main thrust of the joke is to mock women as inveterate wantons. But it might additionally cater to different groups in different ways. Jibes about other husbands would no doubt evoke laughter from men insecure about their own position. In its swipe at married men, patriarchal figures of authority, it might appeal to youths, arguably the largest pool of consumers for jestbooks.[44] But jests, with their depiction of dexterous strokes and parries in the battle of the sexes, also provided useful

---

42. Du Bosc, *Compleat Woman*, G2v.
43. *Taylors Wit and Mirth*, 470.
44. See Reinke-Williams, 'Misogyny, Jest-Books and Male Youth Culture in Seventeenth-Century England'. On women and jesting, see Pamela Brown's illuminating *Better a Shrew Than a Sheep*.

instruction in the art of improvisational wit and offered women a template for how to deflate male complacency and self-righteousness—a lesson imbibed by the witty wives of Windsor.

The Merry Wives of Windsor

The Merry Wives of Windsor is not usually read in conjunction with *Epicene*.[45] At first sight, the gulling of a fat knight disguised as a crone seems the inverse of the triumph of a boy in drag as a young wife, although the final joke in Shakespeare's comedy, when two would-be suitors elope with cross-dressed boys they mistaken for the prize they seek, Anne Page, is built around a similar premise. The antithesis between the urbane world of the West End and the sleepy rural backwater of Windsor does not quite hold either. The social world represented in both *Epicene* or *Merry Wives* is one at the fringes of courtly society, but not quite of it. Admittedly, there are significant differences between the Quarto of 1602 and the Folio version of the play, regarded as authoritative.[46] The Quarto is virtually an urban comedy in which citizens trounce a representative of court corruption, while the setting of the Folio play is ruralized, and an homage to the courtly ceremonies of the Order of the Garter at Windsor Castle is inserted into the Fairy Queen's speech in act 5.[47] What *Epicene* and *Merry Wives* have in common, however, is that both plays satirize facets of the culture of civility.

The inhabitants of Windsor are as preoccupied with status as are the characters in *Epicene*, if on a more provincial note.[48] *The Merry Wives* begins with Justice Shallow and his nephew, Slender, preening themselves on their pedigree in a mixture of mangled Latin and malapropisms to the Welsh parson,

---

45. An exception is Adam Zucker's excellent study, *Places of Wit in Early Modern English Comedy*, 23–53.

46. See Marcus, 'Levelling Shakespeare'. For a different view, see Grav, 'Money Changes Everything', who argues that the Folio version sharpens the critique of pervasive greed in the play.

47. In current criticism, the theory that the play was first performed at the Garter Feast at Westminster in 1597 is no longer in force. Giorgio Melchiori dates the play at the earliest to late 1599. See Melchiori, 'Introduction'. A recent discussion of the political context of the play is Lake, *How Shakespeare Put Politics on the Stage*, 401–16.

48. Useful criticism includes Freedman, 'Falstaff's Punishment'; Hinely, 'Comic Scapegoats'; Erickson, 'Order of the Garter'; Slights, 'Pastoral and Parody in *The Merry Wives of Windsor*', in *Shakespeare's Comic Commonwealths*, 151–70; Barton, 'Falstaff and the Comic Community', in *Essays, Mainly Shakespearean*, 70–90; Korda, '"Judicious oeillades"'; and Brown, *Better a Shrew Than a Sheep*, 43–55. Also see the collection of essays in Gajowski and Rackin, *Merry Wives of Windsor*.

FIGURE 11. Michele Beneditti, *Falstaff at Herne's Oak* (1793). Metropolitan Museum of Art, New York.

Evans, whose patent incomprehension comically sabotages their duet of boasting. Shallow announces that his lineage reaches back three centuries, and Slender embellishes his uncle's statement with the proud claim, 'They may give the dozen white luces in their coat' (1.1.13–14), referring to the heraldic image of fish.[49] Evans assumes they are talking about a real coat, and approves: 'The dozen white louses do become an old coat well' (16). His Welsh accent distorts the fish into lice, which creates further hilarity, puncturing the pomposity of the two country gentlemen. Slender continues to provide rich comic fodder in

---

49. This line might be a joking allusion to the three silver luces that figured on the arms of the Lucy family of Charlecote near Stratford, from whose park, according to legend, Shakespeare is said to have poached venison. Admittedly, the Lucys made do with a fraction of what Shallow boasts on his own coat of arms. See Crane, 'Introduction', 4.

the play, particularly in his inept courting of Anne. Without his book of songs and sonnets, probably a reference to the long outdated *Tottel's Miscellany* (1557), or his collection of riddles, he is literally lost for words, and his amorous discourse shrivels into bluster about the number of his servants: 'I keep but three men and a boy yet, till my mother be dead. But what though? Yet I live like a poor gentleman born' (1.238–40). When Anne does not show the slightest interest in the details of his social standing, he attempts to show off his knowledge of the fashionable art of fencing, but gracelessly dwells on the bruises he has received. In desperation at his lack of success, he resorts to the topic of bear-baiting, by this time a sport that, as Mistress Otter belabours her husband, smacked of a lack of cultivation. Although, in another of his clichéd phrases, he would 'rather be unmannerly than troublesome' (271), he is in fact both.

His competitor, Fenton, on the other hand, is vastly superior in his command of courtly skills. The only character to speak in verse, he is described admiringly by the Host, who has no hesitation in putting his money on him: 'He capers, he dances, he has eyes of youth. He writes verse, he speaks holiday, he smells April and May' (3.2.59–61). He not only possesses courtly accomplishments, but has a mastery of witty discourse. Fenton finds just the right words to woo Anne, to whom he confesses that while originally attracted by her dowry, ''tis the very riches of thyself / That now I aim at' (3.4.17–18). He also courts the favour of his future mother-in-law with a lavish use of Petrarchan imagery: 'Perforce, against all checks, rebukes, and manners, / I must advance the colors of my love / And not retire' (77–79). The Pages remain unimpressed. They persist in their scepticism about the suitability of a match with a former courtier, reflecting the tensions between court and country that would increasingly influence the political development of the nation.

The women in Windsor have not remained untouched by the culture of civility. While Falstaff is unassailable in his conviction that he is irresistible to women, he is observant of Mistress Ford's behaviour in company. 'She discourses, she carves' (1.3.38), he tells his motley band of followers, concluding from her cultured speech and gestures that she is susceptible to his courtly charm.[50] During their encounter, as Mistress Ford admits, Falstaff was the acme of courtesy and propriety: 'he would not swear, praised women's modesty,

---

50. 'Carve' might refer to affected speech or gestures, as in Truewit's Ovidian advice as to how women should present themselves in the best light: if a woman have 'a fat hand . . . let her carve the less, and act in gloves' (*Epi.* 4.1.42–43). See notes to 4.1.42 in the Revels Plays edition. Also see *OED*, s.v. 'carve, v.', III.13.

and gave such orderly and well-behaved reproof to all uncomeliness, that I would have sworn his disposition would have gone to the truth of his words' (2.1.50–54). In wooing the Windsor wives, Falstaff plays up courtliness as his main asset. Promising to make Mistress Ford a lady, he attempts to dazzle her with a cosmopolitan command of fashion, strewing in references to different types of tires or headdresses at the courts of Europe. 'Thou wouldst make an absolute courtier', he flatters her in affected, courtly idiom, 'and the firm fixture of thy foot would give an excellent motion to thy gait in a semicircled farthingale' (3.3.52–54).

Despite being but a shadow of his former, indomitable self in *Henry IV Parts 1* and *2*, as regards verbal ingenuity, Falstaff remains unrivalled in Windsor. When Slender sends his man, Simple, to consult the wise woman of Brentford, Falstaff demolishes him within minutes. Simple has been sent to inquire whether Nim, 'that beguiled him of a chain, had the chain or no' (4.5.25–26). Falstaff reports the words of wisdom ostensibly uttered by the venerable old woman: 'she says the very same man that beguiled Master Slender of his chain cozened him of it' (29–30). Predictably, Simple is too obtuse to grasp that he is being gulled, and continues with his respectful queries. He inquires about the chances of his master's suit to Anne, and whether it be Slender's fortune 'to have her or no' (38–39). Falstaff echoes his words back to him, stating that indeed, Slender would either win her—or not, as the case might be. With a few deft strokes, Falstaff sends up the superstitious ignorance of Slender and his consorts. His asides occasionally sparkle with the former vigour. Contemplating his narrow escape from drowning, he exclaims, 'what a thing should I have been when I had been swelled! I should have been a mountain of mummy' (3.5.14–15), a remark that evokes memories of his duel of wits with the Lord Chief Justice in *Henry IV Part 2*. When the Lord Chief Justice reproaches him with his dissipated way of living, pointing out censoriously, 'Your means are very slender and your waste great', Falstaff memorably twists the meaning of his words and shoots back, 'I would it were otherwise; I would my means were greater and my waist slender' (*2HIV* 1.2.128–31).

As regards imaginative shrewdness, however, the wittiest characters in Windsor are the wives, who devise a concatenation of farcical playlets involving deception and disguise to expose the greed and arrogance of the knight, who assumes provincial wives are his for the taking. They succeed in debunking the erstwhile embodiment of wit so thoroughly that he fears his reputation with his peers will not survive. In an aside he remarks glumly to the audience that should the news of how he has been tricked reach the court, he will be mercilessly pilloried by other courtiers: 'I warrant they would whip me with their fine wits till I were as crestfallen as a dried pear' (4.5.82–83). From the towering personality who once boasted, 'I am not only witty in myself but the cause that wit is in other men' (*2HIV* 1.2.8–9), he has become the butt of the jests of countryfolk.

The jesting of the Windsor wives is somewhat different from that of the gallants in *Epicene*. To be sure, the aim of their jesting campaign is not solely to secure their own position as exemplary wives, but to enhance their prestige in the eyes of their menfolk. In rhyming couplets, Mistress Page pithily sums up the impetus behind their jests: 'We'll leave a proof by that which we will do, / Wives may be merry and yet honest too' (4.2.92–93). They are keen to rupture the association of laughter with licentiousness current in early modern conduct manuals, in which female mirth signalled sexual availability. For Juan Luis Vives, for instance, laughing 'is a signe of a verye lyghte and dissolute mynde'. He cautions young women against sharing laughs with young men, 'whiche none wyll do but she that is nought [wicked], or els a fole'.[51] The connotations of folly and lasciviousness in relation to levity were not restricted to women, and courtesy books do not merely urge their readers to restrain their jesting, but also to rein in their laughter. As one compendium of manners advises, 'Laugh not too much or too Loud, in any publique spectacle, least for thy so doing, thou present thy selfe, the only thing worthy to be laughed at'.[52] For women, however, the stakes were infinitely higher—their honour was inextricably bound up with their reputation for chastity.

Unlike among the wits of *Epicene*, there is no sense of one-upmanship or competition between the women or their helpmeet, Mistress Quickly. On the contrary, they are team players, as is reflected in their frequent use of the first person plural: 'Let's consult together' (2.1.96).[53] What they share with the wits is an infectious pleasure in scheming. The punitive force of their jesting is directed against transgressions of civility. Falstaff is penalized for flouting the laws of hospitality and failing to show respect towards the women of Windsor. The humiliation meted out to him unmasks his rapacity and deflates his delusions of superiority. Master Ford, meanwhile, is publicly rebuked for his manic jealousy and lack of trust in his wife. In contrast to the wits in *Epicene*, the merry wives are not invested in annihilating their victims. In their disciplinary

---

51. See Vives, *A very frutefull and pleasant boke*, D1r.
52. Hawkins, *Youths Behaviour*, B1v.
53. See Belsey, 'Agonistic Scenes of Provincial Life', 34–35.

measures, the women strive to maintain decorum at all times. Ford is not devastated to such an extent that he can no longer maintain his self-respect. Master Page, ally of his wife, astutely curbs any impulse to excessive self-abasement on Ford's part by counselling him, 'Be not as extreme in submission as in offense' (4.4.10). As for Falstaff, both Master and Mistress Page spare no effort to incorporate Falstaff into the festive reconciliation with which the play ends. 'Yet be cheerful, knight', Page urges the (briefly) crestfallen Falstaff, inviting him to accept his hospitality: 'Thou shalt eat a posset [a hot drink] tonight at my house' (5.5.156–57). In the final moments of the play, Mistress Page reiterates the invitation, explicitly including Falstaff: 'let us everyone go home, / And laugh this sport o'er by a country fire, / Sir John and all' (216–18). In *The Merry Wives of Windsor*, Shakespeare does not offer us a cosy vision of a harmonious society. Nonetheless, the Windsor wives utilize humour to forge a sense of communal cohesion, however temporary or fragile. The spirit of community extends to the audience of the early modern theatre, who are invited to join in the laughter at the butts of the jests staged for our entertainment and are welded into a 'community of amusement', at least for the duration of the play.[54]

Jesting as an Agent of Civility

The merry wives are not the only impresarios of jests in Windsor. In a subsidiary strand of narrative, the irrepressible Host choreographs a playlet to torpedo the planned duel between the Welsh priest, Evans, and the French physician, Dr Caius. A possible, buried reference to the pre-eminent medical scholar, Dr John Caius, who provoked Puritan ire for his adherence to the old faith, hints at the grim reality of religious antagonism that ravaged Europe, transposed into a lighthearted, comic key in the play.[55] Shakespeare might have been playing a subtle game with the audience by evoking the memory of a famous physician who embodied the pre-Reformation age while

---

54. See Cohen, *Jokes*, 29.

55. John Caius (1510–73), president of the Royal College of Physicians and physician to three monarchs (Edward VI, Mary, and Elizabeth), was allegedly dismissed by Elizabeth in 1568 on religious grounds. Gonville and Caius College, Cambridge, which he expanded considerably and of which he was master for over a decade, was renamed in his honour in 1557. Caius's treatise, *A boke, or counseill against the disease commonly called the sweate, or sweatyng sicknesse* (1552), is steeped in nostalgia for a lost age of conviviality and good-fellowship 'in the old world, when this countrie was called merye Englande' (D7r). Also see Traister, 'French Physician in an English Community'.

simultaneously undercutting the allusion by turning him into a Frenchman—additionally capitalising on the stock comic device of a funny foreigner. Caius is established as a comically choleric figure from the moment he enters the play, marked by elements of the vainglorious braggart. Prone to violence, he immediately calls for his rapier when he detects the inoffensive Simple hiding in his closet. Mistress Quickly, his housekeeper, identifies him as 'horn-mad' (1.4.44), which could mean being mad with fury without necessarily involving suspected cuckoldry.[56] The description brackets him with Ford, the other compulsive choleric in Windsor. Caius is so eager to nose out offence that he explodes with anger when he hears that Evans is attempting to mediate a match between his nephew and Anne, for whom Caius has set his cap himself. His blundering language brims over with bloodthirsty threats such as 'I will cut his troat' (1.4.97–98), 'I will cut all his two stones' (100), or 'me vill cut his ears' (2.3.55). Caius is very partial to hyperbole: his declaration that he has been waiting six or seven hours at the appointed place shrinks to 'two, three hours' in the very same sentence (2.3.31–32). His ludicrous, if severely restricted, store of epithets for his enemy—'scurvy jackanape priest', 'jack-priest', 'jack-dog priest' (1.4.98; 2.3.27, 55)—are ridiculed in the fantastic appellations attached to him by the Host, who calls him a 'Castalian king urinal' (2.3.29), playing on his profession with an additional glance at 'stale', a term for urine, or 'Monsieur Mockwater' (50–51), a covert slur on his virility and courage. Characteristically, the wily Host packages his insults as compliments. Castalia was the spring on Mount Parnassus sacred to the Muses, while 'mockwater', a nonce word, might just pass as a bland reference to the physician's customary practice of examining a patient's 'water'—and not as a contemptuous allusion to the diluted quality of the blood in his veins, the humour to which courage was attributed. 'Mockwater? Vat is dat?' demands the irritated Frenchman. 'Mockwater, in our English tongue, is valour' (52–53) is the deadpan reply.

The meek parson Evans, on the other hand, is torn between anger and secret terror at the prospect of a duel, which he ventilates in a string of antitheses. 'How full of cholers I am, and trempling of mind! I shall be glad if he have deceived me', he admits (3.1.9–10). His store of threats is as limited as that of Caius: 'I will knog his urinals about his knave's costard [head]', he vows (11–12). To keep up his spirits, he sings garbled snatches of two immensely popular songs, Marlowe's 'Come live with me and be my love' and Psalm 137, juxtaposing lines from each, as in the following snippet: 'Melodious birds sing madrigals.—/ When

---

56. *OED*, s.v. 'horn-mad, adj.', a.

as I sat in Pabylon' (20–21). A parodic allusion to the dated fashion for pastoral love poetry, the passage has been read as an ironic tribute to the spirit of pastoral that imbues the play.[57] It might be seen as another artful compliment by Shakespeare to Marlowe, as in *As You Like It*, when Phoebe recites a line from *Hero and Leander* in an elegiac homage to the 'Dead Shepherd', 'Whoever loved that loved not at first sight?' (*AYL* 3.5.80–81). But Marlowe was the creator of both exquisite erotic lyric, and drama that revelled in cruelty and sectarian hatred—amongst others, *The Massacre at Paris* and *The Jew of Malta*. The jarring intrusion of a fragment from a psalm of religious exile, remarkable for its imagery of violence and hate, might serve as a muted reminder of the backdrop of religious bloodshed to which the comic duel between a Frenchman and a Welshman of possibly opposing (if unspoken) religious affiliations only obliquely gestures.

What *As You Like It* and *Merry Wives* share is a satirical take on the Renaissance vogue for duelling. In *As You Like It*, a fool delivers a travesty of the convoluted rules in duelling manuals, while in *The Merry Wives of Windsor*, the cult of honour is represented by two ludicrous specimens, the Welsh parson and the French doctor.

Throughout *As You Like It*, Touchstone has fun at the expense of courtly manners, despite his boasts to the rustics that he is a pristine exemplar of courtliness. When Jaques casts doubt on his courtly credentials, he produces the evidence: 'I have trod a measure, I have flattered a lady, I have been politic [crafty] with my friend, smooth with mine enemy. I have undone three tailors, I have had four quarrels, and like to have fought one' (5.4.43–46). He mockingly itemizes the typical attributes in courtesy books associated with a sophisticated lifestyle, including the readiness to defend one's honour in individual combat. When Jaques inquires more closely into his alleged duel, the jester declares airily: 'we quarrel in print, by the book, as you have books for good manners' (83–84). In a sideswipe at Jaques's disquisition on the seven ages of man, Touchstone proceeds to relate the seven stages involved in the argument he had with a courtier of whose beard he did not approve. Their slanging match went through an orderly sequence of steps, he explains, from the Retort Courteous, the Quip Modest, the Reply Churlish, the Reproof Valiant, the Countercheck Quarrelsome, to the Lie with Circumstance, and stopped short at the Lie Direct (84–89). Each stage is prefaced by a conditional: 'if I said his beard was not cut well, he was in the mind it was' and so forth (66–67). Touchstone

---

57. See Slights, *Shakespeare's Comic Commonwealths*, 153–54.

is lampooning the solemn instructions outlined in fencing handbooks such as that by the foremost fencing master in London in the 1590s, Vincentio Saviolo. Saviolo expatiates on a diversity of lies, including 'conditionall lyes', which he describes in terms not dissimilar to Touchstone. Saviolo is not happy with devious challenges, urging that 'all such as have any regarde of their honor or credit, ought by all meanes possible to shunne all conditionall lyes, never geving any other but certayne Lyes'. Otherwise, he warns, 'men fal into a world of words'.[58]

Touchstone's spoof on duelling is a caricature of craven knights who are willing to sacrifice their honour to save their paltry lives. But as always with the words of a fool, the thrust of his satire is double-edged. It also ridicules a society in the throes of an obsession with honour. The play itself is honeycombed with the term 'if'.[59] At the denouement, after a litany of lines in the conditional in which the characters hesitantly articulate their desires and fears, Hymen announces the four weddings that will bring the play to a harmonious end, only to add the enigmatic, teasing remark, 'If truth hold true contents' (5.4.121). What we are watching, Hymen hints, is merely a pleasing fantasy, a world of words. Similarly, what Touchstone describes in the duelling scenario built around an 'if' is a social pretence which enables both parties to save face. The way to avoid an actual duel, Touchstone declares mockingly, is by only issuing a hypothetical challenge. 'Your "if" is the only peacemaker', he proclaims (93–94). The entire joke is, like every joke, an elaborate fabrication, a sortie into an 'as if' world.

In *The Merry Wives of Windsor*, the Host takes a similarly dim view of duels. To sabotage the plans of Caius and Evans, he devises a prank, directing the two parties to different trysting grounds, and stages the uncovering of the hoax as an entertaining show for the community of Windsor. Proud of the success of his dissembling, he exults, 'Am I politic? Am I subtle? Am I a machiavel?' (3.1.86–87). In one of Shakespeare's rare references to the Italian political thinker—the others are voiced by the stage Machiavel, Richard, Duke of Gloucester, in *Henry VI, Part 1* and *Part 3*—the Host seems to be alluding to the Machiavellian imperative to adapt to the circumstances at hand and have recourse to dissimulation if necessary, although there is also a hint at Machiavelli's

---

58. Savioli, *Vincentio Saviolo his Practise*, S4r, S3v.

59. The conjunction is a favourite of Touchstone's, but also appears in set pieces by Silvius in 2.4, Jaques's 'Ducdame' song in 2.5, Orlando's duet with the Duke in 2.7, Rosalind's flirtation game with Orlando in 3.2 and 4.1, Rosalind's final catalogue of conditionals in 5.2 and 5.4, and the Epilogue. Also see Ryan, *Shakespeare's Comedies*, 231–32.

subordination of religion to the interests of the state.[60] The Host lays bare the rationale for his action: 'Shall I lose my doctor? No, he gives me the potions and the motions. Shall I lose my parson, my priest, my Sir Hugh? No, he gives me the proverbs and the no-verbs' (3.1.87–90). He has preserved their lives, he announces jokingly, for purely selfish reasons—both the doctor and the clergyman are simply too useful to relinquish. The Host's success in duping the two antagonists serves to boost his own image as local wit. But under the guise of a joke he is also making a subtle point about the interdependence of the members of a community. The denizens of Windsor seem to concur. Caius and Evans are integrated into the communal jest in the forest directed at Falstaff.

The Host is not alone in resorting to pretence in this scene. Flustered at being duped, Caius and Evans whisper to each other, confiding their mutual desire to salvage the shreds of their self-respect while continuing to maintain a facade of hostility. To Evans, Caius says in an aside, 'I pray you, let-a me speak a word with your ear', making 'fritters' of the English language, as Falstaff puts it (5.5.134), while aloud he demands belligerently, 'Vherefore vill you no meet-a me?' (3.1.69–70). Meanwhile, Evans requests him in private, 'Pray you let us not be laughingstocks to other men's humors', while in public he threatens once again to knock out his brains (74–77). Only when they are alone do they admit that they have been gulled. 'He has made us his vlowting-stog [flouting-stock or laughingstock]' (101), Evans laments. The subterfuge practised on them makes them resolve to temporarily set aside their differences and concentrate on tricking the Host in return. To vent their newly found enmity to the Host, they mobilize the same impoverished vocabulary that they previously employed to insult each other. 'I desire you that we may be friends, and let us knog our prains together to be revenge on this scall, scurvy, cogging [vile, despicable, cheating] companion, the Host of the Garter', the parson proposes, and Caius agrees: 'By gar, with all my heart' (101–5). At the end of the scene, it is no longer clear which of the roles they have been playing are the real ones, the role of furious rivals grudgingly agreeing to be reconciled, or that of fellow citizens pretending to be furious to live up to the expectations attached to the cult of honour.

Not that it matters. If the notion that honour is a fiction is unforgettably associated with Falstaff ('What is honour? A word'; *1HIV* 5.1.133), *The Merry*

---

60. The *politique* party in the French religious wars, who advocated a distinction between religion and state, were vilified as endorsing Machiavellianism and, by association, atheism. See Burke, 'Tacitism, Scepticism, and Reason of State', 483.

Wives deploys another fiction, a jest, to call the Renaissance obsession with honour into question. The wit of the subplot lies in a jest that forges a bond between two sworn enemies, all in the name of honour. If, as a later courtesy book asserts, 'more *Duells* arise from Jest then Earnest',[61] the play puts forward an alternative scenario: one in which jesting subverts a duel and buttresses the common good.

Both *Epicene* and *The Merry Wives* suggest that theatricality and fictions are an inescapable component of life. What is decisive is which role we opt to play, and in which fictions we choose to believe. Civility, like jesting, is interlaced with dissimulation: as Kant points out, jokes are built on illusions that momentarily deceive us before dissolving—and spurring laughter.[62] *Epicene* depicts a trio of wits whose jesting aims to humiliate social aberrants of all stripes and explode their pretensions—while exposing the wits as equally under the sway of illusions of superiority. In addition, the play destabilizes audience beliefs, both those of Jonson's contemporaries and our own. The cult of honour might appear a relic of a bygone age, but the irrefutable sense of righteousness and the zeal to take offence on which it was premised appear strangely contemporary. In *The Merry Wives of Windsor*, two resourceful women and a local wag demonstrate how wit can be used to dismantle the deceptions of a motley bunch of dupes, including would-be seducers, horn-mad husbands, and foolish duellists. By permitting them to maintain a facade of self-respect, the jests nonetheless work to forge a sense of cohesion within the community of Windsor.

As the plays indicate, human conflict is an immutable fact. Despite Evan's words, Caius and Evans do not become friends. But for the rest of the play they collaborate and sustain a semblance of esteem for each other. They seem to have made a tacit agreement to allow the other to preserve a veneer of dignity. In a climate of deep suspicion towards surfaces and masks, Shakespeare's play suggests that mutual awareness of role-playing and a pretence of reciprocal respect might offer a mode of living together peaceably within the same community. Pretence, both plays imply, might serve an ethical purpose; implicitly, in its defence of pretence, the theatre is also offering a defence of itself.

---

61. Osborne, *Advice to a Son*, C2r, emphasis original.
62. Kant, *Critique of Judgment*, pt. I, div. 1, p. 54.

Conclusion

CIVILITY, THIS BOOK argues, is a mode of social rhetoric by which we relay mutual esteem and simultaneously present ourselves as worthy of esteem. Throughout history, it has been used either to secure the prestige of a group and mark its members off from others, or to foster a sense of common endeavour in society at large. At the crux of civility is the question of how we might demonstrate respect for those for whom we have none—those outside the wider circle with whom we feel affiliated, but who live in the same society as we do. In an increasingly fragmented world, where genuine esteem for other members of society is thin on the ground, a pretence of mutual respect might be a course to pursue. Dissimulation, this book argues, may bear an ethical charge. In its preoccupation with its own medium, the theatre points to the theatricality of social life. In its concern with spectatorship, it reflects on the pervasive scrutiny of others and ourselves that our social performance entails. And in their reflection on the ethical status of illusion, a number of plays comment on the role fictions, both pernicious and aspirational, play in civil society. But a defence of pretence inevitably spurs questions. What price civility? When does feigned civility segue into servility? And when does it spill over into self-betrayal? In its exploration of the complexity of human dilemmas, drama reveals that in social interaction, it might be impossible to sustain moral certitudes.

Civility, Hypocrisy, and Lying

These considerations have determined the debate about civility from the earliest times to the present. They are closely interwoven with questions of truth and authenticity. In the early modern period, they tap into the burning interest in the issues of lying, dissimulation, and pretence fuelled by the Reformation, which also laid the foundations of a culture of sincerity. The fundamental points of contention are crystallised in one of the most influential controversies of the time and hark back to the early days of Christianity. The dispute was between two giants of the early Church, the apostles Peter and Paul, and two great fourth-century Church fathers, St Jerome and St Augustine. It set the course for all later debates, in the early modern period and beyond.

The biblical episode at issue is described in Galatians 2:11–14. In his epistles the apostle Paul relates how after lengthy missionary travels he returned to the churches he had established in Antioch. He found that tensions had arisen between two groups of converts, the Gentiles and the 'Judaizers', a faction of largely Jewish Christians who sought to reintroduce the strict rules of Mosaic Law into Christianity. Many of these rules related to the segregation of Jews from non-Jews during meals. When a new contingent of Judaizers arrived in Antioch, the apostle Peter, who had hitherto freely shared meals with the Gentiles, withdrew from the latter out of fear of offending the leaders of the Jews. His actions inspired others, including his fellow missionary Barnabas, to follow suit, or as Paul puts it, 'the other Jews dissembled likewise with him; insomuch that Barnabas also was carried away with their dissimulation' (Gal. 2:13, KJV). Paul confronted Peter in public, charging him with hypocrisy for attempting to appease those whose beliefs he did not share. For as Peter knew, Christ had taught that God's grace was a gift granted on the basis of faith, not works or obedience to the ceremonial law. Peter was not only dissimulating to the Judaizing faction, Paul implies—he was lying to himself.

The polemics between Jerome and Augustine centred on their reading of the passage in question. In his commentary on Galatians, Jerome maintained that Paul's denunciation of Peter was a performance, staged for the benefit of the fledgling Christian community in full collusion with Peter. Even as he accused Peter of deception, he was using deception as a tactic himself: Paul opposed Peter so that his hypocrisy 'might be corrected by his own hypocrisy'.[1] He was fully aware that Peter's actions were prompted by considerations of expediency and served the purpose of strengthening the belief of the Jewish converts. Paul, on the other hand, was motivated by the desire to keep the Gentile believers, to whom the epistles were addressed, from wavering in their faith. Both apostles were deploying dissimulation for a higher good. Indeed, on numerous occasions Paul too adopted pretence as a device to win converts

---

1. See Jerome, *Commentary on Galatians*, 104–10, 106. Also see Zagorin, 'Historical Significance of Lying and Dissimulation', to which I am indebted in the following.

to the true faith, justifying his accommodation to a variety of different groups with the assertion, 'I am made all things to all men, that I might by all means save some' (1 Cor. 9:22, KJV)—a verse that Erasmus cites as an opening gambit in *De civilitate*. Jerome's own rationale was to dismantle the slurs cast on the two apostles by Porphyry, a third-century Neoplatonic philosopher who launched a virulent attack on Christianity. Porphyry proclaimed that the anecdote reveals Peter was an ineffectual leader, while Paul was driven by a craving for power, attempting to wrest control within the community. Moreover, the Church leaders were hopelessly divided in their views—all of which served to prove that Christianity was based on a flimsy lie (59–60).

Augustine vehemently disagreed with Jerome. In an exchange of letters he argued that at no point had Paul lied or dissimulated his thoughts. Alleging that the apostles were engaged in pretence would imply that they were wilfully resorting to falsehood. But expediency could never take precedence over veracity, he urged. Admitting that the scriptures condoned lying, even for a higher cause, was fraught with danger—it would undermine the authority of the Word of God as the font of truth. Stories in the Bible that seemed to present examples of deceit were to be read as allegorical or figurative, he claimed. While in his own treatises on lying Augustine set up a taxonomy of lies, graduated according to the degree of depravity involved, lying, he insisted, was always a sin.[2]

Other leading theologians entered the fray. In his own commentary on Galatians, Erasmus sides with Jerome, although he differs with him on some points. Defending Peter against Augustine's severe strictures, he agrees with Jerome that neither had Peter sinned, nor had Paul in reality reproached him. Both had acted out a little charade designed to win over those who were vacillating in spirit. Crucially, Erasmus writes, 'Nor would anyone deny that a righteous man has the right to pretend or feign on occasion', echoing Jerome's views that at times dissimulation was acceptable as an expedient in the cause of human salvation.[3] In his *Ratio*, Erasmus rehearses Jerome's declaration that Christ himself employed pretence. Erasmus compares Christ to Proteus, who dissimulates his true nature as son of God in order to redeem humankind from sin.[4]

Many of the concerns touched upon in the biblical narrative and in the subsequent argument about hypocrisy and dissimulation as opposed to sincerity have left their impact on discussions about civility to the present day. For

---

2. On Augustine's treatises, *On Lying* and *Against Lying*, see chapter 3.
3. Erasmus, *Annotations on Galatians and Ephesians*, 30–41, 40.
4. See Jerome, *Commentary on Galatians*, 108; Erasmus, *Erasmus on Literature*, 77.

many commentators, Peter's conduct points to the limits of civility—in the form of sycophancy and appeasement. If civility is a rhetoric of conduct, it not only involves conveying respect for others, but also *ethos*, presenting ourselves as persons worthy of esteem, whose recognition is of value. Theoretical texts on civility in all cultures, however hierarchical, declare emphatically that civil intercourse is based on reciprocity and mutual deference, not obsequiousness.

Nor does civility entail self-censorship for fear of giving offence. Civility is not, as is sometimes believed, an evasion of conflict. Friction within society is inevitable; civility is about managing our conflicts, not suppressing them. At stake is not whether we disagree, but how we disagree with one another. As Keith Bybee points out, even critics of civility, such as advocates of civil disobedience, do not demand that civility be entirely swept aside. By attacking prevalent canons of behaviour they call for the rules to be changed, not jettisoned.[5] Every society formulates codes of conduct that regulate how we deal with dissension. These principles are not objective truths; they need to be negotiated in interaction with other members of society. Civility is a work in progress. Societal norms are the site of struggle and debate, and are perpetually refashioned and redefined to adapt to new developments in society. In the confusion of human life, there are few simple solutions on offer. This is an insight that literature offers us. And in its exploration of the complexity of human predicaments and the infinite variety of perspectives on every conflict, early modern drama reveals that moral certainties do not hold.

In the early modern period, a period rife with social and religious antagonism, the theatre emerged as a space in which debates about civility, hypocrisy, and lying were played out. If one of the quandaries that haunts social interaction is where the limits of civility lie, another issue is the way a rigid insistence on moral purity can endanger civil society. Plays ranging from comedies, such as *A Merchant of Venice*, to tragedies, such as *Coriolanus*, lay bare how a conviction of moral superiority and a vision of unitary truth impede our ability to live together in amity and cooperate in the shared project of civil life. The culture of authenticity that emerged in the early modern period galvanised the demand for moral absolutes. Tracing its roots back to Augustine, it continues to hold unbroken sway today. A conviction that we are in the sole possession of the truth, and our hankering after authenticity, or a seamless alignment between outer expression and inner truth, impedes our willingness to engage

---

5. See Bybee, 'Rise of Trump'.

with other members of society who are not part of the group with which we identify. But the plays hollow out the idea of authenticity, suggesting it is an illusion. *Every Man Out of His Humour*, for instance, depicts a world in which all characters are busy play-acting, but are mired in self-delusion. Absorbed as they are in pursuing their individual concerns, they are inextricably bound up in a web of relations with one another. *Coriolanus* portrays a protagonist whose dream of an autonomous self is grounded in an unassailable sense of entitlement. He is fiercely committed to upholding his inner truth. What the play presents, however, is a deeply conflicted character, tossed in a maelstrom of continually shifting emotions. But if we are contradictory and changeable, how can we be certain that what we find within is the truth, and not another variety of deceit? The quest for the authentic self, the plays suggest, is always entangled with self-deception. We exist in terms of our interaction with one another, they propose; our lives are inescapably theatrical. Authenticity is merely another performance, if only to ourselves.

In a divided society defined by a hunger for authenticity, commitment to a common stake in civil society is increasingly eroded. Although historically remote from the withering of social relations that political scientists have identified in the modern world, plays such as *Coriolanus* delineate a protagonist 'bowling alone'.[6] In a comic key, a similar sense of radical individualism shadows the city comedies of Jonson and Middleton, governed by the ruthless laws of an emergent market economy. The decay of civil life, however, paves the way for autocratic rule, as Ben Jonson warns in *Sejanus*. Drawing on Aristotle's unerring analysis of authoritarian power, the play shows how in a state in which the bonds of collective life have disintegrated, tyranny flourishes.

For all their scepticism about authenticity, the plays acknowledge that a yearning for truth is intrinsic to human nature; a collective striving for truths plays a crucial role in human society. They make it clear that holding ourselves up to ethical standards remains vital for the well-being of human society. In an age suspicious of illusions and imaginative artefacts of all kinds, early modern playwrights were keen to draw attention to the positive role fictions can play in moulding our world. The ideas around which civil society is built—the common good, for instance, or the human bond—might well be fictions, but they are fabrications on which we anchor a community. As Hobbes reminds us, civil society itself is an invention to facilitate our amicable coexistence. A

---

6. See Robert D. Putnam's classic study of the decline of social intercourse in contemporary America, *Bowling Alone: The Collapse and Revival of American Community*.

collective without aspirational models is particularly susceptible to beliefs which are corrosive of civil society. In today's terms, civility offers a mean between, on the one hand, a rigorous sense of moral righteousness and, on the other, a post-truth notion of moral relativism, where shared standards of truth are abandoned and each person creates their own reality. Civility is a practice of interpersonal behaviour rooted in the underlying idea of a social pact to our mutual advantage. In place of lofty notions of truth, the decisive factor would be keeping faith with one another in our agreements.

It is unfortunate that today the meaning of the term 'civility' has largely dwindled to signify etiquette, in the same way as the concept of decorum, eviscerated of its larger, Ciceronian connotations of common humanity, now evokes the idea of protocol or sclerotic convention. An early modern thinker who grappled with the dilemma of reconciling a desire for authenticity with a commitment to civil society was Montaigne. Writing at the time of the French Wars of Religion, when the nation was torn by fanaticism, anger, and hatred, Montaigne observes how his own moral certainties have crumbled. 'During the present confusion in this State of ours my own interest has not made me fail to recognize laudable qualities in our adversaries nor reprehensible ones among those whom I follow', he remarks. He arrives at the conclusion that both sides owe each other mutual respect (1144). At the same time, he rejects excessive appeasement as equivalent to 'seeking bolt-holes in falsehoods so as to reach a conciliation' (1153).

In one of his last essays, 'On restraining your will', Montaigne looks back on his period in office as mayor of Bordeaux.[7] Despite his palpable hostility to Cicero, whom he describes as 'the vainest man in the world' (1158), he cites his works consistently; in this essay, he draws on Cicero's views in *De officiis* about the obligations imposed by civil society. The ideal man, Montaigne reflects, would find a way of balancing self-love with sociability and engagement in civic life. 'Such a man, knowing precisely what is due to himself, finds that his role includes frequenting men and the world; to do this he must contribute to society the offices and duties which concern him', he opines (1138). In retrospect, Montaigne records that he fulfilled his obligations to those who elected him as mayor punctiliously, and takes pride in the fact that, as he notes, 'if the occasion had arisen, there is nothing I would have spared in their service' (1155). Nonetheless, he is happy that he has been able to participate in public

---

7. Montaigne, 'On Restraining Your Will', in *Complete Essays*, 3.10, pp. 1134–59. On Montaigne and civility, see Hartle, *What Happened to Civility*.

duties without relinquishing his private self. He recommends that we contribute to civil society but reserve our emotional involvement for our own affairs. 'We should husband our soul's freedom', he urges (1135). Citing the *theatrum mundi* topos, Montaigne calls for a degree of distance to one's role in public. 'We should play our role properly, but as the role of a character which we have adopted. We must not turn masks and semblances into essential realities, nor adopted qualities into attributes of our self', he maintains (1139–40).

If we are always performing a part, Montaigne suggests, we should abandon any attempt to fuse the different roles we assume in the divergent arenas of life. A way of maintaining civil relations with others for whom we harbour nothing but disdain, but who are members of the same community, would be to adopt a stance of ironic detachment from the roles we assume in the public sphere. This would involve a show of respect for others, irrespective of our true feelings, and the tacit agreement not to expose one another's performances. More recently, another thinker on issues of theatre, performance, and social interaction, Richard Sennett, has come to a similar conclusion. His book, *The Performer: Art, Life, Politics* (2024), is a summation of his experience as a musical performer and his work on urban space and public culture. Sennett, like Montaigne, sees us all as actors on a social stage; his notion of performance encompasses both individual role-playing and artistic performances. Performing, he insists, is permeated with moral ambiguity: it is 'an impure art'.[8] Like speech, performance can be malign and manipulative, and serve the interests of power. Alternatively, performance can be a tool of freedom, an instrument to challenge power and to forge a community. His sweeping exploration of the relations of art and society ends with a meditation on civility (224–26). Sennett deplores the way art has been infiltrated by a compulsive preoccupation with identity and a quest for purity. A model to emulate, he muses, is civility: performed gestures that create a social bond which is impersonal and not tied to identity. With its repertoire of body language, demeanour, and verbal expression, and its potential to distance us from ourselves, civility, like the theatre, is a performing art. Pretence is at the core of both.

8. Sennett, *The Performer*, ix.

ACKNOWLEDGEMENTS

IN WRITING this book, I have accumulated more debts than I can ever repay. My greatest debt is to two scholars whose tireless encouragement prevented me from abandoning this project at numerous points in the past few years. Quentin Skinner's work is a source of inspiration to scholars all over the world. I am honoured to have been offered his advice and guidance. Rhodri Lewis provides an example of the heights to which literary criticism can still soar. His unflagging support for this book can be attributed only to boundless generosity towards more plodding scholars.

A number of other scholars have invested time and effort in reading parts of the book at various stages of its gestation. Antoinina Bevan-Zlatar, Keith Bybee, Samantak Das, Derek Dunne, Lukas Erne, Neil Forsyth, Heather James, Andrew Johnston, Tony Mortimer, Scott Newstok, Stephen Orgel, Manfred Pfister, Adrian Streete, Keith Thomas, Bart Van Es, Greg Walker, and the late Rick Waswo all read sections of the manuscript. Their sage counsel has been invaluable, even if I haven't always been able to do justice to their suggestions. I am grateful to the anonymous readers for their astute advice in the final phase of the book. Lastly, I wish to thank Ben Tate at Princeton University Press for his faith in the book. I feel deeply privileged to have him as my editor.

For the greater part of my professional life, the University of Fribourg provided a congenial academic environment. It was a pleasure working with scholars like Thomas Hunkeler, Umberto Motta, and Thomas Schmidt. I owe a special word of thanks to Thomas Austenfeld for his support at a crucial stage in my life.

Much of the foundation for this book was laid during a fellowship at the Folger Shakespeare Library in Washington, D.C., and a visiting fellowship at St Catherine's College, Oxford. I am grateful to both institutions for their generous support. I am indebted to the Swiss National Science Foundation for an extremely generous grant to run a four-year research project on 'Civility, Cultural Exchange, and Conduct Literature in Early Modern England, 1500–1700', which provided the unique opportunity to test ideas and exchange thoughts on civility in all its facets in a close-knit group of scholars. It was a pleasure to collaborate with my colleagues in the project, Douglas Clark, Emma Depledge, and Elizabeth Kukorelly.

I have been more than fortunate to enjoy a small group of friends on whose unstinting support I could always count. For friendship during these years, I owe a debt of gratitude to Antoinina Bevan-Zlatar, Guillemette Bolens, Margaret Bridges, Emma Depledge, Lukas Erne, Neil Forsyth, Michael Gorra, Ufuk Zafer Gül, Umut Gül, Peter Holbrook, Andrew Johnston, Karen Junod, Rita Khurana, Silke Lambeck, Didier Maillat, the much missed Ruth Morse, Tony Mortimer, Denis Renevey, Gabi Rippl, Rupa Sengupta, and Pete Smith. My warmest thanks to them all.

Without Walter Wüllenweber, this book quite simply would not have been written.

BIBLIOGRAPHY

Primary Sources

Anon. *Cyvile and uncyvile life*. 1579.

Anon. *A Helpe to Discourse, Or, a Miscelany of Merriment*. 1619.

Aquinas, St Thomas. *Summa theologiae*. Vol. 41. Trans. T. C. O'Brien. London: Blackfriars in conjunction with Eyre & Spottiswoode, 1972.

Aristotle. *The Nicomachean Ethics*. Trans. David Ross. Oxford World's Classics. Oxford: Oxford University Press, 2009.

———. *Nicomachean Ethics*. 2nd ed. Trans. Terence Irwin. Indianapolis: Hackett, 1999.

———. *Nicomachean Ethics*. Trans. H. Rackham. Loeb Classical Library. Cambridge, MA: Harvard University Press, 1934.

———. *On Rhetoric: A Theory of Civic Discourse*. 2nd ed. Trans. George A. Kennedy. New York: Oxford University Press, 2007.

———. *Poetics*. Ed. and trans. Stephen Halliwell. Cambridge, MA: Harvard University Press, 1995.

———. *Politics*. Trans. H. Rackham. Loeb Classical Library. Cambridge, MA: Harvard University Press, 1932.

Ascham, Roger. *The Schoolmaster* (1570). Ed. Lawrence V. Ryan. Ithaca, NY: Cornell University Press, 1967.

Augustine, St. *Against Lying*. Trans. Harold B. Jaffee. In *Saint Augustine: Treatises on Various Subjects*, trans. Sister Sarah Muldowney et al., ed. Roy J. Deferrari, The Fathers of the Church: A New Translation, vol. 16, 113–79. Washington, DC: Catholic University of America Press, 1952.

———. *City of God*. Vol. 1. Trans. George E. McCracken. Loeb Classical Library. Cambridge, MA: Harvard University Press, 1957.

———. *City of God*. Vol. 2. Trans. William M. Green. Loeb Classical Library. Cambridge, MA: Harvard University Press, 1963.

———. *City of God*. Vol. 6. Trans. William Chase Greene. Loeb Classical Library. Cambridge, MA.: Harvard University Press, 1960.

———. *Lying*. Trans. Sister Mary Sarah Muldowney. In *Saint Augustine: Treatises on Various Subjects*, trans. Sister Sarah Muldowney et al., ed. Roy J. Deferrari, The Fathers of the Church: A New Translation, vol. 16, 53–110. Washington, DC: Catholic University of America Press, 1952.

Bacon, Francis. *The Major Works*. Ed. Brian Vickers. Oxford World's Classics. Oxford: Oxford University Press, 1996.

———. *The Works of Francis Bacon* (1857–74). Ed. James Spedding, Robert Leslie Ellis, and Douglas Denon Heath. Cambridge: Cambridge University Press, 2011.

Bodin, Jean. *The Six Bookes of a Commonweale*. Trans. Richard Knolles. 1606.

Braham, Humfrey. *The Institucion of a gentleman*. 1555.

Brathwaite, Richard. *The English Gentleman and English Gentlewoman*. 1641.

Breton, Nicholas. *The Court and Country, or A briefe Discourse betweene the Courtier and the Country-man*. 1618.

Bruto, Giovanni Michele. *The necessarie, fit, and convenient education of a yong gentlewoman written both in French and Italian, and translated into English by W[illiam] P[histon]*. 1598.

Burghley, William Cecil, Baron. *Certaine Preceptes or Directions, For the well ordering and carriage of a mans life*. 1617.

Caius, John. *A boke, or counseill against the disease commonly called the sweate, or sweatyng sicknesse*. 1552.

Castiglione, Baldesar. *A Book of the Courtier*. Trans. Charles S. Singleton, ed. Daniel Javitch. Norton Critical Edition. New York: Norton, 2002.

———. *The courtyer of Count Baldessar Castilio divided into foure bookes*. Trans. Thomas Hoby. 1561.

Cawdrey, Robert. *A Table Alphabeticall*. 1604.

Chesterfield, Lord. *Letters*. Ed. David Robert. Oxford World's Classics. Oxford: Oxford University Press, 1992.

Cicero. *Laelius de amicitia*. In *On Old Age, On Friendship, On Divination*, trans. W. A. Falconer. Loeb Classical Library. Cambridge, MA: Harvard University Press, 1923.

———. *On the Ideal Orator (De oratore)*. Trans. James M. May and Jakob Wisse. New York: Oxford University Press, 2001.

———. *On Invention*. In *On Invention, Best Kind of Orator, Topics*, trans. H. M. Hubbell. Loeb Classical Library. Cambridge, MA: Harvard University Press, 1970.

———. *On Obligations*. Trans. P. G. Walsh. Oxford World's Classics. Oxford: Oxford University Press, 2000.

———. *Orator*. In *Brutus—Orator*, trans. H. M. Hubbell. Loeb Classical Library. Cambridge, MA: Harvard University Press, 1939.

Cleland, James. *Hero-paideia, or The Institution of a Young Noble Man*. 1607.

C[ockeram], H[enry]. *The English Dictionarie: or, An Interpreter of hard English Words*. 1623.

Cooper, Anthony Ashley, 3rd Earl of Shaftesbury. 'Sensus Communis: An Essay on the Freedom of Wit and Humour'. In *Characteristicks of Men, Manners, Opinions, Times*, 2 vols., ed. Philip Ayres, 1:37–81. 1709. Oxford: Clarendon, 1999.

Darell, William. *A Short discourse of the life of Servingmen*. 1578.

Dedekind, Friedrich. *The Schoole of Slovenrie: or, Cato turnd wrong side outward*. Trans. out of Latine into English verse by R. F. Gent. 1605.

Dekker, Thomas. *The Guls Horne-booke*. 1609.

Dekker, Thomas, and Thomas Middleton. *The Roaring Girl*, ed. Coppélia Kahn. In *Thomas Middleton: The Collected Works*, gen. ed. Gary Taylor and John Lavagnino. Oxford: Oxford University Press, 2007.

Della Casa. *The Arts of Grandeur and Submission. Or, A Discourse Concerning the Behaviour of Great men towards their Inferiours: and of Inferiour Personages towards Men of greater Quality*.

Written in Latin by Joannes Casa, Archbishop of Benevento . . . and rendered into English by Henry Stubbe. 1665.

———. *Galateo of Maister John Della Casa, Archebishop of Beneventa. Or rather, A treatise of the manners and behaviours, it behoveth a man to use and eschewe, in his familiar conversation.* Trans. Robert Peterson. 1576.

———. *Galateo or The Book of Manners.* Trans. R. S. Pine-Coffin. Harmondsworth: Penguin, 1958.

———. *Galateo.* Ed. and trans. Konrad Eisenbichler and Kenneth R. Bartlett. Toronto: Centre for Reformation and Renaissance Studies, University of Toronto, 1986.

———. *Galateo, or, The Rules of Polite Behaviour.* Ed. and trans. M. F. Rusnak. Chicago: University of Chicago Press, 2013.

du Bosc, Jacques. *The Compleat Woman.* Trans. N. N. 1639.

Ducci, Lorenzo. *Ars Aulica or The Courtiers Arte.* Trans. Edward Blount. 1607.

Earle, John. *Micro-cosmographie. Or, A peece of the world discovered; in essayes and characters.* 1629.

Elyot, Sir Thomas. *A Critical Edition of Sir Thomas Elyot's* The Boke named the Governour. Ed. Donald W. Rude. New York: Garland, 1992.

———. *The Dictionary of Syr Thomas Eliot knyght.* 1538.

Epictetus. *The Encheiridion.* Trans. W. A. Oldfather. Loeb Classical Library. Cambridge, MA: Harvard University Press, 1928.

Erasmus, Desiderius. *Annotations on Galatians and Ephesians.* Trans. and ed. Riemer A. Faber. In *Collected Works of Erasmus*, vol. 58, gen. ed. Robert D. Sider. Toronto: University of Toronto Press, 2017.

———. *Ciceronianus.* Trans. Betty I. Knott. In *Collected Works of Erasmus*, vol. 28, ed. A. H. T. Levi. Toronto: University of Toronto Press, 1986.

———. *A Declamation on the Subject of Early Liberal Education for Children.* Trans. Beert C. Verstraete. In *Collected Works of Erasmus: Literary and Educational Writings 4*, vol. 26, ed. J. K. Sowards, 291–346. Toronto: Toronto University Press, 1985.

———. *Erasmus on Literature: His* Ratio *or 'System' of 1518/1519 (The* Ratio verae theologiae*).* Ed. Mark Vessey, trans. Robert D. Sider. Toronto: University of Toronto Press, 2021.

———. *The Handbook of the Christian Soldier.* Trans. Charles Fantazzi. In *Collected Works of Erasmus: Spiritualia*, vol. 66, ed. John W. O'Malley, 1–128. Toronto: University of Toronto Press, 1988.

———. 'The Knight without a Horse, or Faked Nobility'. In *Collected Works of Erasmus: Colloquies*, vols. 39–40, trans. and ed. Craig R. Thompson, 880–90. Toronto: University of Toronto Press, 1997.

———. *On Good Manners for Boys / De civilitate morum puerilium.* Trans. and annotated Brian McGregor. In *Collected Works of Erasmus: Literary and Educational Writings 3*, vol. 25, ed. J. K. Sowards, 269–90. Toronto: University of Toronto Press, 1985.

Faret, Nicolas. *The honest man: or, The art to please in court. Written in French by Sieur Faret, translated into English by E[dward] G[rimeston].* 1632.

Fitzgerald, F. Scott. *The Great Gatsby.* 1925. New York: Bantam Books, 1974.

Florio, John. *Florio His firste Fruites.* 1578.

———. *Florios Second Frutes.* 1591.

———. *A Worlde of Wordes.* 1598.

G[ainsford], T[homas]. *The Rich Cabinet*. 1616.

Gesta Grayorum, or, The History of the High and mighty Prince, Henry Prince of Purpoole. 1688.

Gouge, William. *Of Domesticall Duties: Eight Treatises*. 1622.

Gracián, Baltasar. *The Pocket Oracle and Art of Prudence*. Trans. Jeremy Robbins. Penguin Classics. London: Penguin, 2011.

Greene, Robert. *Greenes Groats-Worth of witte, bought with a million of Repentence*. 1592.

Guasco, Annibal. *Discourse to Lady Lavinia His Daughter*. Ed. and trans. Peggy Osborn. Chicago: University of Chicago Press, 2003.

Guazzo, Stefano. *The Civile Conversation of M. Steeven Guazzo*. 2 vols. Trans. George Pettie and Bartholomew Young. 1581 and 1586. London, Constable and Co., 1925.

Hall, Joseph, Epistle VI, Decade VI, To Master I. B. 'A complaint of the mis-education of our Gentry'. In *Epistles, The third and last volume. Containing two decades*, E2r–6r. 1611.

Harrison, William. 'The Description of Britaine'. In Raphael Holinshed, *The Firste volume of the Chronicles of England, Scotlande, and Irelande* (1577), bk. 3, chap. 4, 'Of the degrees of people in the common wealth of Englande', N6r–M2v.

———. 'An Historicall description of the Iland of Britaine'. In Raphael Holinshed, William Harrison, et al., *The First and second volumes of Chronicles* (1587), bk. 2, chap. 5, 'Of degrees of people in the common-weath of England', O5v–P4r.

Harvey, Gabriel. *Letter-Book of Gabriel Harvey, AD 1573–1580*. Ed. Edward J. L. Scott. London: Printed for the Camden Society, 1884.

Hawkins, Francis. *Youths Behaviour, or Decency in conversation amongst men*. 1646.

Hegel, Georg Wilhelm. *Grundlinien der Philosphie des Rechts*. In *Werke*, vol. 7. 1820. Frankfurt a. M.: Suhrkamp, 1979.

Heywood, Thomas. *The Fair Maid of the Exchange; A Comedy*, and *Fortune by Land and Sea; A Tragi-Comedy*, by Thomas Heywood and William Rowley, ed. Barron Field, esq. London: Printed for the Shakespeare Society, 1846.

Hobbes, Thomas. *Leviathan*. Ed. Richard Tuck. Cambridge Texts in the History of Political Thought. Cambridge: Cambridge University Press, 1991.

———. *On the Citizen*. Ed. Richard Tuck and Michael Silverthorne. Cambridge Texts in the History of Political Thought. Cambridge: Cambridge University Press, 1998.

Hume, David. *Selected Essays*. Ed. Stephen Copley and Andrew Edgar. Oxford's World Classics. Oxford: Oxford University Press, 1993.

Isocrates. *Against the Sophists*. In *Isocrates*, vol. 2, trans. George Norlin. Loeb Classical Library. Cambridge, MA: Harvard University Press, 1985.

Jerome, St. *Commentary on Galatians*. Trans. Andrew Cain. The Fathers of the Church: A New Translation. Washington, DC: Catholic University of America Press, 2010.

Jonson, Ben. *The Alchemist*. Ed. F. H. Mares. The Revels Plays. Manchester: Manchester University Press, 1967.

———. *Discoveries*. Ed. Lorna Hutson. In *The Cambridge Edition of the Works of Ben Jonson*, vol. 7, gen. ed. David Bevington, Martin Butler, and Ian Donaldson. Cambridge: Cambridge University Press, 2012.

———. *Epicene, or The Silent Woman*. Ed. Richard Dutton. The Revels Plays. Manchester: Manchester University Press, 2003.

———. *Every Man Out of His Humour*. Ed. Helen Ostovich. The Revels Plays. Manchester: Manchester University Press, 2001.

———. 'Inviting a Friend to Supper'. In *The Norton Anthology of English Literature*, vol. 1, 8th ed., ed. Stephen Greenblatt et al., 1431–32. New York: Norton, 2006.
———. 'An Ode to Himself'. In *The Norton Anthology of Poetry*, ed. Margaret Ferguson et al., 304–5. New York: Norton, 1996.
———. *Sejanus*. Ed. Philip J. Ayres. The Revels Plays. Manchester: Manchester University Press, 1990.
Kant, Immanuel. *Critique of Judgment*. Trans. Werner S. Pluhar. Indianapolis: Hackett, 1987.
La Primaudaye, Pierre de. *The French Academie*. Trans. Thomas Bowes. 1586.
Lipsius. *Sixe Bookes of Politickes or Civil Doctrine*. Trans. William Jones. 1594.
Locke, John. *Some Thoughts Concerning Education and the Conduct of the Understanding*. Ed. Ruth Grant and Nathan Tarcov. Indianapolis: Hackett, 1996.
Machiavelli. *The Prince*. Ed. Quentin Skinner and Russell Price. Cambridge Texts in the History of Political Thought. Cambridge: Cambridge University Press, 1988.
Macrobius. *Saturnalia*. Trans. Robert A. Kaster. Loeb Classical Library. Cambridge, MA: Harvard University Press, 2011.
[Markham, Gervase]. *A Health to the Gentlemanly profession of Servingmen: or, The Servingmans Comfort*. 1598.
Martyn, William. *Youths Instruction*. 1612.
Middleton, Thomas. *Thomas Middleton: The Collected Works*. Gen. ed. Gary Taylor and John Lavagnino. Oxford: Oxford University Press, 2007.
Montaigne, Michel de. *The Complete Essays*. Trans. M. A. Screech. Penguin Classics. London: Penguin, 1987.
Osborne, Francis. *Advice to a Son; or, Directions For your better Conduct*. 1656.
Ovid. *The Love Poems*. Trans. A. D. Melville, ed. E. J. Kenny. Oxford World's Classics. Oxford: Oxford University Press, 1990.
Peacham, Henry. *The Complete Gentleman, The Truth of Our Times, and The Art of Living in London*. Ed. Virgil B. Heltzel. Ithaca, NY: Cornell University Press, 1962.
Peacham, The Elder, Henry. *The Garden of Eloquence*. 1593.
Perkins, William. *A Direction for the Government of the Tongue according to Gods word*. 1593.
———. *The Works of William Perkins*. Vol. 2. 1631.
Plato. *Complete Works*. Ed. John M. Cooper and D. S. Hutchinson. Indianapolis: Hackett, 1997.
Pliny. *Natural History*. Vol. 1. Trans. H. Rackham. Loeb Classical Library. Cambridge, MA: Harvard University Press, 1938.
Plutarch. *Caius Marcius Coriolanus* and *Comparison of Alcibiades and Coriolanus*. In *Lives, Vol. IV: Alcibiades and Coriolanus. Lysander and Sulla*, trans. Bernadotte Perrin. Loeb Classical Library. Cambridge, MA: Harvard University Press, 1916.
———. 'How to Tell a Flatterer from a Friend'. In *Moralia*, vol. 1, trans. Frank Cole Babbitt, 261–396. Loeb Classical Library. Cambridge, MA: Harvard University Press, 1927.
———. *Life of Caius Martius Coriolanus* and *Comparison of Alcibiades with Coriolanus*. In *The Lives of the Noble Grecians and Romans*, trans. Thomas North, selected by Judith Mossman. Wordsworth Classics of World Literature. Ware, Herts: Wordsworth Editions, 1998.
———. *Moralia*. Vol. 8. Trans. Paul A. Clement and Herbert B. Hoffleit. Loeb Classical Library. Cambridge, MA: Harvard University Press, 1969.
———. *Vie de Coriolan* and *Alcibiades et Coriolanus*. In *Les Vies des Hommes illustres*, trans. Jacques Amyot, ed. Gerard Walter. Bibliothèque de la Pléiade. Paris: Pléiade, 1937.

Pontano, Giovanni Giovano. *The Virtues and Vices of Speech*. Ed. and trans. G. W. Pigman III. The I Tatti Renaissance Library. Cambridge, MA: Harvard University Press, 2019.

Puttenham, George. *The Art of English Poesy: A Critical Edition*. Ed. Frank Whigham and Wayne A. Rebhorn. Ithaca, NY: Cornell University Press, 2007.

Quintilian. *The Orator's Education*. Ed. and trans. Donald A. Russell. Loeb Classical Library. Cambridge, MA: Harvard University Press, 2001.

Rankins, William. *A Mirrour of Monsters*. 1587.

Refuge, Eustache de. *A Treatise of the Court or Instructions for Courtiers*. Trans. John Reynolds. 1622.

———. *Treatise on the Court: The Early Modern Management Classic on Organizational Behaviour*. Trans. J. Chris Cooper. Boca Raton, FL: Orgpax, 2008.

R[obson], S[imon]. *The Courte of Civill Courtesie*. 1577.

Rogers, Nehemiah. *Christian Curtesie: or, St Pauls Ultimum Vale*. 1621.

Romei, Annibale. *The Courtiers Academie: comprehending seven severall dayes discourses*. Trans. I. K. [John Keper]. 1598.

Salter, Thomas. *A Mirrhor mete for all Mothers, Matrones, and Maidens, intituled the Mirrhor of Modestie*. 1579.

Sassetti, Filippo. *Lettere di Filippo Sassetti*. Ed. Ettore Marcucci. Florence, 1855.

Savioli, Vincentio. *Vincentio Saviolo his Practise. In two Bookes. The first intreating of the use of the Rapier and Dagger. The second, of Honor and honorable Quarrels*. 1595.

Selden, John. *Titles of Honor*. 1614.

Seneca. 'De Constantia Sapientis'. In *Moral Essays*, vol. 1, trans. John W. Basore, 48–105. Loeb Classical Library. Cambridge, MA: Harvard University Press, 1928.

———. *Epistles 93–124*. Trans. Richard M. Gummere. Loeb Classical Library. Cambridge, MA: Harvard University Press, 1925.

Shakespeare, William. *The Norton Shakespeare*. 3rd ed., ed. Stephen Greenblatt et al. New York: Norton, 2016.

Sidney, Sir Philip. *An Apology for Poetry or The Defence of Poesy*. Ed. Geoffrey Shepherd, revised and expanded by R. W. Maslen. Manchester: Manchester University Press, 2002.

———. *The Countess of Pembroke's Arcadia*. Ed. Maurice Evans. London: Penguin, 1997.

Smith, Sir Thomas. *De Republica Anglorum. The maner of Governement or policie of the Realme of England*. 1584.

Stubbes, Philip. *The Anatomie of Abuses*. 1584.

Tacitus. *The Annals: The Reigns of Tiberius, Claudius, and Nero*. Trans. J. C. Yardley. Oxford World's Classics. Oxford: Oxford University Press, 2008.

Taylors Wit and Mirth. In *Shakespeare's Jest Books*, ed. William Carew Hazlitt. New York: Barnes & Noble, 2017.

T[uvill], D[aniel]. *The Dove and the Serpent*. 1614.

Twyne, Thomas. *The Schoolemaster, or Teacher of Table Philosophie*. 1576.

Vienne, Philibert de. *The Philosopher of the Court*, written by Philbert of Vienne in Champaigne and Englished by George North, gentleman. 1575.

Vives, Juan Luis. *A very frutefull and pleasant boke called the Instruction of a Christen woman*. Trans. Richard Hyrde. 1529.

Washington's Rules of Civility and Decent Behavior in Company and Conversation. Ed. J. M. Toner. Washington, DC: W. H. Morrison, 1888.

Wilson, Thomas. *The Art of Rhetoric (1560)*. Ed. Peter E. Medine. University Park: Pennsylvania State University Press, 1994.

Wright, Thomas. *The Passions of the Mind in General*. Ed. William Webster Newbold. The Renaissance Imagination vol. 15. New York: Garland, 1986.

Secondary Sources

Agnew, Jean-Christophe. *Worlds Apart: The Market and the Theater in Anglo-American Thought, 1550–1750*. New York: Cambridge University Press, 1986.

Anglo, Sydney. 'Systematic Immorality: The Courtier's Art'. In *Machiavelli—The First Century: Studies in Enthusiasm, Hostility, and Irrelevance*, 573–629. Oxford: Oxford University Press, 2005.

Angus, Bill. *Metadrama and the Informer in Shakespeare and Jonson*. Edinburgh: Edinburgh University Press, 2016.

Appiah, Kwame Anthony. *As If: Idealization and Ideals*. Cambridge, MA: Harvard University Press, 2017.

———. *The Honor Code: How Moral Revolutions Happen*. New York: Norton, 2010.

———. *The Lies That Bind: Rethinking Identity*. New York: Norton, 2018.

Archer, John Michael. *Sovereignty and Intelligence: Spying and Court Culture in the English Renaissance*. Stanford, CA: Stanford University Press, 1993.

Arditi, Jorge. *A Genealogy of Manners: Transformations of Social Relations in France and England from the Fourteenth to the Eighteenth Century*. Chicago: University of Chicago Press, 1998.

Arendt, Hannah. 'Lying in Politics: Reflections on the Pentagon Papers'. *New York Review of Books*, November 18, 1971, 1–16.

Arruzza, Cinzia. *A Wolf in the City: Tyranny and the Tyrant in Plato's Republic*. Oxford: Oxford University Press, 2019.

Ayres, Philip J. 'Introduction'. In Ben Jonson, *Sejanus*, ed. Philip J. Ayres, 1–44. The Revels Plays. Manchester: Manchester University Press, 1990.

Ayers, P. K. 'Dreams of the City: The Urban and the Urbane in Jonson's *Epicoene*'. *Philological Quarterly* 66.1 (1987): 73–86.

Bailey, Amanda. '"Monstrous Manner": Style and the Early Modern Theater'. *Criticism* 43.3 (2001): 249–84.

Barish, Jonas A. 'Ovid, Juvenal and *The Silent Woman*'. *PMLA* 71 (1956): 214–24.

Baron, Hans. *The Crisis of the Early Italian Renaissance: Civic Humanism and Republican Liberty in an Age of Classicism and Tyranny*. Princeton, NJ: Princeton University Press, 1955.

Barton, Anne. *Ben Jonson, Dramatist*. Cambridge: Cambridge University Press, 1984.

———. *Essays, Mainly Shakespearean*. Cambridge: Cambridge University Press, 1994.

———. 'Livy, Machiavelli, and Shakespeare's *Coriolanus*'. *Shakespeare Survey* 38 (1985): 115–29.

Bate, Jonathan. *Shakespeare and Ovid*. Oxford: Clarendon, 1993.

Beard, Mary. *Laughter in Ancient Rome: On Joking, Tickling, and Cracking Up*. Berkeley: University of California Press, 2014.

Bednarz, James P. *Shakespeare and the Poets' War*. New York: Columbia University Press, 2001.

Beecher, Donald. 'Introduction'. In *Characters*, by Sir Thomas Overbury (and Others), ed. Donald Beecher, 11–108. Ottawa: Doverhouse Editions, 2003.

Bejan, Teresa M. *Mere Civility: Discontent and the Limits of Toleration*. Cambridge, MA: Harvard University Press, 2017.

Belsey, Catherine. 'Agonistic Scenes of Provincial Life'. In Gajowski and Rackin, *Merry Wives of Windsor*, 27–37.

Berger, Harry, Jr. *The Absence of Grace: Sprezzatura and Suspicion in Two Renaissance Courtesy Books*. Stanford, CA: Stanford University Press, 2000.

———. '*Sprezzatura* and Embarrassment in *The Merchant of Venice*'. In *Shakespeare and the Italian Renaissance: Appropriation, Transformation, Opposition*, ed. Michele Marrapodi, 21–37. Farnham: Ashgate, 2014.

Bevington, David. 'Introduction to *Epicene, or The Silent Woman*', ed. David Bevington. In *The Cambridge Edition of the Works of Ben Jonson*, vol. 3, gen. ed. David Bevington, Martin Butler, and Ian Donaldson, 375–83. Cambridge: Cambridge University Press, 2012.

Boatright, Robert G., et al., eds. *A Crisis of Civility? Political Discourse and Its Discontents*. New York: Routledge, 2019.

Boesche, Roger. 'Aristotle's "Science" of Tyranny'. *History of Political Thought* 14.1 (1993): 1–25.

Boughner, Daniel. 'Jonson's Use of Lipsius in *Sejanus*'. *Modern Language Notes* 73 (1958): 247–55.

Bourdieu, Pierre. *Distinction: A Social Critique of the Judgement of Taste*. Trans. Richard Nice. 1979. Cambridge, MA: Harvard University Press, 1984.

———. *Outline of a Theory of Practice*. Trans. Richard Nice. 1972. Cambridge: Cambridge University Press, 1977.

Bowen, Barbara. *Humour and Humanism in the Renaissance*. Variorum Collected Studies Series. Aldershot: Ashgate, 2004.

———. 'Renaissance Collections of *facetiae*, 1499–1528: A New Listing'. *Renaissance Quarterly* 39.2 (1986): 263–75.

Bradbrook, M. C. 'The Anatomy of Knavery: Jonson, Marston, Middleton'. In *The Growth and Structure of Elizabethan Comedy*, 136–64. London: Chatto & Windus, 1955.

Braden, Gordon. 'Plutarch, Shakespeare and the Alpha Males'. In *Shakespeare and the Classics*, ed. Charles Martindale, 188–205. Cambridge: Cambridge University Press, 2004.

Brett, Annabel, and James Tully, eds. *Rethinking the Foundations of Modern Political Thought*. Cambridge: Cambridge University Press, 2006.

Brooke, Christopher. *Philosophic Pride: Stoicism and Political Thought from Lipsius to Rousseau*. Princeton, NJ: Princeton University Press, 2012.

Brown, Pamela. *Better a Shrew Than a Sheep: Women, Drama and the Culture of Jest in Early Modern England*. Ithaca, NY: Cornell University Press, 2002.

Bruster, Douglas. *Drama and the Market in the Age of Shakespeare*. Cambridge: Cambridge University Press, 1992.

Bryson, Anna. *From Courtesy to Civility: Changing Codes of Conduct in Early Modern England*. Oxford: Clarendon, 1998.

Burckhardt, Jacob. *The Civilization of the Renaissance in Italy*. Trans. S. G. C. Middlemore. Penguin Classics. London: Penguin, 1990.

Burke, Peter. *The Art of Conversation*. Cambridge: Polity, 1993.

———. 'A Civil Tongue: Language and Politeness in Early Modern Europe'. In *Civil Histories: Essays Presented to Sir Keith Thomas*, ed. Peter Burke et al., 31–48. Oxford: Oxford University Press, 2000.

———. *The Fortunes of the* Courtier: *The European Reception of Castiglione's* Cortegiano. University Park: Pennsylvania State University Press, 1995.

———. 'Tacitism'. In *Tacitus*, ed. T. A. Dorey, 149–71. London: Routledge and Kegan Paul, 1969.

———. 'Tacitism, Scepticism, and Reason of State'. In *The Cambridge History of Political Thought 1450–1700*, ed. J. H. Burnes, 479–98. Cambridge: Cambridge University Press, 1991.

Burrow, Colin. *Imitating Authors: Plato to Futurity*. Oxford: Oxford University Press, 2019.

———. *Shakespeare and Classical Antiquity*. Oxford Shakespeare Topics. Oxford: Oxford University Press, 2013.

Bybee, Keith J. *How Civility Works*. Stanford, CA: Stanford University Press, 2016.

———. 'The Rise of Trump and the Death of Civility'. *Law, Culture, and the Humanities* 16.2 (2020): 6–23.

Cain, Tom. 'Introduction to *Sejanus*', ed. Tom Cain. In *The Cambridge Edition of the Works of Ben Jonson*, vol. 2, gen. ed. David Bevington, Martin Butler, and Ian Donaldson, 197–209. Cambridge: Cambridge University Press, 2012.

Calhoun, Cheshire. 'The Virtue of Civility'. *Philosophy & Public Affairs* 29.3 (2000): 251–75.

Carroll, Stuart. *Enmity and Violence in Early Modern Europe*. Cambridge: Cambridge University Press, 2023.

———. 'Violence, Civil Society and European Civilization'. In *The Cambridge World History of Violence*, vol. 3: *1500–1800 CE*, ed. Robert Antony, Stuart Carroll and Caroline Dodds Pennock, 660–78. Cambridge: Cambridge University Press, 2020.

Cavallo, JoAnn. 'Joking Matters: Politics and Dissimulation in Castiglione's *Book of the Courtier*'. *Renaissance Quarterly* 53 (2000): 402–24.

Cave, Richard Allen. *Ben Jonson*. Basingstoke: Macmillan, 1991.

Chakravorty, Swapan. *Society and Politics in the Plays of Thomas Middleton*. Oxford: Clarendon Press, 1996.

Chartier, Roger. 'From Texts to Manners. A Concept and Its Books: *Civilité* between Aristocratic Distinction and Popular Appropriation'. In *The Cultural Uses of Print in Early Modern France*, trans. Lydia G. Cochrane, 71–109. Princeton, NJ: Princeton University Press, 1987.

Chernaik, Warren. *The Myth of Rome in Shakespeare and His Contemporaries*. Cambridge: Cambridge University Press, 2011.

Clare, Janet. 'Jonson's "Comical Satires" and the Art of Courtly Compliment'. In *Refashioning Ben Jonson: Gender, Politics and the Jonsonian Canon*, ed. Julie Sanders, Kate Chedgzoy, and Susan Wiseman, 28–47. Basingstoke: Palgrave Macmillan, 1998.

Cohen, Ralph Alan. 'Introduction to *Your Five Gallants*', ed. Ralph Cohen. In *Thomas Middleton: The Collected Works*, gen. ed. Gary Taylor and John Lavagnino, 594–97. Oxford: Oxford University Press, 2007.

Cohen, Ted. *Jokes: Philosophical Thoughts on Joking Matters*. Chicago: University of Chicago Press, 1999.

Coldiron, A. E. B. 'Form[e]s of Transnationhood: The Case of John Wolfe's Trilingual *Courtier*'. *Renaissance Studies* 29.1 (2015): 103–24.

Colie, Rosalie L. *Paradoxia Epidemica: The Renaissance Tradition of Paradox*. Princeton, NJ: Princeton University Press, 1966.

Connolly, Joy. *The State of Speech: Rhetorical and Political Thought in Ancient Rome*. Princeton, NJ: Princeton University Press, 2008.

Cooper, J. Chris. 'Introduction'. In Eustache de Refuge, *Treatise on the Court: The Early Modern Management Classic on Organizational Behaviour*, trans. J. Chris Cooper, 11–36. Boca Raton, FL: Orgpax, 2008.

Correll, Barbara. *The End of Conduct: Grobianus and the Renaissance Text of the Subject*. Ithaca, NY: Cornell University Press, 1996.

Covatta, Anthony. *Thomas Middleton's City Comedies*. Lewisburg, PA: Bucknell University Press, 1973.

Cox, Virginia. 'Quintilian in Renaissance Italy'. In *The Oxford Handbook of Quintilian*, ed. James J. Murphy and Marc van der Poel, 359–79. Oxford: Oxford University Press, 2021.

———. *The Renaissance Dialogue: Literary Dialogue in Its Social and Political Contests, Castiglione to Galileo*. Cambridge: Cambridge University Press, 1992.

Crane, David. 'Introduction'. In *The Merry Wives of Windsor*, ed. David Crane, 1–27. The New Cambridge Shakespeare. Cambridge: Cambridge University Press, 1997.

Dalrymple, William. *The Golden Road: How Ancient India Transformed the World*. London: Bloomsbury, 2024.

Darwall, Stephen L. 'Two Kinds of Respect'. *Ethics* 88.1 (1977): 36–49.

Davies, Christie. *Jokes and Their Relation to Society*. New York: Mouton de Gruyter, 1998.

Dawson, Mark S. *Gentility and the Comic Theatre of Late Stuart London*. Cambridge: Cambridge University Press, 2005.

Denton, John. 'Plutarch, Shakespeare, Roman Politics and Renaissance Translation'. In 'Shakespeare's Plutarch', ed. Mary Ann McGrail. Special issue, *Poetica* 48 (1997): 187–209.

Destrée, Pierre, and Franco V. Trivigno, eds. *Laughter, Humor, and Comedy in Ancient Philosophy*. Oxford: Oxford University Press, 2019.

Diels, Hermann, and Walther Kranz. *Die Fragmente der Vorsokratiker*. 6th ed. Berlin: Weidmann, 1951.

Dombrowski, Daniel. 'Plato's "Noble Lie"'. *History of Political Thought* 18.4 (1997): 565–78.

Donaldson, Ian. *Ben Jonson: A Life*. Oxford: Oxford University Press, 2011.

Douglass, Robin. 'The Body Politic "Is a Fictitious Body": Hobbes on Imagination and Fiction'. *Hobbes Studies* 27.2 (2014): 126–47.

Drakakis, John. 'Introduction'. In *The Merchant of Venice*, ed. John Drakakis, 1–159. The Arden Shakespeare, 3rd series. London: Bloomsbury Arden Shakespeare, 2010.

Dutton, Richard. *Ben Jonson: Authority: Criticism*. Basingstoke: Macmillan, 1996.

———. *Ben Jonson: To the First Folio*. Cambridge: Cambridge University Press, 1983.

———. 'Introduction'. In Ben Jonson, *Epicene, or The Silent Woman*, ed. Richard Dutton, 1–108. The Revels Plays. Manchester: Manchester University Press, 2003.

Dzelzainis, Martin. 'Bacon's "Of Simulation and Dissimulation"'. In *English Renaissance Literature and Culture*, vol. 1, ed. Michael Hattaway, 329–36. Chichester: Wiley-Blackwell, 2000.

Early Modern Research Group. 'Commonwealth: The Social, Cultural, and Conceptual Contexts of an Early Modern Keyword'. *Historical Journal* 54.3 (2011): 659–87.

Ehrenberg, John. *Civil Society: The Critical History of an Idea*. New York: New York University Press, 1999.

Eisenbichler, Konrad, and Kenneth R. Bartlett. 'Introduction'. In Giovanni Della Casa, *Galateo*, ed. and trans. Konrad Eisenbichler and Kenneth R. Bartlett, xi–xxiv. Toronto: Centre for Reformation and Renaissance Studies, University of Toronto, 1986.

Elias, Norbert. *The Civilizing Process*. Trans. Edmund Jephcott. 1939. Oxford: Blackwell, 1982.
Empson, William. 'Honest in *Othello*'. In *The Structure of Complex Words*, 218–49. Ann Arbor: University of Michigan Press, 1967.
Enterline, Lynn. *Shakespeare's Schoolroom: Rhetoric, Discipline, Emotion*. Philadelphia: University of Pennsylvania Press, 2012.
Erickson, Peter. 'The Order of the Garter, the Cult of Elizabeth, and Class-Gender Tension in *The Merry Wives of Windsor*'. In *Shakespeare Reproduced: The Text in History and Ideology*, ed. Jean E. Howard and Marion F. O'Connor, 116–42. New York: Methuen, 1987.
Ettenhuber, Katrin. *Donne's Augustine: Renaissance Cultures of Interpretation*. Oxford: Oxford University Press, 2011.
Evans, Robert C. *Jonson, Lipsius, and the Politics of Renaissance Stoicism*. Wakefield, NH: Longwood Academic Press, 1992.
———. '*Sejanus*: Ethics and Politics in the Early Reign of James'. In *Refashioning Ben Jonson: Gender, Politics and the Jonsonian Canon*, ed. Julie Sanders, Kate Chedgzoy, and Susan Wiseman, 71–92. Basingstoke: Palgrave Macmillan, 1998.
Farmer, Alan B., and Zachary Lesser. 'What Is Print Popularity? A Map of the Elizabethan Book Trade'. In *The Elizabethan Top Ten: Defining Print Popularity in Early Modern England*, ed. Andy Kesson and Emma Smith, 19–54. Farnham: Ashgate, 2013.
Finkelpearl, Philip J. *John Marston of the Middle Temple: An Elizabethan Dramatist in His Social Setting*. Cambridge, MA: Harvard University Press, 1969.
Finucci, Valeria. *The Lady Vanishes: Subjectivity and Representation in Castiglione and Ariosto*. Stanford, CA: Stanford University Press, 1992.
Fisher, F. J. 'The Development of London as a Centre of Conspicuous Consumption in the Sixteenth and Seventeenth Centuries'. In *London and the English Economy, 1500–1700*, ed. P. J. Corfield and N. B. Harte, 105–18. London: Hambledon, 1990.
Fleming, Sean. 'The Two Faces of Personhood: Hobbes, Corporate Agency and the Personality of the State'. *European Journal of Political Theory* 20.1 (2012): 5–26.
Fontaine Verwey, Herman de la. 'The First "Book of Etiquette" for Children: Erasmus' *De civilitate morum puerilium*'. *Quaerendo* 1 (1971): 19–30.
Fox, Alistair. *The English Renaissance: Identity and Representation in Elizabethan England*. Oxford: Blackwell, 1997.
Frede, Michael. *A Free Will: Origins of the Notion in Ancient Thought*. Berkeley: University of California, Press, 2011.
Freud, Sigmund. *Jokes and Their Relation to the Unconscious*. Trans. and ed. James Strachey. New York: Norton, 1960.
Freedman, Barbara. 'Falstaff's Punishment: Buffoonery as Defensive Posture in *The Merry Wives of Windsor*'. *Shakespeare Studies* 14 (1981): 163–74.
Gajowski, Evelyn, and Phyllis Rackin, eds. *The Merry Wives of Windsor: New Critical Essays*. New York: Routledge, 2015.
Garber, Marjorie. *Shakespeare and Modern Culture*. New York: Anchor Books, 2009.
Ghose, Indira. 'Jesting, Nostalgia, and Agonistic Play'. In *Memory and Affect in Shakespeare's England*, ed. Jonathan Baldo and Isabel Karremann, 124–40. Cambridge: Cambridge University Press, 2023.

———. 'Middleton and the Culture of Courtesy'. In *The Oxford Handbook of Thomas Middleton*, ed. Gary Taylor and Trish Thomas Henley, 376–89. Oxford: Oxford University Press, 2012.

———. *Much Ado About Nothing: Language and Writing*. London: Bloomsbury Arden Shakespeare, 2018.

———. 'Pride'. In *Shakespeare and Emotion*, ed. Katharine A. Craik, 264–74. Cambridge: Cambridge University Press, 2020.

———. *Shakespeare and Laughter: A Cultural History*. Manchester: Manchester University Press, 2008.

———. 'Wit'. In *Shakespeare and Virtue: A Handbook*, ed. Julia Reinhard Lupton and Donovan Sherman, 197–203. Cambridge: Cambridge University Press, 2023.

Gibbons, Brian. *Jacobean City Comedy: A Study of Satiric Plays by Jonson, Marston and Middleton*. 2nd ed. 1968. London: Methuen, 1980.

Gillingham, John. 'From *Civilitas* to Civility: Codes of Manners in Medieval and Early Modern England'. *Transactions of the Royal Historical Society* 12 (2002): 267–89.

Goffman, Erving. *Frame Analysis: An Essay on the Organization of Experience*. Boston: Northeastern University Press, 1974.

———. 'The Nature of Deference and Demeanour'. In *Interaction Ritual: Essays on Face-to-Face Behaviour*, 47–95. New York: Pantheon Books, 1967.

———. *The Presentation of Self in Everyday Life*. London: Penguin, 1959.

Gossett, Suzanne. 'Introduction to *A Fair Quarrel*', ed. Suzanne Gossett. In *Thomas Middleton: The Collected Works*, ed. Suzanne Gossett, gen. ed. Gary Taylor and John Lavagnino, 1209–12. Oxford: Oxford University Press, 2007.

Grav, Peter. 'Money Changes Everything: Quarto and Folio *The Merry Wives of Windsor* and the Case for Revision'. *Comparative Drama* 40.2 (2006): 217–40.

Greenblatt, Stephen. *Renaissance Self-Fashioning: From More to Shakespeare*. Chicago: University of Chicago Press, 1980.

Greene, Thomas M. 'Ben Jonson and the Centered Self'. *Studies in English Literature, 1500–1900* 10 (1970): 325–48.

———. '*Il Cortegiano* and the Choice of a Game'. In Hanning and Rosand, *Castiglione*, 1–15.

Griffith, Mark. 'The Language and Meaning of the College Motto'. *New College Notes* 1 (2012). https://www.new.ox.ac.uk/node/723.

Gross, Kenneth. *Shylock Is Shakespeare*. Chicago: University of Chicago Press, 2006.

Grudin, Robert. 'Renaissance Laughter: The Jests in Castiglione's *Il Cortegiano*'. *Neophilologus* 58 (1974): 199–204.

Guérin, Charles. 'Laughter, Social Norms, and Ethics in Cicero's Works'. In *Laughter, Humor, and Comedy in Ancient Philosophy*, ed. Pierre Destrée and Franco V. Trivigno, 122–44. Oxford: Oxford University Press, 2019.

Gurr, Andrew. *Playgoing in Shakespeare's London*. 3rd ed. Cambridge: Cambridge University Press, 2004.

Hadfield, Andrew. *Lying in Early Modern English Culture: From the Oath of Supremacy to the Oath of Allegiance*. Oxford: Oxford University Press, 2017.

Halasz, Alexandra. *The Marketplace of Print: Pamphlets and the Public Sphere in Early Modern England*. Cambridge: Cambridge University Press, 1997.

Halliwell, Stephen. *Greek Laughter: A Study of Cultural Psychology from Homer to Early Christianity*. Cambridge: Cambridge University Press, 2009.

Hankins, James. *Virtue Politics: Soulcraft and Statecraft in Renaissance Italy*. Cambridge, MA: Harvard University Press, 2019.

Hanning, Robert W. 'Castiglione's Verbal Portraits: Structures and Strategies'. In Hanning and Rosand, *Castiglione*, 131–41.

Hanning, Robert W., and David Rosand, eds. *Castiglione: The Ideal and the Real in Renaissance Culture*. New Haven, CT: Yale University Press, 1983.

Hanson, Elizabeth. *Discovering the Subject in Renaissance England*. Cambridge: Cambridge University Press, 1998.

Hartle, Ann. *What Happened to Civility: The Promise and Failure of Montaigne's Modern Project*. Notre Dame, IN: University of Notre Dame Press, 2022.

Haynes, Jonathan. *The Social Relations of Jonson's Theatre*. Cambridge: Cambridge University Press, 1992.

Heal, Felicity. *Hospitality in Early Modern England*. Oxford: Oxford University Press, 1990.

Heinemann, Margot. *Puritanism and Theatre: Thomas Middleton and Opposition Drama under the Early Stuarts*. Cambridge: Cambridge University Press, 1980.

Herbert, Amanda. *Female Alliances: Gender, Identity, and Friendship in Early Modern Britain*. New Haven, CT: Yale University Press, 2014.

Hill, Tracey. '"He Hath Changed His Coppy": Anti-Theatrical Writing and the Turncoat Player'. *Critical Survey* 9.3 (1997): 59–77.

Hinely, Jan Lawson. 'Comic Scapegoats and the Falstaff of *The Merry Wives of Windsor*'. *Shakespeare Studies* 15 (1982): 37–54.

Hoffman, Manfred. *Rhetoric and Theology: The Hermeneutic of Erasmus*. Toronto: University of Toronto Press, 1994.

Holcomb, Chris. *Mirth Making: The Rhetorical Discourse on Jesting in Early Modern England*. Columbia: University of South Carolina Press, 2001.

Holland, Peter. 'Introduction'. In *Coriolanus*, ed. Peter Holland, 1–141. The Arden Shakespeare, 3rd series. London: Bloomsbury, 2013.

Holloway, Carson. 'Shakespeare's *Coriolanus* and Aristotle's Great-Souled Man'. *Review of Politics* 69 (2007): 353–74.

Hudson, Alexandra. *The Soul of Civility: Timeless Principles to Heal Society and Ourselves*. New York: St. Martin's, 2023.

Hull, Suzanne E. *Chaste, Silent and Obedient: English Books for Women, 1475–1640*. San Marino, CA: Huntington Library, 1982.

Hundert, E. J. 'Augustine and the Sources of the Divided Self'. *Political Theory* 20.1 (1992): 86–104.

Hutson, Lorna. 'Civility and Virility in Ben Jonson'. *Representations* 78 (Spring 2002): 1–27.

———. 'The Displacement of the Market in Jacobean City Comedy'. *London Journal* 14.1 (1989): 3–16.

Itagaki, Lynn Mie. 'The Long Con of Civility'. *Connecticut Law Review* 52.3 (2021): 1169–86.

James, Heather. *Ovid and the Liberty of Speech in Shakespeare's England*. Cambridge: Cambridge University Press, 2021.

James, Mervyn. 'English Politics and the Concept of Honour, 1485–1642'. In *Society, Politics and Culture: Studies in Early Modern England*, 308–415. Cambridge: Cambridge University Press, 1986.

Jardine, Lisa. *Worldly Goods: A New History of the Renaissance*. New York: Norton, 1996.

Javitch, Daniel. '*The Philosopher of the Court*: A French Satire Misunderstood'. *Comparative Literature* 23.2 (1971): 97–124.
———. *Poetry and Courtliness in Renaissance England*. Princeton, NJ: Princeton University Press, 1978.
———. 'Rival Arts of Conduct in Elizabethan England: Guazzo's *Civile Conversation* and Castiglione's *Courtier*'. *Yearbook of Italian Studies* 1 (1971): 178–98.
Jones, Ann Rosalind, and Peter Stallybrass. *Renaissance Clothing and the Materials of Memory*. Cambridge: Cambridge University Press, 2000.
Jones, Emrys. 'The First West Comedy'. *Proceedings of the British Academy* 68 (1982): 215–58.
Jowett, John. 'Thomas Middleton'. In *A Companion to Renaissance Drama*, ed. Arthur Kinney, 507–23. Oxford: Blackwell, 2002.
Judges, A. V., ed. *The Elizabethan Underworld: A Collection of Tudor and Early Stuart Tracts and Ballads*. Key Writings on Subcultures 1535–1727: Classics from the Underworld, vol. 1. 1930. London: Routledge, 2002.
Kahn, Coppélia. *Roman Shakespeare: Warriors, Wounds, and Women*. London: Routledge, 1997.
Kahn, Victoria. *Machiavellian Rhetoric from the Counter-Reformation to Milton*. Princeton, NJ: Princeton University Press, 1994.
———. 'Machiavelli's Afterlife and Reputation to the Eighteenth Century'. In *The Cambridge Companion to Machiavelli*, ed. John M. Najemy, 239–55. Cambridge: Cambridge University Press, 2010.
———. *Rhetoric, Prudence, and Skepticism in the Renaissance*. Ithaca, NY: Cornell University Press, 1985.
———. *The Trouble with Literature*. Oxford: Oxford University Press, 2020.
Kaplan, M. Lindsay, ed., *The Merchant of Venice: The State of Play*. London: Bloomsbury Arden Shakespeare, 2022.
Kapust, Daniel J. 'Cicero on *Decorum* and Morality of Rhetoric'. *European Journal of Political Theory* 10 (2011): 92–112.
———. 'Rethinking Rousseau's Tyranny of Orators: Cicero's *On Duties* and the Beauty of True Glory'. In *The General Will: The Evolution of a Concept*, ed. James Farr and David Lay Williams, 175–96. Cambridge: Cambridge University Press, 2015.
Kay, David W. 'Jonson's Urbane Gallants: Humanistic Contexts for *Epicoene*'. *Huntington Library Quarterly* 39 (1975): 251–66.
Kelly-Gadol, Joan. 'Did Women Have a Renaissance?' In Baldesar Castiglione, *The Book of the Courtier*, ed. Daniel Javitch, 340–52. Norton Critical Edition. New York: Norton, 2002.
Kelso, Ruth. *Doctrine for the Lady of the Renaissance*. Urbana: University of Illinois Press, 1956.
———. *The Doctrine of the English Gentleman in the Sixteenth Century*. Gloucester, MA: Peter Smith, 1964.
Kennerly, Michele. '*Sermo* and Sociality in Cicero's *De Officiis*'. *Rhetorica: A Journal of the History of Rhetoric* 28.2 (2010): 119–37.
Kerrigan, John. 'Coriolanus Fidiussed'. *Essays in Criticism* 62.4 (2012): 319–52.
King, Emily L. *Civil Vengeance: Literature, Culture, and Early Modern Revenge*. Ithaca, NY: Cornell University Press, 2019.
Kinney, Arthur F. *Continental Humanist Poetics: Studies in Erasmus, Castiglione, Marguerite de Navarre, Rabelais, and Cervantes*. Amherst: University of Massachusetts, 1989.

Kirkpatrick, Richard. 'Machiavelli among the Doctors: *The Prince* and Divine Accommodation'. *Reformation & Renaissance Review* 18.2 (2016): 123–36.

Knights, L. C. *Drama and Society in the Age of Jonson*. New York: Stewart, 1937.

Knox, Dilwyn. '*Disciplina*: The Monastic and Clerical Origins of European Civility'. In *Renaissance Society and Culture: Essays in Honor of Eugene F. Rice, Jr.*, ed. John Monfasani and Ronald G. Musto, 107–36. New York: Italica Press, 1991.

———. 'Erasmus' *De civilitate* and the Religious Origins of Civility in Protestant Europe'. *Archiv für Reformationsgeschichte* 86 (1995): 7–55.

Kolb, Laura. *Fictions of Credit in the Age of Shakespeare*. Oxford: Oxford University Press, 2021.

Korda, Natasha. '"Judicious oeillades": Supervising Marital Property in *The Merry Wives of Windsor*'. In *Marxist Shakespeares*, ed. Jean E. Howard and Scott Cutler Shershow, 82–103. London: Routledge, 2001.

Kraye, Jill. 'Moral Philosophy'. In *The Cambridge History of Renaissance Philosophy*, ed. Charles B. Schmitt and Quentin Skinner, 301–86. Cambridge: Cambridge University Press, 1988.

Lagrée, Jacqueline. 'Justus Lipsius and Neostoicism'. In Sellars, *Routledge Handbook of the Stoic Tradition*, 160–73.

Lake, Peter. 'From *Leicester His Commonwealth* to *Sejanus His Fall*: Ben Jonson and the Politics of Roman (Catholic) Virtue'. In *Catholics and the 'Protestant Nation': Religious Politics and Identity in Early Modern England*, ed. Ethan Shagan, 128–61. Manchester: Manchester University Press, 2005.

———. *How Shakespeare Put Politics on the Stage: Power and Succession in the History Plays*. New Haven, CT: Yale University Press, 2016.

Lanham, Richard A. *The Motives of Eloquence: Literary Rhetoric in the Renaissance*. New Haven, CT: Yale University Press, 1976.

Lawrence, Jason. *'Who the Devil Taught Thee So Much Italian?' Italian Language Learning and Literary Imitation in Early Modern England*. Manchester: Manchester University Press, 2005.

Leggatt, Alexander. *Citizen Comedy in the Age of Shakespeare*. Toronto: University of Toronto Press, 1973.

———. 'Middleton, *Michaelmas Term*'. In *Introduction to English Renaissance Comedy*, 89–108. Manchester: Manchester University Press, 1999.

Leinwand, Theodore B. *The City Staged: Jacobean Comedy, 1603–1613*. Madison: University of Wisconsin Press, 1986.

———. 'Introduction to *Michaelmas Term*', ed. Theodore B. Leinwand. In *Thomas Middleton: The Collected Works*, gen. ed. Gary Taylor and John Lavagnino, 334–36. Oxford: Oxford University Press, 2007.

Lenthe, Victor. 'Ben Jonson's Antagonistic Style, Public Opinion, and *Sejanus*'. *Studies in English Literature 1500–1900* 57.2 (2017): 349–68.

Levine, Laura. *Men in Women's Clothing: Anti-theatricality and Effeminization, 1579–1642*. Cambridge: Cambridge University Press, 1994.

Levy Peck, Linda. *Consuming Splendor: Society and Culture in Seventeenth-Century England*. New York: Cambridge University Press, 2005.

Lewis, Rhodri. *Hamlet and the Vision of Darkness*. Princeton, NJ: Princeton University Press, 2017.

———. 'A Kind of Nothing: *Coriolanus*'. In *Shakespeare's Tragic Art*, 290–325. Princeton, NJ: Princeton University Press, 2024.

Lievsay, John Leon. *Stefano Guazzo and the English Renaissance 1575–1675*. Chapel Hill: University of North Carolina Press, 1961.

Lilla, Mark. *The Once and Future Liberal: After Identity Politics*. New York: HarperCollins, 2017.

Lombardini, John. 'Civic Laughter: Aristotle and the Political Value of Humor'. *Political Theory* 41.2 (April 2013): 203–30.

Loxley, James. *The Complete Critical Guide to Ben Jonson*. London: Routledge, 2002.

Luck, George. 'Vir Facetus: A Renaissance Ideal'. *Studies in Philology* 55.2 (April 1958): 107–21.

Lucking, David. '"The Price of One Fair Word": Negotiating Names in *Coriolanus*'. *Early Modern Literary Studies* 2.1 (1996): 4.1–22.

MacIntyre, Alasdair. *After Virtue: A Study in Moral Theory*. London: Bloomsbury, 2013.

Mack, Peter. *Elizabethan Rhetoric: Theory and Practice*. Cambridge: Cambridge University Press, 2002.

———. *A History of Renaissance Rhetoric 1380–1620*. Oxford: Oxford University Press, 2011.

Macpherson, C. B. *The Political Theory of Possessive Individualism*. Oxford: Clarendon, 1962.

Magnusson, Lynne. 'Scoff Power in *Love's Labour's Lost* and the Inns of Court: Language in Context'. *Shakespeare Survey* 57 (2004): 196–208.

Manley, Lawrence. 'London in Jest: From the Jestbooks'. In *London in the Age of Shakespeare: An Anthology*, ed. Lawrence Manley, 119–34. London: Croom Helm, 1986.

Marcus, Leah S. 'Levelling Shakespeare: Local Customs and Local Texts'. *Shakespeare Quarterly* 42.2 (1991): 168–78.

———. *The Politics of Mirth: Jonson, Herrick, Milton, Marvell, and the Defense of Old Holiday Pastimes*. Chicago: University of Chicago Press, 1986.

Marotti, Arthur F. 'The Self-Reflexive Art of Ben Jonson's *Sejanus*'. *Texas Studies in Literature and Language* 12.2 (1970): 197–220.

Marshall, Cynthia. 'Shakespeare: Crossing the Rubicon'. *Shakespeare Survey* 53 (2000): 73–88.

Martin, John Jeffries. *Myths of Renaissance Individualism*. Basingstoke: Palgrave Macmillan, 2004.

Martin, Randall. 'Introduction to *Every Man Out of His Humour*', ed. Randall Martin. In *The Cambridge Edition of the Works of Ben Jonson*, vol. 1, gen. ed. David Bevington, Martin Butler, and Ian Donaldson, 235–47. Cambridge: Cambridge University Press, 2012.

Martinich, Aloysius P. 'Authorization and Representation in Hobbes's *Leviathan*'. In *The Oxford Handbook of Hobbes*, ed. Aloysius P. Martinich and Kinch Hoekstra, 315–38. Oxford: Oxford University Press, 2016.

Maus, Katharine Eisaman. *Ben Jonson and the Roman Frame of Mind*. Princeton, NJ: Princeton University Press, 1984.

———. *Inwardness and Theater in the English Renaissance*. Chicago: University of Chicago Press, 1995.

Mayer, C. A. 'L'Honnête Homme: Molière and Philibert de Vienne's "Philosophe de Court"'. *Modern Language Review* 46 (1951): 196–217.

McCarthy, Dennis, and June Schlueter. *A Brief Discourse of Rebellion and Rebels by George North: A Newly Uncovered Manuscript Source for Shakespeare's Plays*. Rochester, NY: D. S. Brewer, 2018.

McCrea, Adriana. *Constant Minds: Political Virtue and the Lipsian Paradigm in England, 1584–1650*. Toronto: University of Toronto Press, 1997.

McDonald, Russ. 'Jonsonian Comedy and the Value of *Sejanus*'. *Studies in English Literature, 1500–1900* 21.2 (1981): 287–305.

Melchiori, Giorgio. 'Introduction'. In *The Merry Wives of Windsor*, ed. Giorgio Melchiori, 1–117. The Arden Shakespeare, 3rd series. London: Thomson Learning, 2000.

Mendelson, Sara. 'The Civility of Women in Seventeenth-Century England'. In *Civil Histories: Essays Presented to Sir Keith Thomas*, ed. Peter Burke, Brian Harrison, and Paul Slack, 111–25. Oxford: Oxford University Press, 2000.

Miles, Geoffrey. *Shakespeare and the Constant Romans*. Oxford: Clarendon, 1996.

Miller, Stephen. *Conversation: A History of a Declining Art*. New Haven, CT: Yale University Press, 2006.

Miola, Robert S. *Shakespeare's Rome*. Cambridge: Cambridge University Press, 1983.

Moore, G. C., ed. *Gabriel Harvey's Marginalia*. Stratford-upon-Avon: Shakespeare Head Press, 1963.

Motta, Uberto. 'Castiglione e Shakespeare'. In *Letteratura italiana, letterature europee*, ed. Guido Baldassarri and Silvana Tamiozzo, 359–75. Rome: Bulzoni, 2004.

———. 'Il Gentiluomo Innamorato: Petrarca, Castiglione, Shakespeare'. *Studi medievali e umanistici* 15 (2017): 289–314.

Muecke, D. C. *Irony and the Ironic*. The Critical Idiom. London: Methuen, 1970.

Muir, Kenneth. *The Sources of Shakespeare's Plays*. London: Methuen, 1977.

Muldrew, Craig. *The Economy of Obligation: The Culture of Credit and Social Relations in Early Modern England*. London: Palgrave Macmillan, 1998.

Munro, Ian. 'Jestbooks'. In *The Oxford Handbook of English Prose: 1500–1640*, ed. Andrew Hadfield, 343–59. Oxford: Oxford University Press, 2013.

———. 'The Matter of Wit and the Early Modern Stage'. In *A New Companion to Renaissance Drama*, ed. Arthur F. Kinney and Thomas Warren Hopper, 513–28. Oxford: Wiley-Blackwell, 2017.

Newman, Karen. *Fashioning Femininity and English Renaissance Drama*. Chicago: University of Chicago Press, 1991.

Nicholls, Jonathan. *The Matter of Courtesy: Medieval Courtesy Books and the Gawain-Poet*. Woodbridge, Suffolk: D. S. Brewer, 1985.

Nussbaum, Martha C. 'Duties of Justice, Duties of Material Aid: Cicero's Problematic Legacy'. *Journal of Political Philosophy* 8.2 (2000): 176–206.

———. 'Kant and Stoic Cosmopolitanism'. *Journal of Political Philosophy* 5.1 (1997): 1–25.

O'Callaghan, Michelle. *The English Wits: Literature and Sociability in Early Modern England*. Cambridge: Cambridge University Press, 2007.

Oestreich, Gerhard. 'The Main Political Work of Lipsius'. In *Neostoicism and the Early Modern State*, trans. David McLintock, ed. Brigitta Oestreich and H. G. Koenigsberger, 39–56. Cambridge Studies in Early Modern History. New York: Cambridge University Press, 1982.

Orgel, Stephen. 'Devil Incarnate'. In *Spectacular Performances: Essays on Theatre, Imagery, Book and Selves in Early Modern England*, 231–50. Manchester: Manchester University Press, 2011.

———. *Imagining Shakespeare: A History of Texts and Visions*. Basingstoke: Palgrave Macmillan, 2003.

———. 'Venice at the Globe'. In *The Invention of Shakespeare and Other Essays*, 126–37. Philadelphia: University of Pennsylvania Press, 2022.

———. *Wit's Treasury: Renaissance England and the Classics*. Philadelphia: University of Pennsylvania Press, 2021.

Ostovich, Helen. 'Introduction'. In Ben Jonson, *Every Man Out of His Humour*, ed. Helen Ostovich, 1–95. The Revels Plays. Manchester: Manchester University Press, 2001.

Park, Katharine. 'The Organic Soul'. In *The Cambridge History of Renaissance Philosophy*, ed. Charles B. Schmitt and Quentin Skinner, 464–84. Cambridge: Cambridge University Press, 1988.

Partridge, Mary. '"Absolute Castilio"? The Reputation and Reception of Castiglione's Book of the *Courtier* in Elizabethan England'. In *The Routledge Research Companion to Renaissance Literature*, ed. Michele Marrapodi, 312–28. London: Routledge, 2019.

Paster, G. K. *The Idea of the City in the Age of Shakespeare*. Athens: University of Georgia Press, 1985.

Pelling, Christopher. 'The Shaping of Coriolanus: Dionysius, Plutarch and Shakespeare'. In 'Shakespeare's Plutarch', ed. Mary Ann McGrail. Special issue, *Poetica* 48 (1997): 3–32.

Peltonen, Markku. *The Duel in Early Modern England: Civility, Politeness and Honour*. Cambridge: Cambridge University Press, 2003.

———. 'Hypocrisy, Dissimulation, and Education for Civil Life in Pre-Revolutionary England'. In *Forms of Hypocrisy in Early Modern England*, ed. Lucia Nigri and Naya Tsentourou, 15–32. New York: Routledge, 2018.

Pigman, G. W., III. 'Introduction'. In Giovanni Gioviano Pontano, *The Virtues and Vices of Speech*, ed. and trans. G. W. Pigman III, vii–xxvii. The I Tatti Renaissance Library. Cambridge, MA: Harvard University Press, 2019.

Pocock, J. G. A. *The Machiavellian Moment: Florentine Political Thought and the Atlantic Republican Tradition*. Princeton, NJ: Princeton University Press, 1975.

Porter, Annette. 'Philibert de Vienne'. *Bibliothèque d'Humanisme et Renaissance* 27.3 (1965): 702–8.

Posner, David M. *The Performance of Nobility in Early Modern European Literature*. Cambridge: Cambridge University Press, 1999.

Prescott, Anne Lake. 'Humanism in the Tudor Jestbook'. *Moreana* 24.95–96 (1987): 5–16.

Putnam, Robert D. *Bowling Alone: The Collapse and Revival of American Community*. New York: Simon & Schuster, 2000.

Quint, David. 'Courtier, Prince, Lady: The Design of the *Book of the Courtier*'. In Baldesar Castiglione, *The Book of the Courtier*, ed. Daniel Javitch, 352–65. A Norton Critical Edition. New York: Norton, 2002.

Quondam, Amedeo. 'On the Genesis of the *Book of the Courtier*'. In Baldesar Castiglione, *The Book of the Courtier*, ed. Daniel Javitch, 283–95. A Norton Critical Edition. New York: Norton, 2002.

Randall, David. *The Concept of Conversation: From Cicero's Sermo to the Grand Siècle's Conversation*. Edinburgh: Edinburgh University Press, 2018.

Rawls, John. *A Theory of Justice*. Cambridge, MA: Harvard University Press, 1971.

Rebhorn, Wayne A. *Courtly Performances: Masking and Festivity in Castiglione's Book of the Courtier*. Detroit, MI: Wayne State University Press, 1978.

———. 'The Crisis of the Aristocracy in *Julius Caesar*'. *Renaissance Quarterly* 43.1 (1990): 75–11.

———. *The Emperor of Men's Minds: Literature and the Renaissance Discourse of Rhetoric*. Ithaca, NY: Cornell University Press, 1995.

Reich, Klaus. 'Kant and Greek Ethics (I.)'. *Mind* 48 (1939): 338–54.

———. 'Kant and Greek Ethics (II.)'. *Mind* 48 (1939): 446–63.

Reinke-Williams, Tim. 'Misogyny, Jest-Books and Male Youth Culture in Seventeenth-Century England'. *Gender and History* 21.2 (2009): 324–39.

Reiss, Timothy J. *Mirages of the Selfe: Patterns of Personhood in Ancient and Early Modern Europe*. Stanford, CA: Stanford University Press, 2003.

Revel, Jacques. 'The Uses of Civility'. In *A History of Private Life III: Passions of the Renaissance*, ed. Roger Chartier, trans. Arthur Goldhammer, 167–206. Cambridge, MA: Belknap, 1989.

Rhodes, Neil. *The Power of Eloquence and English Renaissance Literature*. Hemel Hempstead: Harvester Wheatsheaf, 1992.

Richards, Jennifer. 'Assumed Simplicity and the Critique of Nobility: Or, How Castiglione Read Cicero'. *Renaissance Quarterly* 54 (2001): 460–86.

———. *Rhetoric and Courtliness in Early Modern Literature*. Cambridge: Cambridge University Press, 2003.

Ricks, Christopher. '*Sejanus* and Dismemberment'. *Modern Language Notes* 76.4 (April 1961): 301–8.

Righter, Anne. *Shakespeare and the Idea of the Play*. Harmondsworth, Middlesex: Penguin, 1962.

Roberts, Hugh. 'Too Paradoxical for Paradoxes: The Role of the Cynics in Two Mid-Sixteenth-Century French Texts, Charles Estienne's *Paradoxes* and Philibert de Vienne's *Le Philosophe de court*'. *French Studies* 58.4 (2004): 459–70.

Rorty, Richard. *Contingency, Irony, and Solidarity*. Cambridge: Cambridge University Press, 1989.

Rosand, David. 'The Portrait, the Courtier, and Death'. In Hanning and Rosand, *Castiglione*, 91–129.

Rose, Mary Beth. *The Expense of Spirit: Love and Sexuality in English Renaissance Drama*. Ithaca, NY: Cornell University Press, 1988.

Ruffini, Marco. 'Alberti on the Surface'. *California Italian Studies* 2.1 (2011). https://doi.org/10.5070/C321009023.

Runciman, David. 'What Kind of Person Is Hobbes's State? A Reply to Skinner'. *Journal of Political Philosophy* 8 (2000): 26–78.

Russell, D. A. *Plutarch*. 2nd ed. London: Bristol Classical Press, 2001.

Ruutz-Rees, Caroline. 'Some Notes of Gabriel Harvey's in Hoby's Translation of Castiglione's *Courtier* (1561)'. *PMLA* 25.4 (1910): 608–39.

Ryan, Kiernan. *Shakespeare's Comedies*. Basingstoke: Palgrave Macmillan, 2009.

Saccio, Peter. 'Introduction to *A Mad World, My Masters*', ed. Peter Saccio. In *Thomas Middleton: The Collected Works*, gen. ed. Gary Taylor and John Lavagnino, 414–17. Oxford: Oxford University Press, 2007.

Saccone, Eduardo. '*Grazia, Sprezzatura, Affettazione* in the *Courtier*'. In Hanning and Rosand, *Castiglione*, 45–67.

Salingar, Leo. *Dramatic Form in Shakespeare and the Jacobeans*. Cambridge: Cambridge University Press, 1986.

Salmon, J. H. M. 'Stoicism and Roman Example: Seneca and Tacitus in Jacobean England'. *Journal of the History of Ideas* 50 (1989): 199–225.

Santosuosso, Antonio. 'Books, Readers, and Critics: The Case of Giovanni Della Casa, 1537–1975'. *La Bibliofilia* 79.2 (1977): 101–86.

———. 'Giovanni Della Casa and the Galateo on Life and Success in the Late Italian Renaissance'. *Renaissance and Reformation / Renaissance et Réforme* 11.1 (1975): 1–13.

Scaglione, Aldo. *Knights at Court: Courtliness, Chivalry, and Courtesy from Ottonian Germany to the Italian Renaissance.* Berkeley: University of California Press, 1991.

Schindler, Kilian. *Religious Dissimulation and Early Modern Drama: The Limits of Toleration.* Cambridge: Cambridge University Press, 2023.

Sellars, John. *Lessons in Stoicism.* London: Allen Lane, 2019.

———, ed. *The Routledge Handbook of the Stoic Tradition.* London: Routledge, 2016.

Sen, Amartya. *The Argumentative Indian: Writings on Indian Culture, History and Identity.* London: Penguin, 2006.

———. *Identity and Violence: The Illusion of Destiny.* New York: Norton, 2006.

Sennett, Richard. *The Performer: Art, Life, Politics.* London: Allen Lane, 2024.

Sherman, Nancy. 'Of Manners and Morals'. *British Journal of Educational Studies* 53.3 (2005): 272–89.

Shrank, Cathy. 'Civility and the City in *Coriolanus*'. *Shakespeare Quarterly* 54.4 (2003): 406–23.

———. 'Masters of Civility: Castiglione's *Courtier*, della Casa's *Galateo*, and Guazzo's *Civil Conversation* in Early Modern England'. In *The Routledge Research Companion to Renaissance Literature*, ed. Michele Marrapodi, 144–59. London: Routledge, 2019.

Simondic, Marko. 'Hobbes on *Persona*, Personation, and Representation: Behind the Mask of Sovereignty'. PhD thesis, University of York, 2011.

Simpson, David. *Engaging Violence: Civility and the Reach of Literature.* Stanford, CA: Stanford University Press, 2022.

Skinner, Quentin. *The Foundations of Modern Political Thought.* 2 vols. Cambridge: Cambridge University Press, 1978.

———. 'Hobbes and the Classical Theory of Laughter'. In *Visions of Politics*, vol. 3: *Hobbes and Civil Science*, 142–76. Cambridge: Cambridge University Press, 2002.

———. 'Hobbes and the Purely Artificial Person of the State'. *Journal of Political Philosophy* 7.1 (1999): 1–29.

———. 'Hobbes on Representation'. *European Journal of Philosophy* 13.2 (2005): 155–84.

———. 'Hobbes and the Social Control of Unsociability'. In *The Oxford Handbook of Thomas Hobbes*, ed. A. P. Martinich and Kinch Hoekstra, 432–52. Oxford: Oxford University Press, 2013.

———. 'Judicial Rhetoric in *The Merchant of Venice*'. In *From Humanism to Hobbes: Studies in Rhetoric and Politics*, 63–88. Cambridge: Cambridge University Press, 2018.

———. 'Machiavelli on Misunderstanding Princely Virtue'. In *From Humanism to Hobbes: Studies in Rhetoric and Politics*, 45–62. Cambridge: Cambridge University Press, 2018.

———. 'Rhetorical Redescription and Its Uses in Shakespeare'. In *From Humanism to Hobbes: Studies in Rhetoric and Politics*, 89–117. Cambridge: Cambridge University Press, 2018.

Slights, Camille Wells. *Shakespeare's Comic Commonwealths.* Toronto: University of Toronto Press, 2009.

Smith, Emma. *This Is Shakespeare.* London: Pelican Books, 2019.

Smith, Ian. *Race and Rhetoric in the Renaissance: Barbarian Errors.* New York: Palgrave Macmillan, 2009.

Smith, James K. A. 'Staging the Incarnation: Revisioning Augustine's Critique of Theatre'. *Literature & Theology* 15.2 (2001): 123–39.

Smith, M. Burdick. '"[P]lain and Passive Fortitude": Stoicism and Spaces of Dissent in *Sejanus*'. *Ben Jonson Journal* 25.1 (2018): 32–51.

Smith, Pauline M. *The Anti-Courtier Trend in Sixteenth Century French Literature*. Geneva: Librairie Droz, 1966.

———. 'Introduction'. In Philibert de Vienne, *Le Philosophe de Court*, ed. P. M. Smith, 9–49. Geneva: Librairie Droz, 1990.

Smuts, Malcolm. 'Court-Centred Politics and the Uses of Roman Historians, c.1590–1630'. In *Culture and Politics in Early Stuart England*, ed. Kevin Sharpe and Peter Lake, 21–43. Basingstoke: Macmillan, 1994.

Smyth, Adam. '"Divines into Dry Vines": Forms of Jesting in Renaissance England'. In *Formal Matters: Reading the Materials of English Renaissance Literature*, ed. Allison K. Deutermann and Andras Kiséry, 56–72. Manchester: Manchester University Press, 2013.

Snyder, Jon. *Dissimulation and the Culture of Secrecy in Early Modern Europe*. Berkeley: University of California Press, 2009.

Stamatakis, Chris. '"With diligent studie, but sportingly": How Gabriel Harvey Read His Castiglione'. *Journal of the Northern Renaissance*, no. 5 (2013). http://northernrenaissance.org.

Steggle, Matthew. 'Charles Chester and Ben Jonson'. *Studies in English Literature, 1500–1900* 39.2 (1999): 312–26.

Stern, Virginia F. *Gabriel Harvey: His Life, Marginalia and Library*. Oxford: Clarendon, 1979.

Stone, Lawrence. *The Crisis of the Aristocracy 1558–1641*. Oxford: Oxford University Press, 1965.

———. 'Social Mobility in England, 1500–1700'. *Past and Present* 33 (1966): 16–55.

Streete, Adrian. 'Polemical Laughter in Thomas Middleton's *A Game at Chess* (1624)'. *English Literary Renaissance* 50.2 (2020): 296–333.

Stroud, Theodore A. 'Ben Jonson and Father Thomas Wright'. *English Literary History* 14.4 (1947): 274–82.

Sullivan, Ceri. *The Rhetoric of Credit: Merchants in Early Modern Writing*. London: Associated University Presses, 2002.

Sullivan, Erin. 'The Passions of Thomas Wright: Renaissance Emotion across Body and Soul'. In *The Renaissance of Emotion: Understanding Affect in Shakespeare and His Contemporaries*, ed. Richard Meek and Erin Sullivan, 25–44. Manchester: Manchester University Press, 2015.

Swann, Marjorie. 'Refashioning Society in Ben Jonson's *Epicoene*'. *Studies in English Literature* 38 (1998): 297–315.

Tague, Ingrid H. *Women of Quality: Accepting and Contesting Ideals of Femininity in England, 1690–1760*. Woodbridge, Suffolk: Boydell, 2002.

Taylor, Charles. *The Ethics of Authenticity*. Cambridge, MA: Harvard University Press, 1991.

———. *Sources of the Self: The Making of the Modern Identity*. Cambridge, MA: Harvard University Press, 1989.

Taylor, Gary. 'Blount [Blunt] Edward (bap. 1562, d. in or before 1632), Bookseller and Translator'. In *Oxford Dictionary of National Biography*, 3 January 2008. https://doi.org/10.1093/ref:odnb/2686.

Taylor, Gary, and John Lavagnino, gen. eds. *Thomas Middleton: The Collected Works*. Oxford: Oxford University Press, 2007.

Teague, Frances. 'Jonson and the Gunpowder Plot'. *Ben Jonson Journal* 5 (1998): 249–52.

Thirsk, Joan. *Economic Policy and Projects: The Development of a Consumer Society in Early Modern England.* Oxford: Clarendon, 1978.

Thomas, Keith. *The Ends of Life: Roads to Fulfilment in Early Modern England.* Oxford: Oxford University Press, 2009.

———. *In Pursuit of Civility: Manners and Civilization in Early Modern England.* New Haven, CT: Yale University Press, 2018.

———. 'The Place of Laughter in Tudor and Stuart England'. *Times Literary Supplement,* 21 January 1977, 77–81.

Trafton, Dain A. 'Politics and the Praise of Women: Political Doctrine in the *Courtier's* Third Book'. In Hanning and Rosand, *Castiglione,* 29–44.

Traister, Barbara. 'A French Physician in an English Community'. In Gajowski and Rackin, *Merry Wives of Windsor,* 121–29.

Trilling, Lionel. *Sincerity and Authenticity.* Cambridge, MA: Harvard University Press, 1971.

Tromly, Fred B. 'Masks of Impersonality in Burlegh's "Ten Precepts" and Ralegh's *Instructions to His Son*'. *Review of English Studies* 66 (2015): 480–500.

Tuck, Richard. *Philosophy and Government 1572–1651.* Cambridge: Cambridge University Press, 1993.

Twyning, John A. 'City Comedy'. In *A Companion to Renaissance Drama,* ed. Arthur Kinney, 353–66. Oxford: Blackwell, 2002.

Ugolini, Paolo. *The Court and Its Critics: Anti-Court Sentiments in Early Modern Italy.* Toronto: University of Toronto Press, 2020.

Ustick, W. Lee. 'Changing Ideals of Aristocratic Character and Conduct in Seventeenth-Century England'. *Modern Philology* 30.2 (1932): 147–66.

Van Es, Bart. *Shakespeare in Company.* Oxford: Oxford University Press, 2013.

Vickers, Brian. *In Defence of Rhetoric.* Oxford: Oxford University Press, 1988.

———. 'Rhetoric and Poetics'. In *The Cambridge History of Renaissance Philosophy,* ed. Charles B. Schmitt and Quentin Skinner, 715–45. Cambridge: Cambridge University Press, 1988.

Vieira, Monica Brito. *The Elements of Representation in Hobbes: Aesthetics, Theatre, Law, and Theology in the Construction of Hobbes's Theory of the State.* Leiden: Brill, 2009.

Vinx, Lars. 'Personality, Authority, and Self-Esteem in Hobbes's *Leviathan*'. *Intellectual History Review* 32.1 (2022): 135–55.

Wakelin, Daniel. '*Gentleness and Nobility,* John Rastell, c. 1525–27'. In *The Oxford Handbook of Tudor Drama,* ed. Thomas Betteridge and Greg Walker, 192–206. Oxford: Oxford University Press, 2012.

———. *Humanism, Reading and English Literature, 1430–1530.* Oxford: Oxford University Press, 2007.

Walker, Greg. *Plays of Persuasion: Drama and Politics at the Court of Henry VIII.* Cambridge: Cambridge University Press, 1991.

———. *Writing Under Tyranny: English Literature and the Henrician Reformation.* Oxford: Oxford University Press, 2005.

Walker, Matthew D. 'Aristotle on Wittiness'. In *Laughter, Humor, and Comedy in Ancient Philosophy,* ed. Pierre Destrée and Franco V. Trivigno, 103–21. Oxford: Oxford University Press, 2019.

Walsh, P. G. 'Introduction'. In Cicero, *On Obligations,* trans. P. G. Walsh, ix–xlvii. Oxford World's Classics. Oxford: Oxford University Press, 2000.

Waswo, Richard. 'Crises of Credit: Monetary and Erotic Economies in the Jacobean Theatre'. In *Plotting Early Modern London: New Essays on Jacobean City Comedy*, ed. Dieter Mehl et al., 55–73. Aldershot: Ashgate, 2004.

Waszink, Jan. 'Introduction'. In Justus Lipsius, *Politica: Six Books of Politics or Political Instruction*, ed. and trans. Jan Waszink, 1–204. Assen: Royal Van Gorcum, 2004.

Watson, Curtis Brown. *Shakespeare and the Renaissance Concept of Honour*. 1960. Westport, CT: Greenwood Press, 1976.

Wayne, Valerie. 'Introduction to *A Trick to Catch the Old One*', ed. Valerie Wayne. In *Thomas Middleton: The Collected Works*, gen. ed. Gary Taylor and John Lavagnino, 373–76. Oxford: Oxford University Press, 2007.

Wells, Susan. 'Jacobean City Comedy and the Ideology of the City'. *English Literary History* 48 (1981): 37–60.

Whigham, Frank. *Ambition and Privilege: The Social Tropes of Elizabethan Courtesy Theory*. Berkeley: University of California Press, 1984.

———. 'Ideology and Class Conduct in *Merchant of Venice*'. In *Shakespeare's Comedies*, ed. Gary Waller, 108–28. London: Longman, 1991.

White, R. S. *Natural Law in English Renaissance Literature*. Cambridge: Cambridge University Press, 1996.

Wikander, Matthew H., '"Queasy to Be Touched": The World of Ben Jonson's *Sejanus*'. *Journal of English and Germanic Philology* 78.3 (1979): 345–57.

Willes, Margaret. *In the Shadow of St. Paul's Cathedral: The Churchyard That Shaped London*. New Haven, CT: Yale University Press, 2022.

Withington, Phil. *Society in Early Modern England: The Vernacular Origin of Some Powerful Ideas*. Cambridge: Polity, 2010.

———. 'Tumbled into the Dirt: Wit and Incivility in Early Modern England'. In *Understanding Historical (Im)politeness: Relational Linguistic Practice over Time and across Cultures*, ed. Marcel Bax and Daniel Z. Kadar, 154–74. Amsterdam: John Benjamins, 2012.

Wittgenstein, Ludwig. *Philosophical Investigations*. Trans. G. E. M. Anscombe, ed. G. E. M. Anscombe and R. Rhees. Oxford: Blackwell, 1953.

Wolfe, Jessica. 'The Cosmopolitanism of the Adages: The Classical and Christian Legacies of Erasmus' Hermeneutics of Accommodation'. In *Cosmopolitanism and the Middle Ages*, ed. John Ganim and Shayne Legassie, 207–30. New York: Palgrave Macmillan, 2013.

Woodhouse, J. R. *Baldesar Castiglione: A Reassessment of* The Courtier. Edinburgh: Edinburgh University Press, 1978.

Worden, Blair. 'Ben Jonson among the Historians'. In *Culture and Politics in Early Stuart England*, ed. Kevin Sharpe and Peter Lake, 67–89. Basingstoke: Macmillan, 1994.

Wright, Louis B. 'A Conduct Book for Malvolio'. *Studies in Philology* 31.2 (1934): 115–32.

Wrightson, Keith. *English Society, 1580–1680*. London: Routledge, 2003.

———. 'Estates, Degrees, and Sorts: Changing Perceptions of Society in Tudor and Stuart England'. In *Language, History and Class*, ed. Penelope J. Corfield, 30–52. Oxford: Basil Blackwell, 1991.

———. 'Sorts of People'. In *Tudor and Stuart England, the Middling Sort of People: Culture, Society and Politics in England, 1550–1800*, ed. Jonathan Barry and Christopher Brooks, 28–51. London: Macmillan, 1994.

Wyatt, Michael. *The Italian Encounter with Tudor England: A Cultural Politics of Translation.* Cambridge: Cambridge University Press, 2005.

Zagorin, Perez. 'The Historical Significance of Lying and Dissimulation'. *Social Research* 63.3 (1996): 863–912.

———. *Ways of Lying: Dissimulation, Persecution, and Conformity in Early Modern Europe.* Cambridge, MA: Harvard University Press, 1990.

Zamalin, Alex. *Against Civility: The Hidden Racism in Our Obsession with Civility.* Boston: Beacon, 2021.

Zubrzycki, John. *The Shortest History of India.* Notaries House, Exeter: Old Street, 2023.

Zucker, Adam. *The Places of Wit in Early Modern English Comedy.* Cambridge: Cambridge University Press, 2011.

———. 'The Social Logic of Ben Jonson's *Epicoene*'. *Renaissance Drama* 33 (2004): 37–62.

INDEX

Page numbers in *italics* refer to illustrations.

accommodation: Bacon on, 157; Castiglione on, 43, 44; in *Coriolanus* (Shakespeare), 132, 135–36; courtiers and, 164; Erasmus on, 15, 74–75, 224–25; Hobbes on, 38; in *Philosopher of the Court* (de Vienne), 114, 117; sincerity and, 126

acting companies: boy actors, 95, 98, 208; Children of Her Majesty's Revels, 200; Children of St. Paul's, 95; Lord Chamberlain's Men, 30–31; Prince Charles's Men, 103

The Advancement of Learning (Bacon), 156–59

aesthetics, 35, 49, 51–52, 52n41, 65, 120–21

affability, 33, 77, 130–32, 175, 190, 191

affectation, 46, 85, 87–88

Against Lying (Augustine), 135, 152–53

'age of dissimulation', 27, 150

aggression: civility and, 18, 18n58, 189; competition and, 139; humour and, 25, 50, 185, 188, 192, 194; wit and, 195, 207

Alberti, Leon Battista, 52–53

Amyot, Jacques, 129–30

Anglo, Sydney, 51–52

animal imagery, 59, 93, 146–47, 173–74

Annals (Tacitus), 154, 172–73, 182

antagonism, 3, 27, 62–63, 133, 138–39, 185–86, 192–93, 195

antiquities, collection of, 81–82

Apophthegmata (Erasmus) (collection of aphorisms), 196

Appiah, Kwame Anthony, 9, 63n62, 105

Aquinas, Thomas, Saint, 135, 153

aristocracy: courtesy texts and, 9–10; in crisis, 13, 18, 42, 77, 80; definitions of, 6, 45; education and, 73, 81; honour and, 131–32, 140–41, 143–44; rivalries in, 138–40; satire of, 69–72

Aristotelianism, 7, 57–58, 77, 104, 131, 141

Aristotle: on affability, 33, 175, 190, 191; common good, 63; on dissimulation, 177–78; on justice, 60; *Nicomachean Ethics*, 33–34, 140, 175, 187–88; on nobility, 76–77; on prudence, 151; on self-love, 63; on truthfulness, 156; on tyranny, 166, 174, 175, 177; virtues of social intercourse, 117, 191; on wit, 187–88, 191; on writing, 52n41

Ars Aulica or The Courtiers Arte (Ducci) (courtesy text), 162–66

art, 7, 66, 67, 81–82

Arundel, Thomas Howard, Earl of, 79, 82

Ascham, Roger, 82, 115

As You Like It (Shakespeare) (comedy), 219–20

attire. *See* fashion

audiences, 82, 90, 92–93, 96, 98, 171–72, 179, 208

Augustine of Hippo, Saint, 7–8, 21, 111, 118, 125, 134–35, 152–53, 224–25

authenticity, 111–12, 111n5, 127, 134, 146, 226–28. *See also* sincerity

257

authorisation, 39, 40
autocratic rule, 51, 77, 174, 227. *See also* tyranny

Bacon, Francis, 44, 82, 105–6, *149*, 156–59
barbarism, 12–13, 20, 59, 123, 139
beauty, 49, 58, 120–21
Beneditti, Michele, 213
betrayal, 55–56, 91–92, 101, 143–45. *See also* faith
Bible, 7–8, 224–25. *See also* Christianity
Blackfriars, 94–95
boasting, 43–44, 156, 188
Boke named the Governour (Elyot) (courtesy text), 75–77, 143–44
The Book of the Courtier (Castiglione) (courtesy text): about, 13–14, 41–45; as inspiration, 16–17; laughter in, 193–95; music in, 64; Shakespeare and, 32–33; *sprezzatura* and, 46–54; translations of, 19–20, 29, 109; women in, 209
Botero, Giovanni, 152, 160
boy actors, 95, 98, 208
Braham, Humfrey, 78–79
Brathwaite, Richard, 84, 103, 210
Bruto, Giovanni Michele, 210–11
buffoonery, 187–88, 192, 193
Burghley, William Cecil, 21, 80, 102
Burke, Peter, 5–6, 16

Caius, John, 217–18, 217n55
Calvinism, 7–8, 21, 116, 125
caricatures, 102, 121–22, 217–18, 220. *See also* satire
Castiglione, Baldassare, 19–20, 29, 30, 51–52. *See also The Book of the Courtier* (Castiglione) (courtesy text)
casual ease. *See sprezzatura*
ceremonies, 123–24, 126–27
Characters of Vertues and Vices (Hall) (book of 'characters'), 90
charactery, 90. *See also* visual codes
charity, 126, 161
chastity, 106, 107, 210, 216

Children of Her Majesty's Revels, 200
Children of St Paul's, 95
Christianity: the Bible, 7–8, 224–25; Christian rulers, 152; Christian thought, 15, 21–22, 56, 74, 117, 131; Cicero and, 116; civility and, 13, 67–68; commonwealth, 86–87; conflict in, 127–28, 224–25; courtesy, 59–60, 62; gentlemen, 84; God, 125–26, 127. *See also* religion
Cicero: Christianity and, 116; common good and, 11; critiques of, 37; on decorum, 111, 151; *De inventione*, 65–66; *De officiis*, 9, 21, 34–38, 43, 118–19, 189; *De oratore*, 40, 43, 65–66, 188, 193; on humanity, 14, 62; on humour, 188–89; on irony, 8n9, 191n12; on justice, 60; *Laelius de amicitia*, 175–76; Lipsius and, 154–55; on magnanimity, 142; Montaigne and, 119n19, 228; on mutual trust, 143; *personae*, 34, 36, 135; on rhetoric, 52n41; Seneca and, 151–52; on wit, 188–89, 188n4, 191
city comedies: about, 72–73; *The Dutch Courtesan* (Marston), 99; *Every Man Out of His Humour* (Jonson), 84–94, 96, 227; *The Fair Maid of the Exchange* (Heywood), 199; *A Mad World, My Masters* (Middleton), 95–96, 98–99; *Michaelmas Term* (Middleton), 95–96, 99–100; personhood in, 88–92; *The Roaring Girl* (Dekker and Middleton), 82; *A Trick to Catch the Old One* (Middleton), 95–96, 100–101; wit in, 95–102; *Your Five Gallants* (Middleton), 95–97, 102
civic humanism, 11, 42, 152
Civile Conversation (Guazzo) (courtesy text), 11, 16–17, 20, 110–11, 125–28, 197
civility: aggression and, 18, 18n58, 189; art and, 67; civilization and, 64; civil philosophy, 74, 156–59; conversation, 4–5, 11, 125, 133, 190–93; in *Coriolanus* (Shakespeare), 128–30; crisis of, 1, 54; cult of, 204; dark sides of, 148; definitions of, 12–13; dissimulation and, 222;

early modern theatre and, 29–32; expediency and, 74; Hobbes on, 38; influence of women on, 210; literature and, 3; selfhood and, 134; society, 4, 9, 11, 40–41, 54; status and, 72–73, 124; throughout history, 5, 5n9, 17–22, 228
civilization, 12–13, 37, 64, 65–66
The Civilizing Process (Elias), 17–18
classical philosophy, 5, 5n9, 117–18
Cleland, James, 81–82, 105, 210
coat of arms, 69, 85, 213
comedies. *See* city comedies; tragicomedies; *individual comedies*
The Comedy of Errors (Shakespeare) (comedy), 30–31
commonality, 11, 13, 37, 62–64, 74
common good, 4, 8, 11, 33–34, 37, 63–64, 74, 154–55
commonwealth, 41, 60, 76, 86–87
competition, 100–101, 139, 164
The Compleat Gentleman (Peacham) (courtesy text), 79, 197
comportment, 6, 15–16, 21–22, 31, 79, 126–27, 157
Contarini, Gasparo, 60
Coriolanus (Petrich), 129
Coriolanus (Shakespeare) (tragedy): about, 111–12, 227; accommodation in, 132, 135; animal imagery in, 146–47; civility in, 128–30; flattery in, 131–34; honour in, 140–43; lying in, 134–37; self-creation in, 137–40; trust in, 143–46
Il Cortegiano (Castiglione). *See The Book of the Courtier* (Castiglione) (courtesy text)
costumes, 87, 99, 100. *See also* fashion
country gentry, 83, 84, 96
court. *See* royal courts
The Courte of Civill Courtesie (anonymous) (courtesy text), 12, 19, 190
courtesans, 98–100
courtesy, 12, 81
courtesy literature: about, 4–5, 13, 16–17; accessibility of, 20, 77; court manuals, 21; *De officiis*, legacy of, 37–38; discussion of, 111–12, 157; *Galateo*, legacy of, 119–20; humour in, 197–98; mocking of, 93, 219–20; purpose of, 9–10, 15, 42–43, 72; trust in, 102; turning tide of, 84; in university curriculum, 109–10; for women, 84, 209–12. *See also individual texts*
Courtier (Castiglione). *See The Book of the Courtier* (Castiglione) (courtesy text)
courtiers: in *Coriolanus* (Shakespeare), 131; courtesy literature and, 13, 19; court ladies, 209; definitions of, 45; goals of, 164, 168–69; ideal, 42, 45, 48–50; the prince and, 44, 48–50, 152, 155–56, 163–65; skills of, 43, 46–47, 168–69
Courtiers Academie (Romei) (courtesy text), 105
credit: trust of creditors and, 71, 85, 101, 102, 103, 141
cross-dressing, 98, 208, 212. *See also* boy actors
cuckoldry, 211
cultural capital, 6, 6n13, 49, 81, 195
Cyvile and uncyvile life (anonymous) (courtesy text), 83

Daniel of Beccles, 9–10, 122
Darell, William, 17, 80–81, 120
Darwall, Stephan, 63
decadence, 79, 112, 183–84
deceit, 47, 118, 155, 156, 158–59. *See also* dissimulation
deception, 47–48, 55–56, 65, 135, 154, 224. *See also* dissimulation; lying
De civilitate morum puerilium (On good manners for children) (Erasmus) (courtesy text), 10–12, 29, 73–75
decorum, 35, 36, 44, 120–21, 124, 148, 151, 193, 196
Dedekind, Friedrich, 122
Dekker, Thomas, 32, 93, 122, 199
Della Casa, Giovanni: *Galateo* (Della Casa), 17, 81, 110, 111, 119–25, 197; *Monsignor della Casa* (Pontormo), 110; *De officiis inter potentiores et tenuiores amicos*, 123

del Sarto, Andrea, 186
deportment, 16, 43, 45, 157, 160
de Refuge, Eustache, 17, 102, 165, 198
'Description of Britaine' (Harrison), 78, 82
de Vienne, Philibert, 110–11, 112–19
Discorsi (Romei), 20
Discoveries (Jonson) (commonplace book), 87–88, 172–73
discretion, 44, 159, 193
dissimulation: aesthetics and, 65; 'age of dissimulation', 27, 150; classical ideas and, 118; in courtesy literature, 111–12; ethics and, 8–9, 74–75, 223; in jokes, 191; power and, 177–79; role of, 7–8, 27–28, 46–47, 63, 117, 148, 154–55; study of, 150–51
distrust, 155, 158. See also trust
Of Domesticall Duties (Gouge) (conduct manual), 21–22
The Dove and the Serpent (Tuvill) (treatise), 153
du Bosc, Jacques, 211
Ducci, Lorenzo, 162–66
duelling, 103–7, 219–20
The Dutch Courtesan (Marston) (city comedy), 99

Earle, John, 85–86, 87
eavesdropping, 171–72. See also spying
education: courtesy literature and, 34, 109; gentlemen and, 18, 78, 81; Greek education (*paideia*), 128–30; Inns of Court, 30, 81, 92, 103n86, 195, 202; nobility and, 11–12, 17–18; purpose of, 16, 73–75; of women, 209–11
Elias, Norbert, 17–18, 150
Elyot, Thomas, 75–77, 143–44
emotions, 125–26, 154, 160, 179–82, 189
England: culture of, 19–20, 76, 82, 86; jeering in, 196–97; roaring, 103; London, 80, 83, 89, 95, 103; Neostoicism in, 167–68
English Gentlewoman (Brathwaite) (courtesy text), 84, 210
Enterline, Lynn, 16

Epicene, or The Silent Woman (Jonson) (comedy), 187, 199–209, 222
Erasmus, Desiderius: *Apophthegmata*, 196; *Ciceronianus*, 192; *De civilitate morum puerilium (On good manners for children)*, 10–12, 29, 73–75; *De conscribendis epistolis*, 15; *De copia*, 15; *De pueris instituendis*, 73; Portrait of Desiderius Erasmus of Rotterdam with Renaissance Pilaster (Holbein), 70; *Ratio verae theologiae*, 74–75, 225; 'The Knight without a Horse, or Faked Nobility,' 69–72, 84–85
esteem, 4, 26, 28, 50–51, 63, 63n62, 117, 141, 223
ethics: aesthetics and, 49, 51–52, 52n41, 64–67; classical ethics, 117; dissimulation and, 8–9, 74–75, 223; expediency and, 36–37; manners and, 33
etiquette, 206, 228. See also deportment; manners
Every Man Out of His Humour (Jonson) (city comedy), 84–94, 96, 227
expediency, 36–37, 74, 114, 148, 151, 224–25

facial expressions, 16, 36, 74, 157, 159
The Fair Maid of the Exchange (Heywood) (city comedy), 199
A Fair Quarrel (Middleton and Rowley) (tragicomedy), 103–4, 104, 106–8
faith, 60–61, 100–101, 143–46, 174, 206. See also religion; trust
Falstaff at Herne's Oak (Beneditti), 213
Faret, Nicolas, 105, 198, 210–11
fashion, 86, 89, 93, 99–100. See also style
fellowship, 36–37, 51, 61, 162
female protagonists, 55–56, 60, 62, 107, 137–38, 204. See also *The Merry Wives of Windsor* (Shakespeare) (comedy)
fictions, 7, 7n15, 63–64, 67–68. See also imagination
first impressions, 44–45
flattery, 131–34, 148, 175–76, 178
Florio, John, 31–32
Florios Second Frutes (Florio) (language manual), 31–32

foreigners, 61, 217–18
fortitude, 128, 153, 176
The Fraternity of Vagabonds (Awdeley) (coney-catching pamphlet), 89
fraudsters, 71, 90, 95–97, 173. *See also* impostors
free will, 117n15, 134
friendship, 33–34, 101–4, 108, 131, 155, 175–76

Gainsford, Thomas, 81, 120
Galateo (Della Casa), 17, 81, 110, 111, 119–25, 197
gentility, 18, 71n4, 72, 77, 81, 83, 85, 89, 96
gentlemen: civility and, 12–13; conduct of, 50–51, 69, 71, 144; from the country, 84, 96; definitions of, 18, 71n4, 78–80; fashion of, 86–87; humour of, 188, 191; instruction to be, 31, 35–36, 80–85; satire of, 72; theatre and, 31–32; value of identity as, 88–89; virtue vs birth, 97; women and, 210–11
gentlewomen, 23, 84, 209. *See also* women
gentry, 18–19, 77–81, 83, 85–86
Gesta Grayorum, 30–31
gossip, 85, 87, 90, 113
The Governour (Elyot), 42. See *Boke named the Governour* (Elyot) (courtesy text)
grace, 111, 116, 121, 124, 130
Gracián, Baltasar, 103, 151, 190
Greenes Groats-Worth of witte (Greene) (satire), 80, 202–3
Grobianism, 121–23
Grobianus (Dedekind), 122
Guazzo, Stefano, 11, 16–17, 20, 110–11, 125–28, 197
The Guls Horne-booke (Dekker) (satire), 93, 122, 199
Gunpowder Plot, 162, 168

Hall, Joseph, 83, 90
harmony, 14, 51, 65, 117–18, 120–21
Harrison, William, 78, 82–83
Harvey, Gabriel, 109–11, 115, 194
Hawkins, Francis, 120

A Health to the Gentlemanly profession of Servingmen (Markham) (courtesy text), 80
heraldry, 69, 73, 85, 213
Hero-paideia (Cleland) (courtesy text), 105
Heywood, Thomas, 199
His firste Fruites (Florio) (language manual), 31–32
Hobbes, Thomas, 3–4, 9, 26, 38–41, 190, 227–28
Hoby, Thomas, 19–20, 23, 209, 4245
Holbein, Hans the Younger, 70
honesty, 131, 159, 176
L'Honneste femme (The Compleat Woman) (du Bosc) (courtesy text), 211
L'honneste-homme ou, L'art de plaire à la cour (The honest man: or, The art to please in court) (Faret) (courtesy text), 198, 210–11
honour: aristocracy and, 140–41, 143; civility and, 131; in *Coriolanus* (Shakespeare), 140–43; duels and, 103, 105, 107, 220; ethics and, 36–37, 63n62, 117; jesting and, 221–22; law of, 104–5
Horace, 65–66, 176
hospitality, 80, 98, 121–22, 139, 217
humanism: Cicero and, 37, 61, 62; education and, 16, 45; ideals, 129; nobility and, 6, 12, 73, 75–76; rhetoric and, 14
human solidarity, 63–64
humour, 25, 185–98, 217. *See also* affability; jestbooks; jesting; laughter; wit

idealism, 11, 49–54
identity: changing, 146–47; sincere self, 125–28, 145, 147, 208; social, 88–89, 103n86, 137, 140–43, 229
imagination, 7, 27, 41, 95n70
impostors, 70–72, 89, 90, 94–95, 97. *See also* fraudsters
individual good, 8, 33–34, 37. *See also* common good
individualism, 13, 100, 105, 227
ingratiation, 3, 51, 114, 202
injustice, 61–62

Inns of Court, 30, 81, 92, 103n86, 195, 202
Institucion of a gentleman (Braham) (courtesy text), 78–79
Institutio oratoria (Quintilian), 15–16, 188–89
The Instruction of a Christian Woman (Vives) (educational manual), 211
irony, 8n9, 75, 188, 191, 191n12, 205; gentlemen, 188
isolation, 147, 159, 170, 175
Italian culture, 19, 32n5, 42, 60, 61, 82–83, 119–23, 196

James I, 105–6
Javitch, Daniel, 115
jeering, 196–97
Jerome, Saint, 135, 224–25
jestbooks, 189–90, 196, 198–99, 211
jesting, 185–87, 189, 193–95, 197, 198n27, 199–204, 210–12, 216–22
Jews, 59, 62–63, 224–25
jokes, 51–52, 92, 98, 120, 185–86, 189–91, 193, 197, 222. *See also* humour; jeering; jesting; wit
Jonson, Ben: *Alchemist*, 108; audience of, 92–93; *Discoveries*, 87–88, 172–73; *Epicene, or The Silent Woman*, 187, 199–209, 222; *Every Man Out of His Humour*, 84–95, 96, 227; *Sejanus His Fall*, 148, 162, 166–74, 179–84, 227
justice, 33–34, 60–61, 63–64, 105, 107, 113–14, 143

Kant, Immanuel, 61, 222
Keper, John, 20, 105
The Knight in Black (Moroni), 2
'Knight without a Horse or Faked Nobility' (Erasmus) (colloquy), 69–72, 84–85

Laelius de amicitia (Cicero), 175–76
Lake, Peter, 167–68
Latin, 16, 45, 97, 203
laughter, 50, 187, 193–95, 216
Letters to His Son (Chesterfield) (courtesy text), 14

Leviathan (Hobbes), 38–41
Libro del Cortegiano (Castiglione). See *The Book of the Courtier* (Castiglione) (courtesy text)
Lipsius, Justus, 152–56, 172–73
Locke, John, 13–14
logic of the market, 24, 88
London, 80, 83, 89, 95, 103. *See also* England
love, 49, 56–59, 126
Luyken, Jan, 167
lying, 27; Augustine on, 21, 134–35, 152–53; ceremonies as, 123–24; civility and, 111–12; in *Coriolanus* (Shakespeare), 134–37, 144–45; in *Sejanus His Fall* (Jonson), 169

Machiavelli, Niccolo, 8, 37, 48, 67, 155, 157–58, 177–78, 220–21
Macrobius, 188n4, 189, 190
A Mad World, My Masters (Middleton) (city comedy), 95–96, 98–99
magnanimity, 44, 104–5, 118, 140n56, 142
manipulation, 178, 181
manners: character and, 14–15; ethics and, 33; as exclusionary device, 20; purpose of, 78, 120–21, 124, 157, 206; respect and, 127; social cachet and, 81
market, logic of the, 24, 88
Markham, Gervase, 80
Marlowe, Christopher, 219
marriage, 71, 100, 200–201, 205, 211
Marston, John, 99
Martin, John Jeffries, 125, 150
Martyn, William, 102–3
Maugin, Jean, 116
megalopsychia, 140, 140n56. *See also* honour; pride
The Merchant of Venice (Shakespeare) (comedy), 32–33, 51, 54–68, 55
The Merry Wives of Windsor (Shakespeare) (comedy), 187, 212–17, 220–22
metatheatre, 7, 54, 90, 97, 98–99
Michaelmas Term (Middleton) (city comedy), 95–96, 99–100

Middleton, Thomas: *A Fair Quarrel* (Middleton and Rowley), 103–4, *104*, 106–8; *A Mad World, My Masters*, 95, 98–99; *Michaelmas Term*, 95, 96, 99–100; *The Peacemaker; or Great Britain's Blessing*, 106; *A Trick to Catch the Old One*, 95, 100–101; *Your Five Gallants*, 95–97, 102
mirrors for princes, 5, 13, 14, 49, 77, 177, 190
misogyny, 50, 57, 58, 206–7
modesty, 44, 84, 214–15
monasteries, 9, 18, 79, 87
Monsignor della Casa (Pontormo), *110*
Montaigne, Michel de, 119n19, 125, 228–29
morals: Bacon on, 158; Christianity and, 62, 152; civility and, 26, 226, 228; in *Coriolanus* (Shakespeare), 111, 145; in *Every Man Out of His Humour* (Jonson), 93–94; expediency and, 33–34; exterior and, 14; manners and, 6, 21–22; moral philosophy, 113, 160; moral virtues, 33–34; nobility and, 71
Moroni, Giovanni Battista, 2
Mother Hubberds Tale (Spenser) (poem), 115
music, 64–67

names, 141–43
Das Narrenschiff (The Ship of Fools) (Brandt) (satire), 122
The necessarie, fit, and convenient education of a yong gentlewoman (Bruto) (courtesy text), 210
Neoplatonism, 23, 48–54, 65, 225
Neostoicism, 21, 153–56, 167–68, 172
Nicomachean Ethics (Aristotle), 33–34, 140, 175, 187–88
nobility: definitions of, 71n4, 75–77; earning of, 42, 69; education and, 11–12, 17–18; humanism and, 6, 12, 73, 75–76; identity as, 14; as myth, 72; parentage, 77; wealth and, 79–80
nonchalance. See *sprezzatura*
North, Thomas, 128–30

observation of others, 148–50, 158, 161–62, 164, 170–71, 178
De officiis (Cicero), 9, 21, 34–38, 43, 118–19, 189
oikeiosis, 34, 63–64, 154
De oratore (Cicero), 40, 43, 65–66, 188, 193
oratory, 15–16, 65–66, 181
Orpheus, 65–66
outsiders, 20, 54–55, 59, 61, 168, 170, 194–95

pagan culture, 117–18
Panaetius, 34–35
Parallel Lives (Plutarch), 128–30
parodies, 93, 94, 98, 100, 122, 179, 199, 206, 219
passions: concealment of, 148, 152, 160; of others, 161–62; Plato on, 7, 187; of rulers, 164, 173, 181
Passions of the Mind in General (Wright), 160–62
Paul, the Apostle, Saint, 74, 224–25
Paul's Walk, 92–93. *See also* print market
The Peacemaker; or Great Britain's Blessing (Middleton) (pamphlet), 106
Peacham, Henry, 79, 81–82, 102, 197
Perkins, William, 22, 153, 196
personae, 34, 36, 135–36
personhood, 38–39, 88–92, 125
Peter, the Apostle, Saint, 224–25
'Le Petit Angevin' (Maugin) (poet), 116
Petrich, Soma Orlai, *129*
Pettie, George, 20
Philosopher of the Court (de Vienne) (satire), 111, 112–19
philosophy, 5, 5n9, 74, 113, 116–18, 156–59, 160
Plato, 7n15, 21, 49, 117, 173, 174, 181, 187
play-acting, 36, 135–36, 156, 159, 208, 229
Plutarch, 128–30, 137–38, 189–90
Pocket Oracle and Art of Prudence (Gracián) (collection of aphorisms), 103, 151, 190
poetry, 65–66
policy. *See* expediency

Politicorum sive civilis doctrinae libri sex (Sixe Bookes of Politickes or Civil Doctrine) (Lipsius), 154–56, 172
politics, 76, 132, 162, 168, 172, 175, 178–79. See also commonwealth
Pontano, Giovanni, 33, 185, 190–93
Pontormo, Jacopo, 110
Portrait of a Lady with a Book (del Sarto), 186
Portrait of Baldassare Castiglione (Raphael), 30
Portrait of Desiderius Erasmus of Rotterdam with Renaissance Pilaster (Holbein), 70
Portrait of Francis Bacon (van Somer), 149
power, 17–18, 36, 38, 166, 181
prestige, 64, 97, 106, 114, 205, 216, 223
pretence, 24–25, 46–47, 131, 134, 222, 223–25. See also dissimulation
pride, 117–18, 130, 140n56
the prince, 44, 48–50, 152, 155–56, 163–65
The Prince (Machiavelli), 48
De principe liber (Pontano) (mirror for princes), 190
print market, 16–17, 19, 20, 69–71, 77, 92–93, 198–99
privilege, 6, 20, 64, 131
prudence, 148, 150–51, 152, 155–56, 158, 160–61
Puritans, 21–22, 153, 206, 217
Puttenham, George, 66, 188n3

Quaestiones convivales (Plutarch) (book of table talk), 189–90
Quintilian, 15–16, 52n41, 188–89, 188n4, 190, 191, 191n12

Rankins, William, 22
Raphael, 30
Rawls, John, 60–61
religion: dissenting faiths, 55, 62–63, 150, 218–19, 224–25; Jews, 59, 62–63, 224–25; pagan culture, 117–18; persecution, 150; Puritans, 21–22, 153, 206, 217; rituals, 127–28. See also Christianity

Renaissance, 9–13, 21, 66, 72, 104–5, 125, 131, 185, 196–99
De Republica Anglorum (Smith) (political treatise), 78
reputation, 37, 44–45, 90, 105–6, 141–43, 160
respect, 4, 8, 35–36, 50–51, 63, 133
rhetoric, 13, 14–16, 35, 57, 67, 157, 179–83, 185–86
Rhetoric (Aristotle), 190
The Rich Cabinet (Gainsford) (commonplace book), 81
rivalries, 138–40, 205
'roaring', 103, 108
The Roaring Girl (Dekker and Middleton) (city comedy), 82
Rogers, Nehemiah, 22
role-playing, 8, 111–12, 135–36, 208–9
Rome, 61, 152, 166, 169–70
Romei, Annibale, 20, 105
Rowley, William, 103–4, *104*, 106–8
royal courts, 9–10, 17–18, 48–50, 51, 112–18, 150
rulers, 44, 48–50, 152, 155–56, 163–65, 168–69. See also tyranny

satire, 69–72, 80, 94–95, 110–19, 122, 220. See also city comedies; *Epicene, or The Silent Woman* (Jonson) (comedy)
Saturnalia (Macrobius) (book of table talk), 189–90
Saviolo, Vincentio, 220
Scholemaster (Ascham) (educational manual), 115
secrecy, 102–3, 159, 161–62, 164
Sejanus, Favourite of Emperor Tiberius, Strangled, and at the Gemonian Stairs, Miserably Abused (Luyken), 167
Sejanus, Lucius Aelius, 163–65, *167*
Sejanus His Fall (Jonson) (tragedy), 148, 162, 166–74, 179–84, 227
self-advancement, 15, 26, 50–51, 91, 93–94, 124, 151
self-help books, 17, 19, 37. See also courtesy literature

selfhood, 88–92, 125–26, 134, 137–41, 145–46, 152
self-interest, 3, 3n4, 37, 41, 48–54, 63–64, 74, 163
self-love, 33–34, 63, 228
self-observation, 89, 148–50, 158
Seneca, 14–15, 87–88, 151–52, 153–54
De sermone (Pontano) (treatise), 185, 190–91
Shakespeare, William: *The Book of the Courtier* (Castiglione) (courtesy text) and, 32–33; coat of arms of, 85; *The Comedy of Errors*, 30–31; *The Merchant of Venice*, 32–33, 51, 54–68, 55; *The Merry Wives of Windsor*, 187, 212–17, 220–22; use of names, 141–42; *As You Like It*, 219–20. See also *Coriolanus* (Shakespeare) (tragedy)
A Short discourse of the life of Servingmen (Darell) (courtesy text), 17, 80–81, 120
'Of Simulation and Dissimulation' (Bacon) (essay), 158–59
sincere self, 125
sincerity, 8, 125–28, 130, 137, 146
Skinner, Quentin, 39, 60
Snyder, Jon, 150–51
social advancement, 18, 20, 42–43, 78–80, 100–101
social bonds, 37, 148, 166, 194–95
social hierarchy, 6, 71, 86–87, 97, 98, 123, 132–33, 137, 192
Socrates, 173, 181, 191
sprezzatura, 2, 13–14, 46–48, 95–96
spying, 144–45, 148, 170–72, 176. See also surveillance
State Formation and Civilization (Elias), 150
St Augustine. See Augustine of Hippo, Saint
St Jerome, 135, 224–25
Stoicism, 34–35, 36, 61, 63–64, 152, 153–54, 174
Stubbes, Philip, 86–87, 99
style, 16, 44, 45, 51–52, 54, 86–87. See also fashion
surveillance, 89–90, 148–50, 170–72. See also spying

table talk, 16, 189, 199
Tacitism, 21, 151–52, 153–56, 167–68
Tacitus, 151–52, 154, 163, 172–73, 182
Taylor, Charles, 1–3
theatre: analogies to, 15–16, 36, 39–40, 44–45, 136, 156, 162, 169; attendance of, 30–32, 171; civility and, 32, 226; fashion and, 87; use of wit in, 187–88
theatres: Blackfriars, 94–95; Globe Theatre, 92; Gray's Inn, 30–31; Inns of Court, 30, 81, 92, 103n86, 195, 202; Red Bull, 103
Thomas, Keith, 13, 141, 175
Thoughts Concerning Education (Locke) (educational manual), 13–14
tragicomedies, 103–4, 104, 106–8
Traicté de la cour, ou instruction des courtisans (*A Treatise of the Court or Instructions for Courtiers*) (de Refuge) (courtesy text), 17, 102, 165, 198
translations, 19–20, 29, 42, 109, 115–16, 119, 129–30
travel abroad, 81–83
Treatise of the Court or Instructions for Courtiers (de Refuge) (courtesy text), 17, 102, 165, 198
A Trick to Catch the Old One (Middleton) (city comedy), 95–96, 100–101
trust, 101, 102, 143–46, 155, 158
truth: absolute, 7, 27, 36, 117; inward truth, 48, 111–12, 126, 127–28, 137, 145–46; truthfulness, 33, 156. See also dissimulation; faith; lying
tyranny, 166, 169, 172–78, 181–82, 227

universality, 3, 63–64. See also common good
universities, 81, 109
urbanisation, 18, 75, 83, 95, 123
Urbanus Magnus (Daniel of Beccles) (courtesy text), 9–10, 122

van Somer, Paul I, 149
Venice, 60–64. See also *The Merchant of Venice* (Shakespeare) (comedy)

virtue, 11–12, 33, 36–37, 48, 83, 118, 128, 151, 154
visual codes, 90
Vives, Juan Luis, 211, 216

Washington's Rules of Civility (Washington) (courtesy text), 120
wealth, 57–58, 78, 79–80, 87, 93–94, 97
William of Wykeham, 6
wit: about, 95n70; Cicero on, 188n4, 191; in city comedies, 95–102; combative, 185, 187, 192–93, 194, 195, 207; jesting vs., 198; the theatre and, 199; urbane wit, 190–91
women: chastity of, 106, 107, 210, 216; courtesans, 98–100; courtesy literature for, 84, 209–12; court ladies, 209; decorum and, 210, 216–17; fashion of, 99–100; female protagonists, 55–56, 60, 62, 107, 137–38, 204; jests of, 210–11; *The Merry Wives of Windsor* (Shakespeare), 187, 212–17, 220–22; *Portrait of a Lady with a Book* (del Sarto), *186*
Wright, John Massey, 55
Wright, Thomas, 160–62, 171, 196–97

Your Five Gallants (Middleton) (city comedy), 95–97, 102
Youths Behaviour (Hawkins) (courtesy text), 120
Youths Instruction (Martyn) (courtesy text), 102–3, 197

Zagorin, Perez, 27, 150
Zeno, 64

A NOTE ON THE TYPE

This book has been composed in Arno, an Old-style serif typeface in the classic Venetian tradition, designed by Robert Slimbach at Adobe.

GPSR Authorized Representative: Easy Access System Europe - Mustamäe tee
50, 10621 Tallinn, Estonia, gpsr.requests@easproject.com

www.ingramcontent.com/pod-product-compliance
Lightning Source LLC
Chambersburg PA
CBHW031803220426
43662CB00007B/512